STAGE SCENERY

THIRD EDITION

STAGE SCENERY
Its Construction and Rigging

A. S. GILLETTE
Emeritus, University of Iowa

J. MICHAEL GILLETTE
University of Arizona

HARPER & ROW, PUBLISHERS, New York
Cambridge, Hagerstown, Philadelphia, San Francisco,
London, Mexico City, São Paulo, Sydney

1817

Sponsoring Editor: Alan Spiegel
Project Editors: Claudia Kohner/Jon Dash
Text and Cover Designer: Helen Iranyi
Production Manager: Jeanie Berke
Compositor: Lexigraphics, Inc.
Printer and Binder: Halliday Lithographic Corporation
Art Studio: Vantage Art, Inc.

Stage Scenery: Its Construction and Rigging, Third Edition

Library of Congress Cataloging in Publication Data

Gillette, A. S. (Arnold S.), Date-
    Stage scenery, its construction and rigging.

    Bibliography: p.
    Includes index.
    1. Theaters—Stage-setting and scenery.   I. Gillette,
J. Michael.   II. Title.
PN2091.S8G5   1981   792'.025   81-568
ISBN 0-06-042332-3   AACR2

To Jo for her assistance, encouragement, and patience

Contents

16. Backstage Organization and Management   *413*

Plate List

Preface

Many changes have taken place in the area of technical theatre since the second edition of this text was published. The use of plastics and metals in scenic construction has greatly increased. There has been a greater emphasis placed on the use of realistic properties in the last nine years. We feel that it is necessary to include this material in this new edition. Those recent innovations and improvements in hand and power tools, both air and electric, that are suitable for scenic work are described and illustrated. The necessary wiring of the shop to take best advantage of these new power tools is described. In answer to requests from students and instructors, a chapter on the techniques of scene painting has been added together with a further expansion of the chapter dealing with special construction and rigging problems.

We are especially indebted to Alan Spiegel of Harper & Row whose advice has helped to guide this present revision. Our special gratitude goes to Elbin Cleveland and Michael Griffith for their assistance and contributions. In spite of their own heavy production schedules, they somehow found the time to suggest many useful ideas and presented us with carefully drawn illustrations of projects that they thought might be helpful. We also appreciate suggestions made in the area of special effects and properties by James Gill, property master of the Old Globe Theatre in San Diego; and for the dancing firelight effect designed by Dan Willoughby, Lighting Designer with the Arizona Theatre Company, Tucson, Arizona. We are extremely indebted to Victor Meyrich the technical director, Sam Bagarella the scenic artist, and Marian Wallace the production stage manager of the Asolo State Theatre in Sarasota, Florida, who were never too busy to answer innumerable questions and who allowed the senior Gillette to roam at will through their shops.

A. S. GILLETTE
J. MICHAEL GILLETTE

1

The Organization of the Production Staff for the Nonprofessional Theatre

We had just heard some of the finest music and operatic voices in the world in a production of *Aida* as it was presented by an internationally known touring company. Like hundreds of others in the audience, we had looked forward to this occasion for weeks. We had driven most of the afternoon to reach the city in time for a leisurely dinner before curtain time. And what was the subject of our conversation at the first intermission? It was not the genius of Verdi, it did not concern the magnificence of the voice or the music we had just heard, nor did it concern any of the details of an otherwise splendid production. All of the entr'acte conversation could be summed up by this one question: "Did you see the stagehand who wandered across the King's courtyard in Act I?"

It was a small enough incident in itself and certainly understandable when one realized that the traveling company had to supplement its regular stage crew with inexperienced members of the local union; but the effect remained, nevertheless. An otherwise flawless production had been marred by a technical error.

This experience illustrates the fact that while average playgoers may know little about the intricacies of backstage organization and management, they are extremely conscious of any interruption of a production that is due to a technical cause. For the most part they are not too severe in their criticism of an actor and are willing to overlook a missed cue or an awkward bit of stage business; but their reaction to a comparable mistake by a member of the backstage personnel is instantly critical. The incident is likely to be an occasion for many amusing and cutting remarks.

It is unfortunately true that in the majority of educational and community productions, and even in some professional productions, the greatest share of attention and energy is expended upon perfecting the script, the acting, and the direction, whereas the technical aspects of the production are relegated to a position of secondary importance. The management has, through thoughtlessness or ignorance, delayed until the last possible hour giving any serious consideration to the problems of technical planning and then often relied on the inspiration of the moment. The risk of such a procedure is both serious and obvious. The standard of a production is lowered when avoidable technical errors occur that detract from the effectiveness of an otherwise carefully planned production.

The primary purpose of this text is to discuss the duties of the technician and the principles of planning, construction, and rigging of scenery. It seems advisable, however, to begin with the topic of organization, since it is essential for the reader to understand just where technicians fit within the general framework of a production staff and to what degree their work will be influenced or affected by the needs of other staff members. This fact is given additional emphasis when it is realized that the office of the scene technician, as it exists in the educational or community theatre, has no counterpart in the production staff of the professional theatre. The technician's duties there have been divided between the personnel of the studios specializing in the construction and painting of scenery and the stage carpenter, electrician, and stage manager of the regular production crew. In some educational theatre organizations the duties of the scene technician are further complicated by the fact that one person will often serve as both scene designer and technician. This fact alone makes it essential that the delegation of duties be understood by all of those working within the framework of a nonprofessional theatre production staff.

The director without a sound knowledge of backstage organization or a clear picture of the duties and responsibilities of various members of the production staff is poorly equipped to assume the authoritative leadership required of the individual who must synchronize all phases of a production. The material offered in this first chapter is therefore concerned with the basic problem of organization.

Within the broad field of the educational, community, and professional theatre it is obvious that there could be no standardization of backstage personnel, with regard to either the number involved or the nature of their assignments. However, whether a production is a simple one-act play produced by an overworked high school teacher or an epic Broadway offering under the supervision of a well-known director aided by a host of specialists, the elements of both productions remain the same.

The successful production of a play is not the achievement of any one or two individuals but the composite result of the work of a number of artists and craftspersons who have labored within their specialized areas with a clear understanding of the importance their particular efforts give to the total effect.

These areas of activity form the component parts of a production and are the elements upon which the organization of a theatrical production staff is formed.

THE ELEMENTS OF A PRODUCTION

The Play, Direction, and Acting

The nucleus around which the entire production centers is the manuscript. The individual usually responsible for breathing life into the script is the director; working through the skill of the actors, the director gives to the production an interpretation of the playwright's ideas. Although it is recognized that the fields of playwriting, acting, and directing demand special skills and training, they are grouped together here as one element because they are inseparably united by the one purpose of conveying the playwright's intention.

Scenery

The element of scenery actually embraces two fields of activity—creative and technical. The creative field is represented by the work of the designer, who is concerned with the problem of interpreting the script through the medium of scenic design and of creating a visual environment for the action of the play. The technical field is represented by the individuals who are responsible for the mechanical operations of drafting, constructing, painting, rigging, and shifting of scenery. Scenery as such may be defined as a series of two- and three-dimensional units that are usually placed on stage to enclose the acting area. When painted, rigged, and lighted, they form the background for the action of the play.

Properties

Properties include all practical or decorative parts of the design that are not structurally a part of the setting. They fall into several classifications, depending upon their size, placement within the setting, and use. Trim or decorative props usually serve no practical purpose other than to help the designer establish the period, nationality, and locale of the setting. They are usually placed against a wall or suspended from it. Set or floor props usually stand upon the stage floor and include all of the furniture normally used by the actors. Hand props are objects carried to and from the stage by the actors or used by them while onstage in the performance of established stage business.

Lighting

Lighting is an essential field that merits its own designer. The subtle control of the distribution, color, movement, and intensity of light greatly effects the audience's perception of a play. Revelation of form, emphasis of scenic and dramatic composition, and enhancement of the emotional content of the play are among the chief contributions that a lighting designer makes to a production.

Costumes

The role of the costume designer is as highly specialized in its own way as is that of the scene designer; both have many factors in common, and both include creative as well as mechanical phases of production work. The costumer strives to incorporate within each costume design features and details that are indicative of the period and country dictated by the script and in accord with the social class and individuality of a specific character.

Business Management

An indispensable part of the work associated with the production of any play concerns the business transactions dealing with budgets, rentals, purchasing, and publicity. Within the professional theatre, where duties of this type are heaviest, they are usually handled by an assistant producer or a general manager. In the educational or community theatre this position is filled by the director of the theatre or some other member of the staff who combines this work with other assignments.

ORGANIZATION CHART FOR THE NONPROFESSIONAL THEATRE STAFF

Plate 1 illustrates the typical basic pattern used for the organization of a production staff for most educational and community theatres. This organizational plan uses the six elements of a production as its foundation. The diagram indicates the departmental heads and lists the members of the production staff whose work will be carried out under their supervision.

Obviously there will be numerous changes in such an organizational chart because of variations in the number of permanent staff members and their particular aptitudes and abilities. Such a diagram is of value when used as a guide and as a means of checking the distribution of the work load among those responsible for specific assignments, but only when it is adjusted to the personnel of each producing group.

PRODUCTION STAFF PERSONNEL AND THEIR DUTIES

The more important members of a theatre production staff are listed below, together with a brief account of the areas in which they work, their duties and responsibilities. There is always a possibility that necessity may force the combining of one or more of these positions on a production staff. This should be done with a full understanding of the duties of each position in order to select combinations of functions that are compatible.

Author

The author is the creator of the script and the individual who, when present during the preparation of the play, assists the director by making revisions in the script or by advising on matters such as characterization or interpretation.

Director

The director is responsible for the interpretation of the play and for the choice of style in presentation. Acting and directing are shaped to express the idea and theme of the play. It is the director's responsibility to see that settings, costumes, props, and lighting are in accord with the acting and directing and that all express the idea of the play.

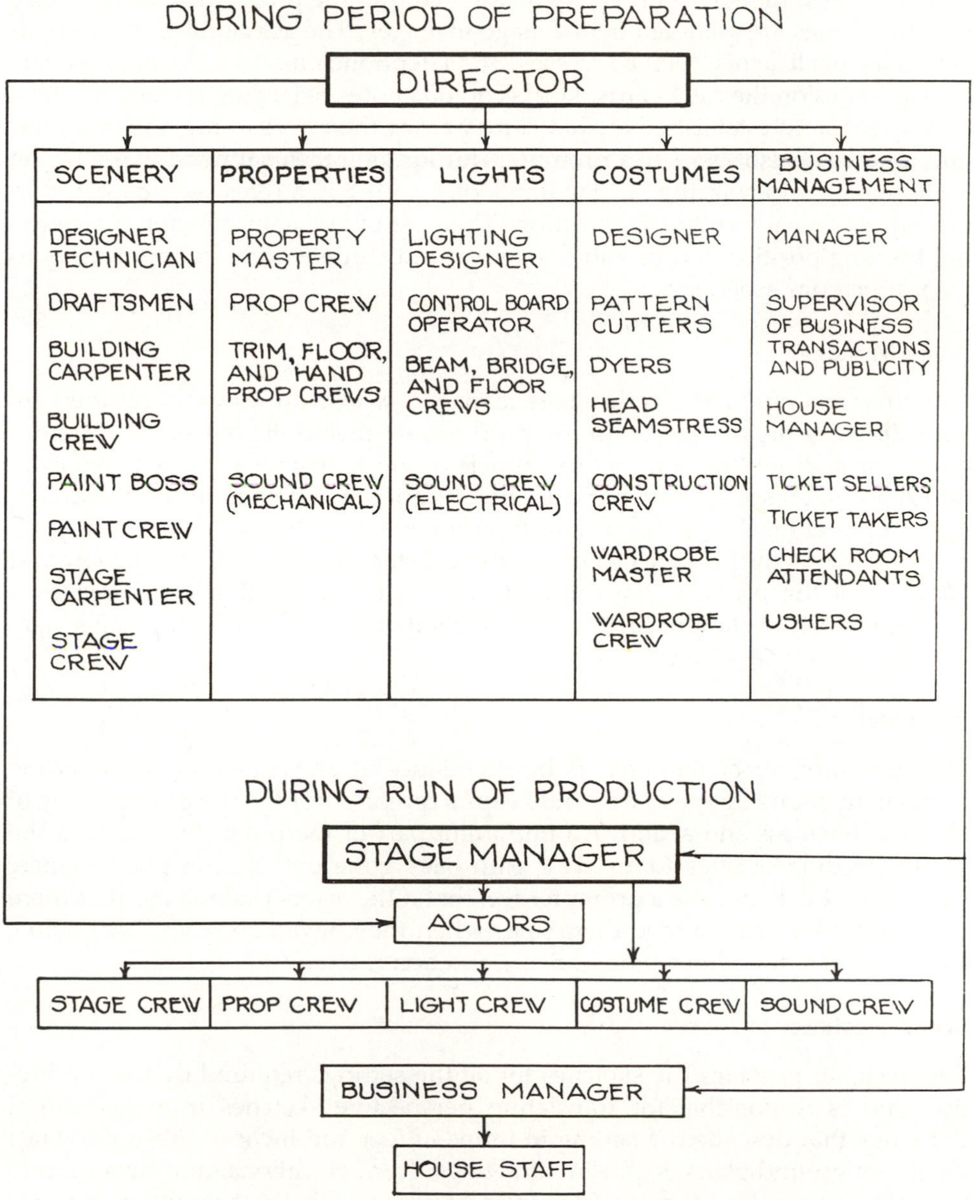

DURING PERIOD OF PREPARATION

DIRECTOR

SCENERY	PROPERTIES	LIGHTS	COSTUMES	BUSINESS MANAGEMENT
DESIGNER TECHNICIAN	PROPERTY MASTER	LIGHTING DESIGNER	DESIGNER	MANAGER
DRAFTSMEN	PROP CREW	CONTROL BOARD OPERATOR	PATTERN CUTTERS	SUPERVISOR OF BUSINESS TRANSACTIONS AND PUBLICITY
BUILDING CARPENTER	TRIM, FLOOR, AND HAND PROP CREWS	BEAM, BRIDGE, AND FLOOR CREWS	DYERS	
BUILDING CREW			HEAD SEAMSTRESS	HOUSE MANAGER
PAINT BOSS	SOUND CREW (MECHANICAL)	SOUND CREW (ELECTRICAL)	CONSTRUCTION CREW	TICKET SELLERS
PAINT CREW			WARDROBE MASTER	TICKET TAKERS
STAGE CARPENTER				CHECK ROOM ATTENDANTS
STAGE CREW			WARDROBE CREW	USHERS

DURING RUN OF PRODUCTION

STAGE MANAGER

ACTORS

STAGE CREW	PROP CREW	LIGHT CREW	COSTUME CREW	SOUND CREW

BUSINESS MANAGER

HOUSE STAFF

Plate 1 Organization of a Production Staff

Assistant Director

The director in the educational theatre may employ the services of a student who serves as assistant director. The assistant is usually in attendance at all rehearsals from the time the play is cast until the production opens, and assists the director in many ways. In more professionally oriented training programs many of these responsibilities are assumed by the stage manager. The assistant director maintains a list of all actors, their addresses, and telephone numbers; posts all rehearsal schedules on the call boards; keeps copious notes regarding the actors' stage movements and established business; may assist the actors in memorizing their lines and may also serve as a prompter during the rehearsal period; assists the stage manager in marking out the limits of a setting in a rehearsal space and in placing rehearsal furniture in position. The post of assistant director is a splendid training position and provides an advanced student with an opportunity to gain directorial experience.

Stage Manager

The director's right hand is the stage manager, whose duties vary considerably with different organizations. In the professional theatre he is usually in attendance throughout the entire rehearsal period and may have some active part in rehearsing mob scenes and bit parts. In educational and community theatre he may take over his duties only a short time before final rehearsals. He is responsible to the director for synchronizing all backstage effects with the action and business of the play. He has authority over actors as well as crew members during the run of the production. On elaborate shows the stage manager may have one or two assistants.

Prompter

The prompter, or bookholder, is in attendance at all rehearsals and aids the actors in memorizing their parts and keeps a careful record in the prompt copy of all stage business and action. An important part of the prompter's duty is the skillful feeding of lines to an actor who has "gone up" during performance. Directors who do not use a prompter feel that if the actors understand that there is nobody backstage to feed them lines when they have "gone up," the actors will memorize their lines more quickly and accurately.

Scene Designer

The designer provides the sketches for all the settings required by the production and is responsible for translating perspective sketches into mechanical drawings that describe the setting in terms of feet and inches. These drawings consist of ground plans, sight-line drawings, front elevations, and detail drawings. The scene designer provides the technician with the general scheme for shifting the settings; supervises the painting of the settings; selects the properties for each set; and is responsible for the final trimming of the settings.

Designer's Assistant

The designer frequently has an assistant who helps with drafting, scene painting, and securing the correct properties and set decorations.

Paint Crew

The paint crew is under the direct supervision of either the designer or the designer's assistant. All of the scenery and special effects are painted by this crew.

Technician

The technician is responsible for translating the designer's plans into working drawings and for the division of the settings into units of scenery capable of easy handling and shifting. He perfects the designer's general scheme for shifting scenery and solves in detail the problems concerned with construction and rigging. He sees that all shop equipment is kept in good workable condition and keeps an adequate supply of building material and hardware in stock at all times. With the aid of the building carpenter and the stage carpenter the technician supervises the building, assembly, and rigging of all scenery. The sound effects and properties that are to be built are constructed under his direction.

Draftsmen

The technician may have one or more draftsmen as assistants in translating the designer's plans into working drawings from which the scenery and special properties are actually made.

Building Carpenter

The building carpenter is the shop foreman, whose duty it is to supervise the actual cutting, covering, and assembling of all units of scenery called for by the working drawings. He keeps the technician advised about the amount of building materials on hand. He assigns work to each member of the building crew and checks the progress of each unit under construction. The maintenance of all hand and power tools is under his supervision. He sees to it that the scene shop is kept clean and that all building materials and hardware are properly stored.

Building Crew

The building crew is usually composed of volunteer workers or students from classes in stagecraft or technical production who work on the crew as part of their laboratory requirement.

Stage Carpenter

In educational or community productions the duties of the stage carpenter are frequently combined with those of the stage manager. The stage carpenter and crew are responsible for the rigging and shifting and storage of all scenery during dress rehearsals and the run of the production. He plans the sequence of shifting operations, designates storage areas, and makes individual crew assignments. He must see that the scenery is kept in good condition during the run of the play and that settings are properly struck and stored at the close of the run.

Stage Crew

The stage crew, like the building crew, is composed of either students or volunteer workers. Students are usually alternated from the building crew of one production to the stage crew of the next to provide them with an opportunity to learn two phases of backstage work and organization.

Property Master

Properties that have been selected by joint agreement of the director and designer are assembled by the property master and crew. Properties are purchased, rented, borrowed, or built by members of the prop crew under the supervision of the property mastery or technician and from working drawings provided by him. Since the moving and storing of properties are carried on simultaneously with the shifting of scenery, the property master and his crew work under the supervision of the technician or stage manager and in close cooperation with stage and light crews.

Property Crew

The members of the property crew, under the supervision of the property master, help in the procurement or construction of all props. During the rehearsal period and the run of the play the crew is usually divided into two sections, one responsible for the placement, shifting, and storing of all decorative and hand props, the other responsible for floor props.

Sound Crew

Ordinary offstage sound effects of a simple nature are usually handled by members of the prop crew. Occasionally a production may require a great many varied and complicated sound effects, or the script may be accompanied in part by a musical score. In such cases it is advisable to have a special crew that can devote its entire attention to synchronizing the sound effects, on the proper cue, to the action and business of the play.

Lighting Designer

The lighting designer works closely with the director, scenic and costume designers in planning the lighting for a production. The duties of the lighting designer include drawing the lighting plot and instrument schedule or hook-up sheet, supervising the hanging and focusing of the instruments, and coordinating the control of the lights during rehearsals and performances.

Light Crew

The work of the light crew is of such a nature that it requires a logical division of the crew into sections for specific purposes. In practice a member of the light crew will work in several if not all of these areas.

1. The hanging crew is responsible for the accurate hanging, circuiting, and coloring of all lighting instruments according to the information contained in the light plot and the instrument schedule.
2. The focusing crew is responsible for the accurate focusing of the lighting instruments so that the light from each instrument is directed to the point specified by the lighting designer.
3. The running crew controls the light board and the specialty instruments, such as followspots, during the rehearsals and performances. It is also

responsible for the movement and relocation of light booms and practical lamps during scene shifts, as well as the necessary repatching of the dimmers and changing of color media during all rehearsals and performances.

Costume Designer

The costume designer submits sketches to the director for all costumes to be used in the play. These may be either rented or made in the theatre's shop. When the latter is the case, the sketches are usually accompanied by material samples and cost estimates. After the director approves the designs, the costume designer determines what stock costumes may be altered for use in the current production and then buys the remaining fabrics and accessories and supervises the making of the costumes. When costumes are rented, the designer places the orders and supervises all necessary adjusting and fitting of the costumes.

Costume Crew

The costume designer usually divides the members of the costume crew into two groups: construction crew and wardrobe crew. The construction crew is concerned with the actual cutting, fitting, and assembling of all costumes. The wardrobe crew assumes responsibility for the completed costumes and their maintenance from the time they are first used in dress rehearsal until the close of the run. Both crews are under the supervision of the costume designer.

Business Manager

The business manager keeps the books and accounts of the organization in order. Cost estimates for costumes, scenery, properties, and lighting are submitted to him by department heads, and he keeps them within established budgets. It sometimes becomes necessary to simplify or alter some phase of the production work to bring the total cost within the limits of these budgets. Changes made for this reason must be approved by the director, and notification of such changes must be given to the department heads whose work is affected by them. All advertising, news stories, and general publicity are handled by the business manager after consultation with and approval by the director. Working under the direction of the business manager is the house staff whose duties are sufficiently described by their titles:

1. House manager.
2. Ticket sellers.
3. Ticket takers.
4. Ushers.
5. Cloakroom attendants.

NEED FOR COOPERATIVE EFFORT

With an organization as large and as complicated as a theatre production staff the necessity for close cooperation between all department heads is obvious. Otherwise misunderstandings or differences of opinion concerning some vital part of the work may result in a performance in which some elements of the production are not in accord.

This cooperation is best achieved by conferences at which problems bearing on the production are discussed. Such meetings should occur frequently enough during the preparation of the play so that those who are responsible for the various phases of the work are conscious of the progress achieved by others, and of any changes that may affect their own work. In this manner many problems that might go unnoticed until the first dress rehearsal can be caught early and solutions found for them. The time thus saved during the dress rehearsal period can well be devoted to the integration of the elements of a production rather than to the correction of needless mistakes resulting from lack of communications.

A well-balanced artistic production can result only when all department heads and various assistants have a complete understanding of the ultimate goal to be attained by the fusion of their individual efforts.

2

The Relationship Between the Scene Designer and the Scene Technician

Perhaps at no place within the structure of a theatre production staff is the need for cooperation more clearly evident than between the scene designer and the technician. Actually the work of the technician is so completely dependent upon the designer's plans that little if anything can be accomplished toward the construction of scenery until the designer's plans are in the hands of the technician. There is nothing unusual about this arrangement: it is simply that those working within the theatre must follow the same pattern used by any group of individuals who are concerned with the general problems associated with designing and building. Whether the object under consideration is a bridge, a house, or a set of scenery, certain basic steps must be taken before construction can actually begin. First, of course, is the actual design of the object, by which its nature and form are determined. Once the design has been established, it is relatively easy to describe it in detail and in terms of specific measurements. These two steps are the responsibility of the designer. Although detailed discussion of the duties of the scene designer is beyond the scope of this book, it is essential that the technician understand just what the designer's plans are and what they are intended to convey, for the obvious reason that the technician must convert these plans into working drawings that will supply all information needed by the building crews in constructing the scenery.

THE DESIGNER'S PLANS

The designer may present his ideas for a proposed setting to the director and to the production staff by either of two methods: (1) he may use a three-dimensional scaled model, or (2) he may represent the setting by means of a colored perspective sketch. In either case it is necessary to supplement the model or sketch with mechanical drawings that describe the setting in greater detail and with greater accuracy. These drawings are known as the designer's plans; they consist of ground plans, sight-line drawings, front elevations, and detail drawings.

The Model

The majority of scene designers prefer to present their ideas by means of colored perspective sketches rather than models, simply because they are easier and faster to make. However, there are occasions when a model is the only practical method of approaching a particularly difficult problem. Settings that are highly irregular in form or that employ forced perspective or that are unusually compli-cated in construction are frequently worked out in detail by the designer with models constructed of clay and cardboard. There are additional disadvantages to the use of models besides the time and skill required to build them. Models are awkward to handle and to carry about, and unless they are very well made they are constantly in need of repairs. Small, detachable parts are easily lost or broken. But despite these handicaps there is no question but that the scaled three-dimensional model provides the production staff and the cast with a much clearer picture of what the proposed setting will be than will a sketch. Some directors prefer to work with a model because it gives them an opportunity to try out stage pictures and groupings of actors by moving miniature-scaled figures about within it.

The Sketch

Whether the designer expresses ideas by means of a model or a sketch, they both serve the same purpose and form the nucleus around which is centered all of the activity associated with the process of planning and constructing scenery (Plate 2).

The sketch of a proposed setting is usually rendered in color and is drawn to represent it as it would appear to a member of the audience who is seated in the center and about halfway back in the auditorium. Usually these sketches are quite complete and represent not only the style and form of the setting but the furniture and property arrangements as well.

The inclusion of a figure of an actor in the sketch can help establish its scale. This is especially desirable if the setting is an exterior scene such as a forest or a river bank or of any scene composed of simple ramps and platforms. In such settings there are usually few keys that aid the viewer in determining just how large or small the setting really is. However, should the setting be realistic in

Plate 2   Perspective Sketch for *The Physicists*

style and include such features as conventional furniture, these features give the proper scale to a sketch and the designer may feel that there is little need to include the figure of an actor.

Frequently the designer may attempt, through his rendering, to give some indication of the proposed lighting scheme. Such a sketch provides all members of the staff and cast with a clear visual representation of what the finished setting will be. Although the general arrangement of the room, the location of such architectural features as doors, windows, fireplace, or stairway are all indicated, the designer's primary concern is with the problem of describing the setting. No matter how accurately the perspective has been drawn or how well rendered the sketch may be, it is nevertheless totally inadequate as a guide to the technician who is concerned with the problem of how to build it. In this respect the sketch can be compared to a photograph: both give a clear picture of what the finished object should look like, but neither provides the necessary information required for its construction. In any event when the sketch is presented to the director for approval it should be accompanied by a ground plan of the setting. On viewing a sketch some of the first questions asked by many directors are likely to be, ''How deep is it; what is its angle of rake; how about sight lines; and do I have room enough to get a wheelchair through that doorway?'' A ground plan with clearly established dimensions answers all of these questions and is a positive step toward the elimination of many misunderstandings.

Perhaps the most critical step in the whole process of designing comes at this point. The sketch or model is complete and it has been approved by the director and the rest of the production staff; yet it in no way gives the technician the necessary specifications and dimensions that will permit him to start construction. If the sketch were his only guide, the best he could possibly do would be to guess at the dimensions the designer might have had in mind, with the result that the completed setting would be only a rough approximation of the designer's intentions. Since this would be a foolhardy procedure at best, the designer must translate his sketch or model into terms of actual feet and inches by means of ground plans, elevations, and detail drawings.

Ground Plans

Scenery is designed not only for a specific play but for a particular stage. It is probably redundant to say that the designer must know the physical characteristics and dimensions of the stage on which she is to work just as thoroughly as a tailor must know the measurements of an individual for whom he is making a suit. Neither can hope for a well-fitted product unless these factors are constantly kept in mind.

There is no agreement among designers on just when the details of the ground plans should be worked out. Some maintain that the ground plans should be made first and the sketches or models based upon these; others declare that they conceive the ideas for their setting in sketch form and then adapt them to the dimensions of the stage. It makes little difference which method is used just so long as it is done, for the ground plans form the key plates on which all other drawings are based.

The ground plan is a scaled mechanical drawing representing the setting in top view as it appears in relation to the stage on which it is to be presented. Perhaps the best way to visualize it is to imagine that you are in a position directly above the setting, from which the ceiling has been removed; what you would see from this vantage point is represented on the ground plan. Such a view should show the exact shape and size of the setting in relation to the proscenium arch and the curtain line, the width and angle of all wall sections, the location and width of all doors and the direction of their swing. The exact placing and dimensions can be shown for such architectural features as windows, stairways, columns, niches, alcoves, and fireplaces. The location and width of all masking backings that will be seen through windows or doorways can be clearly shown in this drawing. In addition, the amount of available storage space for scenery or properties or for the location of lighting instruments can be determined with accuracy (Plate 3).

The production of *The Physicists* was presented in the Studio Theatre at the University of Iowa. The Studio Theatre had at one time been a gymnasium large enough to house a full-sized basketball court. Suspended from overhead beams and attached to the four walls of the gym at a height of 10'-10" from the floor was a running track that provided an encircling balcony. At one end of the gym a 7'-0" by 24'-0" extension had been added to the balcony to form a second-level acting area whenever it was needed. Since the Studio Theatre had no proscenium arch and no front curtain, the balcony front and its extension were used as the architectural feature of the "stage" to which the dimensions of the setting were related. In this manner the exact positioning of the setting within the confines of the gymnasium was established. It will be noted from the ground plan that most of the platforming, a small section of the back wall, and all of the necessary backings were actually under the balcony.

Because all members of the production staff make extensive use of the ground plans, the more complete and accurate they are the less chance there will be for misunderstandings or errors. The director is the first to make use of the ground plans, since the designer presents them at the same time that he submits his sketches. This permits the two of them to discuss the proposed setting or

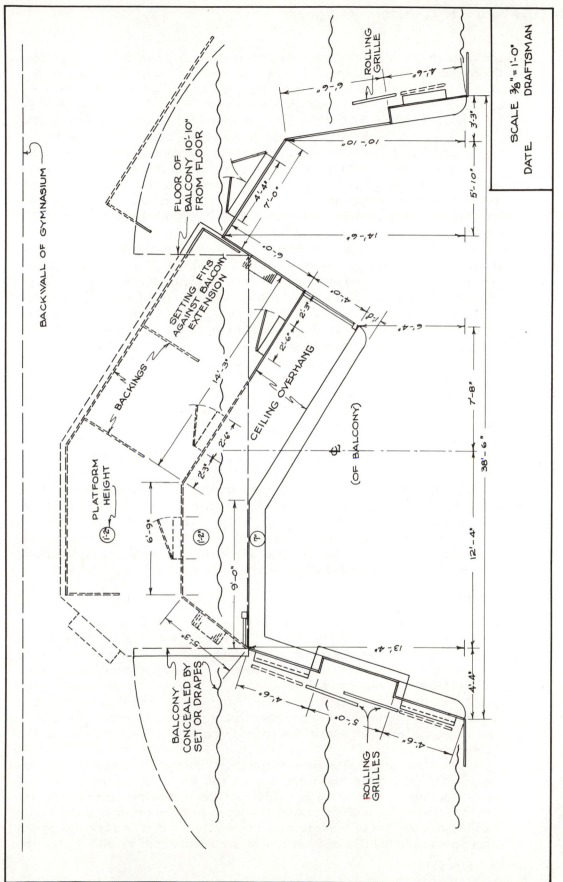

Plate 3 Ground Plan for *The Physicists*

settings in terms of specific measurements rather than generalities. Long before the scenery is either constructed or painted, the director has made use of this drawing by having the plan of the setting marked off on the stage floor for rehearsal purposes. When this procedure is followed, the blocking of stage business and movement and the timing required for actors to move from one part of the set to another can be established early in the rehearsal period.

One of the most important duties of the technician is to analyze a production to determine the method and sequence of construction and decide on what technique will be used to shift the various parts of the setting. At the same time the location of the storage areas for both scenery and properties can be decided on. Only by a careful study of the ground plans can the technician obtain the information that will enable her to make these decisions.

Constant reference is made to the ground plans during the period of construction to make certain that the scenic units are assembled properly and that they comply with the designer's specifications. The final trial setup of the scenery is usually done in the shop and checked against the dimensions and notations contained on the designer's ground plans. At this time not only are the overall dimensions of the scenery verified but the angles of joining are checked, as is the placing of bracing and lashing hardware. Faults in construction or rigging detected by this procedure can be corrected with a minimum loss of shop hours and before the scenery is moved to the paint frame for painting.

Extensive use is also made of the ground plans by the technician, who employs them during the time when the scene shifts are being organized and in order to clarify specific assignments given to individual members of the stage crew. This subject will be treated in detail in a later chapter.

Much of the preliminary planning of two other members of the production staff is based on the information contained in the ground plans; these are the lighting designer and the head of the property crew. Using a duplicate plan of each setting, the lighting designer can locate all major areas of the stage that are to receive light and determine the number, type, and mounting positions of the lighting instruments to be used. The property master, usually in consultation with both the director and the designer, also uses the ground plans to establish the exact location and size of all practical and decorative floor properties.

Sight Lines

Have you ever watched a production from a seat in the auditorium when the setting is so placed on stage that you can see but a part of it, or when some vital scene is played just beyond the limits of your visibility? If so, you will appreciate the importance of adequate sight lines. Determining satisfactory sight lines for a setting is the responsibility of the designer. This step must be taken early in the process of designing, usually at the time the ground plans are formulated. Sight-line drawings assure the designer that all important parts of the setting and all acting areas are within the range of visibility of each member of the audience.

Two separate drawings are required to test the sight lines of any proposed setting. One is a horizontal sectional plan and the other a vertical sectional elevation. Both must be carefully scaled mechanical drawings representing different views of the auditorium with the set in position on stage (Plate 4). By locating the position of the extreme side seats in the first and last row in the orchestra and in the first and last row of the balcony, it is possible to test the

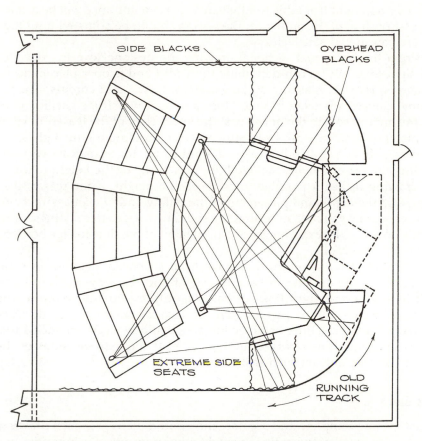

SIGHT LINE PLAN FOR THE PHYSICISTS PRODUCED IN THE STUDIO THEATRE (AT ONE TIME A GYMNASIUM)

HORIZONTAL SECTIONAL DRAWING

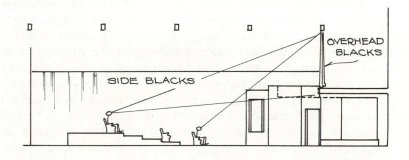

VERTICAL SECTIONAL DRAWING

Plate 4 Horizontal and Vertical Sectional Drawings

sight lines of a setting with surprising accuracy. A straight line drawn from one of these seats past the edge of the proscenium arch and to the setting will reveal how much or how little of the setting is visible to a person seated at that point. If it becomes apparent from this test that an important entrance will be lost to view to a good portion of the audience, the setting should be adjusted until the sight lines are considered satisfactory.

From the horizontal sectional drawing the designer can not only test for good sight lines but he can determine the width and proper placement for the tormentors, returns, masking backings, groundrows, and cutouts. The vertical sectional elevation is used in much the same manner. If a sight line is drawn from the highest seat in the house past the lower edge of the teaser, it will reveal how much or how little can be seen of an actor standing on the highest level of the setting. If this test indicates poor sight lines, these may be corrected by adjusting the teaser height, the depth of the setting, or the height of the levels. This drawing makes it possible to establish the height of the teaser, the light bridge, and the depth and placement of the ceiling and of all masking backings. This is especially valuable in testing the sightlines of exterior settings when it is essential to know the exact height and placement of possible foliage borders, tree silhouettes, and drops.

Unfortunately, some theatres have been so poorly planned in regard to sight lines that no amount of set adjustment and rearrangement can possibly result in satisfactory sight lines. It has been my experience to work within a theatre where, if sight lines were extended from the two extreme side seats past the proscenium arch, little or no acting area could be seen. In such situations there is only one satisfactory solution—rope off the extreme sides of the auditorium and do not sell such seats.

Front Elevations

No matter how complete and accurate the ground plans are, such drawings are lacking in one vital respect: they provide no opportunity for indicating vertical measurements. The designer's front elevations are scaled mechanical drawings representing a front view of the setting as it would appear when drawn in a single plane. Such drawings present the designer with a means of establishing, and showing, all vertical measurements. Drafting these front elevations must not be looked upon as so much "busy work," or a phase of designing that could just as well be omitted, for these drawings form one of the most critical steps in the process of designing. By their means the designer can construct a drawing that will be a proportional reduction of the finished setting. He will be able to see and adjust the relationship and proportion of wall areas to doors, windows, and other architectural features. Through the use of front elevations he can establish exact dimensions of such details as the size and number of repeats of a wallpaper pattern, the proper yardage of material needed for window draperies, and the size and placement of all wall hangings. Every part of the setting visible to the audience should be shown on the front elevations and should be personally checked by the designer as to proper size, proportion, and position. If he is pleased with the compositional arrangement of the setting as it appears in the elevations, and if he has accompanied it with accurate dimensions and concise notations, he may reasonably expect to be pleased with the finished setting (Plate 5).

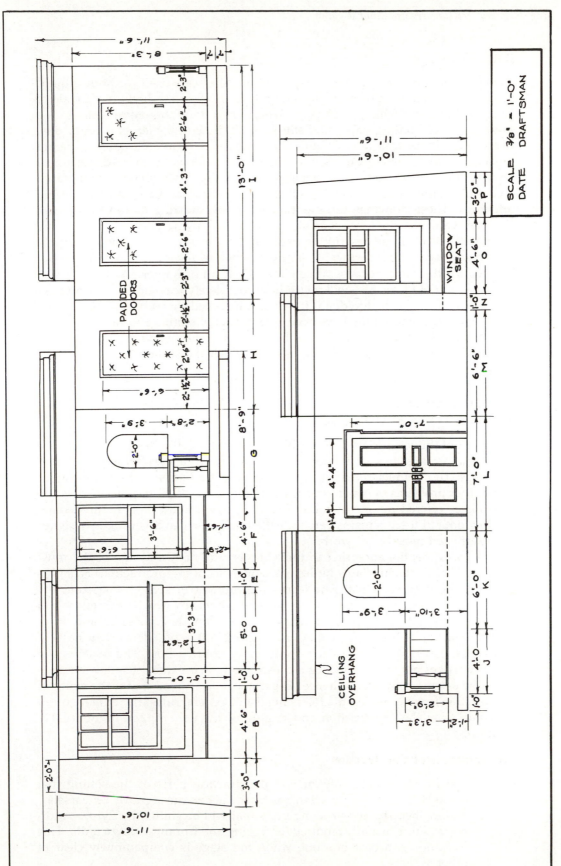

Plate 5 Front Elevations for *The Physicists*

Detail Drawings

Owing to the large size of most stage settings the scale used for both ground plans and elevations is of necessity small. Usually they are drawn on a scale of $3/8''$ or $1/2''$ to $1'-0''$, which permits the designer to draw the entire setting on a single sheet of drafting paper and still keep all dimensions large enough to be easily read. These scales, while quite adequate for plans and elevations, are not satisfactory for showing details and dimensions of smaller three-dimensional units of the setting, such as a fireplace or a stairway. Such objects are redrawn on a much larger scale, usually $3/4''$, $1''$, or $1\frac{1}{2}''$ to $1'-0''$, and are known as detail drawings. These drawings represent an object by showing its top, front, and side views and occasionally a sectional or cutaway drawing. The most commonly used methods of shape description used for this purpose are orthographic projection and isometric drawings. More rarely oblique and cabinet drawings may be used for the same purpose. (See Plates 40, 41 and Chapter 5.)

A study of Plates 2−6 will reveal how completely the setting for a production of *The Physicists* is described. It will also be noted that although the shape, form, and size of the setting have been given in detail, nothing in these drawings tells the carpenter how the set is to be built. The technician and his assistants are responsible for the working drawings from which the scenery will actually be constructed.

THE TECHNICIAN'S ANALYSIS OF A PRODUCTION

The work of the technician cannot really begin until all the designer's plans are in his hands: sketches or model, ground plans, front elevations, and detail drawings. The technician may have had earlier consultations with the designer to consider problems of construction, rigging, or cost, or perhaps to discuss the advantages offered by one method of shifting over another for the immediate production, but there remains very little the technician can do until the designer has completed most of his work.

As was mentioned earlier in this chapter, the first, and one of the most important, of the technician's duties is his analysis of the production. From his study of the designer's plans he learns the number of settings required, the complexity of the building job, and the general scheme by which the scenery will be shifted. He must anticipate the need for special building materials and order them in time for delivery before they are required in the shop. It is on the basis of this study that he determines the sequence of construction. The experienced technician does not necessarily begin construction on the first set simply because it will be seen first by the audience. Experience has proved that if the order of construction is governed by the following list of general rules, the time required for completing the construction and rigging of the scenery can be noticeably reduced.

The Sequence of Construction

1. List for immediate construction the practical parts of the setting that could be used to good advantage by the actors during early rehearsals.
2. Follow these by constructing units that will be shifted by flying. Additional time is usually required for rigging and trimming flown units. This operation can best be done when the stage is comparatively clear of other scenery.

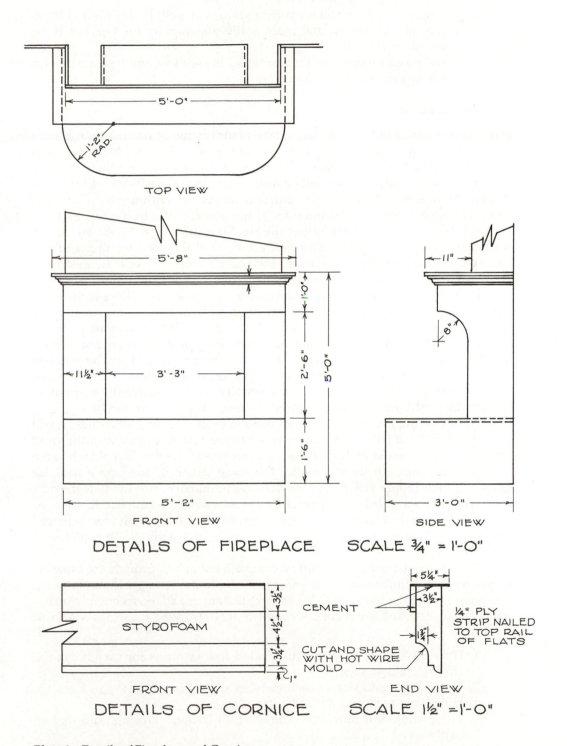

TOP VIEW

DETAILS OF FIREPLACE   SCALE ¾" = 1'-0"

FRONT VIEW

SIDE VIEW

DETAILS OF CORNICE   SCALE 1½" = 1'-0"

FRONT VIEW

END VIEW

Plate 6   Details of Fireplace and Cornice

3. Next in order of construction should be parts of settings scheduled for an elaborate and time-consuming paint job.
4. The order in which the remaining scenery is built is determined by its degree of complexity, the more easily and rapidly built pieces being reserved for the last.
5. Allow adequate time for a trial setup of the scenery and for adjustments in the rigging and stage hardware.

Working Drawings

It has been pointed out that the designer's plans are mechanical drawings used for the express purpose of describing the setting. The designer is interested in representing the front, or onstage side, of the scenery and in the adjustment and placement of the features that will contribute to the compositional effect of the design. Because the details of construction can be shown only by a drawing representing the rear, or offstage side, of the scenery, the technician makes a completely new set of plates called the working drawings. These are scaled mechanical drawings representing the rear view of the scenery; they indicate clearly what material should be used, the size and form of separate members, and how these separate members will be joined to form the whole. They are accompanied by all necessary dimensions and specifications. There is no better way to ensure a true realization of the designer's plans than to have an accurate and complete set of working drawings (Plate 7). The little additional time required to make them is more than offset by being able to detect and correct possible mistakes on the plans before they have been translated into lumber and canvas. A complete set of working drawings is especially desirable for the technician working in the educational or community theatre, where the majority of the building crew will be inexperienced students or volunteer workers.

In comparing the designer's elevations with the working drawings, it will be noticed that the latter not only represents the rear as opposed to the front view, but that the order of the flats has been reversed. The first flats drawn in the working drawings are those forming the stage left wall; successive flats are shown in their proper order, and the drawing terminates with the flats forming the stage right wall. Unless this procedure is followed, the entire setting will be reversed—a mistake that happens with surprising frequency with inexperienced draftsmen. They must train themselves to visualize the setting as they will see it from backstage.

The working drawings should be complete enough to provide the building carpenter with all information she will need to build the setting without frequent conferences with the technician. Verbal instructions are all too frequently inadequate, inaccurate, and unreliable. A complete set of working drawings will show the following:

1. How the setting has been subdivided to form units for easy handling, shifting, and storage.
2. The number and size of each member composing a unit.
3. How these members are to be joined.
4. The placing and number required of all lashing, bracing, and rigging hardware.
5. Proper allowances in size of openings for detachable door or window units or in the width of units to be joined by lashing.

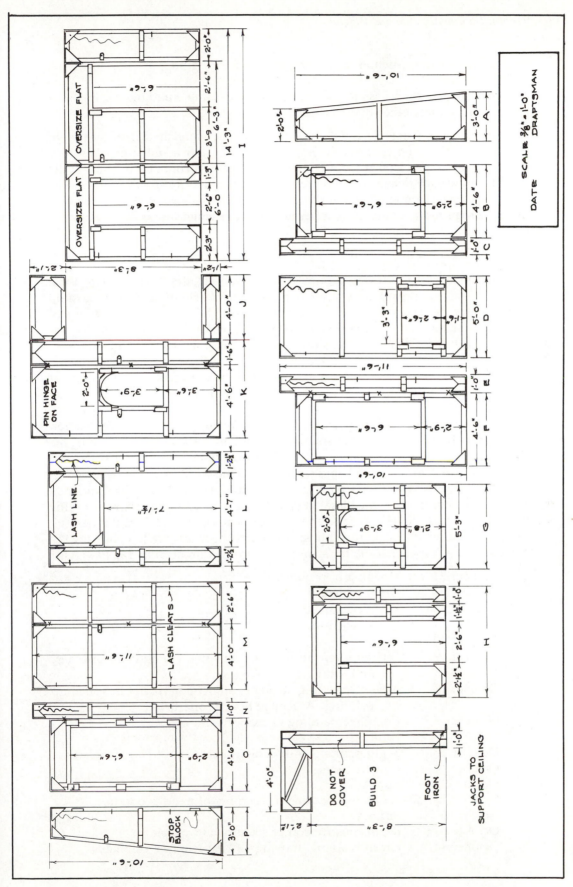

Plate 7 Working Drawings of Partial Flat Work for *The Physicists*

6. Special construction or framing required for rigging, shifting, or flying scenery.
7. Explanatory notes or specifications concerning building materials or procedures other than standard.

Working drawings need not be as complete nor as detailed as those shown in Plate 7. If the shop is under the supervision of a staff member or an experienced shop foreman well acquainted with scenic construction, there will be little need to show such details as the placement of corner blocks and keystones. The drawings can be simplified and drafting conventions established that will reduce the time required to complete a set of working drawings.

WORK SCHEDULE

In many theatrical-producing groups the approach of the opening date for a production is accompanied by a feverish increase of activity in the scene shop and on stage, often culminating in one or two all-night sessions for members of the paint, stage, and light crews. In some weird fashion such activity is associated with the old cliché "The show must go on!" It is looked upon as something of a lark and an indispensable part of the business of producing a play. Nothing could be further from the truth. Rather, it can be looked upon as proof that the technical work has been poorly planned or, more likely, not planned at all.

In the majority of cases the technician can avoid this type of complication by planning his work in advance and then sticking to the dates established by his work schedule. It requires only a little time to make out such a schedule; and there is no greater aid to an even distribution of the work load over a period of time than the use of such a plan. A work schedule is simply a calendar in reverse. It begins with the date the production is to open, then, working backward, it lists the days set aside for dress rehearsals and technical rehearsal, the days required for rigging, painting, construction, and so forth. Following is a sample of the work schedule for a single-set production such as *The Physicists:*

October 24	Opening of production.
October 23	Dress rehearsal.
October 22	Dress rehearsal.
October 21	Dress rehearsal.
October 20	Sunday.
October 19	Technical rehearsal, final adjustment of lights, properties, and setting.
October 18	Assemble setting on stage, adjustment of lights, touch up painting. Assemble floor properties.
October 17	Complete painting of scenery and props.
October 16	Painting.
October 15	Begin painting. All scenic construction to be completed.
October 14	Construction.
October 13	Sunday.
October 12–17	Construction. Begin assembly of hand properties.
October 6	Sunday.
October 5	Begin construction of scenery and props.
October 4	Finish working drawings. Complete cost estimates.

October 3   Begin drafting of working drawings.
October 2   Receipt of designer's plans. Analysis of production. Order
               building materials.

As the number of settings or their complexity increases, the greater becomes the need for a carefully planned work schedule. The technician will soon
learn that it is possible to carry on several phases of the work simultaneously.
For example, the construction of the first setting can be under way at the same
time that he is completing the working drawings for the second set, or the
scenery for act II can be painted while the completed setting for act I is being
rigged.

The dress rehearsals are used by the director to bring together and synchronize all elements of the production. This process of polishing the production
should not be handicapped by frantic last-minute operations by members of the
technical staff and their crews. The technician who has pride in her work will
have so planned and executed her assignment that the dress rehearsals can be
used for the purpose for which they were intended.

3

The Scene Shop

The material offered in this chapter and in Chapter 4 is basic to an understanding of scenic construction. Before any detailed account can be given of construction or rigging techniques, it is advisable for the student to understand to what a great extent his work can be improved and made easier by having a properly planned scene shop and by knowing the characteristics and peculiarities of the tools and materials with which he will be working. This is not meant to imply that good work cannot be done under conditions that are less than ideal—such a statement could be belied by the work of too many producing theatre groups. However, some of the suggestions made here can be adapted and used to improve existing shop conditions and to make possible a better selection of tools and materials.

A study conducted at the University of Iowa reveals that there has been little standardization within colleges and universities in planning and equipping the scene shop—in fact, it appears that very little thought has been given to the subject. Answers to a questionnaire that was a part of this study indicated that the theatre's scene shop could be found in such unlikely locations as an old two-car garage, a church, abandoned barracks, unused classrooms, under the stadium, or in the basement under the stage. Apparently it is felt that any space left over after all other activities of the theatre have been housed is quite satisfactory. This attitude has seriously impaired the efficiency of some otherwise well-planned theatre plants. The scene shop is much more than just a space where scenery can be built; it is in every sense a classroom or laboratory where students are taught the fundamentals of stagecraft and are provided an opportunity to learn the importance of organization and cooperation—a place where they may develop a sense of responsibility.

Thought and care are as important in planning a scene shop as they are in planning laboratories used by physics or chemistry. A fact not appreciated by some who have been responsible for planning our educational theatres is that the number of student hours spent in the shop in building, painting, and assembling scenery will often equal or exceed the total time spent by the cast in rehearsing the production. The efficiency and safety of all operations performed within the shop are dependent upon how well the shop has been planned.

There are two schools of thought regarding the location for the scene shop in college or university theatres. One faction stoutly maintains that the shop should be an integral part of the theatre building, that it should be on the same floor level as the stage, and provided with large soundproof doors giving easy access to the stage. The second faction is just as convinced that the scene shop should be separate from the theatre, preferably in a building some distance removed from the stage. Members of this second group are quick to point out that their system parallels the conditions found in the professional theatre and in many community theatres. Students trained under these conditions are made aware of the importance of planning and building scenery that can be moved and stored easily. They continue with a statement that with the shop in a separate building there is no possibility of shop noises, fumes, or dust disturbing activities on the stage, and if need be, both stage and shop can be in operation at the same time.

Those who advocate that the shop should be in the theatre building argue that this plan permits a smaller staff to supervise the work. They also state that although it is possible for them to build large units of scenery and simply roll it from shop to stage, this is not invariably the rule. They point out that their students receive much practical experience in planning and building scenery that can be moved and stored easily. Their argument continues by pointing out that with the shop and stage in close proximity to each other little time is wasted in the process of rigging and maintaining a production because of the nearness to tools and supplies. And finally, it is pointed out, they save with both the time and the expense required for trucking the scenery from the shop to the stage and they need never wait for inclement weather to pass before beginning the move. It is obvious that sound arguments can be made on both sides of this question. There appears little likelihood that the relationship of the shop to the stage can be settled to everyone's satisfaction and that examples will continue to be found in which successful operations are achieved through the use of each system.

Having worked in scene shops located within a theatre building and in scene shops far removed from the stage, the writers find more to be said for than against the location of the shop inside the main theatre building. Until that time comes when truly effective soundproofing will permit the full simultaneous operation of shop and stage, a careful scheduling of the different types of shop activities will solve most of the problems.

PHYSICAL REQUIREMENTS
OF THE SCENE SHOP

The construction of scenery parallels the pattern of operations found in the manufacture of any product; that is, raw materials enter one end of the shop and after a series of progressive steps the finished product emerges from the other. A list of the operational steps normally accomplished within the limits of the scene shop provides the basis for determining the actual size and form of the space devoted to these purposes. Several of these constructional operations demand much floor space to be accomplished expeditiously. Probably more than any other factor the failure to understand or appreciate these basic requirements has resulted in shops so limited in floor space or height that their efficiency has been greatly reduced (Plate 8). In the following list both the operational steps and the type of space needed to accomplish them are given:

Operational Steps	Type of Space Required
1. Storage of new materials	Horizontal and vertical
2. Storage of stock scenery	Vertical
3. Marking and cutting lumber	Horizontal
4. Framing and alteration	Horizontal
5. Covering	Horizontal
6. Joining	Horizontal
7. Placement of hardware	Horizontal
8. Trial setup	Horizontal and vertical
9. Painting	Vertical
10. Storage of hand tools	Vertical
11. Storage of theatrical hardware	Vertical
12. Placement of power tools	Horizontal

Storage of New Material

Lumber and compositional and covering material constitute most of the new material for which storage facilities should be provided. Of these the placing and the space required for the storage of lumber are the most imporant. The lumber rack should be placed as near the shop-loading door as possible to avoid interrupting building operations that may be in progress at the time the lumber is delivered. Less floor space is required for this storage if some type of lumber rack is developed. One of the better types is a series of shelves formed by strap-iron brackets bolted solidly to the wall. Several comparatively narrow shelves are better than one or two deep ones, as this conserves floor space and provides individual spaces for varying widths of lumber.

Where space permits, compositional material such as plywood and Upson board is stored on its face. Since this material is sold in sheets 4'-0" wide and 8'-0" to 10'-0" long, it may not be possible to allow adequate floor space for storing it. In this case the following substitute can be used: two rigid wood frames about 6'-0" high and 3'-6" wide and bolted 8" apart at right angles to a wall. The compositional material is slipped between these supporting frames and stored on end.

Canvas and muslin covering material are usually sold in rolls of 50 to 100 yards. A pipe slipped through the center of the roll and supported on brackets attached to the end of the template bench makes a convenient way of storing and handling this material.

Storage of Scenery

One of the heaviest cost items in the production of plays is the construction of scenery. The personnel of educational and community theatres have wisely tried to keep this item at a minimum cost by reusing scenery built for previous pro-

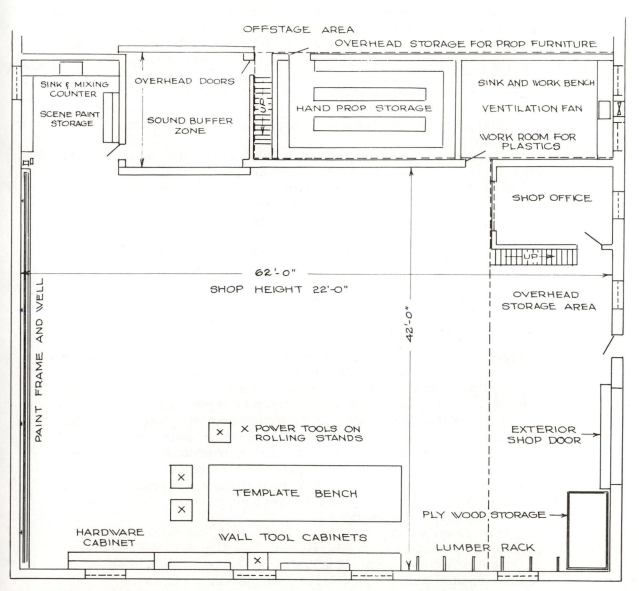

Plate 8   Plan for a Scene Shop

ductions. However, the number of times stock scenery can be reused is largely dependent upon the degree of care given it in handling and the kind of storage provided for it.

There are two basic requirements for scenery storage docks: they should be in or near the scene shop, and they should be designed in such a manner that flats may be taken from them or stored in them with a minimum of effort. Scene docks located on a floor level different from that of the shop or in some distant building are not only inconvenient to use but have a tendency to defeat the very purpose for which scenery is stored, namely its reuse. To prevent damage resulting from mildew, water stains, and warping, care must be used to select a dry, well-ventilated storage space. There is less danger of torn canvas or warped frames if the flats are stored in a vertical position and at right angles to a wall. Pipe or 2" × 4" framing partitions divide the storage area into compartments for different types of flats. Such an arrangement makes it easy to slip a flat in or out of the dock.

The extent of available storage space will determine the amount of bulky three-dimensional scenery that can be kept for possible reuse. Units such as doors, windows, fireplaces, or stairways that are both heavy and space consuming are normally dismantled at the close of a production, and all reusable material salvaged. Experience has proved that units of this type are seldom reused without major alterations.

Both rigid and folding platforms are usually kept as part of the stock scenery. Rigid platforms and the tops of the parallels can be stored vertically by leaning them against a wall. Supporting frames of the parallels are best stored by stacking them one on top of the other.

Measuring and Cutting Lumber

Most new lumber used in the construction of scenery is ordered in the proper width for a specific purpose rather than in a wider width that must then be ripped to size. There are two advantages to this procedure: it eliminates the work of having to rip and dress the lumber, and it is less expensive.

It is important that lumber can be moved from its storage rack to the worktable and the power saw where it will be cut without interfering with other shop operations. The actual selection and marking of material are done by the shop foreman, because of his knowledge of building procedure and materials on hand for reuse, is better qualified to make such decisions. Each piece so marked for cutting is given an identification number or letter that aids in the assembly of the unit and helps avoid possible loss.

Most power sawing of lumber is crosscutting, which can be best accomplished by a pull-over, or radial, saw (see Plate 20, p. 54). When these saws are mounted with the cutting table flush with the top of the adjacent workbenches, an ideal surface is provided for both measuring and cutting.

Unless there are adequate crew members available to assemble the flat frames as the lumber is cut, it is well not to precut more than two or three flats at a time. This will avoid the possibility of some of the cut lumber being misplaced or its being used for other purposes.

Framing and Altering

The process of assembling the cut lumber into flat frames can be greatly speeded up and made less tiring for crew members if a template bench is used. This is a heavy worktable 6'-0" wide and 18'-0" or 20'-0" long. A raised edge along two sides of the bench forms an accurate right angle that can be used to good advantage in aligning flat frames. When the template bench is located near the measuring and cutting table, minimum time is required to move cut material from one to the other. It is extremely important that the template bench be placed in such a position that working space is available on all four sides.

There are two types of templates: one has a solid work top; the other has a partial or skeletal top and is used in many professional studios. Although the latter is admirably suited for mass production of standard flats, it is poorly suited for general work. A template bench with a solid work top is best suited for the nonprofessional theatre, where as much work is done in altering old flats and in building properties as in constructing new scenery.

Rather than having the template bench placed in a permanent position, it is advisable to have it mounted on swivel castors so that it can be moved from place to place. The castors should be equipped with all steel wheels rather than rubber tired wheels, and they should also be fitted with a locking device. Wheels with rubber tires, if they are allowed to stand for any length of time under a heavy load, have a tendency to flatten out at the point of contact with the floor. Because of this they are unsatisfactory for this job. Having the template bench fitted with swivel castors greatly facilitates moving the bench when floor space is needed for other shop operations.

Covering

One of the most critical steps in the construction of scenery is the process of covering the flat frames with canvas or muslin. This operation demands adequate floor space, as the flats must be placed in a horizontal position to receive the covering material. Should the template bench, which is ideal for the purpose, be in use, the flats can be supported on a series of sawhorses or placed on the shop floor. Details of the various steps used in the process of covering flats will be discussed in a later chapter.

Joining

The parts of a stage setting consisting of unbroken wall areas are usually formed by joining two or more standard plain flats edge to edge. Such flats are usually joined by hinging them on the face and concealing the junction and hinges with a strip of canvas or muslin tacked and glued into position. This procedure reduces the number of individual flats that must be handled and the number of lashings that must be made during the shift. The hinged flats form a compact unit that can be folded for easy handling and storage.

Placement of Hardware

After the flats have been joined, they are turned face down to receive the lashing and bracing hardware. This is another operation demanding adequate floor space, because many of the larger units will be composed of two, three, or even four flats hinged together. The exact position for each piece of hardware has been determined by the technician and is clearly shown on the working drawings. It is a wise precaution, however, to check the placement of all hardware to make certain that all items have been properly installed and are correctly aligned. Normally the hardware is not attached to the scenery until the flats have been covered and joined, because the lash lines, stiffening battens, and stop blocks prevent the flats from lying flat and complicate the process of covering and joining.

Trial Setup

Whenever the nature of the design will permit, and there is the necessary floor space within the shop, the technician will arrange for a trial setup. This provides him with the opportunity of seeing that all parts of the setting have been built, that they are of the correct size and shape, and that they fit properly. It also provides him with an excellent chance to double-check the placement of all lashing and bracing hardware and to see the various parts of the setting standing in a vertical position as they will when placed onstage. Frequently he will find that some hardware has been omitted, that lash cleats have been placed too close to toggle bars, making it difficult for the thrown lash line to engage them, or he will find junctions between flats that need additional stop blocks or stop cleats to close them properly.

The trial setup assures the technician, before the painting is started, that he is delivering all parts of the setting to the designer. There is probably no omission quite so disturbing to the designer as the discovery that some small but critical flat has been overlooked in the building and its absence not noticed until the finished scenery is being assembled onstage for the first time. Corrections that must be made in the finished paint job because of such omissions and unforeseen alterations are difficult to accomplish and costly in time and effort. Such mistakes can be detected in advance by the trial setup, and the necessary steps taken to correct them. Should there be inadequate space within the shop to accommodate a full set of scenery, the same information can be obtained by a partial trial setup. Adjacent units of scenery are tested one against the other for proper fit and size.

SCENE-PAINTING EQUIPMENT

Contrary to the practice followed in the professional theatre, where the scenery is built in one studio and painted in another, the scene shop of the majority of educational and community theatres is planned to provide the necessary facilities for both construction and painting of scenery. The reason for this arrangement is twofold: it not only conserves space, but, more importantly, it allows one person to supervise both operations.

The painting of scenery is the last operation to be performed in the shop before the scenery is moved to the stage. This means that in order to reduce the distance the finished scenery must be moved and to avoid interrupting other building operations, the paint frame should be located as near to the stage entrance as possible. Further details on the layout of the paint shop and scene painting equipment are discussed in Chapter 11.

HAND TOOLS

In both community and educational theatres hand tools are owned by the organization. Their selection, care, and storage become the responsibility of the shop foreman or the technician. The hand tools required in the scene shop are the same as those needed for any other type of general woodworking. Most of them can be grouped together under general classifications determined by their use: measuring tools, cutting tools, drilling tools, planing tools, driving tools, clamping tools, wrenches, dismantling tools, and miscellaneous tools. The following lists include those tools most frequently needed in scenic construction. No effort has been made here to present all-inclusive lists; the type of tool selected will vary according to the needs, personal preference, and the experience of the technician.

Measuring Tools

Pocket Tapes with Blades 8', 10', or 12' Long. Carried by all crew members and used for all general measurements. Much less likely to be broken than folding metal or wooden rules (Plate 9).

Outside Calipers. An instrument used for measuring the outside thickness of an object or the distance between two of its points. Especially useful in lathe work.

Inside Calipers. A tool similar to an outside calipers except that it is used to determine the inside measurements of an object.

Dividers. An instrument for dividing lines and transferring measurements.

Venier Calipers. A combination tool by which both inside and outside measurements can be determined as in reading the inside and outside diameters of a pipe. It may also be used to measure the depth of a predrilled hole.

Fifty-Foot Roll-Steel Tape. Required for checking over-all measurements, laying out setting ground plans on stage, and so forth.

Combination Square. Used for checking true 45 and 90° angles and as a guide for marking lumber preparatory to sawing.

Bevel Protractor. The calibrated head permits setting the marking blade at any desired angle.

Steel Square. Required for checking true 90° joints in the assembling of flat frames.

Bevel Set. A tool with an adjustable blade that can be set at any angle. Used as an aid in marking lumber and checking the accuracy of angular joints.

Marking Gauge. A measure tool used in scribing a line parallel with the length of lumber or across the width and thickness of stock.

Level. A tool used in determining true horizontal and vertical planes.

Cutting Tools

Crosscut Saw. A handsaw designed to cut across the graining of wood. The teeth are filed on a bevel of 65° and are sharply pointed. A 26″ saw with 10 teeth per inch is about ideal for scenic work. (See Plate 10.)

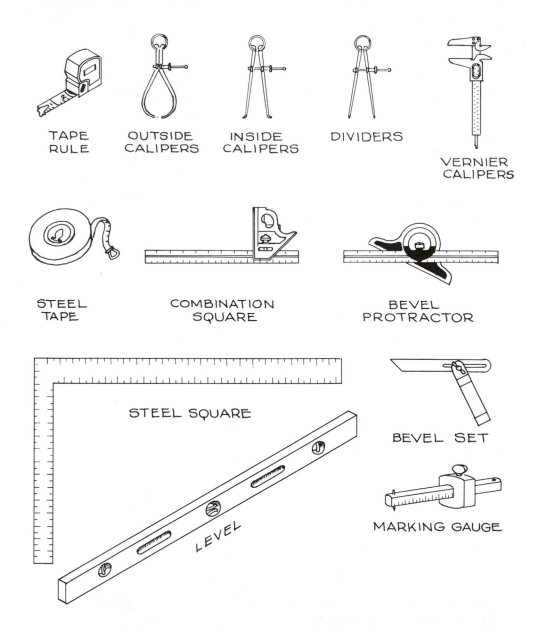

TAPE
RULE

OUTSIDE
CALIPERS

INSIDE
CALIPERS

DIVIDERS

VERNIER
CALIPERS

STEEL
TAPE

COMBINATION
SQUARE

BEVEL
PROTRACTOR

STEEL SQUARE

BEVEL SET

MARKING GAUGE

LEVEL

Plate 9　Measuring Tools

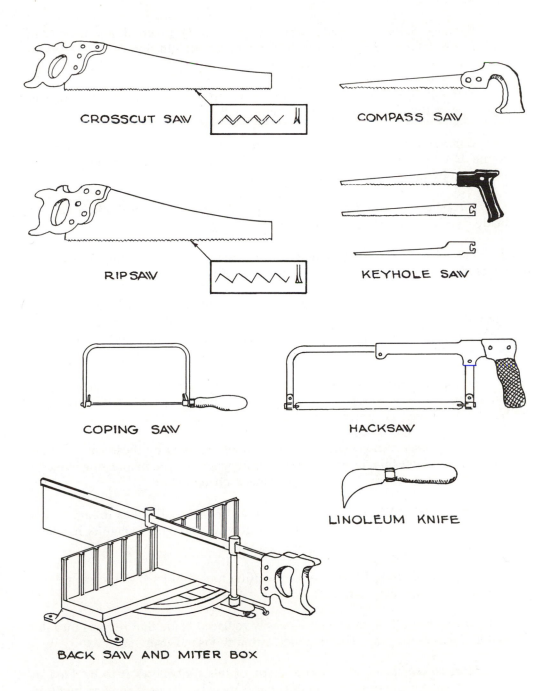

CROSSCUT SAW

COMPASS SAW

RIPSAW

KEYHOLE SAW

COPING SAW

HACKSAW

LINOLEUM KNIFE

BACK SAW AND MITER BOX

Plate 10   Cutting Tools

Ripsaw.   A saw designed to cut parallel with the grain of the wood. The teeth are filed at right angles to the side of the blade, resulting in flat, chisel-shaped cutting edges.

Compass Saw.   The blade of this saw is 12″ to 14″ in length and tapered in width. It is used in cutting arcs or curves and for straight-line cutting in places too small for the ripsaw or crosscut saw.

Keyhole Saw.   A saw similar to the compass saw but with a narrower blade, permitting curvilinear cutting on a smaller radius.

Coping Saw.   A very narrow and thin blade held taut by a spring-back frame. Used for the finest work and cutting highly irregular curves. Depth of cut is limited by distance from blade to back of frame.

Hacksaw.   A saw similar to the coping saw in shape but with a heavier blade that has been tempered to cut metal.

Linoleum Knife.   Although originally designed to cut linoleum, it may also be used to cut or carve many different types of wood or plastic.

Miter or Back Saw and Miter Box.   A fine-toothed crosscut saw with the back edge of the blade stiffened by a steel rib. The blade fits into carriages on the miter box that can be adjusted from 45° to 90° for cuts to either left or right. The carriages hold and guide the saw in making accurate right-angle or angular cuts.

Duckbill Snips.   A tool designed to cut light-weight metal such as tin, aluminum, brass, or copper. The shape of the blades permits left- and right-hand cuts as well as straight cuts (Plate 11).

Compound-Leverage Snips.   The leverage provided by these snips makes them easier to use than ordinary snips. Three types are obtainable; one makes a straight cut, one a right-hand cut, and one a left-hand cut.

Nail-Cutting Nippers.   The 10″ handles of this tool makes it easy to cut through the shaft of most nails; also a very good tool to remove bent or headless nails.

Diagonal-Cutting Pliers.   A wire-cutting tool with jaws shaped to permit cutting wire flush with a surface.

Utility Knife.   A knife with an easily replaced blade that retracts into the handle for safe carrying. This is a tool with a thousand uses.

Mini Hacksaw.   The size and shape of this tool allows it to be used in restricted spaces where a conventional hacksaw is too large. Can even be fitted with broken pieces of hacksaw blades.

Scratch Awl.   Used for scratching marks on sheet metal. Can be used for enlarging holes or starting holes to receive wood screws.

DUCKBILL SNIPS

COMPOUND-LEVERAGE SNIPS STRAIGHT CUT

NAIL-CUTTING NIPPERS

DIAGONAL-CUTTING PLIERS

UTILITY KNIFE

MINI HACK SAW

SCRATCH AWL

CARVING TOOLS

SURFORM TOOL

BOLT CUTTER

Plate 11 Cutting Tools

Carving Tools.   A set of wood-cutting chisels with blades made of hand-forged tool steel, hardened and polished for lasting sharpness. The set usually consists of a bevel chisel, a bent chisel, a "U"-shaped gouge, bent gouge, and a veining tool.

Surform Tool.   These tools come in several different shapes. They provide a fast and easy way of shaping wood, plastics, tile, copper, and aluminum. Replaceable blades can be found for certain types of Surform tools. Surform is a trade mark of the Stanley Tool Company.

Bolt Cutter.   Chrome molybdenum steel jaws plus compound leverage permits the cutting of soft- and medium-hardness metal bolts.

Drilling Tools

Open Rachet Brace.   A tool designed for clamping and turning an auger bit. It is provided with two handles: a pivot handle and an offset crank handle by which the bit is rotated. Better quality braces are fitted with a ratchet, needed for work in close quarters, that permits the bit to be driven forward with a back-and-forth motion of the crank handle. Woodcutting bits increase in diameter by $1/16$" and may be obtained in sizes from $1/4$" to 1". Expansion bits, with an adjustable cutter blade, can be used for drilling holes from $7/8$" up to 3" in diameter. (See Plate 12.)

Hand Drill.   Straight-shanked twist drills are clamped tightly by the jaws of this tool and rotated by turning a small-geared wheel. The chuck of the average hand drill will not accommodate drills with a diameter larger than $1/4$". Twist drills are tempered for work in both metal and wood.

Electric Drill.   The variable speed, reversible motor hand drill is one of the technician's most versatile tools. It not only drills rapidly into wood and metal, but with proper accessories it can be used for doweling, sawing circular holes, driving and removing screws, removing rust and paint, and to buff, sand, and polish.

Breast Drill.   Similar to the hand drill but heavier in construction and capable of handling drills up to $1/2$" in diameter. The gearing of this drill can be shifted from slow to fast speed, and the frame is equipped with a bracket or strap against which the workman can lean to gain greater cutting pressure. To a great extent this tool has been replaced by the portable electric drill.

Push Drill.   A straight-shafted tool fitted with spring return spirals that rotate the chuck and bit by pressure on the handle. Designed for light work.

Auger Bit.   To be used in a brace for drilling holes in wood. The bits vary in size from $1/4$" to 1" increasing in diameter by $1/16$th of an inch. (See Plate 13.)

Spade Bit.   A wood-drilling bit to be used in an electric drill. Without the lead-in screw of a typical auger bit there is no tendency for this bit to overbite.

Twist Drill Bit.   Designed for metal drilling but can be used in wood and in either hand-powered or electric drills.

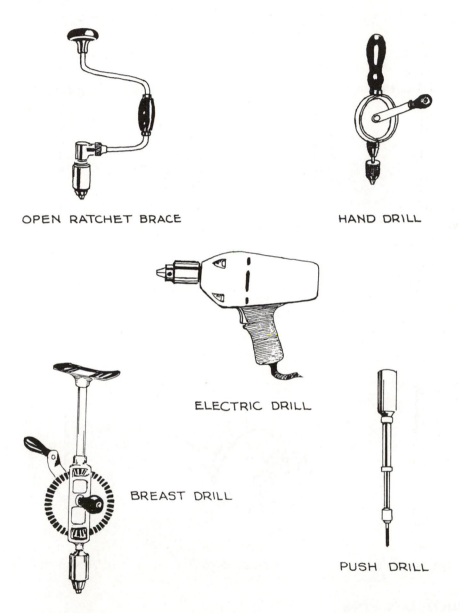

OPEN RATCHET BRACE

HAND DRILL

ELECTRIC DRILL

BREAST DRILL

PUSH DRILL

Plate 12 Drilling Tools

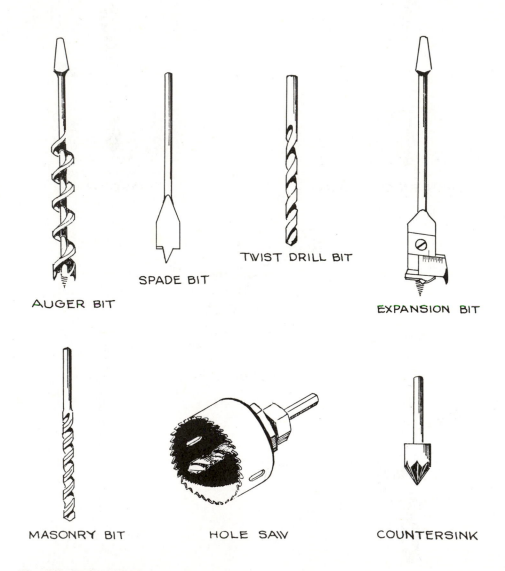

AUGER BIT   SPADE BIT   TWIST DRILL BIT   EXPANSION BIT

MASONRY BIT   HOLE SAW   COUNTERSINK

Plate 13   Drilling Tools

Expansion Bit.   To be used in a brace for woodworking. It comes in two sizes, the smaller cuts holes from ½″ to 1½″ and the larger sizes from ⅞″ to 3″.

Masonry Bit.   A bit designed for use in an electric drill for fast drilling in brick, concrete, and so forth.

Hole Saw.   Can be used in either a portable electric drill or in a stationary drill press; available in over 30 sizes varying from 9/16″ to 6″.

Countersink.   A bit designed to create a flaring enlargement of the upper part of a hole permitting the heads of screws or bolts to be seated flush with the joined material.

Planing Tools

Wood Chisel.   Straight-shafted cutting or paring tool fitted with wooden handles, used by tapping the handle with a mallet or the heel of the hand. Chisels come in a variety of widths from ¼″ to 1½″. They are not used extensively in rough construction work but become essential in handworking many wood joints. (See Plate 14.)

Wood Rasp.   A file with coarse, fast-cutting teeth for rough shaping of wood or plastic.

Metal File.   Metal files are found in different shapes described by their cross section: round, square, knife, flat, triangular, and so on. The coarseness of the teeth falls into three categories, bastard, second-cut, and smooth.

Draw Knife.   Has an elongated cutting edge with handles at each end placed at right angles with the blade. Used for rough shaping or planing.

Rat-Tail File.   A tapered round file used for enlarging holes in metal or wood.

Triangular File.   Obtainable in several different sizes, frequently used in sharpening saws.

Spoke Shave.   The cutting blade of the spoke shave is housed in a metal frame with adjustments for regulating the depth of the cut. It is capable of finer work than the draw knife.

Block Plane.   The cutting blade of the block plane is set in the housing frame at a 20° angle and is capable of fine adjustments. Used for cutting at right angles to the grain of the wood.

Smoothing Plane.   Similar in design to the block plane but has a wider blade and a longer and heavier frame. Used for smoothing faces or edges of lumber. A great variety of planes designed for specific purposes are available, but there is little need for them in normal construction operations of the scene shop.

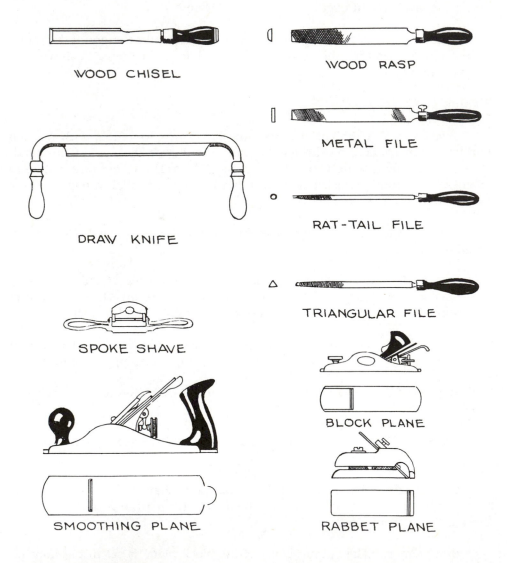

WOOD CHISEL

WOOD RASP

METAL FILE

DRAW KNIFE

RAT-TAIL FILE

TRIANGULAR FILE

SPOKE SHAVE

BLOCK PLANE

SMOOTHING PLANE

RABBET PLANE

Plate 14   Planing Tools

Rabbet Plane. A small plane with the cutting bit placed near the front of the plane. Used for planing into corners.

Driving Tools

Claw Hammer. The two curved jaws extending out from the back of the head are designed for pulling nails and are better suited to this purpose than those found on the rip hammer. (See Plate 15.)

Rip Hammer. The straighter claws of this type of hammer are well suited to prying apart joined lumber.

Ball Pein Hammer. A machinist's hammer. In place of claws this hammer has a second rounded striking face, used in shaping metal or in riveting.

Tack Hammer. Has a light, double-faced head with one face magnetized to hold tacks.

Heavy Duty Hammer. A heavy (one to three pounds) double-faced hammer with one face wedge-shaped, used for pounding and bending strap iron into shape.

Plastic Face Hammer. Replaceable striking faces with varying degrees of hardness are designed for use on soft metals and other surfaces where a nonmarring quality in the hammer is needed.

Ratchet Screw Driver. One of the most useful tools in the scene shop. The spiral shaft of this tool permits screws to be driven or extracted by direct pressure on the handle rather than by rotation of the tool.

Phillips Screw Driver. The bit of this tool is designed to fit the four-sided slot of the Phillips screw.

Nut Driver. The socket at the end of this tool is obtainable in different sizes. It is especially useful in tightening or loosening small-sized nuts.

Spring-Driven Staple Tacker. A stapling gun that operates by pressing a lever that cocks and releases a spring that drives the staple. Easier for the beginner to operate than the staple hammer because the tacker can be carefully positioned before the staple is driven.

Stapling Hammer. Holds a magazine of staples that are automatically placed in position and driven home with each blow of the hammer.

Clamping Tools

Pliers. For holding, clamping, gripping, cutting, or bending and for working in restricted quarters too small to be reached by fingers. Slip-joint pliers, long-nose pliers, diagonal-cutting pliers, and electrician's pliers are considered essential for scene shop work. (See Plate 16.)

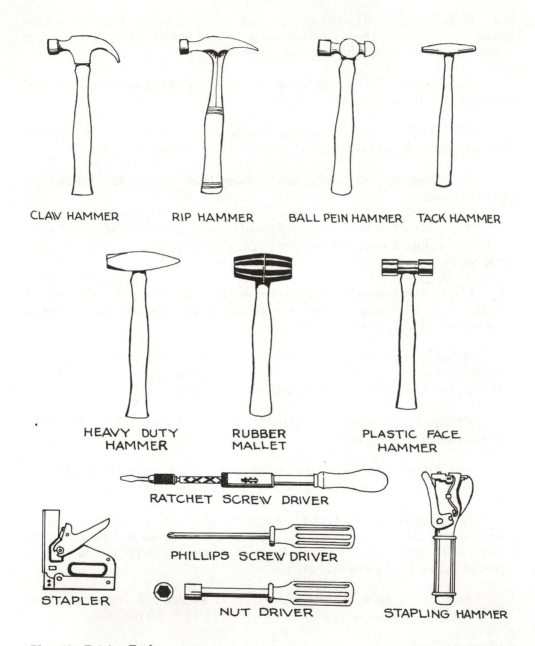

CLAW HAMMER   RIP HAMMER   BALL PEIN HAMMER   TACK HAMMER

HEAVY DUTY
HAMMER

RUBBER
MALLET

PLASTIC FACE
HAMMER

RATCHET SCREW DRIVER

STAPLER

PHILLIPS SCREW DRIVER

NUT DRIVER

STAPLING HAMMER

Plate 15   Driving Tools

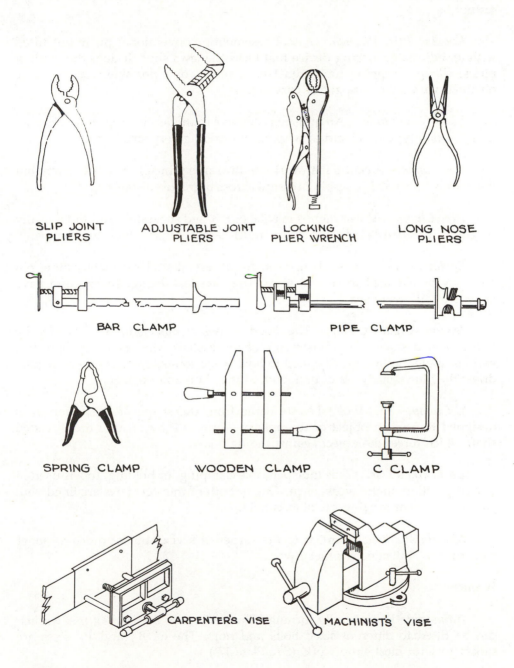

SLIP JOINT
PLIERS

ADJUSTABLE JOINT
PLIERS

LOCKING
PLIER WRENCH

LONG NOSE
PLIERS

BAR CLAMP

PIPE CLAMP

SPRING CLAMP

WOODEN CLAMP

C CLAMP

CARPENTER'S VISE

MACHINIST'S VISE

Plate 16 Clamping Tools

Adjustable Joint Pliers.   The long handles provide tremendous leverage while the parallel position of the jaws allows it to grip round or square objects tightly. It is an excellent general use tool that can be used where many others cannot be.

Locking Plier Wrench.   A tool resembling conventional pliers but fitted with an adjustable locking device that locks the jaws shut. It does the work of pliers, clamps, gripping tool, adjustable wrench, or a portable vise; it can be obtained with either straight or curved jaws.

Long-Nose Pliers.   An indispensable tool in model-making. It is very useful in certain types of electrical work or in gripping very small objects.

Bar Clamp.   A clamp that works on the same principle as the C-clamp but that can be extended to apply pressure across a greater distance.

Pipe Clamp.   These clamps may be purchased separately and fitted to any length of threaded 3/4" pipe. They are much less expensive than bar clamps.

Spring Clamp.   These clamps somewhat resemble a large metal clothes pin and may be obtained in several sizes. They are fast acting, strong, and have dozens of different uses.

Jenson Wooden Clamp.   The wooden jaws of this clamp are activated by two threaded shafts. By adjustments of these shafts the jaws may be set at various angles. Although designed to hold wood joints together while the glue dries, they have many other uses both in the shop and onstage.

C-Clamp.   This tool takes its name from the shape of the frame. It is designed to hold an object or to apply pressure to it by turning the threaded shaft which forces the object against the rigid jaw.

Carpenter's Vise.   This indispensable clamping, or holding, tool is used in a fixed position on the workbench. One or both of the steel jaws are lined with wood to prevent marring the objects held.

Machinist's Vise.   Similar to the carpenter's vise, but of much stronger construction. Intended for metal work.

Wrenches

Adjustable Wrench.   By turning a knurled screw the jaws of this wrench can be fitted to different-sized bolts and nuts. The 6", 8", and 10" sizes are satisfactory for most shop work. (See Plate 17.)

Monkey Wrench.   A wrench with adjustable jaws; in the 12" size can be used for heavier work than the adjustable wrenches described above.

Pipe Wrench.   The jaws of this wrench are made with corrugated teeth to grip a cylindrical form without slipping. It is good to have two of these wrenches on hand, one to hold the pipe, the other to turn the fitting.

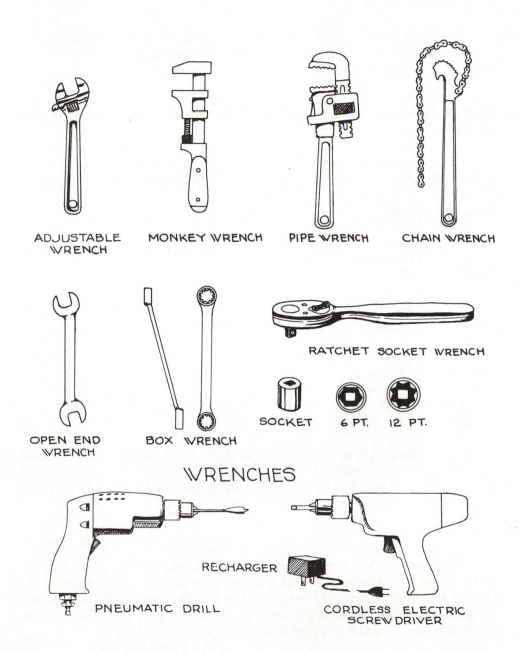

ADJUSTABLE WRENCH   MONKEY WRENCH   PIPE WRENCH   CHAIN WRENCH

OPEN END WRENCH   BOX WRENCH   RATCHET SOCKET WRENCH

SOCKET   6 PT.   12 PT.

WRENCHES

RECHARGER

PNEUMATIC DRILL   CORDLESS ELECTRIC SCREW DRIVER

Plate 17   Wrenches and Drills

Chain Wrench.   Will clamp and hold any pipe from $7/8$" to 4" O.D. or any irregular shape the chain will encompass. The chain wraps around the object to be held and engages the spur on the head of the handle; leverage applied on the handle tightens the chain.

Open End Wrench.   Fast and easy to use. The selection of the right sized wrench for the nut being worked is essential; if it's too small it will not fit; if it's too large it will slip.

Box Wrench.   The head of this wrench entirely surrounds the nut or bolt head. Ideal for breaking loose stubborn fasteners that may be jammed or rusted in a locked position.

Ratchet Socket Wrench.   With a reversible ratched handle the socket wrench is ideal for working in confined places difficult to reach with other tools.

Dismantling Tools

Wrecking Bar.   An indispensable tool used in dismantling heavy wooden platforms. May also be used to pry heavy units of scenery into exact position. (See Plate 18.)

Wonder Bar.   Used in extracting nails, and the thickness of the tool makes it easy to insert between two members of a structure in order to pry them apart.

Nail Claw.   The long handle provides the leverage necessary to extract large nails easily.

Ripping Chisel.   A prying tool with a straight-shafted handle that permits the use of a heavy duty hammer to force the wedging action.

Nail Puller.   A tool for pulling nails whose heads have been driven flush with the surface of the wood. The jaws are driven down on either side of the nail head by striking the hollow metal handle sharply against the stops. The leverage offered by the long handle makes it easy to remove nails.

Miscellaneous Tools

Pop Riveter.   An aluminum or steel rivet is held in the jaws of this tool and inserted into a hole drilled to accommodate the rivet. By activating the handles the outer jacket of the rivet is drawn tight to both clinch the rivet and break off the unwanted portion of the shaft. The riveter permits working on just one face of the materials being joined. (See Plate 18.)

Leather Punch.   This tool is used for punching holes in leather, plastics, rubber, and so forth. A revolving head provides six punches of different diameters.

Grommet Set.   A set consists of a hole punch, anvil, and crimping collar punch. The $3/8$" size is satisfactory for most stage purposes.

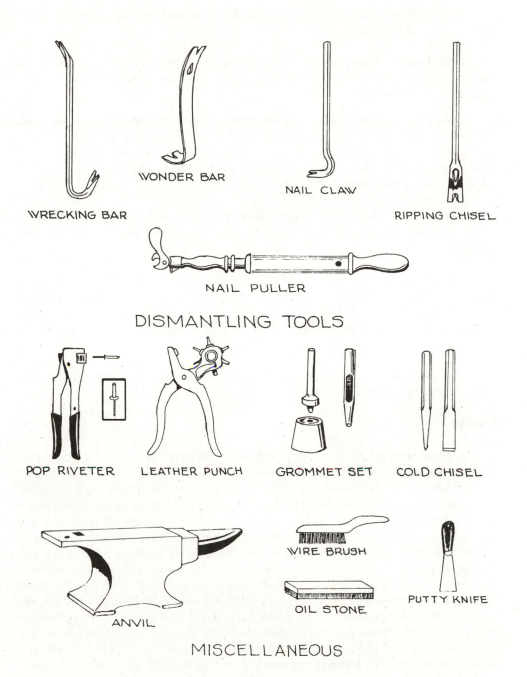

WRECKING BAR   WONDER BAR   NAIL CLAW   RIPPING CHISEL

NAIL PULLER

DISMANTLING TOOLS

POP RIVETER   LEATHER PUNCH   GROMMET SET   COLD CHISEL

WIRE BRUSH

ANVIL   OIL STONE   PUTTY KNIFE

MISCELLANEOUS

Plate 18   Dismantling and Miscellaneous Tools

Cold Chisel. A metal-cutting chisel that can be used to cut the fasteners of bolts that are rusted or frozen in place.

Anvil. The anvil provides a firm and substantial surface on which metal can be worked and shaped.

Wire Brush. This brush is used in cleaning filings, grease, and dirt from the teeth of files or wood rasps. It can also be used in removing rust or paint from metal surfaces.

Oil Stone. An oil stone, usually made of silicon carbide, has two faces. The coarse face is used for fast grinding and the finer face for finishing. With a thin film of oil on it the stone is used to sharpen cutting tools such as plane bits, chisels, and knives. The tool to be sharpened is held firmly against the face of the oil stone and moved in a circular direction.

Putty Knife. Although designed for spreading and forcing putty around window glass, this tool is well suited to spreading most kinds of paste compounds.

Clinch Plates. Six or eight of these plates are needed in even a modestly equipped shop. The clinch plate is made of $^3/_{16}''$ or $^1/_4''$ thick sheet steel cut about 12″ wide and 12″ long. As the frame of a flat is being assembled, the clinch plate is slipped under the frame to bend over, or clinch, the projecting points of the clout nails.

Electric Glue Pot. Basically a double boiler with a thermostatically controlled heating element that makes it impossible to burn glue.

Storage

Storage of Hand Tools. The purchase of the hand tools listed above represents an investment of several hundred dollars. Since the care and maintenance of the tools are the responsibility of the technician, he must prevent their being misplaced, lost, or stolen. Some technicians have attempted to solve this problem by maintaining a tool room with an attendant who issues tools to crew members as they are needed and later checks them in. This scheme has not been too successful because of the difficulty and expense of keeping an attendant in charge at all times. Other technicians have tried issuing individual toolboxes containing the most commonly used tools to crew members and holding them responsible for their return. Such a kit of tools would include a hammer, try square, rule, ratchet screwdriver, pliers, adjustable end-wrench and possibly a small hand drill. However, because students are usually in a hurry when they leave the shop and not always careful about picking up their tools, tool kits are often checked in with some items missing or with a duplication of some tools.

A plan that has proved more satisfactory than most has been used in situations where a graduate student or a full-time shop supervisor is in attendance in the shop throughout the day. Hand tools are under his immediate supervision and are kept in wall cabinets, from which they are selected by workers as they are needed (Plate 19). The supervisor sees that tools are replaced

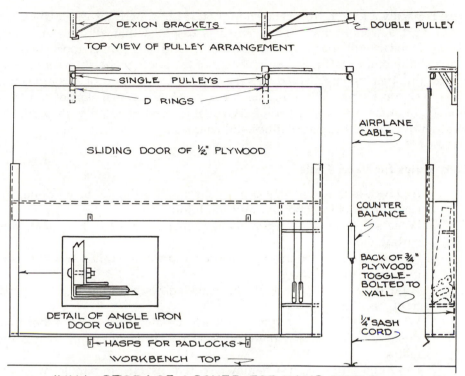

WALL STORAGE LOCKER FOR HAND TOOLS

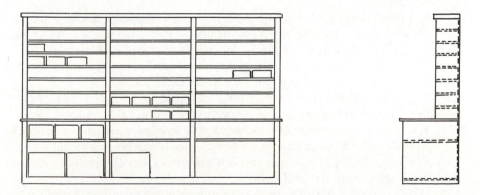

OPEN-SHELF STORAGE FOR STAGE HARDWARE

Plate 19 Hand Tool and Hardware Storage

when they are no longer needed and at the close of the work period makes sure that all tools are checked in before the students leave or the cabinets are locked.

Shop Safety Precautions

There is hardly a tool in the scene shop that, if improperly or carelessly used, cannot hurt a worker. For this reason it is essential that all crew members become familiar with the proper use of both hand and power tools. It is the responsibility of the staff member in charge of the shop or the shop foreman to see that this training is provided. A very satisfactory method of accomplishing this is to set up a series of training sessions prior to the actual start of construction. At this time the proper use of each tool is demonstrated with particular attention devoted to the peculiarities and characteristics of each one.

Safety Rules for Hand Tools

1. Always use the right size and type of tool for the job being done.
2. Keep all tools in good working condition.
3. Wear safety goggles when using punches, chisels, hammers, and cutting tools.
4. Never use a pipe extension over the handle of a wrench as a means of increasing the leverage.
5. Adjustable wrenches should have their jaws clamped tightly against the faces of a nut.
6. When possible, always pull a wrench handle toward you rather than pushing it. In this way there is less chance of losing your balance and falling.
7. Hold and strike with a hammer so that its face is parallel with the surface being struck. Do not strike one hammer against another nor use the side of a hammer for striking. Never use a hammer that has a loose handle.
8. While working with cutting tools that have exposed blades—such as chisels, draw knives, saws, or utility knives—keep them in a safe position so that they cannot be kicked, leaned on, or sat upon.
9. Never use a chisel or punch that has developed a mushroomed striking face. Chips may fly from it with considerable force.
10. Never use screw drivers that have chipped or rounded tips. Square them up on an emery wheel before using them.
11. Tools left on the steps of a ladder above eye level are an invitation to trouble. When the ladder is moved the tools are bound to fall.
12. Work in a well-lighted area and have the work bench and floor cleared of all scrap material and debris.
13. When using a nail puller be sure your hands are properly placed on the hand grips provided; otherwise a badly cut or pinched hand can result.
14. Never use a tool for any purpose other than that for which it was designed.
15. Wear sensible clothes such as slacks and T-shirts. Long hair should be confined in some manner, and loose bracelets or dangling necklaces must be removed.

Storage of Hardware

Open-shelf storage for theatrical and joining hardware is usually satisfactory even in situations where it is impossible for the shop to be locked off from other parts of the theatre. Lightweight wooden boxes 4" high by 7" long are made for each type of item to be shelved. The face of each box is clearly labeled with the name and size of the item, and the boxes are placed on the shelves in alphabetical order. Where possible a sample of the item is fastened to the face of the box for ready identification. This method of storage provides for easy identification of the item and serves as a good teaching aid in giving the students an opportunity to see and handle all types of hardware.

POWER TOOLS

There is no question but that scenery can be built by the use of hand tools alone. However, with the purchase of a few carefully selected power tools the same results can be produced with a tremendous saving in both time and energy. The power tools listed below are mentioned here because experience has proved that these particular tools have been used extensively enough in the construction of scenery to warrant the money invested in them. (See Plate 20.)

The Radial Arm Saw

The pull-over or radial arm saw is one of the most useful and flexible of all circular power saws. It is both safer and easier to use than the conventional table saw, and it is ideally suited for cross-cutting lumber. The motor and blade of this type of saw are mounted on a supporting arm that places them above the cutting table. This feature permits the saw to be placed near a wall with the tops of flanking workbenches flush with the height of the saw's cutting table. Lumber laid on the workbench, preparatory to cutting, is then parallel with the wall and occupies a minimum of space. While the lumber is in this position, it can be measured and marked, then either ripped or cross-cut without moving it from one part of the shop to another. Special accessories can convert this tool into a planer, a shaper, a router, a sander, a grinder, a wood drill, or a polisher.

The Portable Sabre Saw

The sabre saw has been developed and perfected to a point that it is preferred by many to the larger space-consuming jigsaw. The sabre saw was designed for cutting highly irregular shapes that cannot be cut on the band saw. Its narrow blade and its portability make it ideally suited for scenic construction.

The Band Saw

One of the most tedious and time-consuming hand-tool operations is curvilinear sawing. Because the narrow-banded band saw is designed for this purpose, it becomes a power tool high on the technician's list. If equipped with a speed reducer and steel cutting blades the band saw can also be used for cutting metal. Sanding belts 1/2" wide can be used on this machine if desired.

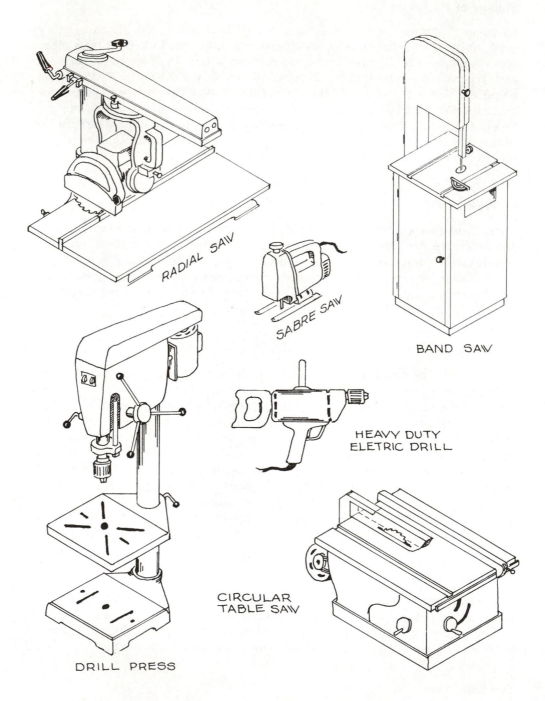

RADIAL SAW

SABRE SAW

BAND SAW

DRILL PRESS

HEAVY DUTY
ELETRIC DRILL

CIRCULAR
TABLE SAW

Plate 20   Power Tools

The Drill Press

The drill press is normally either bench or stand mounted. Although designed for drilling holes in metal and wood, the drill press is similar to the radial saw in that it can be adapted by proper accessories for planing, sanding, carving, routing, shaping, or cutting either dovetail or mortise and tenon joints.

Electric Hand Drills

Much of the heavy drilling that must be done onstage in rigging scenery, or on large units such as rigid platforms, cannot be done with the conventional drill press because it is not portable. For this reason both lightweight and heavy-duty electric drills are considered essential tools by many technicians. The lightweight drill is illustrated on Plate 13, the heavy duty drill on Plate 20. Both types of drills are obtainable with reversible motors and variable controls. In addition to drilling, and with the correct accessories, they can be used for doweling, sawing circular holes, driving and removing screws, and removing rust and paint, as well as sanding, buffing and polishing.

Pneumatic Drill

The pneumatic hand drill is capable of the same multipurpose operations obtainable with the electric drills mentioned above.

Cordless Electric Screwdriver

This tool is extremely useful in rigging operations onstage since it does away with the bother of long extension cords or air hoses. It may also be used as a conventional drill.

Circular Table Saw

The scene shop would be severely handicapped without the services of a reliable table saw. This particular tool is used extensively for ripping lumber. Long lengths of lumber should be supported after leaving the cutting table to prevent the uncut portion from tipping up away from the blade. Be sure to use a push stick when feeding lumber past the cutting blade. Equipped with a dado blade the circular table saw can be used effectively in forming such wood joints as the notched, halved, and mortise and tenon.

Cutawl

This is a power tool similar to the router in size, and like the router, it is hand held. However, it is equipped with a reciprocating rather than a rotary cutting action. It is a simple tool to operate and beautifully designed for cutting small complex patterns. It is ideally suited for cutting a series of stencil patterns at one time. With different types of blades it will cut most compositional materials including plywood. It has adjustments by which the depth of the cutting stroke can be varied (Plate 21).

Router

A compact, high-speed, hand-held shaper tool. There are over 48 different shaper and carving bits that, used separately or in combination, will produce a

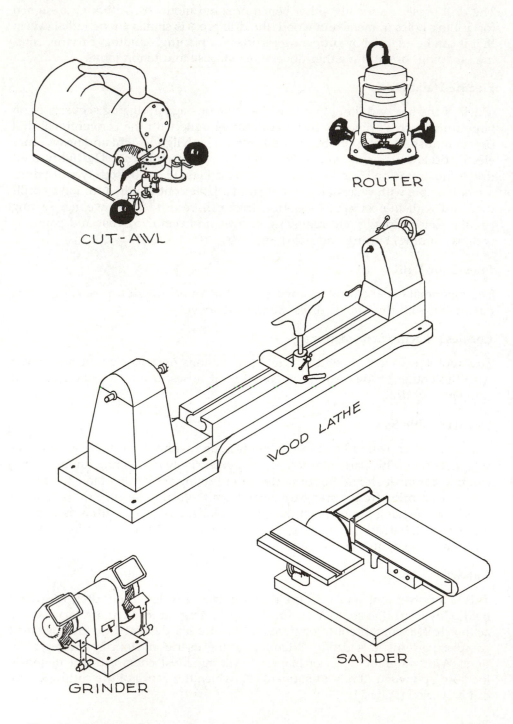

CUT-AWL

ROUTER

WOOD LATHE

GRINDER

SANDER

Plate 21   Power Tools

wide variety of work. It is used for making decorative moldings and for carving three-dimensional designs in wood.

Wood Lathe

A wood lathe is a machine in which material, usually a shaft of wood, is held and rotated while being shaped with especially designed wood cutting tools. It can also be used for sanding and polishing. Variations in the spindle speed are obtained by shifting the position of the driving belt on a cone-shaped pulley from a constant speed motor. The lathe is used for making spindles, bannisters, table legs, decorative lamp bases, and so forth. While the lathe is not used extensively in shop work, it is the only tool that can be used for these purposes.

Grinder

The power grinder equipped with either one or two emery wheels is used for general grinding, for sharpening tools, and smoothing the sharp edges of cut metal. Make sure that it is equipped with shatter-proof eye shields and adjustable tool rests. With proper accessories it can be used for buffing and polishing metal, removing rust or paint from metal surfaces, and for sharpening drill bits.

Sander

This machine with adjustable disc and belt surfaces is used to bevel, surface, or edge-finish wood. The work table for the sanding disc is not only adjustable but removable as well. The sanding belt has a removable back stop and the 6" wide work table tilts and locks at any angle form 0 to 90°. It is a remarkable tool for smooth finished work.

Air Driven Staplers and Nailers

The hand-held power stapler and nailer have found favor with technicians or organizations that have a heavy production schedule and whose budget for tools is ample. Such tools are extremely efficient, not difficult to operate, and provide a faster method of joining flat frames than the more conventional use of a hammer and clout nails. An electrically driven air compressor is best installed in a housing outside of the shop, where the noise of its operation will be muffled and where it can be kept free of shop dust. Trailing air hoses from the compressor to the power tools are constantly underfoot unless strategically placed outlets for the air are provided from overhead pull-down hose reels or from wall outlets placed near the work area. Fast break couplings between the tools and hose are essential.

Divergent (clinching) staples or adhesive coated staples should be used to insure a solid butt joint on a flat frame so that the joint will not pull apart. A good substitute method of making a strong butt joint without either of these two types of staples is to use a regulation straight wire staple and in addition to coat the underside of each corner block and keystone with glue. The one disadvantage with these methods is that the joint is so very strong that it is difficult to tear apart if the flat is to be altered for future use.

Air driven staplers and nailers are just two of many air tools that can be driven from the same compressed air system. Other fastener tools are screwdrivers, nut runners, and impact wrenches. There are the abrasive tools including grinders, belt sanders, orbital sanders, finishing sanders, and buffers; percussion tools such as chipping hammers, needle scalers, and impact chisels. Available cutting tools include a portable circular saw, shears, a bayonet or sabre saw, panel saw, and a router. Needless to say, paint sprayers will operate from the same compressor system.

It should be pointed out that not all of these tools are needed in most scenic work; but should the technician find that her production schedule is excessive and that she needs a particular time-saving air tool, she should be aware of its existence. (See Plate 22.)

Safety Rules for Power Tools

1. If you are unfamiliar with the operation of a power tool, ask the supervisor, instructor, or shop foreman to demonstrate its use before attempting to use it yourself. (The instruction manual that comes with each power tool should be carefully preserved. Before conducting the demonstration, the instructor should study the manual very carefully to make certain he is completely familiar with all subjects covered by it.)
2. Be properly dressed. Beware of loose clothing or any article of apparel that might become entangled in the moving parts of a machine.
3. Wear safety goggles or a plastic face shield.
4. Keep the safety guards of any tool in place at all times.
5. Make sure there is adequate light over the work area.
6. Keep the work area clear of all scrap material.
7. Oversized material on which you are working must be properly supported by a work table extension or by the assistance of a helper.
8. Make certain that adjustment wrenches and chuck keys have been removed before turning on the machine.
9. Use a "push-stick" when feeding material past the blade of a circular saw.
10. Disconnect the power source of a tool before making repairs or adjustments.
11. While using a power tool keep your attention devoted entirely to its operation; do not try to carry on a conversation nor allow your eyes to wander away from what you are doing. If you must talk, turn off the power!

Placement of Power Tools

Because of the wide variety in form and size of stage settings and the resulting need for flexibility of floor space in the shop, every effort is usually made to avoid mounting heavy power equipment in fixed positions. With the possible exception of the radial saw, all power equipment should be mounted on castored tables with lock drawers capable of holding all accessories used by that particular tool. As a safety precaution, lock castors or a lift jack should be used to prevent the tool from creeping as it is being used. The flexibility offered by these rolling units make it possible for power equipment to be moved from one part of the shop to another in order to clear floor space for certain constructional operations, or simply to bring the tool closer to the point of work.

Electrical Power Supply

With the ever-increasing dependency on the use of electrical and air driven tools, the need for having the scene shop liberally equipped with the necessary

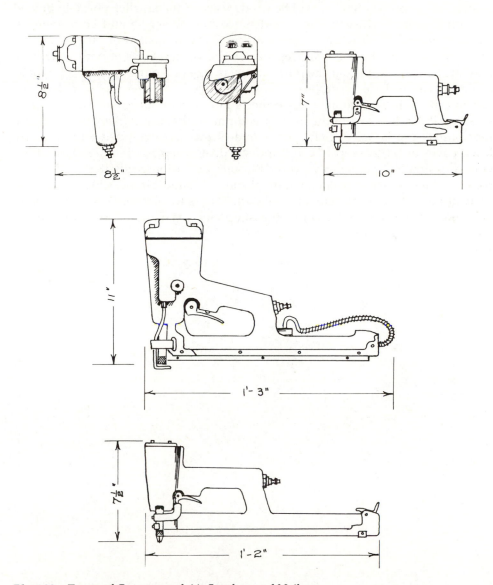

Plate 22 Types of Compressed Air Staplers and Nailers

electrical outlets, both for 110- and 220-volt lines, is apparent. Some heavy power equipment such as a large radial arm saw, sander, router-planer, large air compressor, or electrical welding rig requires a 220-volt line. Because of the size and weight of such equipment it is unlikely that they would be moved from a fixed position. Therefore the circuitry for these units should be routed to the areas of the shop where they will be used. Most of the smaller portable power tools operate from 110-volt lines. Outlets for this power should be numerous and conveniently located in all work areas. Conventional wall outlets can be placed not only on the wall surfaces, but on the vertical faces of both work and template benches. Consider the possible advantage of mounting the wall outlets in conduits at the base-board level. On some power tools there is less risk of the lead-in cable being accidentally disconnected than from outlets mounted higher on the wall. Under some of the heavier equipment that is not likely to be moved floor outlets can be used. Select floor outlets that are equipped with a snap-down cover or lid to keep out dirt and sawdust when not in use. Over other work areas outlets can supply power through extension cords that pull down from a reellike container suspended overhead. It is almost impossible to have too many outlets. Plan the placement of all outlets so as to minimize the use of long, entangling extension cords. All of the shop circuitry should lead through an easily accessible breaker box.

4

Building Materials, Wood Joinery, and Theatrical Hardware

The appearance and the life expectancy of a unit of stage scenery are dependent partly on the quality of the building materials from which the unit is made and partly on the skill and care used in the joining of its various parts. The technician who understands this and, more importantly, puts it into practice, has taken several important steps toward the following goals:

1. Improving the general standard of production.
2. Increasing the life expectancy of stock scenery.
3. Reducing the prorated cost of productions.
4. Reducing the time required for repair work.
5. Increasing the safety factor.

The more thoroughly the technician is acquainted with the characteristics of various kinds of building materials, the better qualified she is to make wise selections of the proper materials for specific jobs. A practice followed by many technicians is to make periodic visits to local lumber dealers to become familiar with the many new building materials being introduced into the market. Some of these products are adaptable for stage purposes and may prove to be excellent substitutes for heavier, weaker, or more expensive materials in current use.

The materials normally used in the construction of scenery fall into three general groups: (1) the lumber from which all supporting frames are constructed, (2) the joining materials used in holding the various parts of the frames together, and (3) the covering materials used to conceal the supporting frames.

LUMBER

Lumber to be suitable for scenic construction must be light in weight, strong, straight grained, easily worked, well seasoned, free from any tendency to warp, and inexpensive. Out of the many woods normally handled by local lumber dealers only a few possess all of these characteristics. Among these are the following:

Norther White Pine.   Northern white pine is excellent in all respects, but unfortunately, the supply is extremely limited and very little of it can be obtained in some areas, such as the Midwest.

Idaho White Pine.   Although the supply of Idaho white pine is somewhat limited, it may be obtained by special order or even found in local markets in certain areas. It is comparable to Northern white pine in its suitability for scenic work.

Ponderosa Pine.   Ponderosa pine, or West Coast yellow pine as it is sometimes called, is well suited for use in scenic construction, although it is somewhat heavier than either of the white pines mentioned. There is an adequate supply of this wood, and it sells at reasonable prices. Ponderosa pine should not be confused with other fast-growing, coarse-grained yellow pines that are too heavy and hard for anything but the roughest kind of stage work.

Redwood.   Like the Ponderosa pine, redwood is a West Coast product and is usually carried in stock by most dealers. Although it meets most of the requirements for stage lumber, some of it is too soft, and it has a slight tendency to splinter and split.

Spruce.   In appearance this wood closely resembles white pine. It is creamy white in color and comparatively fine grained although somewhat heavier than pine. Its resistance to warping and twisting is good, and it can be used successfully for flat framing.

West Coast Red Cedar.   A coarse-grained, lightweight wood, West Coast red cedar can be used for framing and in the construction of properties and trim. Some of it is too brittle to be used for large framing units.

Douglas Fir.   Douglas fir is a coarser-grained and heavier wood than the others mentioned, but it is also the strongest and sells for about half the price of the others. It is used extensively for weight-bearing supports and platform framing. Standard sizes of this wood have a thickness of 2″.

Moldings

Most lumber companies carry a supply of standard moldings. These are normally made from clear Ponderosa pine and have, over the years, been more or less standardized in their design. The descriptive names such as cornice, crown, quarter or half round by which they are known have usually been taken from their intended use or from their shape (Plate 23). Because moldings are made from clear lumber and require special care in their milling and handling, they are quite expensive. However, the technician has found many ways of using molding for purposes other than those for which it was intended. He may use half round molding on the faces of a column to suggest ribbing; cornices and crown molding can be used alone or in combination to form the decorative trim of a fireplace mantel; chair molding can outline panels on the walls of a set or be used as part of a picture frame. In the construction of stage furniture standard moldings have been used in dozens of ways to produce a convincing and finished appearance on pieces that would otherwise be quite undistinguished.

Embossed Moldings. Use of embossed moldings is a great asset to both designers and technicians in adding richness to their finished work. Several of the designs to be found in these moldings are shown on Plate 23. The designs are impressed into the wood to form raised ornamental patterns. These moldings are obtainable in thicknesses varying from 5/16″ to 11/16″ and in widths from 1/2″ to 3 1/8″ and in either straight runs or quarter circles. Embossed moldings have been used very successfully in paneling both the walls and doors of stage sets. Their use in the construction of stage furniture has unlimited possibilities.

Quality of Lumber

Variations in the quality of lumber are designated by a system of grading that uses "A" for perfect, "B" for next best, "C" for lumber with some slight imperfections, such as pin knots, and "D" for lumber with larger sound knots. Below the grade of D the classifications continue with No. 1 Common, No. 2 Common, and so forth. So little available lumber falls within the A and B classifications that for all practical purposes they may be ignored. Not only are these grades almost impossible to obtain, but the price asked for them is prohibitive to all but those with the most expansive budgets. Most scenery is made from C-grade lumber. A few shops may make limited use of D-grade, but it is poorly suited for large framing units or weight-bearing structures.

Dimensions of Stock Lumber

Lumber is obtainable in a variety of standard sizes and dimensions. Thickness and width are designated in inches, and length is specified in multiples of 2 feet. A length of stock lumber 1″ thick by 3″ wide and 14′-0″ long is written as 1″ × 3″ × 14′. Lumber for a specific job is ordered from standard sizes such as 1″ × 3″ or 1″ × 6″ in lengths that will produce the least wastage in cutting. It

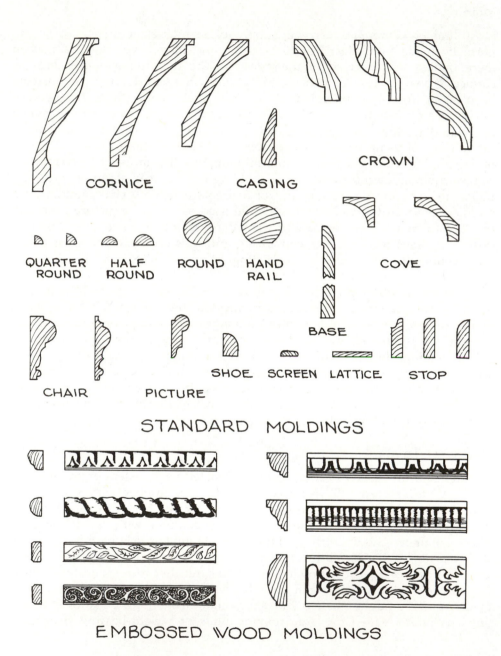

Plate 23   Standard and Embossed Wood Moldings

is important to understand that the lumber will not measure either a full 1″ in thickness or a full 3″ or 6″ in width, though the length will be full measure. Approximately ¼″ is lost from the thickness and as much as ½″ or ⅝″ from the width of all stock lumber during the process of finishing. Finished or dressed lumber has been planed on both faces and edges. There are almost always variations in the dimensions of lumber finished by one lumber mill when compared to that finished by another mill. Because of these variations it is wise to take sample measurements of each new load of lumber delivered to the shop. Knowing the exact size of lumber permits the draftsman to make more accurate drawings since he can now make proper adjustments and allowances for the actual size of the stock.

A list of the common stock sizes of lumber and the purposes for which they are normally used in scenic construction follows:

Stock Size Thickness and Width	General Use
1″ × 2″	Small flat frames, diagonal braces, small cutout frames
1″ × 3″	Standard flat frames
1″ × 4″	Large framing units, battens for drops and ceilings
1″ × 6″, 1″ × 8″	Door and window units, fireplaces, architectural trim
1″ × 10″, 1″ × 12″	Stairways, sweeps, properties, furniture
1¼″ × 3″	Oversized flats, heavy-duty parallel frames
2″ × 4″, 2″ × 6″, 2″ × 8″	Weight-bearing supports, frames, trusses
1″ × 4″, 1″ × 6″ (Tongue and groove flooring)	Platform flooring
1″ × 8″ (Car siding)	Platform flooring

Computing the Cost of Lumber

The price of lumber varies according to its grade, and is usually quoted per 1000 board feet. The board foot is a unit of measure that represents a piece of wood 1″ thick by 12″ wide by 12″ long. Given the price per 1000 board feet the price per single board foot is found by moving the decimal point three places to the left. For example, assuming that the quoted price for C-grade Ponderosa pine is $1000.00 per 1000 board feet, the price per single board foot is found to be $1.00.

Although lumber is sold by board feet, the technician invariably figures the amount of lumber he will need to complete a given job in terms of linear measurement or, for example, how many pieces of 1″ × 4″ × 16′-0″ would be required. It is then necessary for him to convert these linear measurements into board feet to find the cost.

To find the price of an order of 24 pieces of 1″ × 4″ × 16′-0″ C-grade white pine at $1.00 a board foot proceed as follows. Multiply the number of pieces by the length of one piece to get the total number of linear feet. Since a piece of 1″ × 4″ 1 foot long is ⅓ of a board foot, divide the total number of linear feet by 3 to obtain the number of board feet. Multiply the number of board feet by the price per single board foot.

EXAMPLE: Find the price of 24 pieces of 1″ × 4″ × 16′-0″ @ $1.00 per board foot.

$$24 \times 16 = 384$$
$$1'' \times 4'' \times 1'\text{-}0'' = \tfrac{1}{3} \text{ of a board foot}$$
$$384 \div 3 = 128$$
$$128 \times 1.00 = \$128.00$$

An alternate method may be used for determining the price of a lumber order. Find the number of board feet in one length of stock lumber, multiply this by the number of pieces ordered, and multiply this product by the price per board foot. Use the following formula:

T = Thickness
W = Width
L = Length

$$\frac{T \times W \times L}{12} = \text{Board feet}$$

EXAMPLE: Find the price of a lumber order of 24 pieces of 1″ × 4″ × 16′-0″ @ $1.00 per board foot.

$$\frac{1 \times 4 \times 16}{12} = \frac{64}{12} = 5\tfrac{1}{3}\,\text{board feet}$$
$$5\tfrac{1}{3} \times 24 = 128$$
$$128 \times \$1.00 = \$128.00$$

WOOD JOINTS COMMONLY USED IN SCENIC CONSTRUCTION

The speed with which scenery can be built and its strength depend to a great extent upon the types of wood joints used in its construction. For this reason certain types of wood joints have been found more suitable than others for scenic construction (Plates 24 and 25).

In selecting the proper joint for any construction problem, some thought should be given not only to the strength of the joint but to the strength of the lumber itself. The strength of any piece of stock lumber varies according to the position in which it is used and to the direction in which the force or load is applied to it. Consider the following example. A length of 1″ × 4″ placed so that a force is applied against its face is in its weakest position because this force is at right angles to the smallest dimension of the piece of lumber, its thickness. If the position of the 1″ × 4″ can be changed so that the force is against the edge, it will be many times stronger because the force will then be at right angles to the 4″ width. The same 1″ × 4″ is at its strongest position when the force is applied against its ends or parallel to its length.

Lap Joint

A lap joint is the simplest of all wood joints to construct. Two pieces of stock lumber are joined face to face by bolts, screws, or nails. This joint is used in

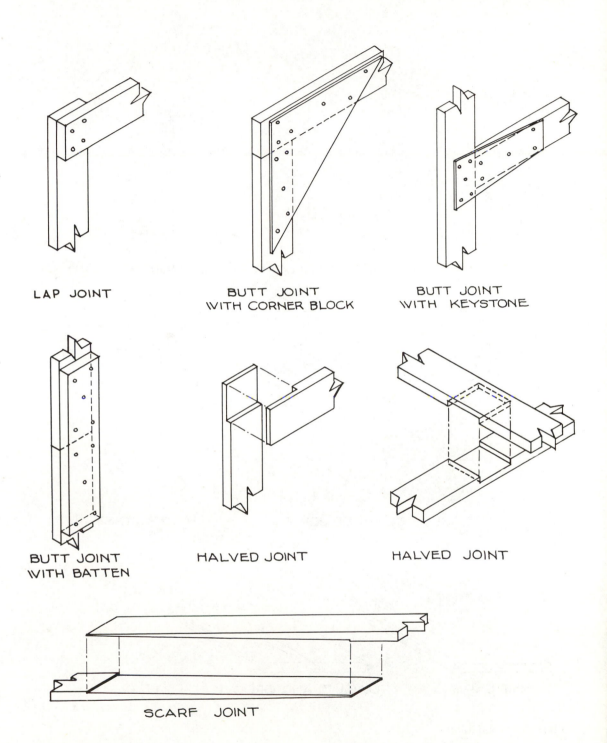

LAP JOINT

BUTT JOINT
WITH CORNER BLOCK

BUTT JOINT
WITH KEYSTONE

BUTT JOINT
WITH BATTEN

HALVED JOINT

HALVED JOINT

SCARF JOINT

Plate 24   Wood Joints

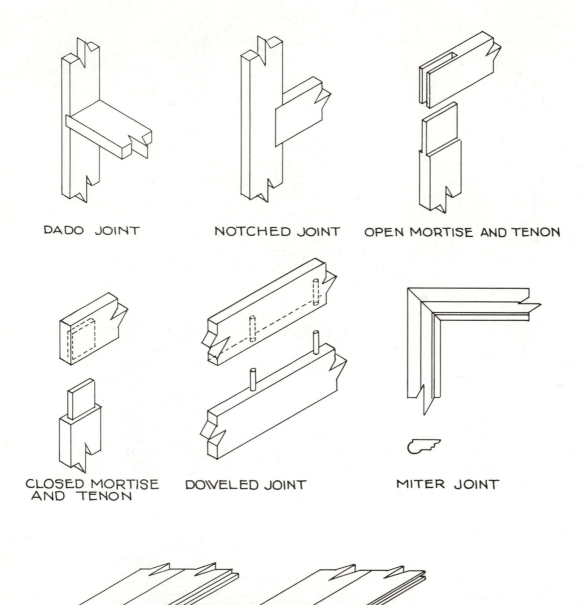

DADO JOINT NOTCHED JOINT OPEN MORTISE AND TENON

CLOSED MORTISE AND TENON DOWELED JOINT MITER JOINT

SHIPLAP TONGUE AND GROOVE

Plate 25 Wood Joints

legging up rigid platforms and in bracing them. It is used extensively in rough offstage framing when it is not important to have the faces of the joined members in the same plane.

Butt Joint

The joint most commonly used in the construction of scenery is the butt joint. It is fast and easy to assemble and it is strong enough to withstand the strains normally placed on scenery by shifting. A butt joint formed between the stile and rail of a flat is made in the following manner:

1. Square the ends of the stiles and rails.
2. Butt the end of the stile against the edge of the rail and check the right angle with a steel square.
3. Cover the butt joint with a full-size (10″) corner block, making sure that the exposed grain of the corner block is at right angles to the joint.
4. Hold the corner block back ³/₄″ from the outer edge of the stile and ¹/₄″ back from the outer edge of the rail.
5. Fasten the corner block to the stile and rail with 1¹/₄″ clout nails driven partially home.
6. Check the accuracy of the right-angle joint with a steel square before clinching clout nails on the face of the frame.
7. To clinch the clout nails insert a plate of ¹/₄″ × 12″ × 12″ sheet metal under the flat frame and hammer home the nails. When the points of the nails strike this plate they will bend over, forming partial hooks that anchor them firmly in place. (Select clout nails that are ¹/₄″ longer than the combined thickness of the corner block and the lumber so that there will be adequate penetration for the point to clinch.)

Halved Joint

The halved joint makes possible the joining of two pieces of wood face to face without increasing the thickness of the lumber at the point of junction, thus permitting the faces of both members to remain in the same plane. This joint is much stronger than a butt joint; it can be made easily with a radial saw equipped with a dado head, or it can be worked with hand tools without requiring too much time. To join two lengths of 1″ × 3″ at right angles by use of a halved joint proceed in the following manner:

1. Square the ends of both pieces of 1″ × 3″.
2. Measure back from the ends of each 1″ × 3″ a distance equal to their width. Using a try square, mark a line at right angles across the faces and edges of both pieces.
3. With a marking gauge set at ¹/₂ the thickness of the 1″ × 3″ scribe a line along the edges and ends until it joins with the width measurement.
4. With the dado blade on a radial saw set for a cut equal to ¹/₂ the thickness of the 1″ × 3″ remove the marked section.
5. Cover the exposed cuts with glue and allow it to dry long enough to become tacky. Then assemble the joint and check the angle for accuracy with a steel square.
6. Allow the glue to set under pressure provided by clamps, screws, or clout nails.

Scarf Joint

It is difficult to obtain white pine in lengths greater than 18'-0". This makes the scarf joint one of the most useful of all joints to the technician because it provides him with a method of joining two lengths of lumber end to end without increasing the thickness. Stiles of flats with a height greater than 18'-0", lengthwise battens of ceilings, and battens used for foliage borders and drops, all are made with the aid of scarf joints. To make a joint of this type proceed as follows:

1. Square the ends of the lumber to be joined.
2. Measure 1'-6" in from the ends of each board and draw a right-angle line across the widths of the boards at this point.
3. Cut a $1/8$" deep saw kerf on this line.
4. Draw a diagonal line on each edge of the board beginning at the bottom of the saw kerf and terminating on the end at a point $1/8$" in from the outer face.
5. Remove all wood above this line by using a drawknife and finish the cut with a block plane or a wood file. Make sure that the face of the taper is perfectly smooth without noticeable high or low points. The faces of both tapers should meet along their full length to insure a strong joint.
6. Cover the faces of both tapers with glue and allow it to dry until it becomes tacky. Then place the tapers face to face, check alignment of the edges to ensure perfect straightness of the joint, and allow the glue to dry under pressure provided by clamps, clout nails, or screws.

Dado Joint

The dado joint provides a method of joining two pieces of wood end to face in a way that is many times stronger than the same junction formed with butt joints. Bookcase shelves, stair treads, and structures that may be subjected to heavy loads are frequently made by use of this joint. To make it, proceed as follows:

1. Mark the vertical member at the desired height with measurements corresponding to the width and thickness of the horizontal member.
2. Remove the wood within the limits of the marks by the use of a dado blade that has been adjusted for the proper width and depth of cut.
3. Cover the face of the notch with glue, insert the end of the horizontal member, and fasten with a cleat, nails, or screws.

Notched Joint

The notched joint is similar to the dado joint in both construction and use, the difference being that the notch is usually cut in the edge of the supporting member rather than in its face.

Mortise and Tenon Joints

Because open and closed mortise and tenon joints are among the strongest of all wood joints, they are used extensively in the construction of furniture and are used by most professional scenic builders for the assembly of all flat frames. However, their shops usually have power equipment designed specifically for cutting this type of joint. The time required to cut and fit it with hand tools alone makes it almost prohibitive for the average unskilled student. As can be seen in the illustration, the open mortise and tenon joint is distinguished from the closed joint by the fact that its tenon, or tongue, is partially exposed on both end and edge when the joint is assembled. When the closed mortise and tenon joint is assembled, the tenon is completely hidden. To make the open mortise and tenon joint with hand tools, proceed as follows:

1. Square the ends of both members.
2. Mark the tenon by measuring back from the end of one member a distance equal to the width of the other. Draw a line across both faces and edges at this point.
3. Set a marking gauge at 1/4 the thickness of the stock and scribe lines along both edges and the end until they intersect the line described in step 2.
4. Remove the two outer marked sections, using a back saw to cut down to the scribed lines. Wood chisels and a mallet are used to complete the operation. To ensure a strong and accurate joint the faces and edges of the finished tenon must be parallel to those of the stock from which it was formed.
5. Mark the member that is to receive the mortise (the slot into which the tongue fits) in exactly the same manner used for marking the tenon. (See steps 2 and 3.)
6. Remove the center section by selecting a drill bit slightly smaller in diameter than the widths of the prescribed lines. Drill a series of overlapping holes down the middle of the center slot. Remove the remaining wood with wood chisels.
7. Smooth up the faces of both tenon and mortise and test the fit. Check right angle with a try square or steel square.
8. Cover both tenon and mortise with glue and allow to dry until it becomes tacky. Then assemble the joint, check its alignment, and fasten with clamps, clout nails, or screws until the glue is dry.

Doweled Joint

When closed mortise and tenon and doweled joints are assembled and compared, it is practically impossible to tell them apart. Although the doweled joint is not as strong as the other, it is much easier and faster to construct. Basically the doweled joint is a method of joining two boards edge to edge, or end to face, by drilling holes in both and inserting glued hardwood cylindrical pegs into them. Hardwood doweling can be bought from most lumber dealers in 30" lengths and in diameters from 1/8" to 3/4". The proper diameter of the dowel is usually 1/2 the thickness of the stock to be used. Two boards can be joined edge to edge by the use of the doweled joint as follows:

1. Place both boards face to face in a wood vise and align their upper edges.
2. Plane the edges of both boards until they are square with the faces.
3. Remove one board from the vise and place its squared edge down on the

squared edge of the second board. Check for high and low places. Plane until both edges fit tightly together.

4. Realign both boards in the vise with the planed edges flush. With a marking gauge set for $\frac{1}{2}$ the thickness of the stock, mark a center line down the edges of both boards.

5. Draw lines at right angles to the center lines with a try square to mark the position for the dowel holes. It is very important that the dowel holes be exactly the same distance apart on both boards. Otherwise the resulting misalignment of the dowels makes it impossible to draw the board edges together.

6. Drill holes about $1\frac{1}{2}"$ deep at each marked position. Be sure that the holes are drilled parallel with the faces of the boards and at right angles with their edges.

7. Cut the doweling into 3" lengths. Cover one-half of each dowel with glue and tap them into the holes along the edge of one of the two boards. Cover the exposed ends of the dowels and the edge of the board with glue.

8. Lay both boards face side down on the workbench. Fit the dowels into the holes of the second board and force the two board edges together with pressure supplied by bar or pipe clamps.

9. Wipe off excess glue squeezed from between the boards and allow them to dry. Plane or sand the surfaces to a smooth finish.

JOINING MATERIALS

Plywood is probably the most useful single building material used in a scene shop. Used primarily as a joining material, it is also used extensively in making irregular contours for a two-dimensional cutout and as a substitute for solid stock lumber when great strength is needed. Plywood is a manufactured product made by bonding together an uneven number of thin sheets of wood. Each sheet is glued to the next, with the graining of one sheet usually at right angles to the adjoining one. It is this alternation of graining that gives plywood its unusual strength. If you test a small piece of $\frac{1}{4}"$ plywood for strength by bending it over the edge of a table, you will notice that when the exposed graining is parallel with the table edge it is possible to bend, or even break it. This does not happen when the graining runs at right angles to the edge of the table. Plywood is much stronger when placed in this position, and for this reason the exposed grain of the corner block or keystone should always be placed at right angles to the junction of the butt joints.

Panelboard, as plywood is sometimes called, is sold by the square foot. It comes in sheets 4'-0" wide and is obtainable in different lengths, though the 8'-0" length is most commonly stocked. Plywood made of fir is the least expensive; it is made in thicknesses of $\frac{1}{4}"$, $\frac{3}{8}"$, $\frac{1}{2}"$, $\frac{5}{8}"$, $\frac{3}{4}"$, and $\frac{7}{8}"$. Plywood made from soft woods such as basswood is obtainable on order in thicknesses of $\frac{3}{32}"$ or $\frac{1}{8}"$.

Corner Blocks, Keystones, and Straps

The wood joint used most frequently in the construction of scenery is the butt joint. When this joint is formed by butting the end of one piece of lumber against the edge of another, it must be reinforced by fastening a third piece over the other two. These reinforcing pieces are made from $^3/_{16}''$ or $^1/_4''$ thick plywood and are called corner blocks, keystones, or straps. The corner block is triangular in shape, with the two right-angle sides 10″ in length. The keystone is 8″ long, 4″ wide at one end and tapers to $2^3/_4''$ at the other. Straps are rectangles of plywood 8″ long by $2^3/_4''$ wide. Ready-made corner blocks and keystones can be purchased from any theatrical supply house, but there is a noticeable saving in cost if the technician cuts them herself. If such is the case she will generally substitute a rectangular strap $2^3/_4'' \times 8''$ for the conventional trapezoidal-shaped keystone because it is much easier to cut. There is no noticeable difference in the strength of the two.

Strap Iron

Strips of malleable iron, $^3/_{16}''$ or $^1/_4''$ thick by $^3/_4''$ wide, are used to join the two lower rails of a standard door flat. Strap iron can be easily cut with a hacksaw and bent to the desired shape by placing it in a machinist's vise and striking it with a heavy hammer.

COVERING MATERIALS

There is hardly a fabric made that has not been used at one time or another for some purpose on stage. Some fabrics, of course, have been found so completely satisfactory for a particular purpose that their use in that capacity has become standard procedure. It is extremely important in selecting a fabric for stage use that it be wide enough for the purpose. The three fabrics listed below are manufactured in widths of 68″, 72″, 81″, and 108″ and sold in bolts containing 50 to 60 yards. They are priced by the running yard rather than by the square yard. If less than a full bolt is ordered, it is necessary to add 10 percent to the current price. Materials that have been flame-proofed will cost an additional 35¢ or 50¢ a yard.

Linen Canvas

Linen canvas is probably the best material that can be used for covering flats. It is expensive, but is remarkably strong, does not snag or tear easily, and will last indefinitely when stored under proper conditions.

Cotton Canvas Duck

An excellent substitute for linen canvas, cotton canvas is used much more extensively than linen for covering flats because it is less expensive and can be easily found on the market. It is manufactured in various weights and is specified by the weight in ounces of a square yard. Eight-ounce canvas is normally used for most scenic work.

Muslin

Heavyweight unbleached muslin is used as a covering material by many technicians who must operate on a limited budget. It is not strong and will stretch and tear rather easily; but since it is lighter in weight and thinner than canvas, it is well suited for the patching needed in altering and reusing stock scenery. Several coats of paint will completely conceal all patches. In spite of its weakness, muslin is surprisingly durable when used as a covering for flats or when made into drops; but it must be shifted and stored with care.

Sisalcraft

Sisalcraft is a substitute for conventional covering fabrics when economy is a prime consideration. It is a building paper made from two sheets of brown craft paper with a layer of asphalt between them. Threads of sisal intermixed with the asphalt give great strength to the product. Sisalcraft comes in widths of 3', 4', 5', 6', and 8'. Although it is heavy and not as easy to apply to a flat as a fabric, it can be used for covering frames of an irregular shape or those that will not be kept as stock scenery.

Compositional Covering Materials

Any unit of scenery that will be subjected to hard usage either onstage or in shifting is ordinarily covered with some stiff self-supporting, compositional material capable of withstanding the stress that will be placed upon it. Plywood is ideal for this purpose, but if cost is a consideration it is essential that the technician become familiar with the characteristics of less expensive compositional materials and learn which are locally available. Such rigid materials, or "boards" as they are sometimes called, are standard building materials used in general construction and cabinet work and so are stocked by lumber dealers. They are sold by the square foot and come in sheets or boards of varying lengths; usually, however, they are 4'-0" wide. They are manufactured from a wide variety of materials—paper pulp, fibers, wood, plaster, asbestos, and even cement. Some have soft finishes, others have hard surfaces, and a few will bend without breaking. Uses of these boards onstage are limited only by one's willingness to experiment with them.

Upson Board.   Upson board is a compressed paper product available in 4' × 8' sheets and in thicknesses varying from 1/8" to 3/16" or 1/4". It is creamy white in color with one face having a pebbled finish while the other face is smooth. The 1/8" thick Upson is called "Easy Curve" and is used for covering curved walls or columns. In use Upson board can be easily damaged or scuffed in shifting; therefore, it is usually protected by having muslin glued to its face. The thicker Upson boards are sometimes used for hard covering of flat frames and for silhouette cutouts such as bushes or mountains that will not be subjected to the hazard of breakage during a scene shift.

Masonite.   This product, sometimes called hardboard, comes in 4' × 8' sheets and can be obtained in 1/8", 1/4" and 3/8" thickness. Masonite is compressed from wood pulp and is a rich brown in color. There are two degrees of hardness obtainable in this product, the untempered and the tempered. The untempered is softer, easier to work, and a lighter brown in color than the tempered. Tempered Masonite is harder, more brittle, less subject to warpage, and can be used for outdoor productions. It is less expensive than plywood and is used in the construction of scenery, props, or stage furniture for which the strength of plywood is not required. Dancing strips, laid down over a rough stage floor, can be made from Masonite. It is tough enough to serve as a raceway for units of rolling scenery.

Hexcel Feather Panel. This product is well named; a 4' × 10' panel 1" thick weighs only 17 pounds. Not only is it rigid and light weight, but it is remarkably strong. It gains its surprising strength from its unique construction. It is made of Kraft material, a paper product, in three layers. The center layer of hexagonal cells is glued at right angles to the two outer layers. This center layer looks somewhat like a honeycomb. In a demonstration to prove its strength a small platform capable of supporting an actor was made entirely from Feather Panel. The sides, center supports, and top of the platform were made from 2" thick material. Feather Panel is manufactured in three different thicknesses: ¹/₂", 1" and 2". The ¹/₂" thick panels are 4' wide and 8' long; both the 1" and 2" thick panels are 4' wide but can be purchased in 8', 10', and 12' lengths.

Particle Board and Fiber Board. These two forms of 4' × 8' compositional boards are not used extensively in scenic work. Since they are prone to chip and disintegrate around the edges, they are poorly suited to withstand the rigors of scene shifting. Both types of board are made from small particles of wood or of fibers of vegetable matter, impregnated with adhesive, and compressed. Celotex, an example of fiber board, has been used as platform padding but it must be protected by a covering of canvas.

Covering Materials for Window Sash

Real glass is rarely used onstage because it reflects too much light, is too heavy and too expensive, and there is too much danger of breakage. Numerous substitute materials provide varying degrees of transparency or translucency. Any one of these materials can be attached to the back of the sash frame by either tacking or stapling it into place.

Bobinette. A very lightweight netting with an open hexagonal weave. It is available in several different colors and should be used when transparency is more important than opacity.

Sharkstooth Scrim. The weave of this material is rectangular in pattern and tighter than bobinette, which makes it more suitable for effects demanding greater opacity.

Marquisette. Another type of netting with a tighter weave than bobinette but a little less transparent.

Screen Wire. Obtainable in either galvanized or japanned finish. Both are transparent. The galvanized finish gives a slight haze to the appearance of the window.

Cel-O-Glass. A galvanized screen wire treated with a coating of cellophane to make it completely translucent.

Cel-O-Cloth. A thin sheet of cellophane with a backing of loosely woven netting and a little less translucent than Cel-o-glass.

Polyethylene Sheeting. This sheeting reflects some light, and care must be used in tacking it to the frames to prevent it from wrinkling. This material is sold in varying thicknesses, the thinner sheets being more transparent.

Cellulose Acetate. A perfect imitation of glass, but it possesses all the disadvantages of glass for stage use except that it will not break.

Covering Materials for General Stage Use

The materials listed below, although not normally used for covering flat frames, have all been used for that purpose. The term "covering material" is used in a broad context here, and applies to fabrics especially suitable for draperies, curtains, and borders used primarily for concealing or masking various parts of the stage.

Cotton Rep. Cotton rep is a heavy-duty cotton fabric with a ribbed weave not unlike that of fine pinwale corduroy. Its characteristics make it the favorite of many technicians. It is inexpensive, available in many colors, strong, drapes well, hangs free of wrinkles, has good opacity, and may be cleaned with either a broom or a vacuum cleaner. It is used primarily for drapery settings, masking drapes of all types, and on occasions when a special draw or fly curtain is needed as part of a setting. Rep has neither the weight nor the opacity needed for the main front curtain or teaser.

Velour. Heavy-duty cotton velour is characterized by a pronounced pile that gives the material a rich appearance. It is available in various colors and in different qualities. Because it is one of the heaviest and longest-lasting materials obtainable, the main front curtain and the teaser are usually made from it. However, it is not suitable for stage draperies or cyclorama sets that must be taken down and stored after each use. It is bulky and heavy and wrinkles when stored for any length of time. Both wrinkles and dirt picked up in the process of storing or hanging the material are difficult to remove.

Sateen. Sateen is an inexpensive, lightweight cotton material manufactured in many colors. One face of the material is finished with a high sheen. Sateen does not possess any great degree of opacity and shows at its best under front lighting. Its light weight makes it difficult to handle as a draw or fly curtain without excessive fishtailing or billowing when the curtains are operated. A chain weight inserted into the lower hem of such curtains will reduce these objectionable effects.

Corduroy. Theatrical supply houses usually do not carry this material but wide, medium, or narrow wale corduroy can be purchased at any large fabric shop in a great variety of colors. It can effectively be used on an interior setting as a substitute for velvet in the construction of decorative window drapes and in upholstering furniture. In addition to these uses it can also be employed, as is rep, in making drapery settings, masking curtains, fly curtains, and so forth. It is, however, more expensive than rep, and it will tear more easily. In some instances these drawbacks will be more than offset by the fact that corduroy takes the light better and will present a richer appearance to the audience.

Burlap. When coarse texturing is required on rocks or tree forms, burlap is frequently used. It is cut into strips, dipped into scene paint containing double strength sizing, then applied to a chicken wire form and molded into the desired shape. Burlap is a loosely woven jute fiber that can be purchased in 36" or 60" widths and in a limited range of colors. When complete opacity or soft draping is not required, burlap can be used for stage curtains.

Monks Cloth. Monks cloth is a very coarsely woven material, but because of its loose weave it is prone to snag. Though it comes in a limited color range, monks cloth receives dye well. It is an ideal fabric, for instance, for covering a decorative screen when an intricate design must be dye painted on the face of the screen. This cloth can also be used for stage curtains and draperies if a certain color, not obtainable in rep, is needed.

THEATRICAL HARDWARE

Much of the hardware used in the construction or rigging of scenery is of standard manufacture and can be purchased from local hardware stores. However, a number of hardware items have been designed and manufactured to meet specialized theatrical needs. The majority of the items in the following list must therefore be ordered from theatrical supply houses (Plates 26, 27).

Nails

One of the most commonly used fasteners is the nail. The three general types are common, box, and finish nails. These categories exclude such highly specialized ones as roofing nails, cut nails, and clout nails. All three types are sold by the pound and can be found in most hardware stores (Plate 26).

Common Nail. A common nail has a large head, and the diameter of its shaft is greater than that of a box nail or finish nail. The heavy common nails are used for general construction work, such as platform and stair assemblies, for bracing and scaffolding, or for any type of building where the heads of the nails are not objectionable. Common nails range in size from 1" (2d or two penny) for the smallest up to 6" in length (60d or sixty penny). The most commonly used nails in scenic work range from 1" up to 3½".

Finish Nail. A very small head and a thin shaft characterize the finish nail. A nail set is used to drive the head of this nail below the surface of the wood; the hole is then filled with putty or plastic wood which completely conceals the hole. Except for the construction of stage furniture and light decorative paneling, finish nails are not used extensively in scenic work.

Box Nail. Because a box nail, like a finish nail, has a small diameter shaft, there is little risk of its splitting lumber. The large head of a box nail prevents it

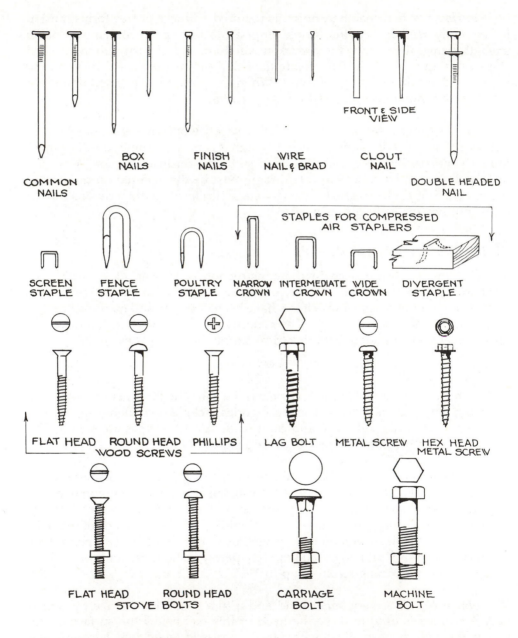

Plate 26   Nails, Staples, Screws, Bolts

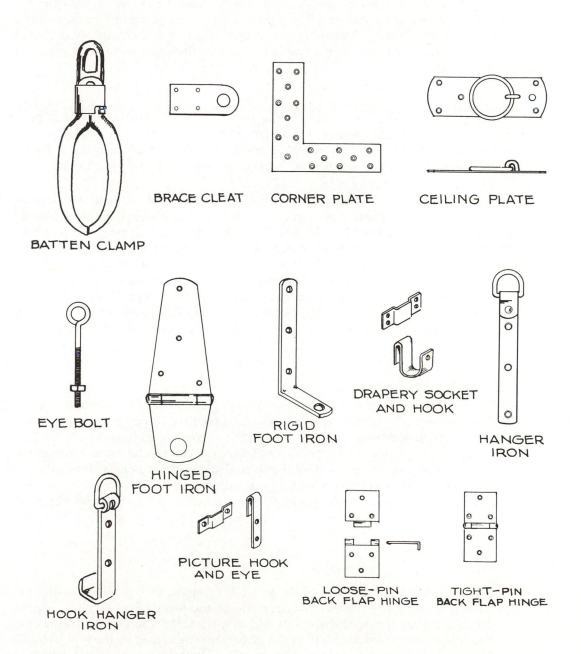

BRACE CLEAT   CORNER PLATE   CEILING PLATE

BATTEN CLAMP

EYE BOLT

HINGED
FOOT IRON

RIGID
FOOT IRON

DRAPERY SOCKET
AND HOOK

HANGER
IRON

HOOK HANGER
IRON

PICTURE HOOK
AND EYE

LOOSE-PIN
BACK FLAP HINGE

TIGHT-PIN
BACK FLAP HINGE

Plate 27   Theatrical Hardware

from pulling through soft compositional material when this material is nailed to a wooden frame.

Coated Box Nail. The readily available coated box nail is used for the same purpose as a clout nail. The adhesive coating is heated by friction as the nail is driven home, exerting a tight grip on the wood fibers and resulting in a firm joint. The point of this nail is clinched in the same manner as that of a clout nail.

Wire Nails and Brads. Box nails less than an inch long are called wire nails; finish nails less than an inch long are called brads. These very small nails are drawn from lightweight wire and range in length from 1/4" to 1". They can be used for model-making, in attaching small decorative molding to stage furniture, and in making small picture frames, as well as for other similar jobs.

Clout Nail. A clout nail is a specialized form not normally stocked by hardware stores. These nails can be purchased from theatrical supply houses and come in lengths of 1", 1 1/4", and 1 1/2". They are used to fasten 1/4" plywood corner blocks or keystones over butt joints in building the frames of flats. The length of the clout nail must be at least 1/4" greater than the combined thickness of the plywood and the framing lumber. In driving a clout nail in place its point is bent over, or clinched, by striking against a 1/4" steel plate (12" × 12") called a clinch plate that has been placed beneath the work. This procedure forms a very firm joint; about the only way a clout nail can be removed is by using a nail puller.

Staples

Fence and poultry staples are not used very often in the scene shop; but when they are needed, there is no good substitute for them. They are needed when fastening chicken wire or hardware cloth to wooden frames and in holding heavy wire in place as a foundation for plastic or papier mâché work. A few of the different types of staples used in air powered staple guns are illustrated on Plate 26. Either a narrow crown coated staple or a divergent staple can be used in place of clout nails to hold cornerblocks and keystones in place when building flat frames. Wide crown staples are used in place of tacks when covering flats with muslin or canvas.

Screws

Because they are much less likely to work loose, screws produce a stronger joining between two pieces of wood, or metal and wood, than do nails. Screws are more easily removed than nails and they have the additional advantage of being reusable. Screws are sold by the box and are described by the type of head, by the length of the screw, and by the diameter of the shaft which is designated by number. Most stage hardware has been drilled to receive a No. 8 or No. 9 flat head screw. Technicians in some scene shops have switched from the use of a standard slotted-head screw to a Phillips screw because they feel that there is less damage to the latter from power equipment.

Bolts

Stove bolts, either flat or round headed, are used when the strongest type of fastening is required. A hole the same diameter as the bolt shaft is drilled through both the members to be fastened; the bolt is then inserted into the hole and tightened in place with a nut and washer. These bolts are obtainable in $^3/_{16}$″, $^1/_4$″, $^5/_{16}$″, or $^3/_8$″ diameters; they vary in length from 1″ to 6″. See Plate 26 for illustrations.

Carriage Bolts. Carriage bolts have a rounded head and beneath the head are sloping shoulders that are wider than the shaft. Striking the head of the bolt with a hammer will seat the shoulders into the wood and prevent the bolt's turning. One of the most common uses of carriage bolts is fastening in place the 2″ × 4″ legs of platforms. These bolts vary in size from $^1/_4$″ to $^3/_4$″ in diameter and from 1″ to 24″ in length.

Machine Bolts. Machine bolts are used for joining metal to metal as in bolting a safety winch to its supporting bracket; or they can be used to bolt two pieces of wood together provided a washer is placed under both the head and the nut. Machine bolts have either square or hexagonal heads, the diameters of the shafts vary from $^1/_4$″ to 1″ and the length from 1″ to 6″. Two wrenches are required to tighten or loosen a nut on this type of bolt.

Batten Clamp, or Drop Holder (Plate 27). A clamp used for attaching drops or borders to a set of lines in preparation for flying them. The jaws of the clamp are designed to open and fit around the wooden batten at the top of a drop. These clamps may be attached or removed rapidly and without damage to the canvas.

Brace Cleat. The cleat is screwed to the stile of a flat and provides a fast and easy method of engaging the hooks of a stage brace required for bracing standard scenery.

Corner Plate. Corner plates are 1″ or $1^1/_8$″ wide with 6″ sides and are cut from solid plate. They are used to reinforce the joints of a detachable door or window unit or as a substitute for corner blocks.

Ceiling Plate. Used in joining cross battens to the lengthwise battens of a book or roll ceiling and to provide the necessary rings by which the ceiling can be flown.

Eye Bolt. Used to provide a solid anchor for lines, piano wire, or turnbuckles. Varies in price according to size.

Hinged Foot Iron. Used for bracing or locking scenery directly to the stage floor by means of stage screws. The hinged feature adapts this type of foot iron for use on scenic units that do not stand at right angles to the stage floor. The free half of the foot iron can be folded out of the way for shifting or storage.

Rigid Foot Iron.   Used for the same purpose as the hinged foot iron; it lacks the hinged feature but is stronger.

Drapery Hangers.   The socket and hook arrangement of drapery hangers permits the fast and easy shifting of door or window draperies. The sockets are screwed to the face of the scenery and the hooks are screwed to each end of the drapery pole, permitting one stagehand to handle drapes, pole, and hooks in one operation.

Hanger Iron.   The hanger iron is bolted to the back and near the top of scenery that is to be shifted by flying. It provides a strong metal ring to which the snatch lines can be attached. It is used alone only on very light scenic units; on heavier scenery it is used in conjunction with the hook hanger iron.

Hook Hanger Iron.   Provides a means of attaching a snatch line to a heavy unit of scenery so that it can be flown under compression. It is attached to the back of the flat with the lower rail resting in the hook. At the top of the flat, directly above the hook, is placed a hanger iron. The snatch line feeds through the ring of the hanger iron and is tied off at the bottom of the flat to the ring of the hook hanger iron.

Picture Hook and Eye.   Lightweight hooks and sockets used for fastening decorative or practical properties to the face of the scenery. Properties so attached may be removed and replaced with a minimum of effort and time.

Loose-Pin Back Flap Hinge.   The loose-pin hinge is used when a temporary union is required between two pieces of scenery that must be separated during a scene shift or for storage. Removal of the pin makes this operation both easy and fast. These hinges are available in two sizes, $1\frac{1}{2}'' \times 3\frac{1}{2}''$ and $2'' \times 4\frac{1}{2}''$. The smaller size is used on units made of $1'' \times 2''$ framing and the larger on frames constructed from wider stock.

Tight-Pin Back Flap Hinge.   These hinges are used when a permanent union is required, such as that between two or more flats joined edge to edge to make up an expanse of unbroken wall. Junctions between flats and hinges are concealed by a strip of canvas glued and tacked in place over them. Available in the same sizes as loose-pin hinges.

Lash-Line Cleat.   Attached to the inner edges of flat stiles and used when a temporary joining of two flats is to be made by lashing. (See Plate 28.)

Lash-Line Eye.   Used for attaching the lash line to the flat. The eye is attached to the inner edge of the stile just beneath the upper corner block; one end of the lash line is passed through the eye and knotted to provide a firm anchor for the line. Use of this cleat can sometimes be avoided by drilling a $\frac{3}{8}''$ hole in the corner block, inserting the lash line, and knotting it.

Lash-Line Hook.   A substitute for a conventional lash cleat when the structural nature of the flat prohibits the use of the latter.

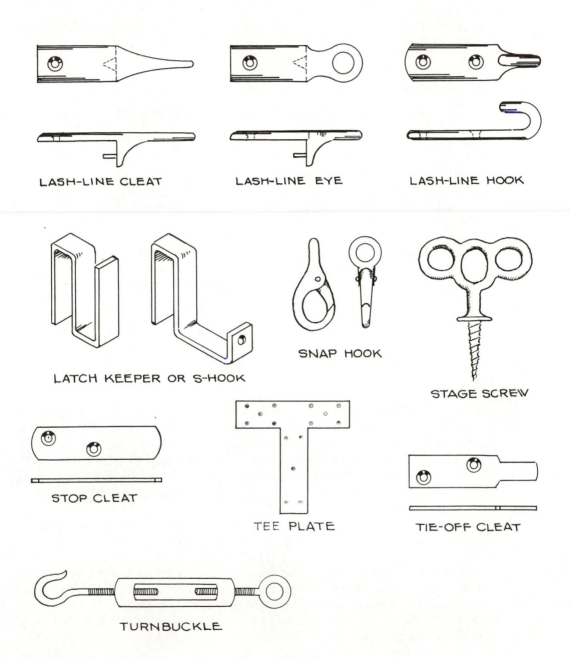

LASH-LINE CLEAT   LASH-LINE EYE   LASH-LINE HOOK

LATCH KEEPER OR S-HOOK   SNAP HOOK   STAGE SCREW

STOP CLEAT   TEE PLATE   TIE-OFF CLEAT

TURNBUCKLE

Plate 28   Theatrical Hardware

Latch Keeper.   Two or more latch keepers are placed over the toggle bars on the rear of a two- or three-fold flat. A stiffening batten placed in the open halves of the hooks serves to keep the flats rigid and in a single plane.

Snap Hooks.   Snap hooks provide a fast and safe method of attaching one object to another, eliminating the risk associated with hastily tied knots.

Stage Screw.   A heavy, hand-operated floor screw used in conjunction with a brace cleat and stage brace in bracing scenery.

Stop Cleat.   Used to assure the perfect vertical alignment of two flats that are to be joined by lashing. The cleats are screwed to the back of the stiles with their ends projecting ³/₄″ beyond the outer edges. This arrangement prevents one flat from slipping past the other.

Tee Plate.   A substitute for a keystone in the assembly of a butt joint. It is cut from solid plate and is 1¹/₈″ × 6″ × 6″.

Tie-Off Cleat.   Two cleats placed opposite each other at the 3'-0″ level on two flats to be joined by lashing; the lash-line knot is formed around them. The angular edges of this cleat prevent the lash line from slipping during the process of tying off.

Turnbuckle.   Turnbuckles are sometimes attached to the end of snatch lines, thus making easy the final trim of a flown unit. More frequently the turnbuckle is used for stretching taut a wire or rope. Varies in price according to size.

Improved Stage Screw.   In some theatres regular stage screws are not used because they have a tendency to tear up the floor; but the improved stage screw can be used in their place (Plate 29). The improved stage screw consists of two parts, a plug threaded both inside and out and the screw which threads into the plug. To use the device drill a ⁹/₁₆″ hole into the floor, insert the plug, and, using the screw as a tool, drive the plug into the hole until it is flush with the floor. Remove the hand screw, and the plug is ready for use. At the close of the production the plug can be removed by using a large screw driver. The hole can then be filled with a short length of ⁹/₁₆″ hardwood doweling.

Roto Lock, Heavy Duty.   The Roto Lock, or casket lock as it is sometimes called, is simple in design and compact in size. It is used as a butt joint fastener when it will be necessary at times to separate the parts so joined. The Roto Lock is ideal for locking platforms together or for joining the parts of a double-faced wall that must be separated for shifting.

Torque Washer.   Sometimes the sloping shoulders beneath the head of a carriage bolt will rotate in the wood making it difficult either to tighten or to loosen a nut. This problem can be avoided by the use of a torque washer. It fits over the shaft of a carriage bolt with the bolt shoulders slipping into the squared center hole. The four projecting teeth of the washer bite into the wood preventing the bolt head from turning.

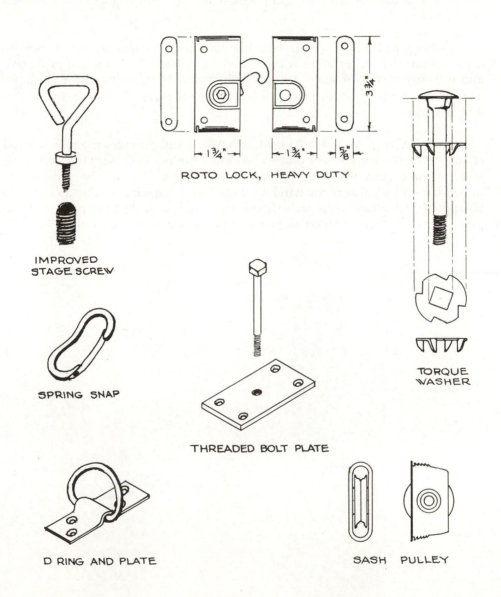

Plate 29 Theatrical Hardware

Spring Snap. These snaps provide an excellent method of attaching draperies or curtains to the travellers of a curtain track.

Threaded Bolt Plate. The bolt plate furnishes a simple solution to the problem of bolting an object to a surface when only one side of the surface can be reached. The plate is screwed into position and the bolt engages the threaded center hole.

D-Ring and Plate. A D-ring may be used separately or it can be clamped into a fixed position with its covering plate. This ring is inexpensive and has many uses on stage. It can, for instance, be substituted for a hanger iron when attaching small pieces of scenery to the lines by which the pieces will be flown.

Sash Pulley. An old-fashioned sash pulley still provides the best method of counter-balancing a heavy practical window if it not necessary to remove the window unit from the window flat during a scene shift. The pulleys are imbedded on each side of the window at the top of the window thickness piece. Sash cords are attached to each side of the window sash; they pass over the pulleys and are then attached to the weights necessary to balance the window.

5

Mechanical Drawing

It should be apparent from the preceding chapters that the ability to read and to make a set of mechanical drawings is essential for anyone concerned with the technical aspects of a production. Certainly the designer cannot describe his setting accurately without this knowledge, and the same may be said for the technician who must convert the designer's plans into working drawings. Whatever is built in the scene shop, whether it is scenery or properties, must first be delineated by a scaled mechanical drawing that gives the shop foreman and the crew members all the essential information on what the finished unit looks like, what its dimensions are, what materials it is made from, and how its various parts are assembled.

NEED FOR A KNOWLEDGE
OF MECHANICAL DRAWING

As a means of communication humanity has developed many different languages, but there still are times when the written or spoken word is not enough. This occurs when it becomes necessary to describe in great detail the physical appearance of an object. The more complicated the object becomes, the more essential it is to supplement the spoken or written word with some other method of shape description. Diagrams, freehand sketches, or well-executed perspective sketches are a tremendous asset to understanding—witness the rough diagram a filling station attendant may make while showing us how to reach a given address. These forms of graphic description may give a general picture of what a proposed structure should look like, but they are not accurate enough to indicate exactly the intended size or proportions of the structure. Mechanical drawing came into being in order to furnish this more accurate form of shape description.

Mechanical drawing, or engineering drawing as it is sometimes called, is essentially what the name implies. As opposed to freehand drawing, it is a form of graphic description that represents an object or structure by a series of different views drawn to an appropriate scale where each line has been formed by the aid of a drafting instrument of some kind.

DRAFTING MATERIALS

For the type of mechanical drawing required for scenic work, the list of equipment is neither elaborate nor expensive. Such a list would include the following: an architect's scale rule, a drawing board, a T square, triangles, dividers, compasses, a French curve, drawing paper, drafting tape, pencils, and an eraser. It is suggested that good-quality drafting instruments should be purchased. If given proper care they will give excellent results and will last almost indefinitely, whereas cheap instruments are difficult to control, are soon worn out, and are a source of constant annoyance. This is especially true of the dividers and compasses. Because a student draftsman has little need for many of the instruments included in a complete set of draftsman's instruments, it is recommended that the beginner not get a complete set, but rather buy separately dividers and compasses of very good quality. Usually it is not necessary to ink the drawings used in scenic work, which eliminates the need for ruling pens and pen attachments for compasses. There is no question but that an inked drawing produces clearer blueprints or Ozlite copies; it is also true that quite acceptable prints can be made from heavily penciled originals. To ink a drawing satisfactorily requires considerable skill and time; while it is hoped that this step in drafting will eventually be mastered, it is a step that can be bypassed for most scenic work—certainly by a beginner.

Architect's Scale Rule

Perhaps the draftsman's most important tool is his scale rule. Any object that is too large to be drawn to full scale on a single sheet of drafting paper must be proportionally reduced in size. Proportional reduction, which may sound ominous to the uninitiated, is accomplished quickly and easily by the use of an architect's scale rule. Although this scale comes in several different forms, the one most frequently used for scenic work is triangular shaped rather than flat. It has in addition to a regular linear foot, which occupies one face of the rule, ten reduction scales imprinted along the five remaining faces. These reduction scales consist of the following: $3'' = 1'\text{-}0''$, $1\frac{1}{2}'' = 1'\text{-}0''$, $1'' = 1'\text{-}0''$, $\frac{3}{4}'' = 1'\text{-}0''$, $\frac{1}{2}'' = 1'\text{-}0''$, $\frac{3}{8}'' = 1'\text{-}0''$, $\frac{1}{4}'' = 1'\text{-}0''$, $\frac{3}{16}'' = 1'\text{-}0''$, $\frac{1}{8}'' = 1'\text{-}0''$, and $\frac{3}{32}'' = 1'\text{-}0''$. (See Plate 30.)

Perhaps the easiest way to understand proportional reduction is to imagine that a regular linear foot has been reduced in length to correspond to one of the scales on the rule. Examine the architect's rule for a moment. Except for that edge of the rule that has the regular 1-foot measure, each face of the rule has two scales imprinted on it. The identifications of scale are printed near the end of the rule and are paired off in the following groupings: the $3''$ and $1\frac{1}{2}''$ appear on one face, the $1''$ and $\frac{1}{2}''$ on another face, the $\frac{3}{4}''$ and $\frac{3}{8}''$ on the third face, the $\frac{1}{4}''$ and $\frac{1}{8}''$ on the fourth face, and the $\frac{3}{16}''$ and $\frac{3}{32}''$ on the fifth face. Although two scales are printed along the same face of the rule, there is little chance to confuse the

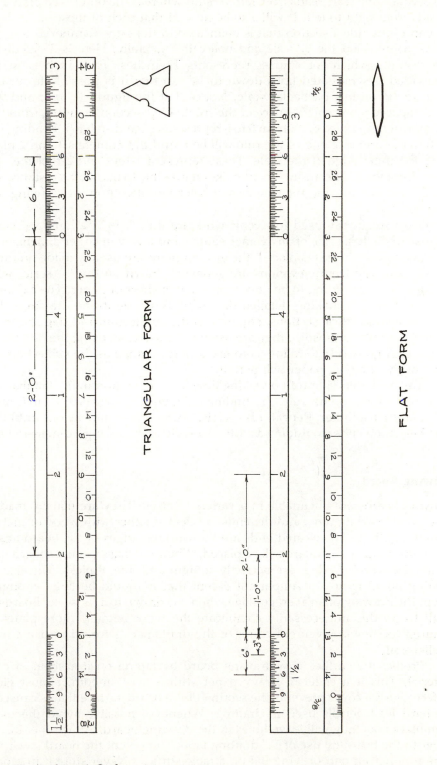

Plate 30 Architect's Scales

two because one scale reads from left to right, whereas the other is so placed that it reads from right to left. It will also be noticed that each of these scales has at the end of the rule a section that is delineated in the same manner as a regular foot measure. Find the 3″ scale and notice this carefully. Here is 3″ subdivided into twelfths which, of course, represents 12 inches. Each inch is in turn subdivided by graduated lines down to $\frac{1}{8}$″, so that it is possible to measure down to $\frac{1}{8}$″ on this particular scale. Notice that the figures 0, 3, 6, and 9 are evenly spaced along this 3″ space of the subdivided section. Reading from the 0 to 3 represents a space of 3″; from 0 to 6 represents 6″; and so forth. Reading from the 0 to the opposite end of the rule will be found the numerals 1 and 2 placed along the inner edge of the scale. These represent 1-foot and 2-foot measurements from the 0. The arrangement makes it possible to mark off a distance such as 2′-6″ without moving the rule once it has been placed on the drawing. (See Plate 30.)

Most frequently used for scenic work are the 1″, $\frac{1}{2}$″, $\frac{3}{4}$″, and $\frac{3}{8}$″ scales. Because of the large size of an average setting and the even larger dimensions of the stage upon which it is placed, the ground plans are usually made on the $\frac{3}{8}$″ or $\frac{1}{2}$″ scale. The front elevations are generally drawn on the $\frac{1}{2}$″ scale, which permits an entire setting to be drawn on a single sheet of paper. The $\frac{3}{4}$″ and 1″ scales are used in making detailed drawings. Since sight-line drawings, both horizontal and vertical sections, require that the auditorium and stage be shown in their proper relationship, they are usually drawn small using the $\frac{1}{4}$″, $\frac{3}{16}$″, or $\frac{1}{8}$″ scale. A good rule to follow is to use as large a scale as the subject and the limits of the drawing paper will permit.

The beginner will profit by taking time to become thoroughly familiar with the various scales on his rule. Try finding a dimension such as 9′-7″ on first one scale and then another. Repeat this exercise with various dimensions until there is no hesitation either in finding a particular scale or in reading a dimension from it.

Drawing Board

Drawing boards are obtainable in a variety of sizes. They are usually made of bass wood or white pine, and the ends are cleated either with wood or metal to prevent splitting. The cleated ends are the working edges of the board against which the head of a T square will be placed. When purchasing a new board make certain the working edges are perfectly straight and free of nicks. The size of a drafting board is not too important except that it should be large enough to accept the drawing of an average stage when it is drawn to a $\frac{1}{2}$″ scale. Boards too small to do this unnecessarily complicate the work because more plates are required to show a given structure, or the draftsman is forced to use a much smaller scale.

Protect the surface of a drawing board by taping on it a sheet of cover material. This is a sheet of heavy paper with a very smooth, almost glossy surface. Such a cover prevents the scoring of the board surface that is caused by the hard lead pencils used in drafting. Whenever possible avoid the use of thumbtacks, as they will leave holes in the drawing board. Attach the drawing paper to the board by use of $\frac{3}{4}$″ drafting tape. To prevent the board's warping, store it either on end or lying flat on a table surface. Never store it in a damp place or behind a radiator—this is asking for trouble.

T Square

The basic tool used for the construction of all horizontal lines is the T square and, in combination with various triangles, it is used for making vertical and angular lines (Plate 31). Because it plays such an important role in drafting, the selection of a good T square becomes a matter for careful consideration. T squares are made of hardwood with a head attached to a shaft by both glue and screws. Make sure the head is firmly attached to the shaft at a true right angle and that there is no looseness or play between the two. The shaft should be long enough to cover the width of your drawing board and it must be absolutely straight and free of nicks. The straightness of a shaft can usually be checked by squinting down its length or by placing a steel square against the shaft. If your budget will permit it, a T square with transparent edges is preferred to a solid wood shaft.

Triangles

The beginning draftsman will find two triangles adequate for most of his work. Although triangles can be purchased in many different sizes, the 8″ 45° and the 10″ 30° −60° are best suited for general work. All vertical lines are constructed by using these triangles and a T square. The base of a triangle is placed against the T square shaft with the vertical edge of the triangle facing the left. Assuming that the light source is from the left, this position of the triangle will eliminate the shadow that would be cast by it if its position were reversed. All vertical lines are drawn from bottom to top of the triangle. Triangles smaller than those specified require that both T square and triangle be shifted either up or down in order to draw a long vertical line. By placing one of these triangles against the other and guiding both with a T square, two additional angles can be formed, the 15° and the 75°. See Plate 31 for the proper placement of triangles.

A very worthwhile addition to the draftsman's set of instruments is an adjustable triangle or set square. A conventional 45° triangle is divided into two unequal parts joined by a plastic protractor reading from 0° to 45°. A threaded bolt and thumbscrew permit the locking of the two sections at any desired angle. Without an adjustable triangle the draftsman must resort to the use of a protractor to establish angles other than those possible with his two triangles (Plate 32).

Dividers

The divider is a two-legged metal instrument with each leg terminating in a needle point; it is capable of fine adjustment (Plate 33). This instrument is used to transfer measurements or to divide a line into any number of equal parts. It is especially useful in transferring measurements from a three-dimensional set model to a drawing, or vice versa. It is frequently impossible to place a scale rule on a small model in a position that permits the draftsman to read a dimension. Dividing a line into, say, thirds by use of the divider is accomplished as follows. Separate the legs by what you estimate to be one-third of the length of the line and "walk" the dividers along the line. Should the final step of the divider be too long, this overlength is divided by three and the distance between the divider points shortened by that much. If the final step is too short, the underlength distance is again divided by three and the distance between points lengthened to conform.

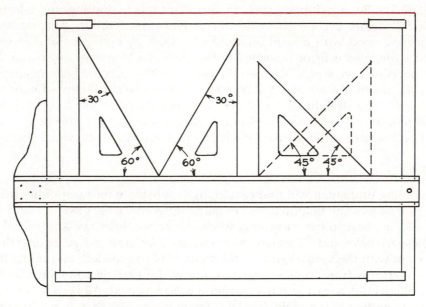

DRAWING BOARD – T SQUARE
AND TRIANGLES

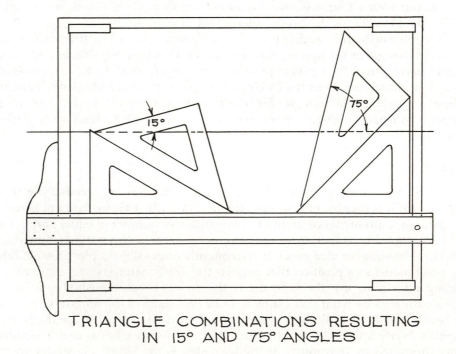

TRIANGLE COMBINATIONS RESULTING
IN 15° AND 75° ANGLES

Plate 31   Drawing Board, T Square, and Triangles

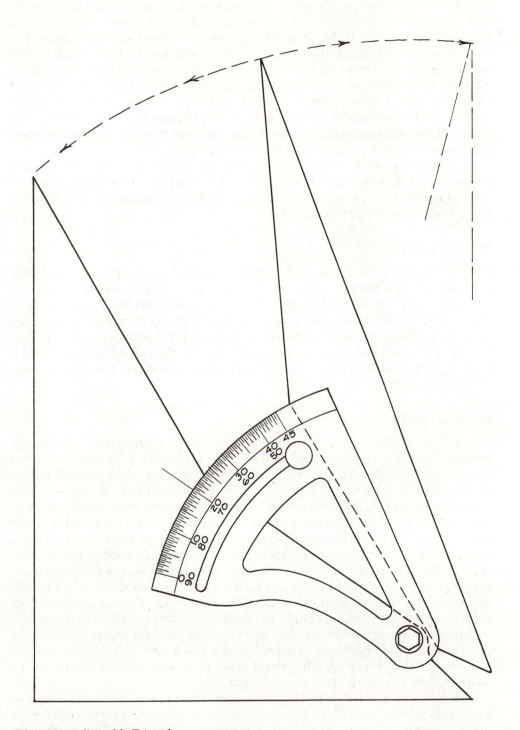

Plate 32 Adjustable Triangle

Compasses

The compass is similar to the dividers in general shape and form but differs in that one of its legs is equipped with a removable pencil-lead attachment. A regular 6″ compass is capable of drawing circles up to about one foot in diameter. For circles or arcs larger than this the pencil attachment is removed and a lengthening bar is inserted into the compass; the pencil attachment is then attached to the end of the lengthening bar. For very small circles a smaller compass, called a bow compass, is used. The very smallest circles are drawn with a special instrument called a drop bow compass (Plate 33). The special design of this instrument permits the pencil lead to be brought closer to the pivot point needle than is possible with the other compasses.

Should the student's budget be severely limited, it is possible to omit buying a pair of dividers and to substitute a 6″ compass. This compass can be used in much the same way as dividers to transfer measurements or to divide a given distance into equal parts.

French Curves

Irregular curved lines, those that cannot be formed by a compass, are drawn with the aid of a French curve. This is basically a trial-and-error procedure. Establish a series of points through which the irregular curve will pass and draw the curve freehand, being careful not to obliterate the location points. Once the desired line is established in satisfactory form, apply a French curve to it; find that section of the French curve that coincides with the curved line and draw it in. The position of the French curve may be changed several times in drawing a single curved line (Plate 34).

Drafting Pencils

The highest quality of graphite lead is used in the manufacture of drawing pencils. They range in degree of hardness from 9H, which is the hardest, down through 8H, 7H, 6H, 5H, 4H, 3H, 2H, H, to medium at F, then through HB, B, 2B, 3B, 4B to 5B, which is the softest. The softer leads are used only for sketching or rendering and should be avoided when one is doing mechanical drawing. Very soft lead rubs off from the drawing onto the underside of the triangles and the T square and onto the draftsman's hands, resulting in a drawing that has a graphite "shadow" smeared over its surface. Harder leads such as the 2H, 3H, and 4H are best suited for general drafting. It is, however, possible to select a lead that is too hard. Pencils with too hard a lead have a tendency to cut or tear the paper and to leave marks that are difficult to erase. The hardest leads will even score a drawing board should too much pressure be applied to the pencil. Pencils used in mechanical drawing must be kept pinpoint sharp. This may be done with a good sharpener or a knife and a sandpaper block that is used to achieve the final pointing. The pencil leads of a compass are sharpened by shaping them to a sharp bevel on sandpaper.

Several mechanical pencils are designed for drafting. Each has a hollow barrel into which a lead of the desired hardness is inserted. A metal chuck grips the lead firmly allowing a portion to extend beyond the grip. This lead can be sharpened to a fine point by placing it into a rotary lead sharpener.

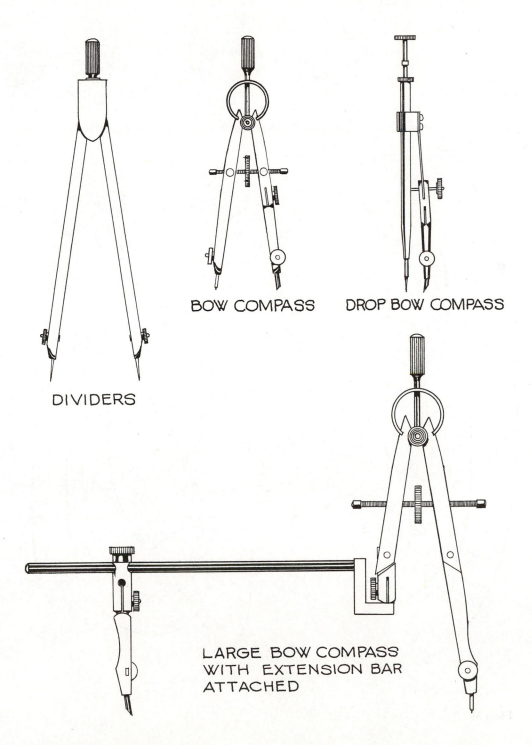

BOW COMPASS   DROP BOW COMPASS

DIVIDERS

LARGE BOW COMPASS
WITH EXTENSION BAR
ATTACHED

Plate 33 Dividers and Compasses

Plate 34   Types of French Curves

Drafting Tape

Do not confuse regular masking tape with drafting tape. They look somewhat alike, but drafting tape has much less adhesive than the other and can be removed from a drawing without roughening the paper surface or tearing it.

Align the drawing paper with the board and T square before fastening it to the board with short lengths of drafting tape placed across each corner. Make sure that the top edge of the paper is parallel to the T square shaft when the head of the square is held firmly against the working edge of the board. Hold the paper in position with one hand while with the other you apply the drafting tape to the corners.

DRAFTING SYMBOLS AND CONVENTIONS

Any written composition is given additional clarity by the use of various punctuation marks. So it is with mechanical drawing. Drafting symbols and conventions make a drawing much easier to read and understand. Some of these symbols have been carried over from engineering or architectural drawing, whereas other have been developed to meet the special need of theatre work.

A freehand drawing is composed of various types of lines, each used to describe better the features of an observed object. The same is true in mechanical drawing, where the draftsman makes use of a particular type of line in order to clarify the details of an object he is drawing. There are about a dozen standardized variations of line forms, each with its own meaning, that are normally accepted as drafting symbols or conventions (Plates 35·and 36). They are as follows:

Margin Line. A heavy solid line used to form a border about a completed plate. It is sometimes used to separate several unrelated objects appearing on a single sheet of paper.

Construction Line. A solid line of medium weight used to describe the shape or contour of an object.

Hidden Construction Line. A medium-weight line broken into a series of equal length short dashes that shows the shape of that part of an object that is concealed in the given view.

Drapery Line. A wavy line of medium weight used to indicate the placement of draperies as they would appear when seen in top view.

Extension Line. A lightweight line placed at a right angle to a surface or part of an object to show the terminal points of a dimension. Extension lines are separated from a construction line by a slight space, or placed at right angles to the terminals of a given line.

Dimension Line. Lightweight lines placed on either side of a dimension which extend to a contact point with the extension lines. The contact point is emphasized by arrowheads.

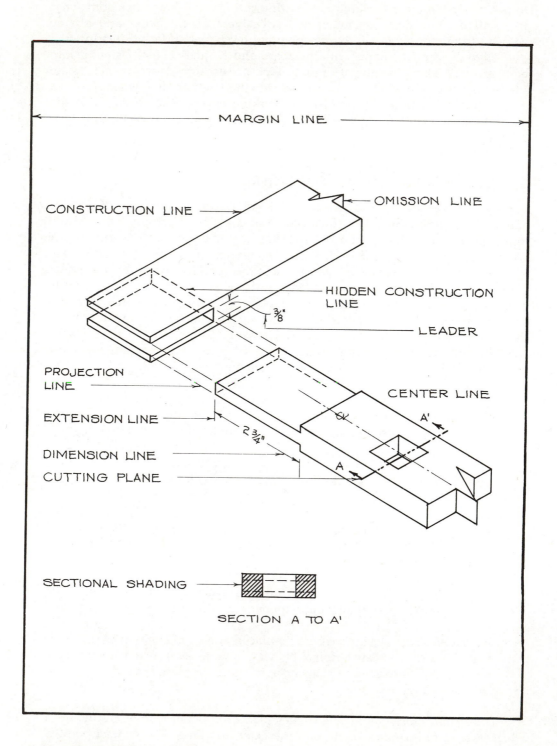

Plate 35   Drafting Conventions

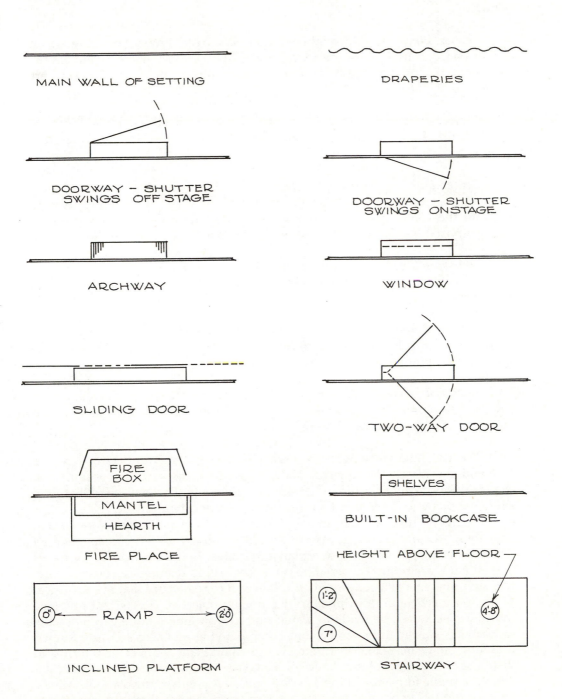

Plate 36 Drafting Conventions for Ground Plans

Dimension Encircled.   A circle drawn about a dimension indicates the height of an object above the horizontal plane on which it is resting. It is used extensively in indicating height levels when drawing ground plans of a stage setting.

Leader Line.   A lightweight straight or curved line terminating in an arrowhead. It is used when the space between two extension lines is too limited to permit the proper insertion of the printed dimension. The dimension is printed at the head of the leader.

Projection Line.   A series of lightweight dashes that is used to indicate the relationship of various parts of an object as they would appear when seen from different views.

Center Line.   A lightweight line composed of alternating long and short dashes so placed as to describe the center of an object. Frequently used to indicate the center line of a stage setting. The letters C and L (center line) superimposed one on the other are drawn directly over the center line.

Omission Line.   A medium-weight line interrupted at intervals by angular breaks; used to indicate that a part of an object has been omitted from the drawing.

Cutting Plane.   A heavyweight line composed of a series of long dashes followed by two short ones and terminating in arrowheads; used to show the imaginary cutting plane of a sectional drawing.

Sectional Shading.   A series of lightweight, evenly spaced lines drawn at 45° used to emphasize a cross-sectional view of an object drawn as it would appear at the point indicated by the cutting plane.

These symbols should be as easily recognized and understood as are conventional punctuation marks. They serve much the same purpose in that they make a drawing clearer and easier to understand. Become so familiar with these various line forms that their use becomes almost automatic.

No matter how carefully an object is drawn or how many views are used in describing it, the drawing may mean little unless it is accompanied by dimensions and perhaps a few explanatory notes. Both dimensional numerals and all notes are printed to avoid possible mistakes in reading caused by poorly formed numbers of illegible longhand. It is well to remember that the basic goal of a good mechanical drawing is to describe an object so clearly and precisely that no mistake can be made in visualizing it. The time required to make the drawings is wasted if the dimensions accompanying them are so badly formed that they can be misread. The numerals shown on Plate 37 are of such form and distinction that there is little chance of mistaking one for another. Pay particular attention to the formation of the 3, 5, 6, 8, and 0. A poorly formed 6 can easily be mistaken for an 8, or even for a 0, and vice versa. Notice that each numeral is formed either by a straight line, a part of a circle, a full circle, or some combination of these. A little practice in forming these numerals pays large dividends in the speed with which they can be drawn.

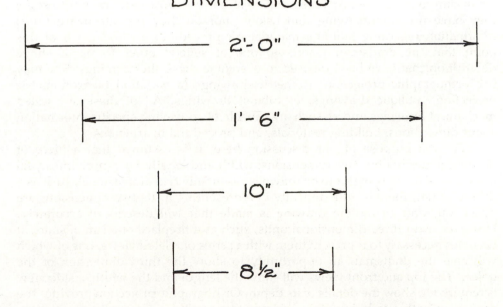

UPPER CASE

ABCDEFGHIJKLMNOPQRSTUVWXYZ

Lower Case

abcdefghijklmnopqrstuvwxyz

NUMERALS

1234567890

¼ ½ ¾

DIMENSIONS

|← —————————— 2'-0" —————————— →|

|← ————————— 1'-6" ————————— →|

|← ———— 10" ———— →|

|← —— 8½" —— →|

Plate 37   Alphabets-Numerals-Dimensions

There are no rules pertaining to the placement of dimensions on a drawing other than that they are usually positioned so that they read from left to right or from bottom to top. This means that anyone reading them would do so as he would read anything else, from left to right. By turning the drawing one quarter turn to the right, those dimensions written from bottom to top now read from left to right. One other general rule that makes sense is to place the dimensions where they can most easily be read. This may mean that some are placed within the contour lines of a drawing, and others are placed at the sides, the bottom, or the top. Be careful not to use overly long extension lines that must pass through or over the contour lines of a drawing.

Two other drawing conventions are the symbols used to indicate feet and inches. A single prime placed to the right and slightly above a numeral denotes feet; a double prime in the same position indicates inches. An even number of feet, such as six feet, is written 6'-0". Should the dimension be six and one-half feet, it would be written as 6'-6", never 6½'. The only time that a fraction is seen on a drawing is when it represents the fractional part of an inch. Dimensions such as five inches or eight inches are written as 5" and 8". It is unnecessary to signify that there are no feet.

SHAPE DESCRIPTION

Freehand sketches, perspective drawings, even photographs, serve admirably in presenting a clear idea of what the shape of an object is intended to be, but none of these forms of shape description carries sufficient information to enable a technician to build from it. These drawings, for the most part, are not to scale; they have no accompanying dimensions, nor do they provide instructional information regarding building materials or procedural methods. It is at this point that the draftsman resorts to one of several other forms of shape description that have been devised to overcome these shortcomings. She may use orthographic projection, isometric drawings (a variation of axonometric projection), oblique drawings, or cabinet drawings. All of these are scaled mechanical drawings and as such are capable of conveying specific information about dimensions, building materials, and procedural instructions.

For the purpose of our discussion here, it is assumed that a piece of drafting paper has but two dimensions: width and length; we ignore the actual thickness of it. If the object to be drawn is essentially two dimensional, such as a drop or a flat, there is little difficulty in representing it. Its two dimensions are scaled off, and an outline drawing is made that will describe it accurately. However, with three-dimensional units, such as a fireplace or a run of stairs, it becomes necessary to represent them with a series of related views, one of which will give the draftsman an opportunity to show the third dimension of the object. The top and front views will show the length and the width; a side view is required to show the details of its depth. Orthographic projection provides the draftsman with a technique that achieves this result.

Orthographic Projection

Watch a person inspect a small unfamiliar object. He is very likely to turn it over and around several times before he is satisfied that he has seen all of its various sides. He feels its texture, probably even guesses at its weight. Should the object have any movable parts, he probably tries in various ways to test the movements. A draftsman does exactly the same thing with anything he proposes to draw. He describes the object by drawing different views of its various faces; he appends dimensions and explanatory notes where necessary. In short, he resorts to orthographic projection to describe an object by a series of different but related views.

The easiest way to understand the relationship of these different views is to imagine an object, for example, a run of three steps, enclosed in a transparent box with each of its sides hinged one to another so that they all can be flattened out into a single plane. If we look down on the top of the stairs through the box, we can see their width and length but not their height or the baseboard. Should we project lines from the four corners of each step to the top plane of the box and connect all of these points with lines, we would have an accurate drawing of them. Drawings of the front, the back, and the two sides can be projected from the stairs to the corresponding planes of the box in a similar manner. When the transparent box is flattened out into a single plane, it becomes two dimensional as is our drawing paper. There is, however, a definite relationship between the various views of the steps as they appear on our drawing paper. Each represents a different view of them and each is drawn as though the observer was viewing them at a true right angle; he can see only one face of the stairs at a time. It is obvious that several different views are required to describe the stairs completely.

One of the advantages of orthographic projection is the speed with which an object can be drawn. As can be seen in the example (Plate 38), the arrangement of the different views of the stairs is such that it will permit transferring a scaled measurement from one view to another by means of a T square or triangle. There is no need to use a scale rule for this purpose.

A majority of the designer's drafting is accomplished through the use of orthographic projection. This is true because the size of a conventional stage setting is too large to be drawn by any other means. The ground plan, although drawn on a separate sheet of paper, represents the top view; the elevations, again on a separate sheet, describe the front view. The same is true of detail drawings; they show a smaller segment of the setting by giving not only the dimensions of its width and length but of its depth as well.

Isometric Drawing

Some parts of a setting may be so complicated in form that some other type of pictorial drawing is required to describe it adequately. Axonometric projection, from which isometric drawing is derived, is a form of drafting that assumes that the object to be drawn has been both tilted and rotated into a position that permits the observer to see three faces of it at once. It is apparent that an object can be placed in an infinite number of angles when arranged in this manner. The simplest of these positions occurs when equal angles are employed, resulting in what is called the isometric position. It is also apparent that a drawing made of an object in this position would be represented by foreshortened lines. The isometric drawing, however, ignores the foreshortening that actually occurs and allows each line to be represented at full scale.

Isometric drawings are based on three lines representing three edges of an object placed in the position described above. These lines, one vertical and the

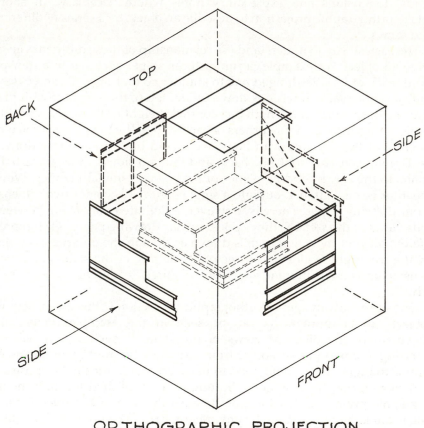

ORTHOGRAPHIC PROJECTION

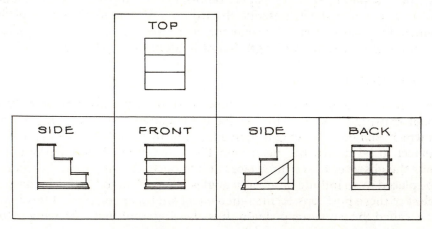

RELATIONSHIP OF VIEWS

Plate 38   Orthographic Projection and Relationship of Views other two drawn on either side of it at a 30° angle to it, are called the isometric axes. Lines drawn in this fashion are separated by 120°—again, "equal measure"—or isometric axes. Any line drawn parallel to any one of the axes is called an isometric line and as such can be measured at its true length (Plate 39). The various surfaces bounded by the isometric lines are called isometric planes. Lines not parallel to any of the axes are called nonisometric lines, and cannot be measured directly. They may be drawn by plotting their measurements, as they would appear in an orthographic view, and transferring these measurements to the corresponding isometric plane. A line drawn between the points so established will represent the desired angle or nonisometric plane.

Circular forms are drawn in much the same manner. When a circle is enclosed in a square, it will be noticed that the circumference of the circle is in contact with the square at midpoints on each side of the square. Locate the enclosing square in its proper isometric plane, then establish the contact points between circle and square. Using these four contact points as guides, the elliptical shape of a circle may be approximated freehand or by use of a French curve.

A much more accurate ellipse can be drawn by use of a compass as illustrated in Plate 39. An isometric drawing of a square has two obtuse angles (an angle greater than a right angle) and two acute angles (an angle less than right angle). From the apex of both obtuse angles A and B, draw lines to the center of opposite sides of the isometric square; these centers correspond to the contact points between the circle and the square. The contact points are identified by the figures E, F, G, and H shown in the illustration. Two of these four lines will intersect at C and the other two at D. Place the point of a compass on C and adjust the second arm to a distance equal to C-G. Draw an arc from G to H. Without disturbing the compass reading place the pivot point at D and lay in an arc from E to F. This will complete opposite halves of the isometric circle. Place the compass point at A and measure the distance to H. Draw in the arc from H to E. Repeat this process with the compass point at B and draw an arc from F to G to complete the circle.

It is important to recognize that some objects do not lend themselves well to representation by isometric drawings. This form of drafting does not recognize either the actual effects of foreshortening or the laws of perspective; hence some drawings done in this manner may appear distorted. This is especially true of large objects: the larger the object and the drawing, the more obvious the distortion becomes. Irregular shapes that do not conform to isometric planes or objects with curvilinear details are difficult to draw isometrically, and if drawn, may be so distorted as to be of little value.

Oblique Drawing

Objects with many curvilinear details are most easily represented by an oblique drawing (Plate 40). This is a form of drafting that combines both orthographic and isometric principles. The most complicated face of an object is selected for emphasis by representing it as though the observer were viewing it at right angles, much as the front view of an orthographic would represent it. This, of course, greatly simplifies drawing the true shape of any curved or circular form. An oblique drawing resembles an isometric in that three views of the object are shown in one drawing. The top and side views are drawn to the left or right of

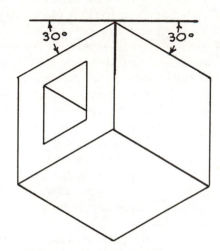

ISOMETRIC AXES
OBJECT BELOW
EYE LEVEL

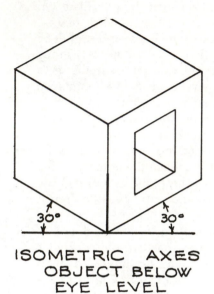

ISOMETRIC AXES
OBJECT ABOVE
EYE LEVEL

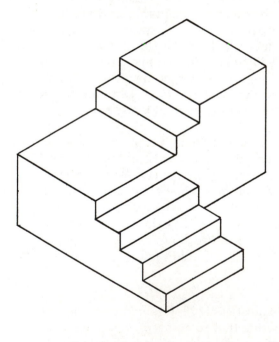

ISOMETRIC DRAWING

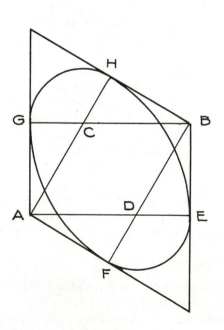

ISOMETRIC CIRCLE

Plate 39 Isometric Figures

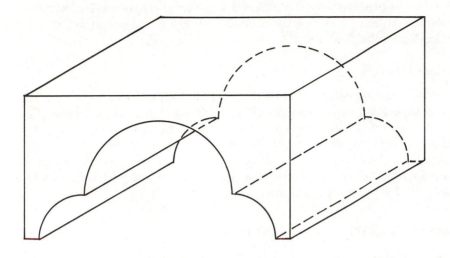

PROJECTED 30° TO THE RIGHT
OBJECT BELOW EYE LEVEL

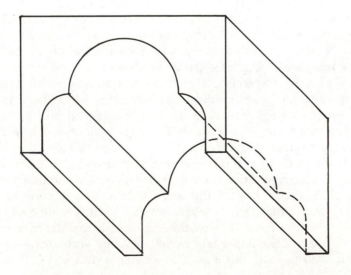

PROJECTED 45° TO THE LEFT
OBJECT ABOVE EYE LEVEL

Plate 40 Oblique Drawings

the front view at angles of 30° or 45°. When these angles are extended upward, the drawing will appear as though the object had been placed below the observer's eye level. When the angles are extended downward, the object will appear to be placed above the observer's eye level. This convention permits the draftsman to select that view of an object, either top or bottom, left or right, that will best describe the subject.

Cabinet Drawing

A cabinet drawing is infrequently used, but it does provide a drafting technique that is especially well suited for solving certain types of problems (Plate 41). Cabinet drawing is similar to an oblique drawing in all details of construction and appearance except one. All dimensions shown on the oblique angles are reduced one half. This, to a great extent, reduces the distortion that appears when the object drawn is overlong, as would be the case with the Colonial bench shown in the illustration (Plate 41).

DRAFTING LAYOUT AND SPACING

Before actual drawing begins it is good to spend a little time in planning the arrangement or layout of the various drawings that are to appear on a single sheet of drafting paper. This procedure may well help the beginner avoid some of the more common faults that seem to plague his work. He will not, for instance, find all the different views crowded into one corner of his sheet of paper; nor will he find out too late that there isn't room enough on the paper for all of his drawing.

In analyzing a drafting problem, a student must first determine how many separate views will be required to describe the object completely. He must then select the drafting technique that depicts what must be shown: an orthographic, isometric, oblique, or cabinet drawing, or a combination of several of them. If necessary he must make rough freehand sketches of each view he thinks will be required and plan the placement of them as they appear on the final drawing.

With the general layout in mind, the next step is to select an appropriate scale. This he can easily determine by simple addition and subtraction. He tentatively selects a scale, such as $3/4'' = 1'-0''$, and determines how much space will be required to draw the different views needed to solve the problem. He then subtracts this total from the amount of space provided by a sheet of drafting paper. It may be discovered that there isn't enough space and that the layout will be crowded. So he drops down to the next smaller scale and uses the $1/2'' = 1'-0''$. On the other hand, it may become apparent that a larger scale could be used. A good general rule to follow is to select the largest scale that the dimensions of the object and the size of the paper will permit. A large-scale drawing is not only easier to draw and to read, but it assures greater accuracy.

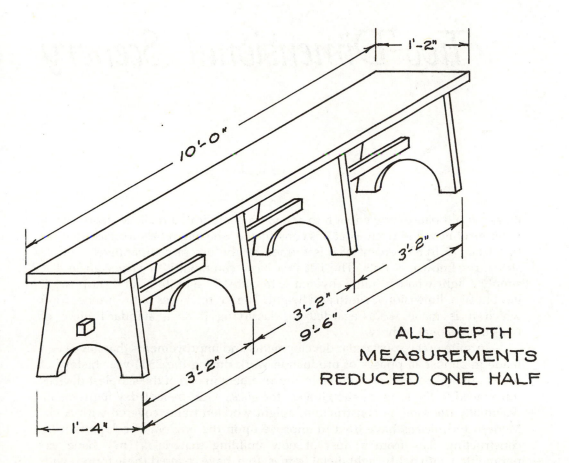

Plate 41 Cabinet Drawing

6

Two-Dimensional Scenery

If one would pause long enough to analyze a complicated realistic stage setting in terms of how and from what it is constructed, she might be surprised to learn that from 75 to 85 percent of it is formed by the use of comparatively simple structures known as flats. The flat is a basic commodity of stagecraft and is simply a light wooden frame covered with cloth. To all intents and purposes it has but two dimensions, width and height. The ³/₄″ thickness of the lumber from which it is made is disregarded in classifying it as a standard piece of two-dimensional scenery.

In spite of the spectacular developments and improvements that have been made in almost all phases of production work during the 2500-year history of drama, there has been no noticeable improvement in one of the simplest devices introduced to the stage by the Greeks, the *pinak*. Our present-day flat remains essentially the same in construction, a light wooden frame covered with cloth. Modern technicians have tried to improve upon the original Greek pattern by constructing flats from a host of new building materials. They have experimented with lightweight metal frames; they have covered these frames with plywood, beaver board, compositional materials of all kinds, and with various plastics and fabrics. In a few cases these experimental flats possess certain worthwhile features; but the good points are, more often than not, offset by limitations imposed by the materials from which they are built. The acceptability of any device proposed as a substitute for a flat must be tested by the factors governing the construction and rigging of scenery.

FACTORS GOVERNING THE CONSTRUCTION AND RIGGING OF SCENERY

The only points of similarity between stage carpentry and general carpentry or construction work are in the tools employed and some of the wood joints and building materials used. In all other respects there is very little in common. The characteristics of scenic construction which dictate the method by which scenery is built are the following:

1. Scenery is constructed to be used for a comparatively short time.
2. Scenery must be planned for rapid construction.
3. Scenery is often planned for possible alteration and reuse.
4. Scenery is usually built in one place and used in another.
5. Scenery is constructed in easily portable units and assembled onstage by temporary joining.
6. Scenery is generally finished on one side only
7. Scenery must be light in weight and capable of compact storage.
8. Scenery must be strong enough for safe usage and safe handling.
9. Scenery must be constructed as inexpensively as possible and still comply with the requirements mentioned above.

FLATS

Size Limitations of Stock Flats

Actually there is no limit as to how wide or how high a flat can be made except the limit placed upon it by the dimensions of the shop and stage where it is built and used. On one occasion I constructed flats 36'-0" high, so high in fact that they had to be pulled upright by the counterweight system. (These flats were later cut in half to become part of the 18'-0" set of stock scenery.)

Normally the width of a standard flat is limited to 5'-9", which is the maximum width of most readily available canvas or muslin. Flats wider than 5'-9" are difficult to handle or store and usually require that strips of the covering material be sewed together before it can be attached to the frame. The minimum width of a flat is usually 1'-0", occasionally even as little as 9" or 10". A narrower width is supplied by using solid stock lumber.

The height of stock scenery used in the educational and community theatres is determined in part by the sight lines from the auditorium to the stage and in part by the fact that such scenery will be built and shifted by inexperienced personnel. Stock scenery 12'-0", 14'-0", or 16'-0" high is most commonly used. Flats 18'-0" high or over are not only awkward to shift and store, but should be constructed from stock lumber with greater rigidity and strength than that provided by 1" × 3" stock. This additional rigidity can be obtained by building the frame from 1" × 4" or 1¼" × 3" stock. In many parts of the country it is difficult to obtain 1" × 3" white pine in lengths greater than 16'-0", which necessitates the use of scarf-jointed stiles for all flats over 16'-0" in height. The ease with which a flat over 20'-0" in height can be handled can be increased by building scarf-jointed stiles that taper in thickness. The lower sections of the stiles are made from 1¼" × 3" stock, and the upper parts from 1" × 3" stock.

Standard Flats—Plain Flats (Plate 42)

The conventional flat consists of the following members: rails, stiles, toggle bars, and diagonal braces. The rails are the top and bottom horizontal members, the stiles the outside vertical members. Toggle bars are the inside horizontal members that hold the stiles equidistant. Diagonal braces are placed at the top

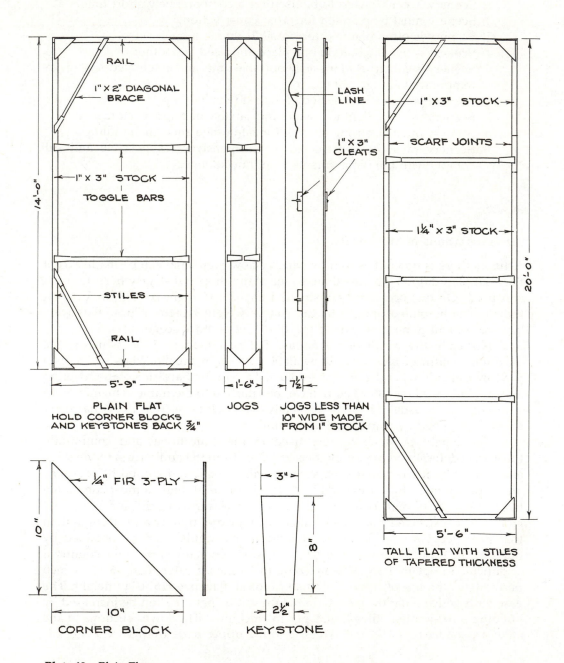

Plate 42   Plain Flats

and bottom on the same side of the flat at an angle with rails and stiles to give the flat greater rigidity and strength. The various parts of a standard flat may be assembled by the use of mortise and tenon or halved joint, but most flats are made by using butt joints reinforced with corner blocks and keystones. To build a standard flat frame 5'-0" wide by 14'-0" high, proceed as follows:

1. Cut all rails, stiles, and toggle bars from 1" × 3" lumber, grade C or better.
2. Cut the two rails each 5'-0" in length.
3. Cut the two stiles 14'-0" minus the combined widths of the two rails.
4. Butt the ends of the stiles against the edges of the rails. This method of assembly forms a skid of the lower rail and eliminates the possibility of splitting the end grain of the stile by having it come in contact with the floor.
5. Place a 3-ply corner block over the butt joint with the exposed grain of the corner block at right angles to the joint. Test the accuracy of the joint with a steel square. Hold the corner block back from the outer edges of the stiles by ³/₄" and from the outer edges of the rails by ¹/₄". Nail the corner block in place by using 1¹/₄" clout nails clinched on the face. See Plate 24 for the proper placement of nails.
6. Cut the toggle bars 5'-0" in length minus the combined widths of the two stiles.
7. Space the toggle bars no farther apart than 5'-0". Insert them between the stiles, check for true right-angle butt joints, and join them to the stiles with keystones and clout nails.
8. Cut the diagonal braces of 1" × 2" stock, grade C or better. Insert them at approximately a 45° angle between the rails and stiles at both top and bottom of the flat and on the same side. Fasten them in place with strips of plywood or with a keystone that has been ripped lengthwise.

The process of covering a flat frame with canvas or muslin is one of the most critical steps in building scenery. Should the covering material be stretched too tight, there is danger that the frame will be pulled out of alignment by shrinkage of the material when it is painted. Should the material be too slack, the surface of the flats will billow and shake each time a set door is opened or closed. Being conscious of these two possible faults is the first step in avoiding them. The normal steps in covering a flat frame are as follows:

1. Place the frame, face up, on the template bench, sawhorses, or the floor.
2. Unroll enough canvas to cover the length of the frame plus a 2" or 3" overhang at each end. Cut or tear the canvas to this length but do not attempt to precut it in width.
3. Preliminary tacking or stapling is required to hold the canvas to the frame so that it is free of wrinkles while it is being glued in place. Align the selvage edge of the canvas with the outer edge of one stile. Tack it at 1'-0" intervals along the inner edge of the stile with 4-ounce upholsterer's tacks or with wire staples.
4. Move to the opposite side of the flat. Starting in the center, pull the material snug and tack to the inner edge of the stile. Working from this center point pull the material snug and at a slight angle toward the ends of the flat and tack. Make due allowance for the shrinkage of the material

when it is painted. Small semicircular wrinkles will appear around the heads of the tacks when the material has been pulled too tight.

5. Complete the preliminary tacking at either end of the flat by tacking along the inside edge of each rail. Make what adjustments are necessary to eliminate any wrinkles appearing within the area now enclosed by tacks. Tacks whose heads have been driven flush with the canvas may be removed easily by inserting the corner of a screw driver under the head and prying.

6. Turn back the loose flap of canvas over one of the stiles and apply canvas glue directly to the wood. Smooth the flap down over the glue and press it firmly into place with the heel of the hand or with a small block of wood. Work one side of the flat at a time to avoid having the glue congeal before the canvas can be pressed into it.

7. Tack along the outer edges of the stiles and rails with 4-ounce up-holsterer's tacks or wire staples, spacing them so that they fall between those already in the flat. This method will space the tacks about 6″ apart, alternating between the inside and the outside of the stiles and rails.

8. Allow the glue to dry before attempting to trim excess canvas from the flat. This can best be done by running a sharp knife along the outer edge of the frame while pulling the excess canvas taut with the other hand.

Three formulas are most commonly used in mixing a good canvas glue. Full-strength glue cannot be used without running the risk of having it seep through the canvas and darken or discolor the paint job.

White-Flake Glue. White-flake glue is the strongest of the three mixtures and the easiest to prepare, but it is also the most expensive. To prepare it place dry-flake glue in the upper container of a double boiler, cover the glue with water, and heat until it has dissolved. This glue must be applied to the frames while it is hot, as it congeals rapidly when allowed to cool. Care must be taken to avoid getting this glue onto the face of the canvas because it will stain or ''bleed'' through and darken any paint placed over it.

Ground-Amber Glue and Whiting. A very satisfactory canvas glue can be made from a mixture of 50 percent whiting and 50 percent ground-amber glue. Prepare the glue by covering it with water and heating it in a double boiler as described above. Place the dry whiting powder in a separate container and add sufficient water to work it into a heavy paste that is free of all lumps. Add the hot liquid glue to the paste; this will thin the latter sufficiently for immediate use. This mixture must be applied to the frames while it is hot. Both of these first two glue mixtures will congeal into a solid mass when allowed to cool overnight. Reheating them in a double boiler will return them to their original consistency without the need to add more water.

Cold-Water Paste and Amber Glue. Although not as strong as the first two, this formula has the advantage of being less expensive and it does not require reheating after each use. The formula is approximately ⅔ cold-water paste to ⅓ hot amber glue. Prepare the ground-amber glue as previously described. Cold-water paste is sold in a dry powdered form and must be mixed with water before the hot liquid glue is added. To avoid the small globules and lumps of paste that sometimes form when mixing cold-water paste, be sure to stir and sift the dry paste into a bucket containing the water.

Jogs. For the sake of convenience in both the cataloguing and storing of scenery, many technicians divide their plain flats into two groups. Flats from 5'-9" wide down to and including those 3'-0" wide are classified as plain flats. Those less than 3'-0" wide are considered jogs. The only difference in construction of plain flats and jogs is that diagonal braces can be omitted from jogs less than 2'-0" wide.

Window Flats (Plate 43)

The window flat is but a slight variation of the plain flat. The two toggle bars are adjusted in height to correspond to the top and bottom of the window dimensions and are fastened with keystones and clout nails to the stiles of the flat. The vertical sides of the window are formed by additional lengths of 1" × 3" called window stiles. These are carefully placed according to the specified dimensions, checked for true right-angle butt joints, and fastened in place with keystones and clout nails.

Covering a window flat follows the same procedure as canvasing a plain flat. First, cover the whole flat with canvas. Then tack along the outside edges of the window stiles and toggles. Cut the canvas from the window opening by running a sharp knife along the inside of the window-framing members and removing the unwanted canvas. Make a 45° cut about 3" long in the canvas at each of the four corners of the window opening. This will permit turning back the resulting canvas flap for the application of canvas glue to the framing members. Press the canvas down into the glue and tack along the inside face of the window stiles and toggles.

Door Flats (Plate 44)

The only difference between constructing a window flat and a door flat is the substitution of a reinforcing band of strap iron for part of the lower rail. This band is called the sill iron and is made from $3/16$" or $1/4$" by $3/4$" strap iron, cut 1'-6" longer than the over-all width of the door flat. Each end is drilled with four to six holes, countersunk to accommodate the heads of 1" No. 9 flathead screws. After drilling the sill iron, place it in a vise and put right-angle bends in it 9" from each end. Fit and countersink these 9" sections along the outer edges of each stile. Screw the sill iron to both the stiles and the lower rails. Make sure that the heads of the screws that were driven into the rails do not project beyond the face of the sill iron to snag or tear the floor cloth.

A door flat may be covered in one of two ways: by a single piece of material, following the same procedure outlined for canvasing a window flat, or by piecing the material together on the frame. Should the second method be used, it is well to canvas the section of the flat above the door first and then to cover the sections on either side of the door, overlapping the canvas to the full width of the toggle that forms the door top.

Archway Flats (Plate 45)

The construction of a doorway with a rounded or arched top follows the same steps used in building a door flat. The only variation between the two is the

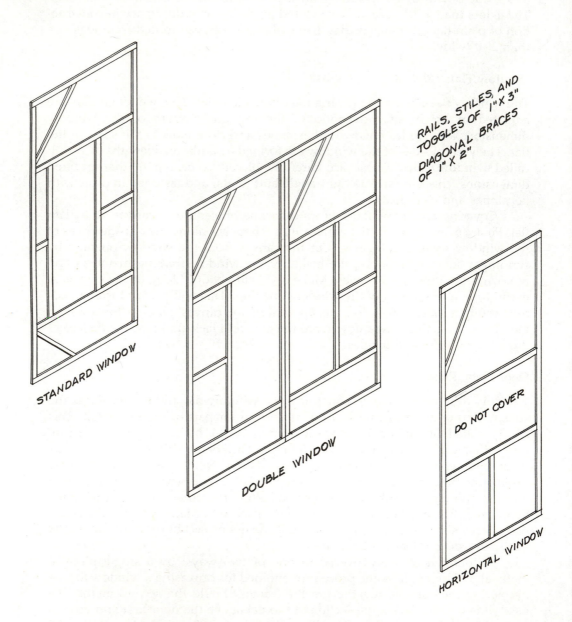

STANDARD WINDOW

DOUBLE WINDOW

RAILS, STILES, AND
TOGGLES OF 1" X 3"

DIAGONAL BRACES
OF 1" X 2"

DO NOT COVER

HORIZONTAL WINDOW

Plate 43   Types of Window Flats

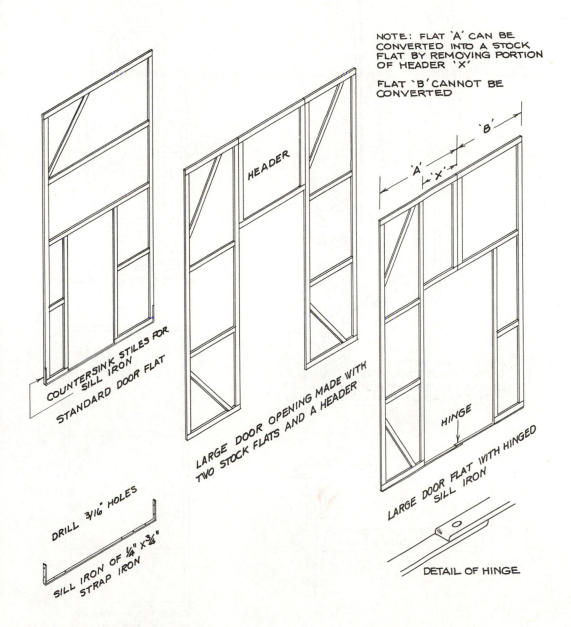

NOTE: FLAT 'A' CAN BE CONVERTED INTO A STOCK FLAT BY REMOVING PORTION OF HEADER 'X'

FLAT 'B' CANNOT BE CONVERTED

COUNTERSINK STILES FOR SILL IRON

STANDARD DOOR FLAT

HEADER

LARGE DOOR OPENING MADE WITH TWO STOCK FLATS AND A HEADER

HINGE

LARGE DOOR FLAT WITH HINGED SILL IRON

DRILL 3/16" HOLES

SILL IRON OF ¼" X ¾" STRAP IRON

DETAIL OF HINGE

Plate 44   Types of Door Flats

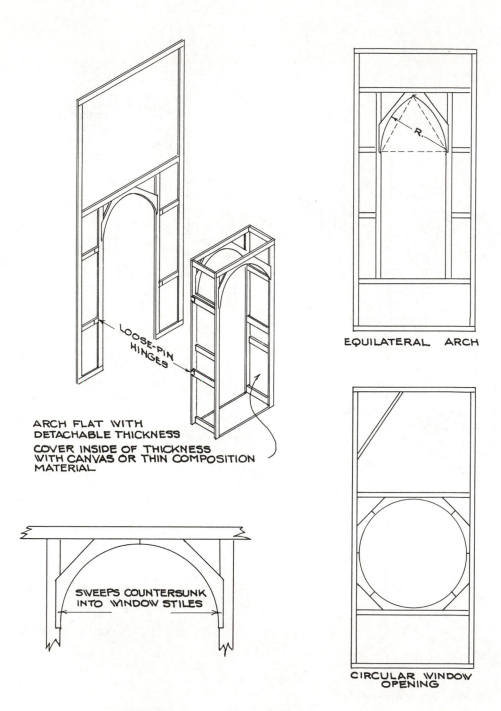

LOOSE-PIN
HINGES

ARCH FLAT WITH
DETACHABLE THICKNESS

COVER INSIDE OF THICKNESS
WITH CANVAS OR THIN COMPOSITION
MATERIAL

EQUILATERAL ARCH

R.

SWEEPS COUNTERSUNK
INTO WINDOW STILES

CIRCULAR WINDOW
OPENING

Plate 45   Types of Arch Flats

addition of curved sweeps inserted at the top of a door opening to provide the desired shape.

Most arches, such as Roman, Gothic, or Tudor, are laid out on geometric patterns and may be easily adapted to door openings of specific sizes. Freehand or irregular arches are transferred from the designer's plans by graph. These scaled drawings are divided into 6″ or 1′-0″ squares that provide a series of reference points at the intersections between the contour lines of the arch and either the vertical or horizontal graph lines. When the full-scale arch is laid out in the shop and graphed into 6″ or 1′-0″ squares, surprisingly accurate enlargements of the arch can be obtained by using the designer's graphed drawings as a guide. First, make a heavyweight paper pattern of the arch, then test it in the door opening to see that it fits properly and is of the desired shape. Next, lay out the pattern and outline it on a wide width of lumber. If the arch is unusually wide, it may be necessary to have each sweep composed of two or more segments. Be sure to leave a reinforcing strip of 3/4″ at the terminal points of each sweep to prevent it from splitting when nailed to the door stiles or toggle. Allow for this 3/4″ reinforcing strip by an adjustment of the door toggle and by countersinking it into the door stiles. See Plate 45 for details.

Irregular Flats (Plate 46)

Flats of irregular shape include such standard stage units as wood wings, groundrows, set pieces, and profile settings. These are all two dimensional in form and follow as closely as possible the building procedure used in constructing conventional rectangular flats. Most irregular flats fall roughly into two classifications, vertical or horizontal. In planning the framing of such units it is advisable to carry one or two framing members the full height or width of the structures for added strength and stability. The remaining parts of the frame follow as closely as possible the shape of the unit, but at the same time must adhere to the principles of good construction and sound joinery. Overlapping the full width of the outer framing members and extending beyond the frame by not more than 6″ is the lightweight compositional material or plywood. This material is nailed to the framing members, then marked and cut to give the unit its distinctive shape or profile. Upson board may be used for this purpose, but it will not withstand rough handling. A much stronger, but more expensive, material used for the same purpose is 3/32″ or 1/8″ plywood of either bass or pine. With the frame completed and the profile edges cut to shape, the whole assembly can be covered with muslin or canvas. Allow the canvas glue to dry thoroughly before attempting to trim the canvas with a sharp knife.

CEILINGS

Ceiling pieces will do more toward completing the appearance of a realistic interior than any other single piece of two-dimensional scenery. No matter how cleverly designed and beautifully painted the setting may be, any convincing illusion of reality is shattered when a series of wrinkled cloth borders is used in lieu of a ceiling. Borders are a heritage of the old drop-and-wing setting and as such are as much out of place in today's realistic settings as kerosene headlights would be on a modern automobile.

Two other advantages of the use of ceilings should be mentioned: (1) There

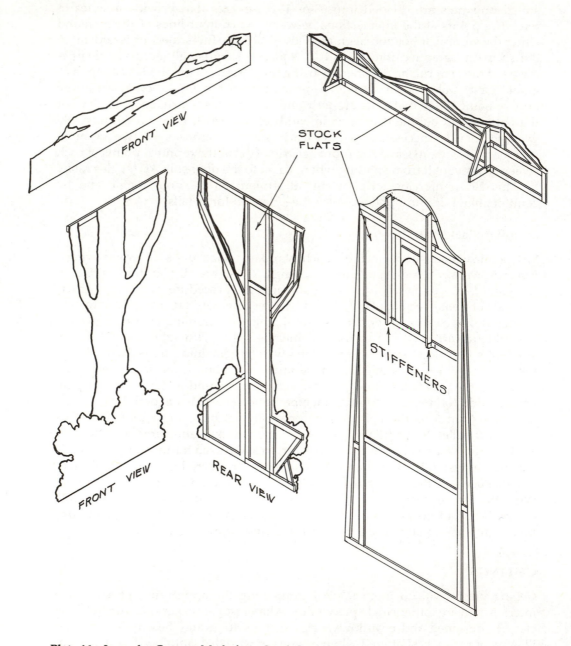

Plate 46   Irregular Cutouts Made from Stock Scenery

is a noticeable improvement in the ease with which an actor can project her voice toward the audience when a ceiling has been lowered in place on the three walls of a conventional box setting. Sound waves are reflected in part from the ceiling instead of being lost in the space overhead. (2) Additional stability and bracing are given to the setting by the weight of the ceiling resting on the flats. Most settings are braced at a point about two-thirds of the distance between the lower and upper rails by standard adjustable stage braces. This leaves the upper third of the scenery free to move or shake under the impact of a closing door or on contact by an actor. The weight of the ceiling serves to counteract this movement.

Any one of these reasons gives a sufficient justification for the construction and use of a ceiling piece. The ceiling should be considered a permanent piece of stage equipment and be designed with the idea that it will be used on any number of settings that will differ radically in both size and shape. Perhaps the most common mistake in planning a ceiling is making it too small.

The average depth of the back wall and the average angle for the placement of the sidewalls, as determined by the sight lines of a theatre, can be found by a study of ground plans of previous productions. With these averages established, it is comparatively simple to determine the size of a ceiling. It is important to allow the ceiling to overhang the side and back walls of an average set by at least 2'-0". This liberal allowance of overhang permits the ceiling to be shifted in any direction to provide the necessary coverage required by alcoves, niches, or bay windows that may extend beyond the average depth or width of most settings. It is unnecessary to disturb the permanent rigging of the ceiling to accomplish this shifting of position. An extended stage brace placed against one side of the ceiling just before it is lowered into place is usually adequate to shove it into the desired position.

The Roll Ceiling

There are two types of ceilings in common use: the roll ceiling and the book ceiling. The roll ceiling (Plate 47) is the easiest to build and rig and, as the name implies, it can be dismantled and rolled into a compact bundle for storage. Should the space set aside for the storage of the ceiling be too short, the length of the ceiling can be reduced one-half by hinging the lengthwise battens on the face with 10" strap hinges and folding the ceiling before it is rolled. The steps in the construction of a roll ceiling follow:

1. Make the outside framework, consisting of lengthwise battens and outer cross battens, of 1" × 4" stock.
2. Scarf-joint the lengthwise battens to the proper length. Allow an additional 1'-6" for each scarf joint in determining the amount of lumber required.
3. Make the inside cross battens from 1" × 3" stock. Cut these battens to the specified depth minus the width of the two lengthwise battens.
4. Assemble the various parts of the framework in their proper positions and check the over-all dimensions and angles. Mark the junction between each part with identification numbers to facilitate reassembly.
5. Place ceiling plates over each butt joint and mark their position.
6. Attach ceiling plates permanently to each end of the cross battens by $^3/_{16}"$ stove bolts, with the heads of the bolts on the face of the ceiling.

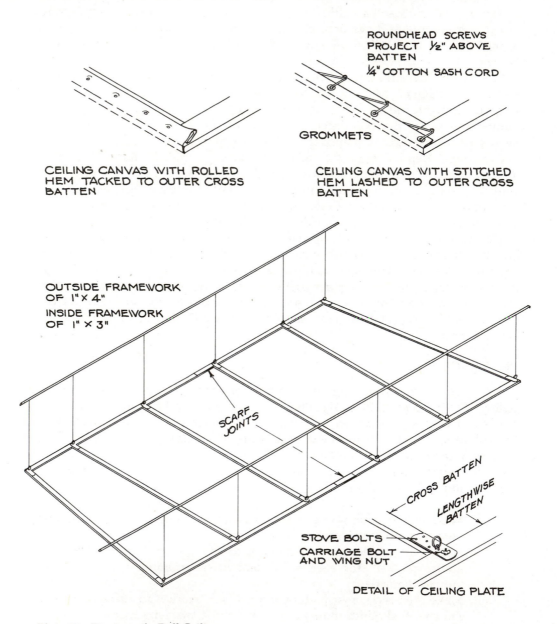

ROUNDHEAD SCREWS
PROJECT ½" ABOVE
BATTEN

¼" COTTON SASH CORD

GROMMETS

CEILING CANVAS WITH ROLLED
HEM TACKED TO OUTER CROSS
BATTEN

CEILING CANVAS WITH STITCHED
HEM LASHED TO OUTER CROSS
BATTEN

OUTSIDE FRAMEWORK
OF 1" × 4"

INSIDE FRAMEWORK
OF 1" × 3"

SCARF
JOINTS

CROSS BATTEN

LENGTHWISE
BATTEN

STOVE BOLTS
CARRIAGE BOLT
AND WING NUT

DETAIL OF CEILING PLATE

Plate 47   Rigging of a Roll Ceiling

7. Bolt ceiling plates to the lengthwise battens by a single $3/8'' \times 1 1/2''$ carriage bolt fastened with a wing nut.
8. Sew the covering material into a single piece, with seams running lengthwise. Allow at least a 12" extension of the material beyond each outside cross batten.
9. Turn the assembled frame over. Then tack and glue the covering material to the two lengthwise battens only.
10. Turn the ceiling over on its face. Fold the cloth extensions into a hem and tack them to the top of the outer cross battens. An alternate method of stretching the covering material is provided by lacing it to the outer cross battens. The hem is folded and sewn, then fitted with $3/8''$ grommets spaced 10" apart. A lash line threaded through the grommets engages the projecting heads of roundhead screws driven into the top of the outer cross battens.
11. To dismantle the ceiling remove the tacks or unlace it from the outer cross battens. Remove all cross battens. Turn the ceiling paint-side up and roll tightly around one lengthwise batten.

The Book Ceiling

There is one disadvantage to the use of a roll ceiling. The supporting battens of the counterweight system are placed directly above the lengthwise battens of the ceiling. Since the ceiling may be as much as 14'-0" to 16'-0" in depth, this means that all sets of lines located between the two supporting battens become inoperative. To offset this handicap, the book ceiling was devised (Plate 48). This type of ceiling employs three adjacent battens in its rigging rather than two widely separated ones.

The book ceiling consists of two oversized plain flats hinged together in such fashion that when not in use they can be folded together and suspended above the stage with their length parallel to the proscenium arch. The overall shape and size of the book ceiling is governed by the same factors as the roll ceiling. The difference between the two lies in the fact that the book ceiling has four lengthwise battens instead of two and that the covering material is permanently glued to both the outer cross battens and the lengthwise battens. When not in use the book ceiling is simply folded and stored in the flies. Should circumstances make this inadvisable, the book ceiling may be constructed so that it can be dismantled and rolled into a compact bundle. In this case, the covering material must be temporarily attached to the outer cross battens by either lacing or tacking; this permits the removal of these battens.

DROPS

Drops have long been a favorite device of the scenic designer. They were originally introduced into theatre service about the middle of the sixteenth century with Serlio's experiments in perspective. The drop is a large unframed area of cloth supported by wooden battens at top and bottom to hold the material free of wrinkles. Drops present the designer with a wide expanse of unbroken material upon which scenes can be painted. The advantages of a drop are obvious: they are neither difficult nor expensive to make, they require little stage space, and they may be quickly and easily shifted by flying.

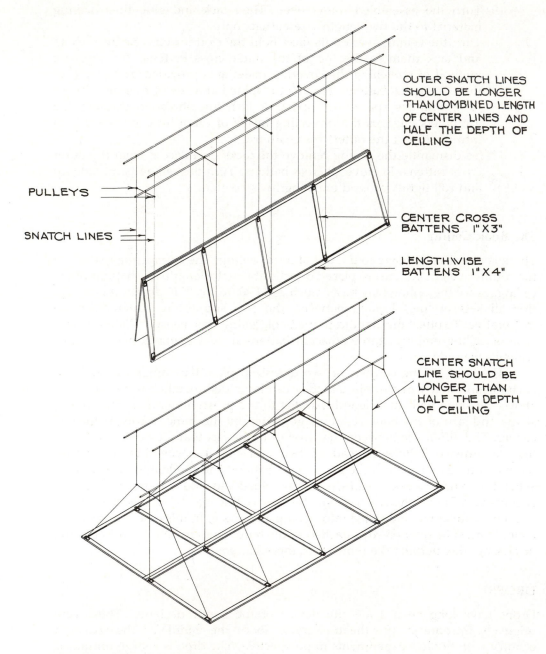

OUTER SNATCH LINES
SHOULD BE LONGER
THAN COMBINED LENGTH
OF CENTER LINES AND
HALF THE DEPTH OF
CEILING

PULLEYS

SNATCH LINES

CENTER CROSS
BATTENS 1"X3"

LENGTHWISE
BATTENS 1"X4"

CENTER SNATCH
LINE SHOULD BE
LONGER THAN
HALF THE DEPTH
OF CEILING

Plate 48　Rigging of a Book Ceiling

The effects obtained by the use of drops can be varied greatly by the material used in their construction, the ways in which they are painted, and the manner of lighting them. The opaque or standard drop is made of muslin, canvas, or velour, with the seaming of the material running parallel to its length. The upper edge of the drop is glued and tacked to the face of a 1" × 4" batten. A second 1" × 4" batten is then placed over the first, and the two are screwed tightly together. It is advisable to bevel the outer edges of both battens to prevent creasing the drop when it is rolled. The lower edge of the drop can be finished in one of two ways: a 1" × 3" scarf-jointed batten can be glued and tacked to the back of the drop, or a deep hem can be made into which the 1" × 3" batten can be slipped. Given a flat coat of light-blue paint, such a drop can serve as a substitute for a cyclorama, or designs of any type can be transferred to it and painted in detail.

Translucent Drops

This type of drop is usually made of extra-wide muslin rather than heavy canvas. It may be painted with a combination of opaque paint and dye. The areas painted with dye will permit back lighting, which results in a degree of translucency and a sense of depth impossible to achieve in any other manner. By alternating the lighting from front to back the same drop may be used for different effects. Occasionally an unpainted translucent drop is used in much the same manner as a movie screen with projections thrown upon it from backstage.

Scrim Drops

These drops are made from bobinette or sharkstooth scrim. So-called transformation scenes are accomplished by use of this type of drop. The drop is painted with either dye or very thin scene paint, and when angular front lighting is used the drop appears opaque or solid. By dimming the front lighting and raising the intensity of lights back of it, the design painted on the drop seems to disappear. Drops made of bobinette or scrim must be handled with great care because they snag or tear easily. They cannot be patched or sewed without having it show.

Cutout Drops

A three-dimensional quality can be imparted to a scene by a series of cutout drops placed at varying distances from the curtain line (Plate 49). Designs are first painted on the drops, and unwanted sections of material are then cut out and removed, permitting the audience to see sections of each drop. Any part of the design not supported by the natural hang of the drop material must be reinforced by netting.

BORDERS

Borders are vertical masking pieces of cloth suspended over the stage to prevent the audience from seeing into the loft area or the grid. Borders extend the full width of the stage and may vary in height from as little as 2' or 3' to 10' or 12'. Two types of borders are in common use: the drapery border and the painted border. The drapery border is usually matched in both color and material to a set of stage draperies and is pleated to hang in folds. The top of such a border has a reinforcing band of webbing provided with grommets and tie strings. The

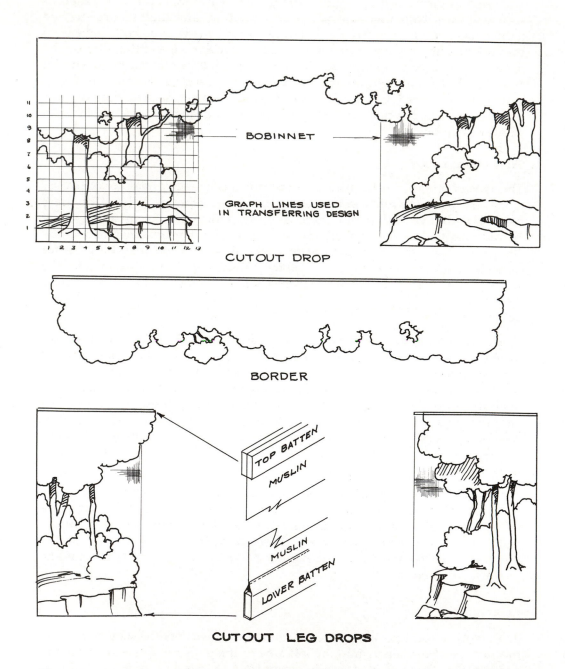

Plate 49   Cutout Drops, Border, and Leg Drops

border is tied directly to the pipe battens of the counterweight system. The painted border not only serves as a masking device but becomes an integral part of the stage setting and may take any form, such as clouds, banners, or tree foliage. The painted border is hung without fullness and is glued and tacked to a wooden batten by which it is supported.

STAGE DRAPERIES

Probably no single item of unframed two-dimensional scenery is as versatile and useful as a set of stage draperies. They are used to enclose the acting area on occasions when no scenery is required and when it is desirable to mask backstage equipment from the view of the audience. They also provide an excellent alternate for a sky cyclorama in productions requiring a neutral background.

To achieve maximum service from a set of draperies the following factors should be considered:

1. The material selected should be strong, drape well, and hang free of wrinkles.
2. The weave must be tight enough to avoid the necessity of backlining, yet the drapes should not be so heavy and bulky that they are hard to handle and store.
3. The material should be free of both nap and pile, so that it may be brushed free of dust and lint.
4. A novelty fabric with a pronounced pattern, high sheen, or light color should be avoided.

One of the most satisfactory materials for stage curtains is cotton rep, which can be purchased through most theatrical supply houses in 50″ widths in a wide variety of colors. Velour, duvetyne, monk's cloth, velveteen, sateen, and cotton flannel are sometimes used for draperies, but in one respect or another they fail to give the satisfaction of rep.

A set of stage draperies will consist of a long back wall, two side walls, and perhaps one or two borders. It is best to have the draperies made up in comparatively small sections, 6′-0″, 8′-0″, or 10′-0″ wide. These widths can be handled more easily than fewer but wider sections, and they can be rigged in a greater variety of ways. Each section of curtain should be made with at least 50 percent fullness gathered into pleats and sewn to reinforcing webbing along the upper hem. Through both webbing and curtain material are fitted ³/₈″ grommets spaced on 10″ centers and supplied with tie lines of ⅛″ diameter cord. The lower hem should contain a chain weight to prevent the curtains from blowing and to help them hang free of wrinkles.

STOCK SCENERY

In an effort to keep down production costs many theatre organizations reuse their scenery many times. Scenery thus saved for possible reuse is called stock scenery; usually it consists of two-dimensional flat framing in the form of jogs, plain flats, and window and door flats. Although the term "stock scenery" implies a certain standardization of measurements, this applies only to the matter of height, which is determined partly by the sight lines of a given theatre and partly by convenience of shifting and storing. An organization may possess several sets of stock scenery with standardized heights of possibly 18'-0", 14'-0", and 10'-0", or 12'-0", 10'-0", and 8'-0". Because the width of most two-dimensional scenery can be altered with comparative ease, no effort is made to standardize this dimension.

Alteration of Stock Scenery

It is possible to alter the size and type of a flat and to repaint it many times before it becomes necessary to wash off excess scene paint or to recover the frame with new material. Scenery can be altered without damaging its value or in any way impairing its expected life. The following suggestions are offered as a guide in the alteration of stock scenery:

1. Risk of damage to the flats can be reduced if the clinched clout nails are withdrawn with a nail puller. When performed with this tool, this operation preserves the corner blocks and keystones for future use and reduces the chances of splitting the framing members.
2. A plain flat can be converted into a window flat by adjusting the position of the toggle bars to form the top and bottom of the window and by inserting two additional vertical stiles to form the window sides. Before removing the old canvas from the window opening, tack along the outside edge of the window-framing members. Run a sharp knife along the inside of the window opening to cut away the canvas. Glue and tack the canvas remaining on the flat to the faces of the window-framing members.
3. The width of a flat can be increased a few inches by nailing or battening strips of 1" stock of the desired width to the flat stiles. Cover the cracks with strips of canvas or muslin called dutchmen; tack and glue into position.
4. A plain flat or a window flat can be altered into a door flat by the following procedure. Move the toggle bar to correspond to the desired height of the door. Determine the exact location of the door opening; measure and cut two vertical door stiles and nail them into place by using corner blocks and keystones. Remove the part of the lower rail between the inner edges of the door stiles. Reinforce the bottom rail with a sill iron made from 1/4" by 3/4" strap iron. Remove the canvas from the door opening and tack and glue the canvas remaining on the flat to the door stiles and toggle.
5. A window or door flat can easily be converted into a plain flat. No effort is made to alter the framing assembly of a window flat—a patch is simply placed over the window opening. Care should be taken in selecting the material for the patch to see that it matches the material already on the flat; otherwise, the difference in surface texture will be noticeable under the final paint job. If new material must be used as a patch on an old flat, it should be given several coats of paint to reduce the contrast in texture with the surrounding surface. The framing of a door flat can also remain unaltered when it is converted into a plain flat. The patching can be done by inserting a section of lower rail into the space between the door stiles, then applying the patch with glue and tacks. Sometimes it may be advantageous to rebuild the door flat in part

by removing the sill iron and door stiles and replacing the lower rail before applying the covering material.

6. Because most stock scenery has been standardized with respect to height, the technician will avoid altering this dimension if at all possible. If he reduces the height of a flat, he also reduces his opportunities to reuse it. If he increases the height of a unit by battening on an additional frame, he does so at the expense of both weight and strength.

Variations in the Use of Stock Scenery

The rectangular form of two-dimensional scenery lends itself well to a wide range of uses. The technician soon becomes adept in using stock scenery in any number of ways to reduce building time and production cost. Even such highly irregular forms as a two-dimensional tree cutout, a random board fence, or a series of mountain groundrows, each may have as its foundation one or more pieces of stock scenery used in some unusual manner. The drawings in Plate 46 provide several such examples.

Notice that these variations in form were achieved by one of two methods: irregular contours were added to the sides or top of a flat, or the flat was turned to rest upon its stile rather than its rail. The following description of a false proscenium may be taken as another example.

THE TWO-DIMENSIONAL FALSE PROSCENIUM

The false proscenium is a large decorative archway that spans the full width of the stage and is normally placed just upstage of the main curtain and parallel with it (Plate 50). Usually it has a distinctive silhouette that is appropriate for a particular production. Through it the audience views the entire action of the play.

Because the budgets of many community and educational theatres are limited, the management might well consider the construction of such a large unit of scenery too costly. However, it is quite possible to build one at only a fraction of its expected cost by using a series of standard flats that can be taken from the theatre's supply of stock scenery. Five of the seven flats used in the construction of the arch illustrated here were taken from stock. Only the curved sections F and G were newly constructed, and even these were made from lumber salvaged from previous productions and covered with parts of an old drop. The only cost of this archway was that incurred in painting it.

A few moments spent in studying the drawing will reveal that the false proscenium is really nothing but an oversized door flat with contour-forming segments added to the top of the door opening on each side. In this particular case the sides of the arch were formed from two 5'-0" × 18'-0" stock flats. The header across the top was made by hinging three other stock flats end to end. Two of these flats were 14'-0" long, the third was 12'-0" long, and all were a uniform 3'-6" wide.

The problem of transporting such a large unit from the shop to the stage was solved by building the archway in three sections, the header forming one and the two 18'-0" side flats, to which the curved segments had been hinged, the other two. The sections were laid out face up on the stage floor and centered in relation to the regular proscenium arch. The three sections were joined with

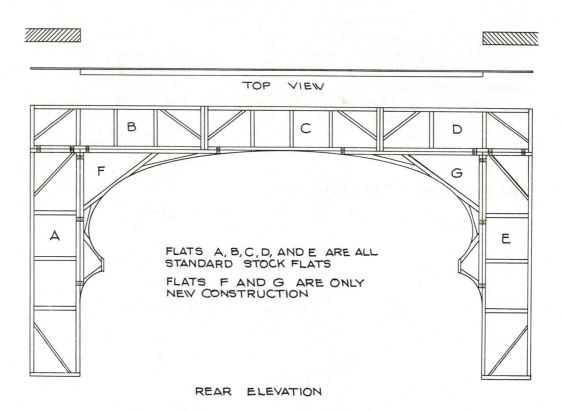

TOP VIEW

FLATS A, B, C, D, AND E ARE ALL
STANDARD STOCK FLATS

FLATS F AND G ARE ONLY
NEW CONSTRUCTION

REAR ELEVATION

Plate 50   Construction of False Proscenium by Using Standard Flats tight pin hinges that were concealed by gluing and tacking over them a prepainted dutchman.

The arch was pulled into an upright position and supported by one of the battens of the counterweight system. This batten was lowered to the stage floor, and ³/₈″ manila snatch lines were tied from it to hanger irons spaced across the rails of the header. To prevent the leg stiles of the arch from breaking as the batten was raised, it was necessary to provide support for them by "walking them up."

CATALOGUING SCENERY

The cost of a production can certainly be materially reduced by altering and reusing stock scenery, but to reuse scenery at all it is first necessary to know how many pieces are available, how many of each type there are, what the exact dimensions are, and what the condition of each piece is. All of this information can be kept in a card catalogue with a number assigned to each piece of scenery. Any convenient method of classification may be used, but one of the simplest is to divide the scenery into types of uniform height, such as 14'-0″ jogs, 14'-0″ plain flats, and so forth. Should the theatre possess a second set of stock scenery of a different height, this would be catalogued and filed separately. The catalogue can be extended to cover all items of scenery kept for possible reuse (Plate 51).

Selecting a catalogue number can be simplicity itself. Consecutive numbers from 1 to 200 or 300 are jotted down in a record book. Each piece of scenery is assigned a number, which is then painted on the back of the unit in some conspicuous place. In the case of a flat, the number is painted on both stiles about 5'-0″ from the floor, so that no matter which way the flat is stored in the scene dock the number can be readily seen. To indicate in the record book that a particular number has been assigned, a very brief description of the flat follows the catalogue number—for example, No. 124, 2'-6″ × 14'-0″ jog. A 4″ × 6″ filing card is used to record the complete description of the unit. Across the top of the card from left to right is the catalogue number, the type of unit, and the over-all dimensions. Immediately below and to the left are listed the date of construction, kind of lumber and covering material, color, or special construction details. On the opposite side of the card is a freehand working drawing that gives all key dimensions. Cards representing flats or units of the same type and height are then filed together under their proper index.

As the technician makes her working drawings, she will have at her fingertips the complete history and all information she will need concerning each piece of scenery kept in stock. As she makes her selection of units, she jots down the name of the production on the card of that unit and files it under a separate "current production" index. This eliminates the possibility of planning to use the same unit of scenery more than once in a production. Should she find it necessary to alter the unit in any way, she makes corresponding changes in the drawing and dimensions on the card. This keeps the catalogue accurate and up to date. With the close of the production, all of the cards are withdrawn from the "current production" index and redistributed into their proper classifications. If a unit of scenery has been so altered, or is in such condition that there is little use in keeping it in stock, it is dismantled for salvageable material and its card is destroyed. The corresponding number in the record book is freed for reassignment by simply erasing the unit description.

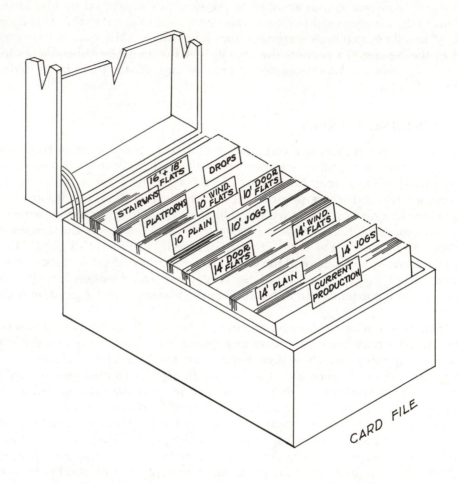

CARD FILE

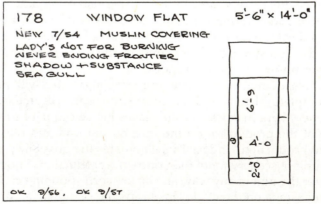

178   WINDOW FLAT   5'-6" × 14'-0"

NEW 7/54   MUSLIN COVERING
LADY'S NOT FOR BURNING
NEVER ENDING FRONTIER
SHADOW + SUBSTANCE
SEA GULL

OK 9/56, OK 9/57

SAMPLE CARD

Plate 51   Card Catalogue

The time and effort required to establish a card catalogue and to keep it accurate are more than repaid by the advantages it offers:

1. The technician can thumb through a pack of cards rather than a stack of scenery to get the information he needs.
2. There is a great saving of time at the drafting board when units requiring the least alteration can be selected.
3. There is a saving of man-hours in the shop where these units are assembled.
4. The cost of the production can be held at a minimum.
5. Unnecessary constructional duplication is avoided.

7

Three-Dimensional Scenery

Three-dimensional scenery includes all architectural features and weight-bearing structures that impart to a setting a sense of solidity or depth. They are constructed separately and are usually handled separately from the two-dimensional scenery against which they may be placed. The factors governing the construction of three-dimensional scenery are identical with those listed for the construction of two-dimensional scenery.

TYPES OF STAGE WINDOWS

The variety of form and size of stage windows is almost limitless; it may range from a slot window in a prison cell to an elaborate stained-glass window in a cathedral. Most stage windows are made from three basic parts—casing, jamb, and sashes. The casing is the practical or decorative framework that overlaps the wall surface and encases the window opening. The jamb, more frequently called the thickness piece in stage terminology, is the frame, which is usually placed at right angles to the casing to simulate the actual thickness of the wall. The sashes are the movable parts of a window—the frames that support the glass. Disregarding the matter of variety of form, stage windows fall into four distinct types: fake, dependent, independent, and practical.

The Fake Window

For lack of a better name a simple opening in a flat might be called a fake window (Plate 52). It is an impractical affair that is literally no more than a hole in the flat. The muntins, or crossbars, if any, are likely to be made of twilled tape tacked to the back of the window opening. The casing, and in some cases even the thickness pieces, is painted on the face of the flat. Windows of this type are used

134

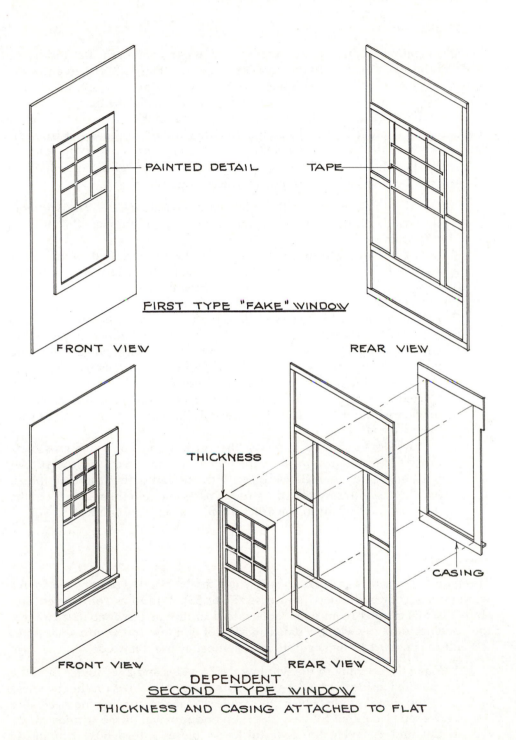

PAINTED DETAIL

TAPE

FIRST TYPE "FAKE" WINDOW

FRONT VIEW

REAR VIEW

THICKNESS

CASING

FRONT VIEW

REAR VIEW

DEPENDENT
SECOND TYPE WINDOW

THICKNESS AND CASING ATTACHED TO FLAT

Plate 52 Types of Windows

only when the director wishes to capitalize on staging conventions of a previous era, or when a realistic effect is not essential.

The Dependent Window

As the name implies, this type of window is an integral part of the flat and can be made to appear as realistic as the occasion demands (Plate 52). Its advantage in construction is the ease and speed with which it can be assembled. The disadvantages are (1) its additional weight which, added to that of the flat, makes it a difficult unit to shift and store; and (2) it cannot be saved as part of the stock scenery because it must be completely dismantled to remove it from the flat. Windows of this type are generally used when it is unnecessary to shift the setting or when the setting can be shifted by some form of rolling. A dependent window can be constructed by following these suggestions:

1. Cut two thickness pieces the height of the window stiles; cut two more the width of the window opening plus an additional 1½″ for the necessary overlap.
2. Screw or nail these four pieces on edge to the back and to the inside faces of the window stiles and toggles. The box thus formed around the window opening on the offstage side of the flat represents the thickness of the wall.
3. Apply the casing to the face of the flat after the frame has been covered with muslin or canvas. Cut two pieces of 1″ thick lumber of the proper width and equal in length to the height of the window. Cut top and bottom casing pieces the width of the window opening, plus the combined widths of the two side casing pieces.
4. Place the casing pieces over the window stiles and toggles and nail them in place with finishing nails. Countersink the nails and fill the holes with plastic wood.
5. The window sash and muntins (the vertical and horizontal crossbars) can be assembled as a separate frame and inserted into the proper position inside the thickness piece. If the design of the sash is simple, it may be easier to assemble the various parts and join them directly to the thickness piece than to construct them as a separate frame.

The Independent Window

This window is made as a separate unit which can be inserted or removed from a window flat with both speed and ease (Plate 53). Windows constructed and shifted in this manner require that adequate clearance be provided in the size of the opening cut in the window flat. This kind of window and window flat is not difficult to construct if the suggestions given below are followed:

1. Make the opening in the window flat 3″ wider and 2¼″ higher than the specified inside dimensions of the window. This allows for the thickness of the lumber from which the window is made and for the necessary clearance required for easy insertion and removal of the window unit.
2. Cut and assemble the four thickness pieces into a box with inside dimensions corresponding to those specified by the designer's plans.
3. Assemble the window sash as a separate frame, or build it as an integral part of the thickness frame as previously described.

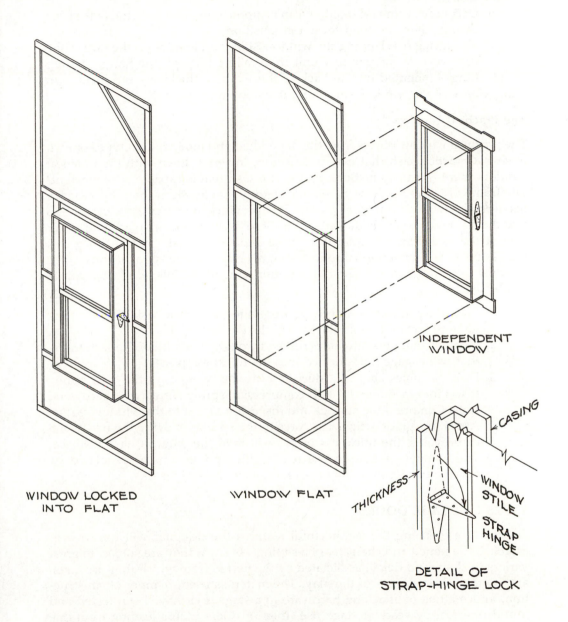

WINDOW LOCKED
INTO FLAT

WINDOW FLAT

INDEPENDENT
WINDOW

CASING

THICKNESS

WINDOW
STILE

STRAP
HINGE

DETAIL OF
STRAP-HINGE LOCK

Plate 53 Window Flat and Independent Window

4. Join the casing directly to the edge of the thickness piece with 1½" No. 9 flathead screws with the heads countersunk and covered with plastic wood. (Putty cannot be used, as the oil in it will discolor the water-soluble scene paint.)
5. With large-angle irons reinforce the back of the butt joints formed by the casing.
6. Decorative trim and molding can be applied directly over the face of the casing. Glue and brad these into position.
7. The casing overlapping the window stiles and toggles on the face of the flat prevents the window unit from falling through the flat, and strap hinges mounted on the back of the window thickness and locking in back of the window stiles hold it solidly in place.

The Practical Window

The practical window differs from the dependent and independent types only in having a practical sash that may be raised or lowered. Even with the practical window there is usually just one part of the sash that is capable of movement. The frame of the movable sash is made slightly less in width than the distance between the two side thickness pieces. This provides the necessary clearance so that the frame can be easily moved. Strips of ³/₈" × ³/₈" wood are placed on either side of the sash frame to hold it in place and to serve as guides. Since it is impossible to use conventional counterweight balances or tension lifts on a stage window to hold the sash in a raised position, one of the following alternatives can be used:

1. Place the guide strips tightly against either side of the sash, thus creating enough friction to hold the sash at the desired level.
2. Fit metal plungers into holes drilled through the width of the sash frame that will engage holes drilled into the thickness pieces.
3. Drill ⁷/₁₆" holes about ⁷/₈" deep into the outer edges of the sash frame. Insert into each hole ³/₈" × 1" compression springs fitted with hardwood caps. Compress the springs and insert the sash into the window frame. Attach the guide strips. The force of the springs shoving the hardwood caps against the thickness pieces will hold the window sash in place. The amount of tension exerted by the springs can be regulated by varying the depth of the holes into which the springs fit.

TYPES OF STAGE DOORS

Doorways are among the architectural features the designer will use to help establish the period and character of a setting. As such, they are subject to great variety in shape and detail, as dictated by the period from which they are taken and by the circumstances of the play. The materials used, manner of construction, and method of attaching hardware to a stage door have been tested and found practical by years of stage use. Interior doors (doors leading from one room to another) are hinged on the offstage side of the thickness pieces; when located in a sidewall, they are mounted so that they will swing offstage and upstage. This arrangement provides the following advantages:

1. Having the door swing offstage makes it easier for an actor to make a fast exit or entrance.

2. Valuable onstage floor space is reserved for the movement of actors or the placement of props or furniture.
3. The door itself serves as a partial backing.
4. It permits the audience to see the thickness pieces of the doorway when the door is closed.
5. The door is finished on only one side, thus permitting the use of lighter-weight lumber and giving a faster method of joining.

The method of building doors and door frames falls into the same pattern of types as that used in building windows.

Fake Door

This type of door is completely artificial in appearance and is the counterpart of the fake window previously discussed. The door is made as a simple canvas-covered flat hinged flush with the face of the door flat. The casing and thickness are usually painted on the flat; frequently even the lower rail of the flat is left in place, forcing the actors either to step or trip over it.

Dependent Doorway

Doorways of this type are built as an integral part of the door flat (Plate 54). These doors can be easily and quickly built, but their additional weight makes the door flat difficult to shift and store. The door is the only part of the doorway that can be saved for possible reuse, as the thickness pieces and casing must be dismantled to remove them from the flat. The thickness pieces and the casing for the door are assembled in the same manner as those for the dependent window. (See Steps 1 through 4 on page 135.) Follow the steps listed below in building an unpaneled or flush door:

1. From 1″ × 4″ lumber cut two rails 1½″ longer than the width of the door opening. Cut the door stiles the same length as the height of the door opening minus the combined width of the two rails. Cut the center toggle to fit between the stiles.
2. Assemble the various parts of the door in their proper positions. Test the accuracy of all right angles and join the parts by fastening with corner blocks and keystones.
3. Cover the face of the door with a single sheet of Upson board or ¼″ fir plywood. Use 1″ wire brads to fasten covering to frame.
4. Hinge the door to the back of the thickness piece with 6″ or 8″ strap hinges. See Plate 54 for method of bending the hinges and attaching them.
5. Use a rim latch lock assembly attached to the back of the door. The catch is mounted on the end of a short length of 1″ × 4″ attached to the outside face of the thickness (Plate 54).

To build doors with recessed panels, follow the same general method of assembly as that used for flush doors but with these differences: the width of the lumber used is specified by the designer, and the covering material, usually ¼″ plywood, is fastened to the back of the door by clout nails or ⅞″ No. 9 flathead screws.

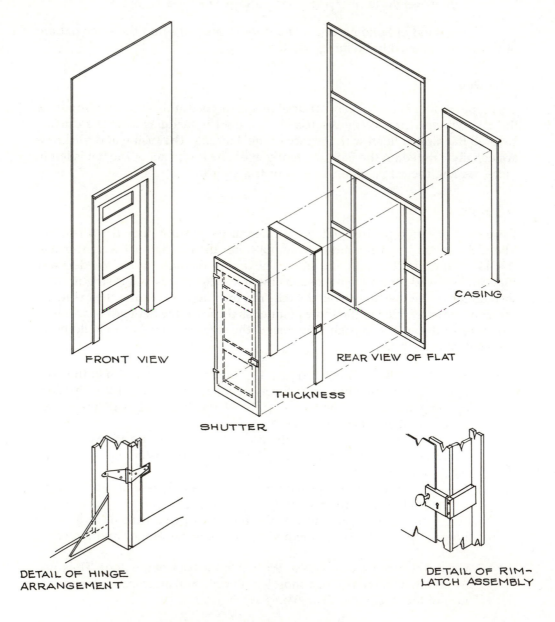

FRONT VIEW

SHUTTER

THICKNESS

REAR VIEW OF FLAT

CASING

DETAIL OF HINGE
ARRANGEMENT

DETAIL OF RIM-
LATCH ASSEMBLY

Plate 54   Dependent Door, Permanently Attached to Door Flat

Independent Door and Frame

The independent door and its supporting frame are made as a single unit that is separable from the door flat (Plate 55). Be sure that adequate clearance has been allowed in the width and height of the opening cut in the door flat for easy insertion and removal of the door unit. The only variation in construction between this and the dependent doorway is that the bottom of the independent door frame needs to be reinforced with a threshold piece. This may be made of either 1″ stock lumber cut to the same width as the thickness piece or of $^3/_{16}$″ × $^3/_4$″ strap iron. A 9″ section on each end of the strap iron is bent at right angles and screwed to the outer face of the thickness piece.

Independent Archway and Door

The thickness pieces of a doorway with an arched or irregularly shaped top must be constructed differently; this doorway is jointed to the flat in a different manner than are rectangular doors and windows. Two additional sets of sweeps and door stiles, identical with those in the arch flat, are cut and assembled into separate frames. The bottom of each frame is reinforced with a sill iron attached to the stiles. To provide the desired thickness the frames are joined together by 1″ × 3″ cross members. Canvas is used as a covering material for the inner face of the assembled thickness frames. The door may be hinged inside the thickness frame to swing onstage, or it may be butted against the back of the frame and hinged to swing offstage. The thickness frame and door are joined to the back of the archway flat by loose-pin hinges.

Exterior Door and Frame

An exterior door differs from a conventional stage door in that it is designed to swing into the setting, thereby exposing both of its faces. A door of this type may be used with either a dependent or an independent frame. The parts of the exterior door can be made from 1$^1/_4$″ stock that has been joined by halved, doweled, or mortise and tenon joints. Plywood panels $^1/_8$″ or $^3/_{16}$″ thick are cut to fit between the framing members. These panels are held in place by decorative moldings placed on either side of the panels and nailed to the edges of the framing members. The thickness of the 1$^1/_4$″ stock will permit the use of a mortise latch assembly.

The flush type of exterior door is made with a framework of butt-joined 1″ × 2″ on edge, with plywood or Upson board covering on both faces. Additional wooden reinforcement is added to the framework where the mortise latch will be inserted. All exterior doors use conventional butt hinges countersunk into both the thickness frame and the edge of the door. A special stop molding placed inside the thickness piece on the offstage side prevents the door from tearing loose from the hinges and avoids light spills.

Sliding Doors

Standard sliding doors are suspended from overhead tracks concealed within the thickness of the walls (Plate 56). This method of mounting cannot be used onstage because the walls of a setting have no practical thickness. Moreover, the weight and movement of the doors would be transferred to the supporting flats and would result in the visible movement of the scenery each time the doors

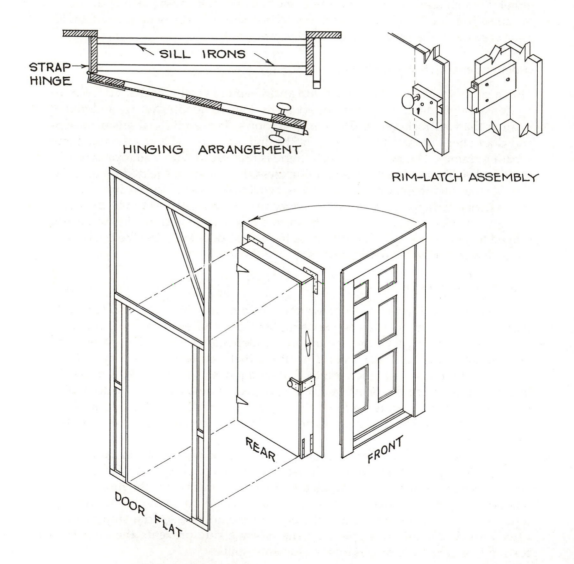

STRAP HINGE

SILL IRONS

HINGING ARRANGEMENT

RIM-LATCH ASSEMBLY

DOOR FLAT

REAR

FRONT

Plate 55　Door Flat and Independent Door Unit

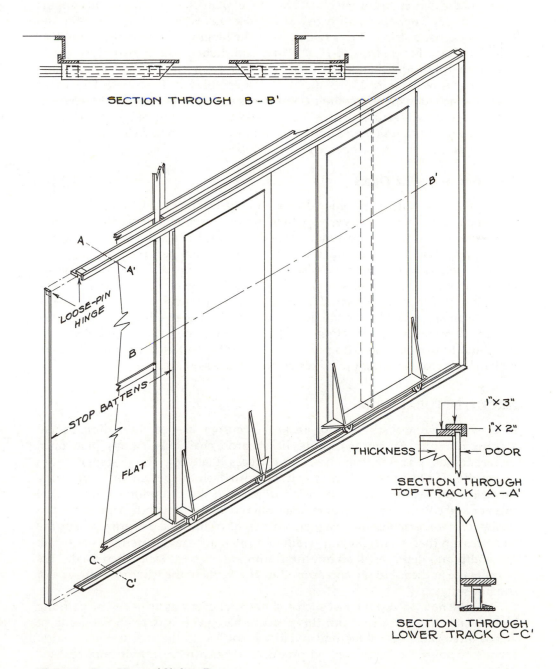

SECTION THROUGH B - B'

LOOSE-PIN HINGE

STOP BATTENS

FLAT

1"X 3"

1"X 2"

THICKNESS

DOOR

SECTION THROUGH TOP TRACK A - A'

SECTION THROUGH LOWER TRACK C - C'

Plate 56   Rear View of Sliding Doors

were moved. Sliding doors for stage use ride on castors mounted on the bottom of each door and are guided by wooden tracks at top and bottom. Rigid castors with wheels 3″ in diameter are bolted to a 1″ × 6″ wooden plate, which is then screwed to the back of the door in a position to allow a ³/₄″ clearance between the floor and the bottom rail of the door. The 1″ × 6″ plate is given additional support by blocking it from above with two triangular pieces of 1″ × 6″. To make the lower track, use a strip of ¹/₄″ plywood twice the length of the combined width of the two doors. Bevel strips of 1″ × 2″ and nail them to the plywood to form a groove slightly wider than the width of the castor wheel. The top track is made from lengths of standard 1″ × 3″ and 1″ × 2″ assembled as illustrated. The upper track is attached to the top of the thickness piece; the lower track can be screwed to the stage floor. Retaining strips are screwed to the offstage edge of each door to engage the thickness pieces and to prevent the doors from rolling beyond the halfway point of the door opening.

Two-Way Swinging Doors

Barroom doors, waist-high office doors, and old-fashioned swinging doors like those sometimes found between kitchen and dining room are no more difficult to build than double-faced exterior doors (Plate 57). The special two-way spring hinges required for mounting this type of door can be obtained from any well-stocked hardware store. Be sure to get the type of hinge that has an adjustment for the spring so that the rate of swing can be controlled. The swinging door is hinged from the center of the thickness piece and is free to travel in an arc of 180° before the door strikes the face of the thickness. A greater arc can be provided by mounting a vertical batten in the center of the thickness piece and hinging the door from this. The wider the batten, the farther the door will swing before striking the edges of the thickness pieces.

ARCHITECTURAL TRIM

A conventional realistic interior makes extensive use of three-dimensional architectural trim. Such trim includes baseboards, chair rails, panels, plate rails, picture molds, pilasters, columns, and cornices (Plate 58). The designer makes use of these in two ways: (1) they help him establish the period and nationality on which the setting was patterned; and (2) with the exception of the vertical pilaster and column, the horizontal lines offered by the remaining trim serve as a means of counteracting the exaggerated height of most stage settings. For the same reason that the height and width of a room are exaggerated for stage use, the width and depth of all architectural trim are proportionally increased. This permits the audience to see and appreciate the detail of the trim from all parts of the house.

In the not-too-distant past such architectural trim was achieved by painting on the face of the scenery, but this practice has given way to the building of actual three-dimensional facsimiles that are applied to the face of the scenery. Unquestionably the latter method produces a much more convincing, realistic effect.

The problem associated with the use of three-dimensional trim is not one of construction but one affecting the cost, method of rigging, and manner of shifting. Assuming that the budget is liberal, the single-set production can be dressed with as much trim as the design and the work schedule will allow. When

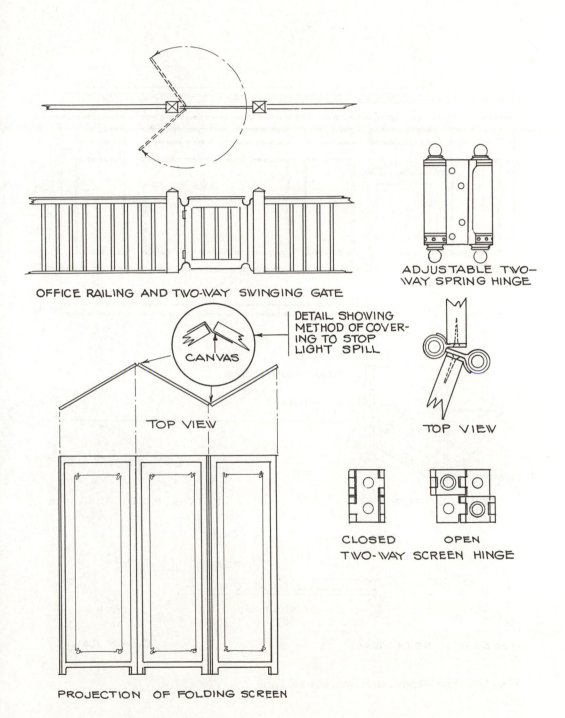

OFFICE RAILING AND TWO-WAY SWINGING GATE

ADJUSTABLE TWO-WAY SPRING HINGE

DETAIL SHOWING METHOD OF COVER-ING TO STOP LIGHT SPILL

CANVAS

TOP VIEW

TOP VIEW

CLOSED   OPEN

TWO-WAY SCREEN HINGE

PROJECTION OF FOLDING SCREEN

Plate 57   Two-Way Hinging

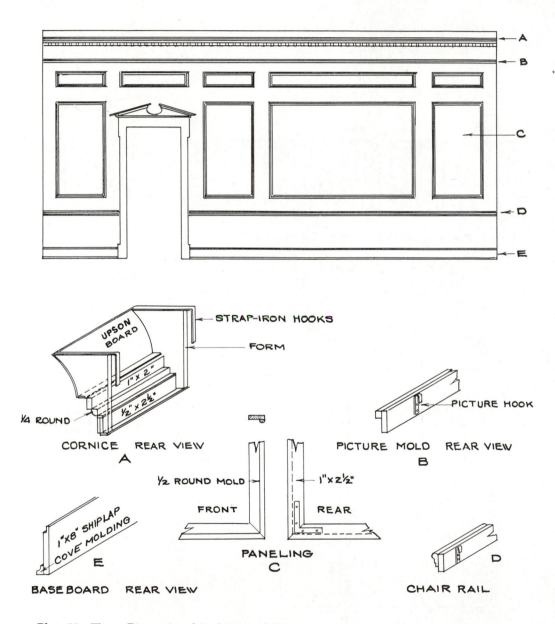

Plate 58   Three-Dimensional Architectural Trim

the setting is to be shifted, attention must be given to the manner of rigging the trim. Hinged flat scenery with three-dimensional trim mounted across its face cannot be folded unless the trim is temporarily removed. If trim remains in place, the scenery must be moved by either flying it or rolling it.

Baseboard

The baseboard, sometimes called the mopboard, is a projecting board or wide molding that is placed against the wall at its junction with the floor and extends completely around the room. An inexpensive baseboard can be made from 6", 8", or 10" carsiding or shiplap. Additional molding or strips of wood can be nailed to the face of the baseboard if a more elaborate pattern is required. The baseboard can be permanently attached by screwing or nailing it to the face of the scenery. If it must be removed during a scene shift, it should be attached by picture hooks and eyes. A single hook and eye near the end of each section of baseboard is all that is required to hold it in place.

Chair Rail

The chair rail is a projecting rail or decorative molding extending around the walls of a room to protect them from damage from the backs of chairs. It is usually placed at a height of 2'-4" to 2'-10" from the floor. An effective but inexpensive chair rail can be made from 1" × 3" and 1" × 2" stock joined at right angles to each other, with the face of the 1" × 2" nailed to the edge of the 1" × 3"; this forms an overhanging lip of 1". If a more decorative rail is desired, additional molding, dentils, or even strips of varying widths of Upson board can be nailed to the face of the 1" × 3" beneath the projecting lip. The completed chair rail can be attached to the scenery by picture hooks and eyes or permanently attached by screws or nails.

Panels

The paneling of a room is the division of various parts of the walls into areas, usually rectangular in shape, with their centers recessed or outlined with decorative molding. The recessed panel can be made in one of two ways: (1) The panels can be formed within the framework of a flat with additional horizontal and vertical members. The covering material is mounted on the back of the panel section and the rest of the covering is placed on the face of the flat. This method of construction necessitates major alterations of all stock scenery used for this purpose and results in an increased cost and weight of each unit. However, (2) a recessed panel can be faked by fastening rectangular frames of decorative molding to the face of a flat and painting the enclosed area a little darker than the rest of the surrounding surface. At points where the panel frames cannot be fastened to the stiles or toggles of the flat, additional battens are added to the back of the flat for support of the frames. If the setting must be shifted, the panels can either be attached by picture hooks and eyes and so removed, or they must be so placed that they will not interfere with the folding of any hinged units. The insertion of a tumbler between two hinged flats will provide adequate clearance for the panel frames when the flats are folded face to face.

Plate Rails and Picture Molding

Trim of this type is constructed and mounted in much the same manner as chair rails. Every possible effort should be made to avoid removing this type of trim from scenery during a shift, as it is usually mounted so high that it cannot be conveniently reached without a ladder. When such trim is essential and it is necessary to shift the scenery, the trim is permanently mounted in place, and the wall sections are shifted by flying them or rolling them on tip jacks, outriggers, or wagons.

Picture Toggle

During the process of dressing a setting a designer may discover that there is no toggle bar nor stile in a position that allows a picture to be hung at a particular point. This presents a problem that is easily solved with the addition of a picture toggle. Cut a length of 1" × 3" to fit between the two stiles of a flat; clout nail, staple, or screw a keystone to each end of the 1" × 3" and allow the keystones to overhang by 2½". Predrill the overhanging portion of each keystone to receive ⅞" No. 8 or 9 flathead screws. The picture toggle can be placed at any desired height and easily screwed into position, or it can also be secured to the flat by using a pneumatic stapler.

Ceiling Beams

In a setting where period and circumstances justify their use, there is probably no more distinctive architectural trim than ceiling beams (Plate 59). A one-set show, of course, offers no major problem concerning either the construction or the manner of rigging the beams—they are simply attached to the cross battens of the ceiling. However, when the same ceiling must be used for several settings in a production, or when the production is to be taken on the road, some other method of construction and shifting must be devised. Plate 59 illustrates one possible solution to these problems.

The beaming of this particular setting, a midwestern farmhouse, consisted of three types: horizontal timbers that followed the contour of the room, diagonal beams that paralleled the sloping roof line, and the main ceiling beams that depended upon the diagonals for support. The horizontal wall timbers were of flat construction with a 4" plywood thickness and were attached to the side walls by picture hooks and eyes. These timbers were placed low enough on the walls to allow stagehands to attach them to the setting while standing on the floor. The diagonal beams were of the same construction, but they were attached to the walls by strap-iron hooks that engaged the upper rails of the sidewall flats. Two rigging poles were used to raise these beams into position and slip the hooks over the flat rails. The rigging poles eliminated the need for ladders and proved to be a fast and satisfactory method of handling the units.

This play was to be taken on the road, and the handling of the main ceiling beams presented two difficulties: Their three-dimensional shape required more space than the trucking van would permit; and because the main beams had to depend upon the diagonal beams for support, the frames had to be constructed so that they would not sag. The first difficulty was met by building them as two-folds with detachable frames that locked the two flats together at the proper angle when the pins were inserted into the loose-pin hinges. By removing the locking frames the two flats could be folded back to back in order to conserve valuable trucking space. The possibility of sagging was overcome by trussing the vertical face of each beam. This diagonal bracing greatly increased the rigidity of the units and prevented any noticeable sagging even under the weight of the

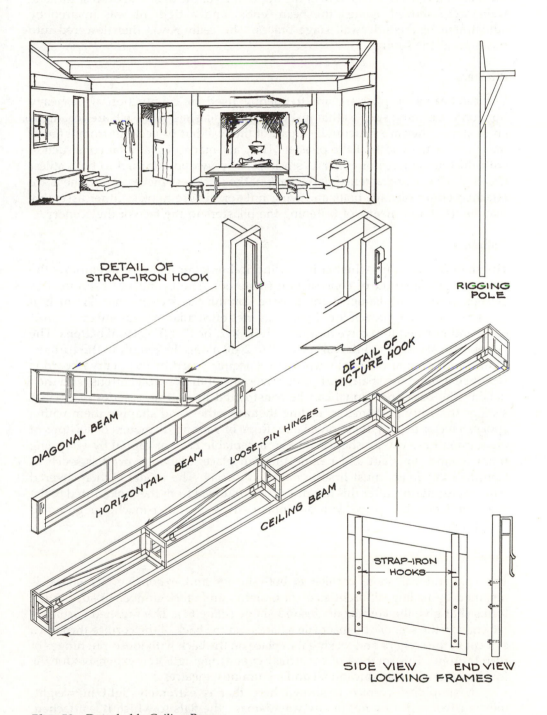

DETAIL OF
STRAP-IRON HOOK

DETAIL OF
PICTURE HOOK

RIGGING
POLE

DIAGONAL BEAM

HORIZONTAL BEAM

LOOSE-PIN HINGES

CEILING BEAM

STRAP-IRON
HOOKS

SIDE VIEW
LOCKING FRAMES

END VIEW

Plate 59 Detachable Ceiling Beams

thickness flats that were attached to them. Two stagehands placed these main beams into position with the aid of the rigging poles. As soon as the hooks on the end frames were lowered over the upper rails of the diagonal beams, the side walls were shoved against the beam ends, and a tight fit was insured by adjustment of the side wall stage braces. The ceiling was then lowered into position on the setting.

Pilasters

Vertical beams or pilasters are frequently used in conjunction with heavy horizontal beaming such as that just described. Pilasters (Plate 60) are rectangular in shape; they are structurally a part of the wall but project out from it about one-third of the width of the pilaster. They are made of plain flat construction with thickness pieces of either 1" stock or ¼" plywood attached to both stiles. Cleats of 1" × 3" are fastened to the back of the thickness pieces and to these are attached either carriage bolts and wing nuts or picture hooks. Either assembly may be used as a means of fastening the pilasters to the face of the scenery.

Columns

The shaft of a column, whether it is cylindrical or tapering in form, employs the same general method of construction (Plate 60). The cylindrical column uses sweeps of identical diameter; the tapered column has sweeps that diminish in diameter as they approach the capital. A series of circular sweeps are cut from 1" stock and notched to receive four or more 1" × 2" or 1" × 3" vertical battens. The sweeps are attached at intervals of 2'-0" to 2'-6" along the length of the battens. Thin compositional material such as ⅛" Lacquer board or Easy-curve board is wrapped around the shaft, butt-joined over one of the vertical battens, and then nailed. The base and capital can be constructed by cutting a series of circular sweeps that vary in diameter, nailing them together, and shaping them with a spokeshave or turning them on a lathe. Rope of varying diameters or sections of old garden hose can be shaped into an acceptable base or capital by wrapping them around the shaft and nailing them in place. Elaborate capitals, such as Corinthian or Ionic, must first be modeled in clay. The model is then covered with papier-mâché; after this has dried, it is removed from the mold, fitted to the shaft, and glued in place with additional strips of papier-mâché or gummed paper tape.

Cornice

The conventional stage cornice is both heavy and expensive. Its shape is obtained by nailing different sizes of molding and stock lumber to supporting forms that give the cornice its desired shape (Plate 61). The finished cornice is attached to the scenery by inserting a batten on the back of the cornice through a slot cut in the scenery and locking it in place on the back with loose-pin hinges or turn buttons. This method of construction and rigging is too expensive for the low budgets of most educational and community theatres.

A simplified cornice is shown here that is extremely light in weight, inexpensive, and does not in any way damage the flats to which it is attached. Supporting forms that give the desired shape to a cornice are cut from 1" stock and placed at intervals of about 3'-6" along each section of cornice. The forms are

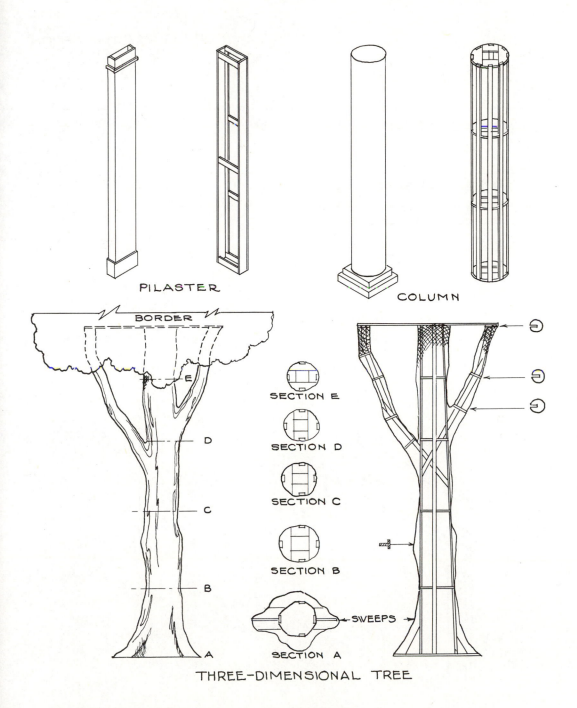

PILASTER

COLUMN

BORDER

SECTION E

SECTION D

SECTION C

SECTION B

SECTION A

E

D

C

B

A

SWEEPS

THREE-DIMENSIONAL TREE

Plate 60 Pilaster, Column, and Three-Dimensional Tree

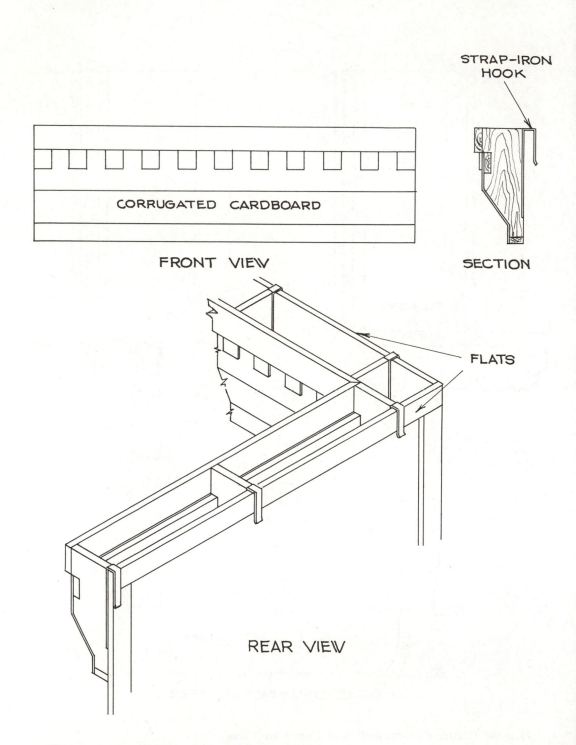

STRAP-IRON HOOK

CORRUGATED CARDBOARD

FRONT VIEW

SECTION

FLATS

REAR VIEW

Plate 61   Cornice Supported by Strap-Iron Hooks

joined together by two lengthwise battens, one being nailed to the bottom of each form and the other countersunk at the top and back of each form. These battens provide needed rigidity for the cornice and also present a solid wooden face to which the covering material is nailed. Corrugated cardboard, a surprisingly tough and inexpensive material, is used for covering. It comes in sheets 4'-0" wide and from 6'-0" to 10'-0" long and costs only a few cents per square foot. If care is used to crease or score it parallel to its length, it can be bent at angles as great as 90° without breaking the outer layer of paper. When a single section of this material has been scored and bent to the desired shape and then nailed to the patterned forms, the resulting cornice is both rigid and strong. A supporting form should be placed at the junction of each section of cardboard. The two edges of the cardboard are butt-joined over the form, nailed, and the junction concealed with gummed paper tape or a muslin dutchman. The forms should be placed far enough in from the end of each section so that they will not interfere with the miter joints that will be used at each break of plane. It is best to cut the miters and fit the cornice to the setting after the set has been assembled for a trial setup, as it is difficult to precut the miter joints of the cornice sections with any assurance of obtaining an accurate junction.

The finished cornice is attached to the setting by strap-iron hooks made from $^3/_{16}$" × $^3/_4$" stock. Each hook is screwed to the top and back of the forms and extends out in back just far enough to engage the upper rail of the flat. The cornice may be locked in place by drilling and screwing through the back of the hook into the offstage side of the upper rail.

STAGE PLATFORMS

Few features of a stage setting delight both the director and the actors more than the extensive use of varied acting levels. These make possible variety in stage movement and grouping not otherwise possible. Three types of platforms are normally used for this purpose; two are folding platforms of different types, and the third is a rigid platform. The third type is preferred by most technicians.

The Rigid Platform

The rigid platform has many advantages: it is easier and much faster to build, it is less expensive, it may be easily varied in height, it can be made much stronger by the addition of extra legs, it may be readily converted into a wagon, and two or more may be bolted together in numerous ways (Plate 62). The only serious disadvantage of the rigid platform is that it is heavier, and when it is legged up and ready for use, it is both bulkier and more space consuming than a parallel or folding platform.

The supporting frame of the rigid platform can be built of either 1" × 4" or 1" × 6" white pine or 2" × 4" or 2" × 6" fir. If economy is the first consideration, it would be good to consider the use of 2" fir, for, although it is somewhat heavier than white pine, it is about half as expensive. Assemble the outside frame first, placing the framing member on edge for greater strength and butt-joining them with common 12-penny nails. The inside supporting members should run parallel with the length of the platform and should not be spaced farther apart than 2'-0". The platform top can be made of white pine tongue and groove flooring, either nailed or screwed to the supporting frame. A much stronger platform top is made by flooring the frame with $^3/_4$" 5-ply fir. The top of the

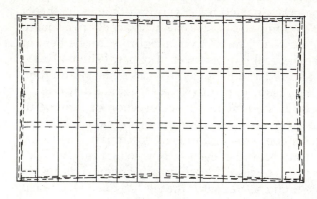

TOP VIEW

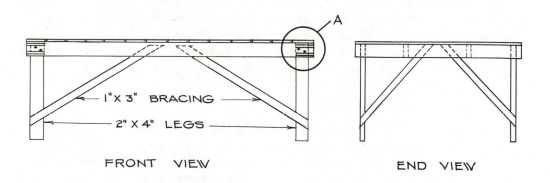

A

1"x 3" BRACING

2" X 4" LEGS

FRONT VIEW

END VIEW

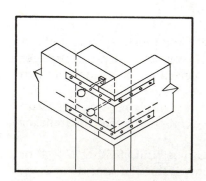

DETAIL A
PERFORATED STRAP-IRON
REINFORCEMENT FOR CORNER

Plate 62   Rigid Platform

platform should be padded with either felt or jute; if the budget is limited, an old rug or even several layers of folded newspapers can be used, tacked in place to prevent their shifting under the covering material. Heavyweight muslin, or preferably canvas, is used as covering for the padding, allowing sufficient width and length so that it may be carried down and glued and tacked to the sides of the frame. There is little chance of snagging or tearing the covering when it is attached in this manner.

The height of a platform can be varied by bolting 2″ × 4″ legs to the inside corners of the frame with ³⁄₈″ × 3¹⁄₂″ carriage bolts. Sets of legs of different heights can be kept for future use, provided that some method is found to identify them with their position on the platform. Any platform over one foot in height should have the legs diagonally braced by lengths of 1″ × 3″ against the inner face of the platform sides and ends.

The Continental Parallel

The two types of folding platforms just mentioned are the continental parallel and the standard parallel. Both have removable tops and supporting frames that can be folded. The general pattern of construction is similar in both; the principal difference lies in the fact that the center supports of the continental parallel are removable and it has a different hinging arrangement (Plate 63). These factors give it three major advantages over the standard: (1) Because the center supporting frames are detachable, they do not interfere with the folding of the outside frames. This permits the center frames to be placed closer together, thus providing greater strength and support for the platform top. (2) The hinging arrangement permits the supporting frames to be folded into a compact unit no longer than the platform, thus requiring less storage space. (3) It is possible to build these parallels to larger dimensions than is practical with the standard parallel.

The supporting frames for a continental parallel are made of 1″ × 3″ stock lumber assembled by mortise and tenon joints, halved joints, or butt joints reinforced by corner blocks and keystones. It will be noticed in the illustration that each outside end frame is made in two sections and hinged to fold inside the side frames. The center frames are slipped into place between two pairs of 1″ × 1¹⁄₂″ vertical battens that are screwed to the inner face of the outside side frames. The center frames are equipped with strap-iron hooks countersunk at each end of the top rail. The hooks engage the top of the side frame, which should be notched to accommodate the ³⁄₁₆″ thickness of the hooks. This permits the top to rest solidly against the supporting frames. The hooks are essential for two reasons: they prevent the center frames from slipping out of their grooves when the assembled parallel is picked up and moved, and they serve to hold the side frames equidistant from each other.

The removable tops of these platforms are made either from tongue and groove white pine flooring or from a single sheet of ³⁄₄″ fir plywood. Battens of 1″ × 4″ are screwed into place on the underside of the top ⁷⁄₈″ or 1″ in from its outer edges. When the top is placed in position, the 1″ × 4″ battens fit down inside and against the faces of the supporting frames. This holds the top in place and prevents the frames from folding. The parallel top is padded and covered in much the same manner as the rigid platform, allowing a sufficient overhang of the covering material so that it can be pulled over the edges and tacked to the underside of the platform top.

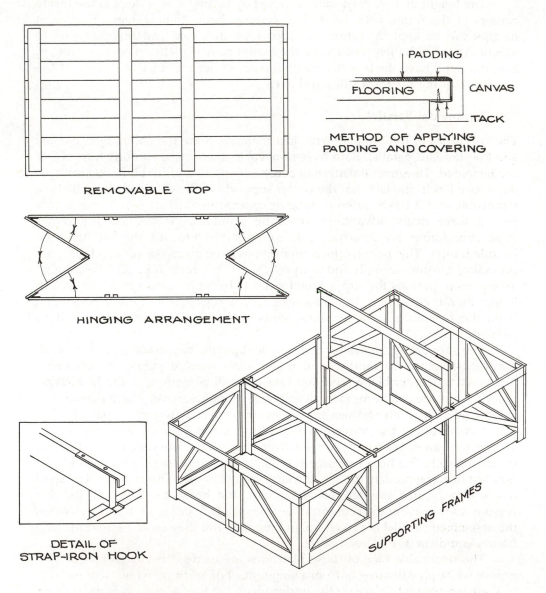

REMOVABLE TOP

PADDING

FLOORING   CANVAS

TACK

METHOD OF APPLYING
PADDING AND COVERING

HINGING ARRANGEMENT

SUPPORTING FRAMES

DETAIL OF
STRAP-IRON HOOK

Plate 63   The Continental Parallel

The Standard Parallel

As already noted, the similarity between the standard and continental parallel is great: both are folding platforms, both have removable tops, and both have hinged supporting frames. It is evident from Plate 64 that the length of the standard parallel is increased by its width when the frames are folded together. It is equally evident that when more than one inner supporting frame is used, they will bind against each other to such a degree that it is impossible to fold the side frames into a compact unit. These two facts limit both the size and the strength of this type of parallel. However, it possesses one advantage: it can be more quickly shifted because all of the supporting frames are hinged into a single unit.

The cost of building materials and the time required to construct either the standard or continental parallel make this a relatively expensive unit of scenery. For this reason the dimensions of a single parallel, or a set of them, should be determined more by the possibility of future reuse than by the dictates of a specific production. One method of achieving this standardization is to establish the height of the parallels in multiples of the average step riser, either 6" or 7". The width and length might be standardized by dimensions that best combine with each other and with the over-all dimensions of the stage on which they will be used.

STAIRWAYS

Stairways for stage use are generally classified as dependent, independent, and curved. Such details as the pitch of the stairs, height of the risers, and depth of the treads are determined by the designer; the manner of construction and method of shifting are the responsibility of the technician. Any type of stairway consists of risers, treads, and carriages. The treads are the horizontal planes, the risers are the vertical faces of the steps, and the carriages are the supporting frames to which treads and risers are attached (Plate 65).

Dependent Stairs

Because dependent stairs are structurally skeletal in form and are dependent on a platform for support, they are most frequently used as offstage stairs, out of sight of the audience. To conserve both space and weight they are seldom wider than 2'-0", which permits the use of only two carriages. These may be made of 2" × 6" boards placed on edge, with 2" × 4" cleats nailed or screwed to their inner faces as support for the treads. The risers are left uncovered. Five-ply ³/₄" fir plywood is used for treads. The upper end of each carriage is countersunk to receive a 1¹/₄" × 3" horizontal batten, which in turn rests upon a similar batten bolted to the platform legs. Cleats on the upper batten prevent the stairs from slipping off the supporting batten.

Independent Stairs

Independent stairs carry their own supporting base and do not depend on a platform for support. The carriages are spaced on 1'-6" to 2'-0" centers and are cut from 1" × 10" or 1" × 12" stock. If scrap material is used in constructing the carriages, as illustrated, the cost of construction can be reduced. There is a supporting base of 1" × 3" framing for each carriage. The bases are joined to the

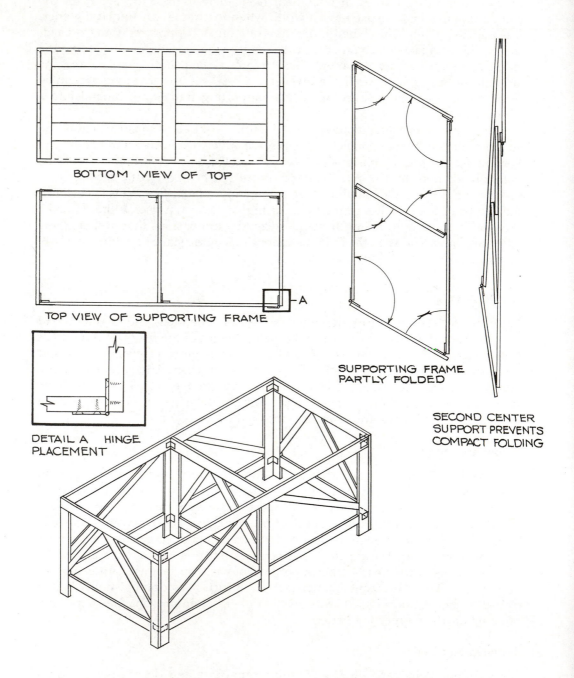

BOTTOM VIEW OF TOP

TOP VIEW OF SUPPORTING FRAME

A

DETAIL A HINGE PLACEMENT

SUPPORTING FRAME PARTLY FOLDED

SECOND CENTER SUPPORT PREVENTS COMPACT FOLDING

Plate 64   Standard Parallel

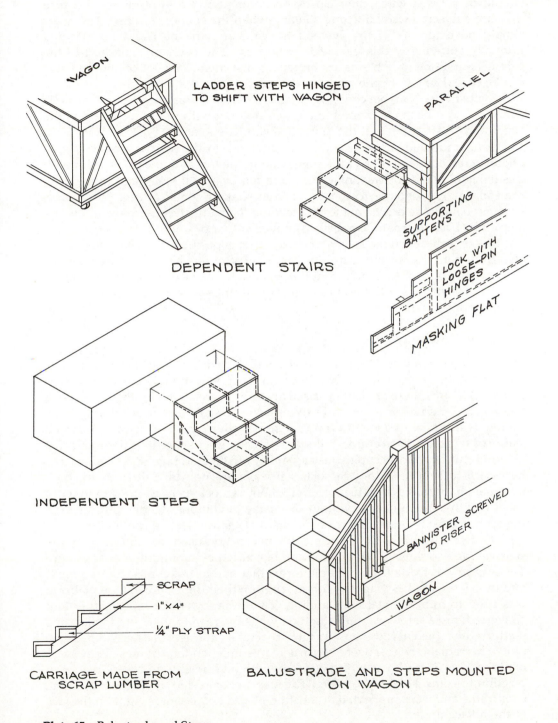

WAGON

LADDER STEPS HINGED
TO SHIFT WITH WAGON

PARALLEL

SUPPORTING
BATTENS

DEPENDENT STAIRS

LOCK WITH
LOOSE-PIN
HINGES

MASKING FLAT

INDEPENDENT STEPS

SCRAP

1"x4"

¼" PLY STRAP

CARRIAGE MADE FROM
SCRAP LUMBER

BANNISTER SCREWED
TO RISER

WAGON

BALUSTRADE AND STEPS MOUNTED
ON WAGON

Plate 65 Balustrade and Steps

carriages by placing corner blocks and keystones on the inner faces of the carriages. This provides an unbroken outer face for the side of the stairs, which should be covered with either Upson board or plywood—not fabrics, because they are subject to wrinkling and shaking when the stairs are in use. The risers should be made of ¼" fir plywood to withstand the heel and toe scuffing normally suffered by this part of the stairway. The risers are attached to the carriages first; then the treads are butted against them. The bottom of the risers can be nailed solidly to the edges of the treads.

Balustrades can be constructed in one of two ways: (1) A detachable balustrade can be made by building a masking flat with the same shape as the stairway and attaching to it the individual bannisters, newel post, and handrail. The balustrade and masking frame are attached to the stairway by loose-pin hinges screwed to the back of the frame and to the treads of the stairs. Although this balustrade has the advantage of being removable, it is difficult to join it to the stairs rigidly enough to prevent it from shaking when in use. (2) A much stronger balustrade can be made by attaching the bannisters permanently to the step unit. Each alternate bannister is moved into a position on the step where one face of its base is flush against the riser. In this position it can be nailed to the step from both the bottom and side. The other alternate bannisters are attached by doweling or nailing them through their base to the face of the treads. Such a stairway assembly is heavy and difficult to shift unless it has been mounted on a wagon or a set of lift jacks.

The Curved Stairway

The curved stairway adds a distinctly decorative element to settings in which its use can be logically justified. Directors and designers should, however, recognize the fact that there are certain disadvantages associated with the use of such a stairway, and unless some extensive use can be made of it as an additional acting area, it might be well to consider some other type of stairway. A curved stairway requires an exceptional amount of stage floor space in order to reach a given elevation, and occupies just as much offstage storage space when it is necessary to shift it. Although such stairways are not difficult to build, their irregular shape makes it difficult to store them as stock scenery, or even to reuse them in other productions without extensive alterations. Under these conditions, they may well become luxury units that many theatres can ill afford.

Plate 66 illustrates the principle of construction used in building a curved stairway. It also shows how the unit can be shifted by mounting it on a wagon. The wagon was made from rigid platforms that had been kept as stock scenery, and they were used as wagons without altering their dimensions. One platform was used to form the stairway landing. Two others were bolted together and converted into a single wagon 7" high on which were mounted both the landing platform and the curved steps. Wagon B actually formed the first step of the unit. The radial carriages were constructed as independent frames. They were made of 1" × 3" stock cut to the desired width and height, and were placed in position to coincide with the risers. The step treads rested upon the top of one riser frame and were supported by a batten placed at the same height on the face of the adjacent frame.

A solid curved balustrade was used on each side of the step unit. These balustrades were made of Upson board sheets temporarily nailed into position, marked to the desired shape and height, then removed and cut. They were

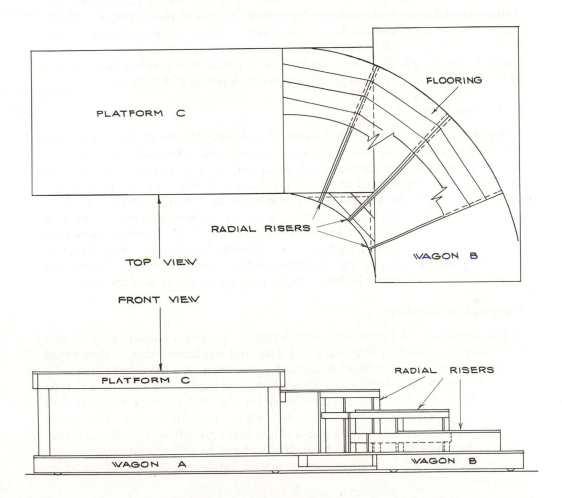

Plate 66 Framing and Assembly for a Curved Stairway

permanently nailed into place and reinforced on the upstage sides by vertical 1″ × 3″ battens screwed to the face of the riser frames. The 4″-wide handrail that formed the horizontal top of the balustrade was made of strips of ¼″ plywood that were first bent into position, marked, and then cut to shape and nailed to the tops of the vertical reinforcing battens. The junction between the handrails and the wall faces was covered with strips of muslin glued into place.

FIREPLACES

Designers often use fireplaces as a means of giving additional interest and distinctive detail to their settings. Although fireplaces may appear radically different from each other in design, an analysis of their structural form reveals that they generally fall into one of two categories. They may be built as an integral part of the wall or they may be constructed as independent freestanding units. An example of each type of fireplace is illustrated in Plate 67.

Dependent Fireplace

A dependent fireplace is much the easiest and fastest to build. The flat used in building the firebox opening, such as that illustrated, is basically nothing but a door flat, and the construction is identical with it. The mantel is constructed separately and attached to the flat by bolting it to the stiles or to a special supporting toggle. Should the mantel interfere with shifting or storing the flats, it can be attached to them by picture hooks and eyes or with carriage bolts and wing nuts, and removed for the shift. The backing of the firebox opening is made of three small flats hinged together and locked to the back of the fireplace flat with loose-pin hinges. The remaining details, such as cupboard doors and planked facing, can either be built into or painted on the face of the flats.

Independent Fireplace

In the illustration of the independent fireplace, the lower section consists of a small wagon, an arched flat, two small flats, and a practical mantel. Supported by the mantel is the overmantel assembly, consisting of a plain flat flanked by two solid lengths of 1″ × 8″, and a decorative shield made from Celotex, a fibrous composition material. Three-dimensional trim in the form of molding and decorative pilasters is applied over the face of the flat frames. The whole assembly is permanently joined into a single unit and shifted by rolling. It may be locked to the wall flats against which it is placed by one or two carriage bolts that project through any conveniently placed toggle or stile and fastened by wing nuts.

TREES

Three-dimensional trees, either half-round or completely circular, can be made by following rather closely the procedure outlined for the construction of columns and shown in Plate 60. A series of sweeps duplicating the shape and dimensions of sections taken through the tree at given heights are constructed from 1″ stock and notched to receive 1″ × 3″ vertical battens. The flaring roots at the base of the tree or irregularities in the contour of the trunk can be added by cutting 1″ stock to the desired shapes and attaching them to the outer faces of the vertical battens. Large branches are constructed in the same manner as the trunk

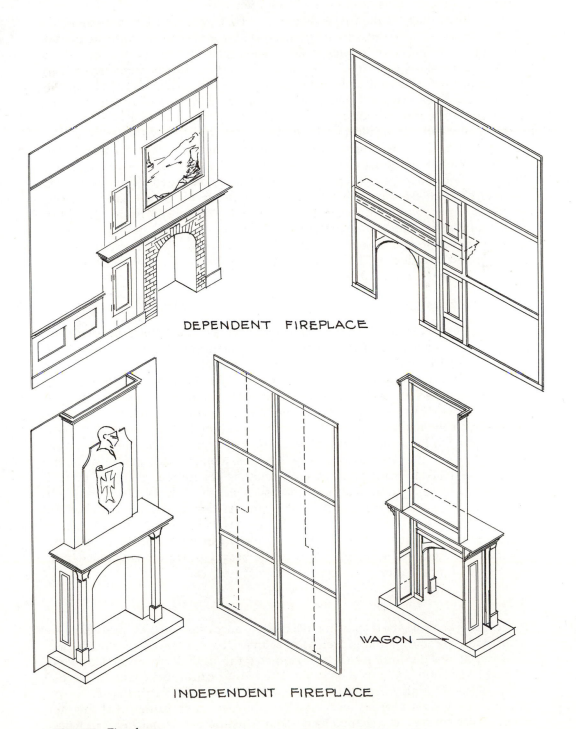

DEPENDENT FIREPLACE

INDEPENDENT FIREPLACE

WAGON

Plate 67 Fireplaces

of the tree. The vertical battens of the branches are interlocked with those of the tree by extending them from one side of the tree trunk to the other and fastening them in place with bolts, screws, nails, or even wire.

The final shape of the tree is determined by 1" mesh chicken wire molded, shaped, and stapled to the wooden framework. Over the chicken wire are placed three or four layers of papier-mâché. This can best be done by tearing newspapers into strips about 4" or 5" wide, covering one side of them with a 25 to 75 percent mixture of hot amber glue and cold-water paste, and applying the strips to the chicken wire. If difficulty is encountered in making the first layer of paper adhere to the oily surface of the wire, the paper may be broken or torn occasionally and the resulting tabs folded around individual strands of the chicken wire. This procedure ensures that the papier-mâché will follow the molded contours of the wire. Allow each layer of paper to dry before applying the next. Since the papier-mâché is brittle and easily damaged after it has dried, it should be protected by strips of muslin applied in the same manner as the layers of paper. Bark texture can be worked into the muslin by pinching the material into the desired shape after it has been applied to the papier-mâché. If the shape of the branches is highly irregular, the width of the paper and muslin strips should be reduced. The narrower the strips the more easily and smoothly they can be applied to an irregular shape.

CURVED WALLS

A setting designed with curved walls is undoubtedly an aesthetic pleasure, but the technical problems associated with the construction and shifting of convex or concave wall sections make their use questionable. Curved wall sections are not difficult to build, but they are expensive, too bulky to be kept as stock scenery, and too heavy to shift easily unless it is possible to mount them on an outrigger or wagon. Plate 68 shows the general method of assembly. Reinforced sweeps are made for the top and bottom of the curved section. If the arc is wide, it may be necessary to form each sweep from a series of segments battened together. Vertical 1" × 3" battens are spaced on 2'-0" centers along the circumference of the sweep and nailed in place so that their 3" width is at a right angle to the curved edge of the sweep. Additional horizontal sweeps are made by fitting between the vertical battens segments cut on the same radius as the top and bottom sweeps. Make sure that both vertical battens and horizontal sweeps are so placed that the beaver board covering material can be nailed to them. The junctions formed by the butted edges of the beaver board are covered with a muslin dutchman or gummed tape.

ROCKS

Stage rocks may be used only for decorative purposes, or they may have to withstand the movement and weight of actors. Decorative rocks are made of a lightweight wooden frame that approximates the desired shape and covered with chicken wire and papier-mâché (Plate 69). Practical rocks usually have a series of slanting platform surfaces supported by a solid frame that form the practical or weight-bearing surfaces. Vertical faces and planes that are not practical are covered and shaped by chicken wire and papier-mâché. A practical rock, such as the one illustrated, could be shifted in one of two ways: it could be constructed as three separate units and moved manually, or it could be built as a single unit on an irregularly shaped wagon, and rolled.

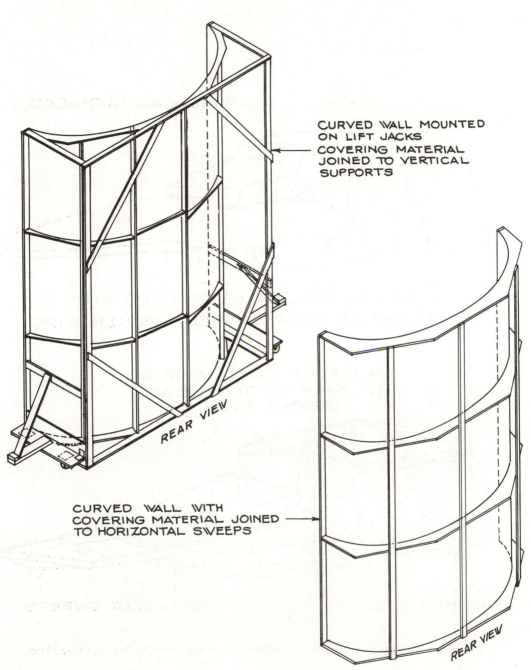

CURVED WALL MOUNTED
ON LIFT JACKS
COVERING MATERIAL
JOINED TO VERTICAL
SUPPORTS

REAR VIEW

CURVED WALL WITH
COVERING MATERIAL JOINED
TO HORIZONTAL SWEEPS

REAR VIEW

Plate 68 Curved Wall

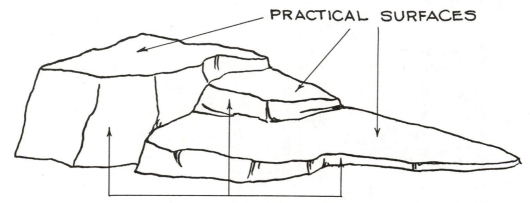

PRACTICAL SURFACES

NEAR VERTICAL FACES COVERED WITH
PAPIER–MÂCHÉ OVER SHAPED CHICKEN WIRE

PLATFORM TOPS MADE OF
¾" 5-PLY OR TONGUE AND
GROOVE FLOORING

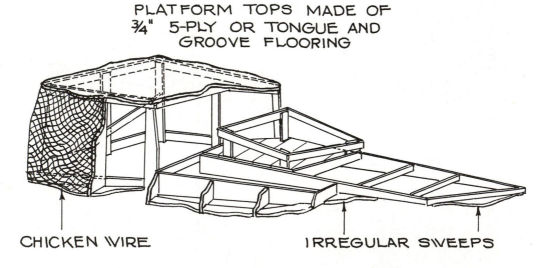

CHICKEN WIRE   IRREGULAR SWEEPS

Plate 69 Irregular Framing Used in Building a Practical (Weight-Bearing) Stage Rock

8

Plastics

The use of plastics in the theatre has increased dramatically over the past ten years. Many types and forms of plastics have come into common use in even the most modest scene shops. Almost every college or community theatre now uses some form of plastic, even if it is only as a small plastic flower arrangement, plastic picture frame, or a vase. Other more elaborate productions may have the entire setting covered with pour-in-place and spray foams.

While the new shapes and textures of the various types of plastics offer a genuine artistic challenge to the designer or technician they also raise safety problems that were not previously found in the scene shop. The processes used to work plastics—catalytic reaction, compound mixing, heating of plastics, and so forth—almost invariably release some sort of vapor or fume. Many types of plastics, as well as the solvents and binders used to work them, produce fumes that are either noxious or toxic. The inhalation of vapors or contact with the plastic material before it has cured can have harmful effects on the technician and those in the working area. The constantly repeated warning to work only in a well-ventilated area, preferably outdoors, and to wear appropriate respiratory- and eye-protective devices cannot be overstressed. Some plastic formulas, such as the urea formaldehyde foam compounds, are known carcinogens. Vapors from the burning or heating of polyurethane are toxic. Acetone and alcohol, which are solvents for a variety of plastics, are highly flammable and have a strong drying effect on the skin. If proper safety precautions are observed when working with the various forms of plastics used in the theatre, the technician will find that the use of plastics can be extremely rewarding, as there are shapes, forms, and textures that are available in plastics that cannot be achieved using more traditional materials.

The following section on the various types of plastics will show construction techniques as well as discussing the safety procedures to be observed when working with each type. The types of plastics selected for inclusion in this chapter are intended to be representative rather than exhaustive, as a thorough discussion of all types of plastics for use in scenic construction would be too lengthy for this text. Some of the publications listed in the bibliography will provide similar, as well as different, methods for working the particular types of plastics described in this chapter. Further reading in plastics technology is advised for the serious student, because as with any craft material, the more familiar one becomes with the properties and characteristics of the material to be worked, the more creative one can become in the application of that material.

POLYETHYLENE

Polyethylene comes in three basic forms that are easily applicable to theatrical use: film, foam, and pipe.

Polyethylene Film

In almost any community, polyethylene film can be seen on construction sites as the plastic sheeting that is used to cover materials that are stored on the job location. It is commonly used as a plastic drop cloth when painting either at home or in the shop. The material is generally available from lumber companies and hardware stores and can be purchased in a variety of thicknesses and widths. The most useful thicknesses for stage and shop use are .004" and .006", although it is readily available in .002", .008", and .010" as well. It is generally available in rolls with widths of 10', 12', and 20' and lengths of 50' and 100'. It can be obtained in black, clear, or white.

This film can be used in a variety of ways. It is waterproof and is an excellent nonabsorbent drop cloth. The pour-in-place and spray foams will not adhere to it, thus making it an excellent drop cloth when working with these materials. In addition to its more utilitarian applications, polyethylene film can be used as curtain material, covering material for flats, and the white film can be utilized as a projection screen surface.

Polyethylene film can be bonded by heat welding. The pieces of film to be joined are laid on top of each other then pressed together using an iron set on medium heat. Aluminum foil must be used between the film and the sole of the iron to prevent the film from melting and sticking to the iron. Seams similar to chain pockets in fabric drops can be welded to the edges of a section of film and rope; lumber or thin wall conduit can be inserted into the pocket and used to support or stretch the film. Grommets can also be used if support ropes are to be attached to the material. It is advisable to reinforce the area to be grommeted by heat welding and adding layers of film to the area to be grommeted.

Because of the flexibility and extremely slick surface of the film, traditional paints will not adhere to the surface very well. The only paint that the authors have found that firmly adheres to the polyethylene film surface is ROSCO Labs vinyl acrylic Roscopaint.

Polyethylene Foam

Polyethylene foam is generally known as "Ethafoam," which is a trade name of the Dow Chemical Company. It is an expanded flexible foam that is more limber than polystyrene foam but slightly stiffer than the polyurethane foam that is used in sofa pillows. The smooth surface of polyethylene foam feels moderately slippery or greasy. The material is available in a variety of shapes, but because of its relatively high expense the only shape that is generally used in the theatre is the flexible rod. Polyethylene foam rod is available in diameters of ¼" to 6". Larger diameters are available but the high cost makes their use impractical. Available lengths vary as the smaller diameters, up to 2", are generally delivered in coils or rolls similar to garden hose, while the larger diameters are normally provided in straight lengths of 6' to 8'.

Polyethylene foam can be cut using a knife, razor knife, or a band saw equipped with a regular woodworking blade. Rigid adhesives that are effective with polyethylene foam are white glue, hot glue gun adhesive, and construction mastic. About the only adhesive that is effective when the material is flexed is the hot glue gun adhesive.

The flexibility of the small-diameter polyethylene foam rod makes it an ideal material to use in fabricating ornate decorations on columns, capitals, large picture frames, wrought iron fences, and banisters. To make curved panel moldings on flat surfaces, the rod may be split on a band saw by the use of a simple wooden jig as shown in Plate 70. The resulting half round can then be attached to the surface in the desired pattern using a hot glue gun. To create a free-standing form such as the curl on a wrought iron fence, the rod can be split halfway through and a stiff armature wire inserted into the slit, which is then resealed using a hot glue gun or other flexible adhesive. The foam-wire form can then be shaped into the desired finished configuration.

As the slick flexible surface of polyethylene foam rejects most standard paints, it must be coated with a sealing material prior to painting. The traditional method of using several layers of cheesecloth or gauze bonded onto the surface with white glue works well but requires a considerable amount of time for the glue to dry between coats. It also results in a rough surface texture dictated by the cheesecloth. Armorcoat, a product of ROSCO Labs, can be painted onto the surface and sanded to a smooth metallic finish. An equally effective solution can be achieved by thinning plastic auto body putty to the consistency of heavy cream and painting the polyethylene foam with the mixture. The putty should be thinned to the appropriate consistency before adding the cream hardener.

Polyethylene Pipe

Polyethylene pipe is black flexible water pipe that is available in a variety of diameters generally ranging from ½" to 2". Available from lumber companies, plumbing shops, and hardware stores, it is usually sold in 50' or 100' rolls, although some hardware stores may sell it by the foot.

There are two principal uses of polyethylene pipe in the theatre. The most obvious use is as a temporary water distribution system whenever it is necessary to use water onstage. A variety of plumbing fittings is available in hardware stores, plumbing shops, and plant nurseries that sell drip irrigation supplies. Water-tight joints are made by using tubular inserts that fit inside the pipe. These inserts are held in place by hose clamps. The other main use of polyethylene pipe is in constructing sweeping curves such as those found on the balustrade handrails of curved staircases. To attach the pipe to the balustrade, holes are cut into the underside of the pipe to accept the tops of the banisters. After the pipe is fitted to the banisters a nail is driven through the top of the pipe into the banister to secure the pipe in place.

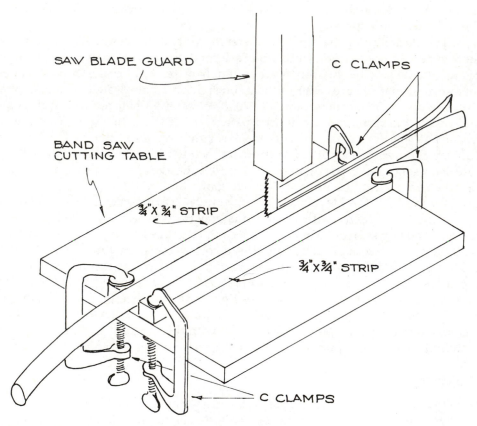

SAW BLADE GUARD

C CLAMPS

BAND SAW
CUTTING TABLE

¾" X ¾" STRIP

¾" X ¾" STRIP

C CLAMPS

Plate 70   Jig for Splitting Polyethylene Foam Rod

POLYESTERS

There are two general categories of polyesters. These are the saturated and unsaturated polyesters.

Saturated Polyesters

Saturated polyesters are generally found in manufactured products such as polyester film. Mylar, a registered trade mark of the E. I. Dupont Company, is an example of polyester film. A variety of coatings may be applied to the surface of this polyester film. These coatings determine the use of the film. Products utilizing polyester film as a base include recording tape, color media for lighting instruments, and an aluminized polyester film which has the same properties as a one-way mirror. These materials are available from a variety of sources.

Unsaturated Polyesters

Of all the plastics available to the scenic technician, unsaturated polyester resin is probably the most available, versatile, and useful. In addition to being the resin used in fiberglass reinforced plastics, it can be used as a glue or bonding agent for a wide variety of materials. It can also be utilized as a paint or surface treatment. It is readily available in hardware stores, lumber yards, boat repair shops, commercial plastics houses, and paint stores. The solvent for polyester resin is acetone.

Fiberglass Reinforced Plastics

Polyester resin for use in reinforcing fiberglass is available in four basic formulae: (1) polyester resin; (2) laminating resin; (3) sanding resin; and (4) finishing resin.

Polyester Resin. This is straight polyester resin without additives or special properties. It can be used for all applications involving the reinforcement and finishing of fiberglass reinforced plastics in the theatre. Straight polyester resin is the only type needed in the average scene shop. The specialized resins need to be used only if a special application warrants their purchase.

Laminating Resin. The laminating resin produces a porous, slightly tacky surface so that the next coating of resin will firmly adhere to it. ͗

Sanding Resin. The sanding resin has wax added to the resin. During the curing process the wax rises to the surface to form a very thin skin. This skin enables the resin to cure to a hard slick surface that will not clog the face of the sand paper.

Finishing Resin. Finishing resin contains leveling agents as well as additives to promote a smooth, nonporous, extra-hard surface. It also contains additives to retard the ultraviolet deterioration of the polyester molecule chain.

The inherent value to the theatre technician of polyester resin reinforced fiberglass is that it can be shaped into almost any form using almost any means of construction. It can be molded or built up. It can be worked on with scissors or a utility knife immediately after the resin has gelled. After the resin has hardened, it may be cut using tin snips, saws, or other light metal cutting tools.

The reinforcing material—fiberglass—comes in a variety of forms: cloth, mat, strands, and powder. Almost any conceivable shape can be created using the appropriate form of reinforcing glass with the resin.

An almost limitless variety of fillers may be added to the resin to create different textures and surface treatments. Almost any organic or inorganic material ranging from sawdust, kaolin, breakfast cereal, string, and shredded cardboard to filings from a metal lathe, sand, pebbles, and wire mesh screen can be mixed with the catalyzed resin or imbedded in the surface of the resin after it has been applied to the basic form. The filler materials will then become part of the surface of the finished object. The definition of the finished surface can be softened by applying additional coats of resin over the filler coat.

The resin can be colored using commercially available transparent and opaque coloring agents. Dry scenic pigments and bronzing powders can also be mixed with the resin to create interesting mottled surface treatments resembling tarnished metal.

Safety Procedures

Always work in a well-ventilated area. No smoking or open flames should be allowed in the workshop. When working with polyester resin and its solvent acetone, thin disposable rubber gloves should be worn to avoid the extreme drying effects of the resin and acetone. When working with the fiberglass, reinforcement goggles and a dust mask must be worn as the glass fibers or powder can cut or severely abrade the eyes and lungs.

CONSTRUCTION TECHNIQUES FOR FIBERGLASS REINFORCED PLASTICS

All fiberglass reinforced plastic construction relies on the basic principle of interlocking the strengths of the two components. The fiberglass reinforcement has a high tensile strength or resistance to flexing, but compresses relatively easily. Polyester resin has a strong resistance to compression but is quite flexible. When the two components are bonded together they result in a combination that has a great deal of strength and rigidity. The rigidity and strength of the structure to be built are directly proportional to the amount of fiberglass reinforcement in the mixture. Regardless of the construction technique used to fabricate an object from fiberglass, all methods work on the following principles. A minimum of two or three layers of fiberglass reinforcement (cloth, mat, strands, or powder) are laminated together. Units requiring greater strength will need more layers of reinforcement. The nature of the form and the construction technique being utilized will determine whether all of the reinforcing glass can be laminated at one time, or whether the individual resin-impregnated laminates must be allowed to dry between coats. After the laminated sandwich of reinforcing glass has cured for an hour or two, the finishing coat or coats can be applied.

The catalyst, usually methylethyl ketone, is added to the resin in the generally recommended ratio of 1 part hardener to 50 parts of resin. Always read the instructions on the container to find the recommended ratio for the particular hardener and resin purchased. The working life of the catalyzed resin is about

20–40 minutes. By slightly reducing the amount of catalyst, the working life of the resin can be extended with no adverse effects to the resin. Increasing the amount of catalyst above the prescribed ratio is not recommended, as it will decrease the working life of the mixture, will generate an excessive amount of heat, and will increase the chances of cracking or crazing the resin coat.

Molding

When working with molds, a release agent must be applied to the working surface of the mold prior to the application of any resin to prevent the resin from sticking to the mold. Petroleum jelly or commercial release agents provide this function for both male and female molds. Aluminum foil can be used with male molds. The foil will become imbedded on the inside of the finished object, but will prevent the resin from sticking to the mold.

The detail and shape of the mold dictate the type of fiberglass reinforcement that must be utilized. For large smooth surfaced molds, lightweight fiberglass cloth or mat can be used. If the mold is intricately detailed, then the use of cut strands or fiberglass powder would be appropriate.

When using female molds, the first coating applied after the release agent will be the finished surface coating. This coat is brushed or poured into the mold and allowed to gel or "kick off." After it has gelled the reinforcing layers may be added to give the unit strength. The finished object may be removed from the mold when it has hardened to the point that it cannot be dented by pressing it with your thumbnail.

Armature

Fiberglass can be built up over almost any type of armature or core. Wire, cardboard, papier-mâché, chicken wire, or hardware cloth can be shaped to the desired configuration and the fiberglass applied over the core to create the desired finished product. If a hollow final product is desired, water soluble materials can be carved to shape, covered with resin and fiberglass, and then the core can be removed by melting it with hot water. Free-hanging sheets of resin impregnated glass cloth can be held in place using wire clips and clothespins attached to strings to stretch the material into the desired finished shape. After the fiberglass has cured, if necessary, portions can be cut away to create the required finished shape.

POLYSTYRENES

Two very common plastics used in the theatre belong to the polystyrene family. Polystyrene sheet, specifically high-impact polystyrene, is the principal material used in heat or vacuum forming. Expanded polystyrene foam, commonly called Styrofoam, a trade name registered by the Dow Chemical Company, is the least expensive of the expanded foams and will take a variety of common surface treatments and paints. It is the most commonly used rigid foam in scenic construction. Adequate ventilation must be used when working with either polystyrene sheet or foam, as small quantities of toxic gas are released when the material is heated. Goggles and a dust mask should be worn when cutting the material with a power saw.

High-Impact Polystyrene

High-impact polystyrene sheet is available in thicknesses ranging from .010″ to .187″. The thicknesses most applicable to theatrical use are .010″, .015″, and .020″. The size of the sheets are generally standardized at 40″ by 72″. This plastic must be purchased from a commercial plastic supply company as it is a specialty item and is not available through hardware stores or similar local outlets.

High-impact polystyrene becomes soft and limber when heated to between 150° and 200° Fahrenheit. When the heated sheet is shaped around an object and cooled to room temperature, it will retain the shape of the object over which it has been molded. The most convenient way to accomplish this molding process is through the use of a vacuum forming machine. This machine, shown in Plate 71, consists of an oven to heat the polystyrene sheet and a vacuum table to draw the limber plastic around the male mold to be copied. In his excellent book on the subject, *Thermoplastic Scenery for the Theatre*, Nicholas Bryson supplies full plans for the construction of a vacuum forming machine. Commercial models of vacuum forming machines are also available.

Almost any type of paint, with the exception of dry pigment and binder, will adhere to the surface of high-impact polystyrene. The metallic spray paints, both enamel and lacquer, impart a very high gloss metallic finish to the material.

Expanded Polystyrene Foam

Expanded polystyrene foam is available in a large variety of sizes. Thickness normally ranges from ¹/₂″ to 6″ with sheet sizes standardized at 4′ by 8′. Sheets with thicknesses of 1″, 1¹/₂″ and 2″ and 4′ by 8′ size are generally available from lumberyards as the material is quite frequently used as building insulation. Non-flame-resistant polystyrene foam is normally supplied only in white. Flame-resistant foam is colored light blue for easy identification. The foam is available in a variety of densities. The lighter density foams are perfectly suited for theatrical use as all foams generally look the same when viewed from a distance, and the less dense foams are less expensive and easier to carve. It is not necessary to stock a variety of thicknesses of foam as the 1″ material is easily laminated to greater thickness using white glue, flexible glue, mastic, or latex-based contact cement.

Polystyrene foam can be cut in a variety of ways. Knives can be used to cut and carve the material. Serrated-edged knives cut the material more easily than straight-edged knives, but they do not make as clean a cut as the smooth-edged blades. Band saws and table and radial arm saws can also be used to work the foam. Smooth cuts can be obtained by slowly feeding the material through the saw while the blade is turning at a relatively high speed. The most efficient method of cutting polystyrene foam is with a heat cutter. Hot wire cutters, hot wire lathes, soldering guns, and soldering pencils all work very well to cut the foam. An effective small hand-cutter can be made by using 6″ to 8″ piece of 18 gauge Nichrome wire in a 150-watt pistol-grip soldering iron. The wire can be inserted in place of the soldering tip and bent to the desired cutting shape.

A note of caution should be added here: hot wire cutters should never be used on urethane foams, since the gas released during the burning of the urethane is highly toxic. If there is any question as to the composition of the foam being cut, use mechanical cutting devices rather than hot wire cutters.

Adhesives that work with polystyrene foam are any of the animal, casein,

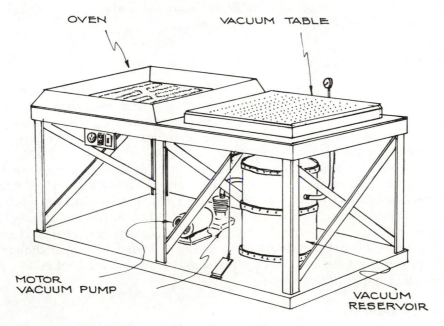

OVEN

VACUUM TABLE

MOTOR
VACUUM PUMP

VACUUM
RESERVOIR

Plate 71   Vacuum Form Table

or white polyvinyl glues, rubber cement, latex-based contact cement, and several of the construction mastics. The painting of polystyrene foam is relatively simple when compared with other plastics. Casein, latex, and alkyd paints all adhere to the foam. The problem with direct application of paint to the foam does not come from the inherent characteristics of the foam or paint, but from the abuse to which the foam will be subjected during the production run. The foam itself is not strong and will chip if subjected to even moderate abuse. If the material is to be shifted or if a different surface texture than that provided by the foam itself is desired, a number of options are available to the technician. The foam can be covered with muslin, cheesecloth, or other fabric and glue. Objects that will be handled or subject to wear can be covered with plastic auto body putty and sanded to a smooth metallic finish. If a smooth surface is not desired, then additional treatments can be applied to the body putty covering. A mixture of white glue and water, to which a filler such as whiting, sand, or styrofoam beads is added, can be applied to the foam with the nature of the filler determining the finished surface of the foam.

POLYURETHANE FOAMS

Polyurethane foams are available in a wide variety of forms. Rigid sheets similar in texture to polystyrene foam can be purchased from insulation and lumber dealers. Flexible polyurethane foam for use in upholstery is also available in a wide variety of shapes. Additionally the components for producing the foam in the scene shop are also available.

Heat-cutting or open flames should never be used on any of the urethane foams as the gas emitted by burning urethane is highly toxic. High volume ventilation should be used when working with pour-in-place and spray foams as the gas emitted during catalyzation is also toxic. When stirring or applying spray or pour-in-place foams, the use of goggles and an activated charcoal mask is advised. Good ventilation should also be provided when cutting urethane foam with power saws as toxic gas is released by friction-caused heat as the blade passes through the foam.

Rigid Urethane Foam

Rigid urethane foam is available in two basic modes. It can be purchased in manufactured blocks, slabs, and other shapes. The A-B components of the foam can also be purchased to hand mix and pour in the shop. A discussion of the uses of the pour-in-place urethane foams can be found later in this section.

Manufactured rigid urethane foam comes in a variety of thicknesses including 3/4" and 1". Sizes of the sheets vary, but the material is available in 4' by 8' sheets from insulation suppliers and some lumberyards. Rigid urethane foam has a stronger resistance to compression and is generally stronger than polystyrene foam. The uses of block and slab rigid urethane parallel those of polystyrene foam. The advantages of using urethane over polystyrene foam are that virtually all adhesives will adhere to the urethane, and the foam is stronger than the polystyrene foam.

If a shop stocks both polystyrene and urethane rigid foams in blocks or slabs, there is always the possibility that an unsuspecting worker may select a piece of urethane instead of styrene foam and use a hot wire cutter on the material. To avoid the possibility of such an accident occurring, it is recommended that rigid urethane foam not be kept in stock, and that it be purchased only when the need for the increased strength of the material makes its use advisable.

Flexible Urethane Foam

Flexible urethane foams for theatrical use are available in three basic forms: manufactured blocks, slabs, and other shapes; pour-in-place foams; and spray packages.

Manufactured Flexible Urethane Foam. Manufactured flexible urethane foam can be purchased in a wide variety of shapes and sizes. The bulk of the foam used in cushioned upholstery is urethane foam. It is available in many sizes of blocks and slabs as well as a wide variety of special shapes such as pillows and bolsters. These shapes can be cut with knives, and the thinner slabs can be cut with scissors. Band saws equipped with a knife blade or a very fine-toothed blade will cut these foams if the material is fed into the saw very slowly. Soaping the blade will aid in decreasing the chances of the blade snagging the material.

Pour-in-place Foams. The A-B elements of urethane foam can be purchased in containers for hand-mixing and pouring. The pour-in-place foams have almost limitless uses. They can be poured onto almost any cloth and can be rolled up or walked on without any appreciable deterioration. Because the foam will adhere to almost any surface except polyethylene, it makes an excellent all-purpose glue. Bronzing powders and graphite flakes will adhere to the surface of the foam if sprinkled on while the foam is still wet. Dry pigment can be added to the A component prior to catalyzation to color the foam. The cured surface can be painted with almost any paint including casein, latex, vinyl acrylic, alkyd, and enamel. As stated earlier, pour-in-place foams are available in both rigid and flexible formulations. By mixing the A components of the rigid and flexible formulations in varying proportions, the amount of flexibility of the produced form can be similarly varied.

Spray Packages. The two component elements of urethane foam, the relatively inert portion designated A, and the catalyst designated B, can be purchased in portable disposable spray packages such as the Insta-Foam Froth Pak. These spray packages are available from commercial plastics houses and some insulation shops. The spray urethane foam can be used to create surface treatments resembling weathered rock, dirt, plaster, stucco, and many other forms. It can be sprayed on muslin covered flats and other surfaces such as cardboard and wire screen. The finishing of the spray foams is identical to those listed for the pour-in-place foams. A specific advantage of the spray foams over the pour-in-place urethane foams is that the spray can very easily be applied to vertical surfaces.

ACRYLIC

While the predominant use of acrylic in educational and community theatre is as a glass substitute, other scenic and property uses of the material can be found. The main problem with the extensive use of acrylic is the relatively high expense of the material when it is used in quantity. Acrylic is available in sheet, rod, tube, and a number of extruded configurations. Acrylic sheet is available in a variety of thicknesses and sizes. Thicknesses normally range from .030″ to 4.25″. A thickness of .125″ provides a good glass substitute for small-size window panes. Greater thickness is required for large windows, as the flexing of the acrylic can be a distraction. Sheet sizes vary depending on the supplier. The material can be purchased in almost any size up to 10′ by 12′. Acrylic sheet is available in clear, white, black, and a large number of colors. It is also available in mirrored finish, decorative patterns, and a wide variety of textured surfaces. Rod is available in diameters ranging from ¹⁄₁₆″ to 8″ with standard lengths of 4′ to 8′, although longer lengths can be ordered. Acrylic tubing is available in a wide variety of diameters and wall thicknesses ranging from ¹⁄₈″ to 2′. Standard lengths are 4′ to 8′, although longer pieces can be purchased. Acrylic can be obtained through a variety of outlets including hardware stores, lumberyards, and plastic supply houses.

Cutting

Acrylic can be cut using conventional power tools that are equipped with blades designed to cut acrylic. If these specialty blades are unavailable, blades for use with soft nonferrous metals such as copper, aluminum, and brass can be used. In all cases the blades should have a high number of teeth per inch, and the teeth should be close set for maximum performance. Power saw blade speeds should be set at normal woodworking speed. The plastic should be fed slowly into the blade, and the acrylic must be well supported in the area of blade contact to avoid chipping, cracking, or crazing the material.

Power drills will work well provided that the hole is drilled slowly and a wooden backing support is provided directly under the area to be drilled. The paper backing that is applied to most acrylic sheet should be left on while drilling and sawing the material to avoid scratching the relatively soft surface of the acrylic. If the paper has been removed, the surface can be marked with a china marker or grease pencil.

Heat Bending

Acrylic becomes soft and pliable when heated to approximately 350°. Unusual objects can be formed by bending the acrylic when it is hot. In all cases the paper backing should be removed prior to heating the acrylic. The material can be heated in an oven for a few minutes and formed over wooden jigs into a variety of shapes.

Gluing

Acrylic can be bonded together through the use of adhesives or heat. Commercially available acrylic solvent cement bonds the pieces to be joined into a single unit and is a very effective method of joining. By heating the sheet to approximately 600°, the acrylic becomes soft. If pressed to another piece of acrylic at this temperature the pieces will bond together. Heat bonding requires more practice and specialized equipment than does the use of solvent cement and should probably be thought of as a backup means of joining acrylic to acrylic.

Acrylic sheet that is to be used as a glass substitute in windows can be attached to the window or door using brads or screws to hold it in place. If the window rattles or moves too much, a small dab of caulking compound at each corner will cushion the sheet and prevent it from moving within the window frame.

CELASTIC

Celastic is a felt cloth impregnated with pyroxylin plastic, which is extremely useful in scenic, property, and costume construction. When dipped in an acetone-based solvent Celastic becomes limp and can be formed into almost any shape. When the solvent evaporates, the pyroxylin plastic in the cloth becomes quite rigid. The material can easily be cut with scissors before it has been dipped, and it can be worked with a sharp utility knife after it has set. The material is self-adhesive when wet and can be layered to increase the rigidity of the unit being constructed. It is generally available in two weights from most theatrical supply houses. Celastic is commonly used to construct masks, armor, and decorative properties.

The plastics that have been discussed in this chapter are not the only ones used in the theatre. They are a representative list of the types of materials available to the technician and should only be considered as a guide to the use of plastics in the theatre. The effective use of plastics, or any material, can occur only if the technician takes the time to experiment with the materials, find their potentials and drawbacks, and then make a creative application of their specific properties in the solution of a particular scenic construction problem.

9

Metal and Metalworking

The use of metal in the scene shop has increased greatly since the first edition of this book in 1959. At that point there was little creative use of metal in even the most advanced scenic shops. The predominant use of this material was in the structural use of strap steel to brace door openings in flats, and in the traditional use of nails, screws, and stage hardware. Since that time there has been a rapid growth in the use of structural and decorative metals. Even modest scene shops now possess some type of metalworking equipment such as an oxy-acetylene welding outfit, or at least there will be a propane torch or an electrical soldering iron or gun available.

In many situations the vastly superior structural strength of steel or aluminum makes the material much more desirable to use than wood. Generally, technicians tend to avoid the use of metal because of a lack of knowledge of how to work the various types and forms of metal and because of the relatively high cost of the material itself. While new metal generally costs more than lumber, there are many sources for used pipe, tubing, sheet metal and fencing in almost every community. The use, and reuse, of new and recycled metals further reduces the over-all cost of scenic construction in metal to the point where the cost factor can be compatible with even a modestly budgeted production program.

USES

Structural

Steel can often be substituted for wood. The increased strength of steel allows a piece of smaller cross-sectional area to be substituted for a larger piece of wood.

Plate 72 shows the use of 16-gauge, 1″ square tubing as a substitute for 2″ × 4″ lumber in the construction of a 4′ × 8′ rigid platform. This platform also makes use of small pieces of ³/₁₆″ × 3″ × 3″ angle stock as support brackets for the 2″ × 4″ lumber legs. The angle stock has ³/₈″ holes drilled in it to accept bolts which are used to attach the 2″ × 4″ legs to the platform. The use of the thin wall square tubing results in a lighter platform of equal strength that will not weaken with use and age. The use of the angle stock leg supports also allows for the reuse of platform legs.

Many productions require the use of irregularly shaped wagons. The framing for these units can be welded from square tubing or angle stock, and the castors can be welded to the frame assuring that they will be held in permanent alignment.

Metal can also be substituted for wood in the framing of flats. For flat construction, square tubing or angle stock is welded into the appropriate configuration and then the entire surface of the flat is covered with ³/₁₆″ or ¹/₄″ plywood or similar rigid material using self-drilling, self-tapping screws and a power screwdriver or by drilling through the plywood into the tubing or stock and using metal screws to firmly attach the wood to the frame. The raw surface of the wood can then be finished as desired. Stage hardware can be attached to the frame with bolts or by welding.

Decorative

The decorative uses of the various forms of metal are myriad. They range from the use of small-diameter copper tubing for the construction of decorative elements on properties, through the use of rebar, or reinforcing rod, as the structural element in a decorative chandelier, to the use of thin wall conduit for gracefully curved structurally oriented items such as ironwork grills and gussets. The decorative uses of the various forms of metal depend to a great extent on the designer's knowledge of the forms and characteristics of the various types of metal, as well as the technician's knowledge and ability to work the requisite material.

TYPES OF METAL

While there are literally thousands of types of metals and alloys available for purchase, there are only a few that are of specific interest to the designer-technician. Plate 73 shows some of the more useful basic shapes in which the following types of metals are available.

Steel

There is no other metal that is as useful to the technician as steel. In addition to its more prosaic use as the material from which nails, screws, hinges, and other stage hardware are made, steel can perform many functions better than any other material for the technician. Mild steel will satisfy almost every stipulation imposed by the requirements of theatrical construction. It is a general purpose steel that can be drilled, cut, or welded easily; can be forged or worked cold; and will retain a good structural integrity after being worked. Steel is available in all of the basic shapes shown in Plate 73 plus many other specialized shapes as well. A fuller knowledge of the types and forms of steel available to you can be obtained by consulting with the steel supplier in your community.

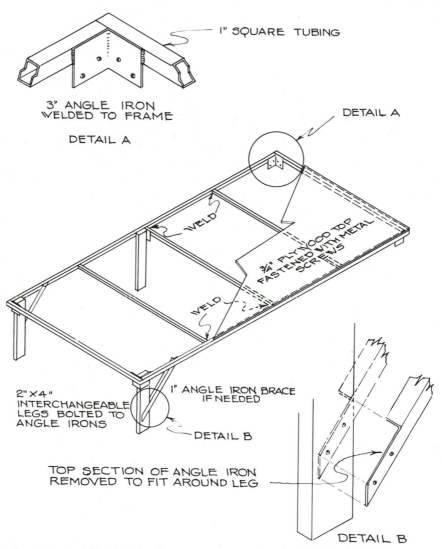

1" SQUARE TUBING

3" ANGLE IRON
WELDED TO FRAME

DETAIL A

DETAIL A

WELD

3/4" PLYWOOD TOP
FASTENED WITH METAL
SCREWS

WELD

2"X4"
INTERCHANGEABLE
LEGS BOLTED TO
ANGLE IRONS

1" ANGLE IRON BRACE
IF NEEDED

DETAIL B

TOP SECTION OF ANGLE IRON
REMOVED TO FIT AROUND LEG

DETAIL B

Plate 72 Tubular Metal Platform with Interchangeable Wooden Legs

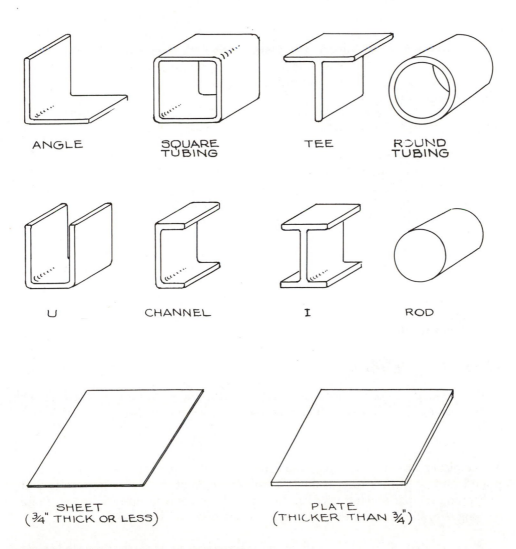

ANGLE   SQUARE TUBING   TEE   ROUND TUBING

U   CHANNEL   I   ROD

SHEET
($\frac{3}{4}$" THICK OR LESS)

PLATE
(THICKER THAN $\frac{3}{4}$")

Plate 73   Standard Structural Metal Shapes

Copper

Copper is available in a variety of forms, but the primary shapes used in the theatre are sheet, tubing, and wire. While expensive, the structural characteristics and finish of copper make it a very useful metal for the designer-technician. The form of copper most frequently used in the theatre is tubing. Copper tubing is available in both soft and rigid alloys and in diameters from 1/8" to 6" and larger. The soft form of tubing can easily be bent into intricate curves and soldered into position. Douglas C. Taylor in his excellent book *Metalworking for the Designer and Technician* indicates that when the soft tubing has been shaped into its desired configuration, the work can be "stiffened by filling the bent tubing with low melting point Cerrobend or Hydrocal plaster." Copper is very easily worked and can be cut and drilled with ease. The most efficient manner of binding copper is by soldering.

Aluminum

Aluminum is a useful decorative metal for the designer-technician. In its harder alloys it is an efficient structural metal, but generally the cost of these high-tensile-strength alloys in comparison to the cost of mild steel makes their use unadvisable. The soft- and mild-tensile-strength alloys are available in a wide variety of standard forms including all of those illustrated in Plate 73 and others, including decorative screens and panels. Aluminum is readily available in hardware stores and some lumberyards, as well as metal supply houses. It can be worked easily in the average scene shop using ordinary hand and power tools. The easiest methods of joining aluminum are by screwing, bolting, or riveting. The material is not easily soldered, and while it can be welded, it takes a very experienced welder to successfully work the material unless she has specialized welding equipment.

METHODS OF JOINING

There are a variety of methods of joining metals, and each type of metal has its own working characteristics as detailed in the previous section.

Mechanical

Mechanical methods of joining metals involve drilling or tapping the pieces to be joined and then inserting a sheet metal screw, bolt, rivet, or pop rivet and tightening the particular device until the metal has been securely fastened. Plate 26, page 78, illustrates the various types of mechanical fasteners.

Sheet Metal Screw. The sheet metal screw is a very coarse threaded screw that is used to hold two or more pieces of sheet metal together. Its use is generally limited to binding thin sheets of metal together, as it is not designed for use on thick sections of plate metal.

Bolt. The use of bolts to fasten metal together follows the same procedures as when working with any other type of material. A hole of the same diameter or slightly larger than the shaft of the bolt is drilled in the work, the bolt is fed through the hole, a washer and lock washer is applied, and a nut fitted to the end of the bolt and tightened.

Rivet. Unlike screws and bolts, rivets are permanent nonremovable fasteners. The rivet is inserted into a hole drilled in the work, and the shaft of the rivet is braded to form another head on the underside of the work thus permanently binding the pieces together.

Pop Rivet. The pop rivet is an improvement on the basic riveting technique. The pop rivet has a hollow tube shaft through which a thin rod passes. The rod terminates at its lower end in a ball which is slightly larger than the hollow shaft of the rivet. After the rivet is placed in position, a set of special tightening pliers are attached to the upper end of the rod. By drawing the rod upwards through the hollow shaft, the shaft is collapsed and forms a head on the underside of the work. When fully tightened the excess rod is cut off to form a smooth, flat-topped rivet. The pop rivet is an extremely useful fastener because it can be used in the blind, as when the underside of the work is covered.

Soldering

Soldering is the process of binding pieces of metal together by heating them and applying solder which melts at a lower temperature than the work. The solder binds to the surface of the metal and holds the pieces together. For soldering to be effective, there must be a good mechanical bond between the various pieces of the work, as the solder itself is not strong and works only as a bonding agent to hold the pieces together. The metal to be soldered must be free of grease and oxidation for the solder to adhere to the material. To aid in the cleansing of the surface, flux is applied to the metal. Flux cleans the surface of the metal and prevents oxidation from occurring as the metal is heated. The two principal types of flux are acid flux and rosin flux. Rosin flux is used on electrical and electronic connections and components, while acid flux is used on all other types of soldering work. Flux is available in paste, powder, and liquid forms and also as a core in rolls of solder.

Heating of the metal may be accomplished by the use of an electrical soldering iron or gun, or by using a propane torch. The thickness and composition of the metal to be soldered will generally determine the size or wattage of the soldering iron to be used. Lower wattage irons, 25 or 40 watt, are generally used only on small wire projects or electronic soldering, as they do not put out nearly as much heat as the larger 125- to 1000-watt soldering irons.

Welding

Welding is the process of melting the edges of the pieces to be joined so that they flow into each other and form a permanent bond. This fusion process can take place only when a very intense high heat is applied to the metal. The heat is provided by an oxy-acetylene flame or an electrical arc. The problems of oxidation mentioned in connection with soldering are equally prevalent in welding. To create a stronger weld, the molten metal must be shielded from the oxidizing effects of the air surrounding the work. This is accomplished in a variety of ways. A paste or powdered flux can be used with the oxy-acetylene flame. The warm welding rod is usually dipped into the paste or powdered flux. The burning of the flux forms a gaseous shield surrounding the molten metal to prevent oxidation. In arc welding the welding rods are coated with flux. In MIG (metal inert gas) or TIG (tungsten inert gas) arc welding the area immediately surrounding the contact zone of the arc is bathed in a stream of inert gas which shields the molten metal from the atmosphere.

Oxy-acetylene Welding.   Oxy-acetylene or gas welding is accomplished by mixing oxygen and acetylene to produce a flame of approximately 6000° Fahrenheit. This flame is hot enough to melt any metal that is used in theatrical construction. In gas welding the torch is held in one hand directing the flame at the work. The welding or filler rod is held in the other hand. The filler rod is applied to the welding point, and as the rod melts it flows and becomes part of the weld. This is referred to as the two-handed method of welding.

The oxygen and acetylene are stored in steel tanks or cylinders under tremendous pressure. Regulators are attached to the top of each tank to allow the operator to vary the pressure of the gas that is fed to the torch. The torch is connected to the regulators by long—usually 25'—hoses. The torch itself has small valves for adjusting the amount of oxygen and acetylene to be fed to the flame. Plate 74 shows a typical oxy-acetylene welding outfit. Notice that the tanks are secured to a rolling hand truck. This dolly insures that the tanks, which are the most cumbersome part of the system, can be moved with ease and safety.

When welding with an oxy-acetylene outfit it is advisable to wear a long-sleeve shirt and trousers, leather welders' gloves, and a heavy leather apron. This protective clothing will prevent any sparks or pieces of molten metal from striking the skin. The heavy protective clothing is very important if any cutting is to be done, as many sparks and splashes of molten metal are blasted from the cut zone when using the cutting torch. Protection for the eyes is essential. Goggles must be worn to protect the eyes from the harsh light produced by the flame and to protect the eyes from pieces of molten metal.

Arc Welding.   In arc welding intense heat is generated by creating an electrical arc between the rod of the electrode and the work. The effect of this 12000° to 13000° Fahrenheit heat is to melt the metal in the contact zone of the arc almost instantly. If the arc is struck at the junction point between two pieces of metal, both will be melted immediately and will flow into each other. The flux-coated electrode rod also melts, and the metal filler core of the electrode flows into the weld seam while the burning flux creates the necessary shield to protect the molten metal from the atmosphere. As the melting electrode automatically provides filler metal for the weld, the use of an additional filler is not necessary. Since the operator needs to use only one hand to accomplish arc welding, the technique is referred to as single-handed welding.

The protective clothing mentioned for oxy-acetylene welding also applies to arc welding. But there is an additional reason for protecting the operator and observers or helpers from the effects of the arc. When an arc is struck, a much more intense light is emitted than with oxy-acetylene welding. This light contains strong ultraviolet rays, and the skin and eyes of the operator must be protected from the harmful effects of the rays. For this reason the operator must wear a welding hood when using an arc welder. The welding hood has a dark glass filter to shield the operator from the ultraviolet rays. To protect the people in the area surrounding the work space of an arc welder, fireproof portable screens should be set up to shield the work from the rest of the shop.

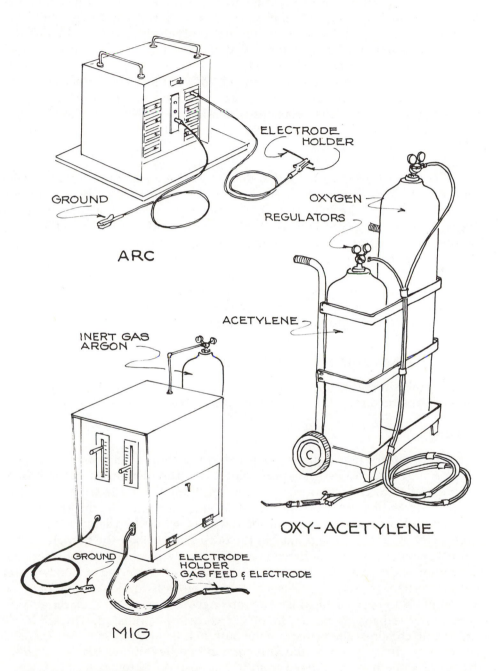

ELECTRODE
HOLDER

GROUND

OXYGEN

REGULATORS

ARC

ACETYLENE

INERT GAS
ARGON

GROUND

ELECTRODE
HOLDER
GAS FEED & ELECTRODE

OXY-ACETYLENE

MIG

Plate 74   Welding Rigs

MIG (Metal Inert Gas) Arc Welding. MIG is an arc welding process that is increasing in popularity. As previously indicated, MIG is an arc welding process in which a stream of inert gas—usually carbon dioxide—is directed on the arc contact zone. This inert gas provides the necessary shield to prevent contamination of the molten metal by the atmosphere. The electrode in MIG is a consumable wire which is automatically fed through the electrode holder at a rate which is set by the operator and determined by the composition and thickness of the material being welded.

The positive aspects of single-handed MIG welding are that a clean weld on a wide variety of materials can be accomplished by operators with little experience in welding. The problems of working with MIG are the relatively high initial expense of the equipment and the fact that the equipment is bulky and not particularly portable.

TIG (Tungsten Inert Gas) Arc Welding. TIG arc welding uses a basically nonconsumable tungsten electrode in the electrode holder instead of the consumable wire of the MIG system. The electrode holder directs an inert gas shield at the welding contact zone. As the electrode does not act as a filler rod, the operator must manipulate the filler rod in the same manner as used for oxy-acetylene welding.

It cannot be emphasized strongly enough that anyone attempting to work with welding equipment should first receive thorough instruction in the safe and effective use of the equipment from a competent instructor.

SPECIAL CONSTRUCTION CONSIDERATIONS

Because of the increased use of metal in theatrical construction, there are several types of construction techniques that should be mentioned.

Trussing

Lightweight steel trusses can be fabricated in the shop when it is necessary to bridge a large span between support points. The truss derives its strength from the transfer of forces within the interlocking triangles of the truss form. If a downward force is exerted on the apex of an equilateral triangle, the force will be diverted and passed equally down the outside legs of the triangle. When the force traveling down the legs reaches the outside corners of the triangle, it will be further redirected into a direction approximately parallel with, and moving away from, the base of the triangle. If this triangle is constructed of wood or steel and the corners are securely fastened, the net effect is to redirect the forces so that they are applied against the strongest part of the material—the compression-expansion factor. In other words, the initial downward force attempts to compress the material in the outside legs, and pull apart the material in the base. In addition to the structural properties of the triangle, further strength for the truss is derived from the opposition of forces in the bases of adjacent triangles. The expansion force applied against the base of one triangle will have a tendency to equalize the expansion force applied against the base of an adjacent triangle.

The principles previously outlined should be used as a guide to understanding the strength of the truss form. As the practical strength of a truss depends on the inherent strength of the material and fasteners, as well as the design of the truss, it would be advisable to consult a mechanical engineer prior to constructing a load-bearing truss for theatrical use.

Gusset

A gusset, which is a solid triangular metal brace, can be used to reinforce the junction between the intersecting members of any object, such as the longitudinal stringer and legs of a rigid platform. The gusset will function to increase the rigidity of the structure, but should not be thought of as a substitute for diagonal bracing of tall legs on a platform.

SPECIALTY ITEMS

There are a variety of "metal lumber" materials on the market. Three of the most widely available brand names are:

Dexion. This material is made of slotted angle that has holes stamped in it at regular intervals. It may be bolted together to form any number of shapes and structures.

Unistrut. Unistrut is fabricated from U-shaped channel that must be secured using special fasteners. It is a very versatile material, and it can be used for almost any type of scaffolding or support structure.

Telespar. Telespar is a system of square tubing that works on the telescoping principle of slipping a smaller tube inside a larger tube. The sides of the tubes are perforated with holes through which bolts may be placed to secure the tubing into position.

Roto-Lock. A special fastener designed to work with standard-size pipe is the Roto-Lock. This fastening device will securely hold pipe at a 90° intersection and is very useful for constructing temporary scaffolding and movable cross arms on lighting booms.

10

Stage Properties

Carefully selected properties can greatly enhance the impression created by an environmental setting. The full significance of this statement is self-evident to anybody who has been associated closely with a production and has seen a setting when it was first finished and put on stage—before the selected properties were placed in it. Perhaps the setting was used for several rehearsals before the props were ready and nothing more than make-do rehearsal furniture was used as a substitute. It is at this time that the designer's attitude toward her setting is likely to reach its ''low'' point. She can't help but wonder, ''What sort of monstrosity have I created?'' The total visual effect is dreary beyond words. There is no denying the additional value and meaning that properties give to a setting. Indeed, it cannot really be considered finished, nor can it be judged, until all the properties are in place. In training young designers, the point should be made early that the success of a stage design, typical of a given period and country, depends just as much on the selection of correct prop furniture as it does on the use of distinctive architectural features and interesting floor plans.

Remember that the first glimpse of a stage setting creates an immediate impression on an audience who sees it. Long before they have a chance to meet the entire cast, long before they become aware of the plot and before they know whether or not the production has been blessed with good acting and good direction, the setting has been silently creating a mood suggesting a place and time for what is to follow. To achieve this goal the setting and all of its appointments must be in complete accord—each in its own way telling its part of the story.

Properties are the joint responsibility of the designer and the director. The designer is principally concerned with the visual contributions the properties can make to his setting: Are they of the proper period and style? Is the color of the upholstery acceptable? Do they give an audience some insight into the personalities of the play's characters? The director is not only involved with these same visual aspects, he is equally concerned that the properties meet the physical demands of the planned stage business: Is the sofa large enough to seat three people without crowding? Are the arms of an antique chair strong enough for an actor to sit on one of them? Is a particular piece of furniture light enough to be moved easily by an actress?

Decisions on the construction or selection of properties should be made early, and work started upon them at the same time that construction of scenery is begun. Unfortunately, there is a tendency to postpone making final decisions on properties until there is inadequate time left to do a thorough job on them. This is understandable. The director may delay his decisions on properties because he has not yet completed blocking all the stage business, and he may not be sure that he needs a sofa that will seat three or that he even wants an actor to sit on the arm of a chair. So he delays making up his mind. The designer, however, is not only entitled to an early decision from the director, he must have it if he is to do the best possible job of creating a satisfactory background for the play. For this reason he should, during this early stage of the game, keep in close and frequent touch with his director and insist that the important decisions be made on time. As soon as he knows the director's requirements, he should immediately proceed to finalize his own plans so that the work on props can progress in as orderly a fashion as the building of the set itself. The point regarding the need for an early start on properties is made here especially for the benefit of those who have had little practical experience to guide them. Time will teach them that there never seem to be enough hours to complete all work before the date of the first dress rehearsal.

CLASSIFICATION OF PROPERTIES

There seems to be some confusion regarding which parts of a setting are scenery and which are properties. Properties fall within several distinctive classifications:

Decorative or Dress Properties

The furnishings of a setting that have been selected by the designer to help establish the period and country in which the play is laid are considered decorative or dress properties. They are usually attached to or hung from the walls and include such items as door and window draperies, pictures, tapestries, decorative glassware such as bottles, plates, or vases displayed on a mantel, a plate rail, or a window sill. Sometimes they have been chosen not only for their distinctive period style but because they add a helpful accent to the color scheme of the design. Because these properties are often permanently attached to the scenery, they are shifted by members of the stage crew, although they were procured and assembled by the property crew. Decorative properties are seldom handled by the actors, and serve no other purpose than to reinforce the visual image the designer has chosen to depict.

Floor Properties

Floor properties, sometimes called set properties, include all of the heavy furniture within a setting and all that is normally used by the actors. As the name implies, such pieces are supported by the stage floor rather than by the scenery, although some of them may be placed against a section of the set walls as would be the case with a kitchen work counter. Occasionally too some heavy floor prop may have been selected because of its decorative value and not be used by the actors at all. This could well be the case with a china closet or an ornate bookcase. Basically, however, this group consists of such items as chairs, sofas, tables, a grandfather clock, cabinets, desks, stoves, a kitchen sink, rugs, and other special floor coverings.

Hand Properties

Any object that is picked up and used by an actor in the performance of his stage business is classified as a hand property. It might be a box of cigarettes that is picked up from a coffee table by one actor and offered to another. Hand properties also include those small objects carried onstage by an actor. Packages of many kinds, briefcases, umbrellas, a tray of drinks, or place settings for a table would all be so classified. Hand properties should not be confused with accessories that rightfully are part of a costume ensemble. Hats, coats, scarves, handkerchiefs, swords, and side arms, although worn or carried onstage and used by an actor, are considered essential parts of a costume and are the responsibility of the costume designer and costume crew.

It is easy to see how there might be some confusion about the classification of a property and about whose responsibility it is to look after it. Fortunately the nonprofessional theatre is not plagued by strict union rules governing situations of this type. In case an argument develops between crew heads over who should handle a particular object, the stage manager should determine if it would be more advantageous to have the object handled by a member of the stage crew or by a member of the prop crew. Once this determination is made, work should progress harmoniously without time-wasting arguments—better an occasional mistake in judgment than a continual, disruptive battle.

It should also be pointed out that the actor should be willing to accept some responsibility for the care of her personal hand props and costume accessories. Unless the play's action demands it, these things should not be left wherever they were last used but should be turned over to some member of the prop or costume crew. If all concerned, including the actor, understand where, how, and by whom a prop is to be handled, and if they all cooperate to see that the prop is there, it will eliminate many a frantic last-minute search while the audience waits impatiently for the curtain to open.

ORGANIZATION OF THE PROPERTY CREW

The property crew is headed by a property master. He should be appointed early in the production organization so that he may be present at all production meetings when discussions are conducted on the type, style, and nature of all properties. In productions that depend heavily on properties, the property master should be in attendance at early rehearsals to become familiar with how a particular object is being used. For instance, he may learn from watching a rehearsal that the old butter churn is actually used and discovers, further, that the churn must be small enough for an actor to move it easily and store it on a shelf in a closet. In addition to attending the early production meetings the property master must keep in close contact with the director and the designer concerning any essential practical features of a property as well as its style, form, and color. In short, the more he knows about each property the easier it becomes for him to find the right one.

There is another advantage in having the property master become familiar with the requirements of each prop early in the production schedule. He may discover that his theatre does not have a suitable prop and that it cannot be found locally; the only alternative is to construct it. Knowing this fact early leaves him with the time required to make working drawings of it and to build it.

Depending upon the relative complexity of the production and the number of properties required for it, the property master is given a crew that may range in size from one or two to as many as six or more. All crew members assist the property master in finding the props. Arrangements must be made, once the properties have been located, to have them at the theatre a day or two prior to the first technical rehearsal. When things must be constructed in the scene shop, some of the crew members are assigned to this phase of the work rather than to help with the location of properties.

Shortly before the first technical rehearsal, the property master divides her crew members into groups: one group to look after the decorative props, another to be responsible for the floor props, and still another to care for hand props. Since no two productions are likely to have the same problems, there would be little value in outlining a rigid standardization in the form of a property crew organization. A production with a single setting may require only enough crew members to look after hand properties once the play is in production. A multiset production, on the other hand, will obviously need a larger crew, with members assigned to each of the three divisions: decorative, floor, and hand props.

Organization of the Property Shift

The property master, the stage manager, and the technical director work out the sequential order and details for each shift of scenery and properties. For a multiset production with numerous floor properties the procedure used in most cases is that discussed in the following account. At the command of "strike," given by the stage manager, members of the prop crew remove from the set walls all decorative props not handled by the stage crew and move all furniture to a downstage position near the curtain line. This procedure clears the stage floor to leave sufficient space for the folding and moving of scenery. When one wall section has been removed, the floor props can be taken easily from the stage to their proper storage areas. This avoids the congestion and possible damage that can result if floor props are removed from the stage by passing them through a normal-sized stage door. As rapidly as possible the floor props for the following scene are then taken to the stage and stored in the same downstage center position. This can usually be done before the walls of the second setting are assembled. When the walls are in place the floor props for that scene can then be put in their proper positions. Extra-heavy pieces of furniture such as a large desk or sofa are best shifted by placing them on a small wagon, perhaps 2'-9" wide by 7'-0" long, and rolling it off or onstage. Working simultaneously with the floor prop crew members are those assigned to look after the hand properties. In many cases small hand props are carried onstage by actors and left there according to planned stage business. Because these props are likely to be small and easily broken or lost, they are picked up by a crew member who makes a fast circuit of the setting, and if the props are too numerous to be carried safely in his hands, he carries them in a lightweight container such as a wicker basket or a cardboard box. These props are returned to the property table for safe keeping.

Positioning Floor Properties

During the first technical rehearsal the property master and the director or the stage manager will find time to place all floor props in exactly the spot desired. Frequently the placement of furniture is critical to the movement and the grouping of actors. To make sure that the furniture is in the same place for each performance the property master will see that the position of each key floor prop is plainly marked. This process is called spiking. A key property is one to which other properties take a relative position. This could well be a dining table with four chairs equally spaced around it. Placing the table on its marks also assures the proper placement of the chairs. This spiking for a property can be done in several ways. Small bits of black plastic tape can be used to mark the position of chair legs; when a painted floor cloth is used, small dots of color can be used for the same purpose, or upholsterers' tacks can be driven into the floor to mark the spot for each leg. Should marking the stage floor be impractical for any reason, the spot for a property can be ascertained by measurements that relate it to some feature of the setting. A sofa, for instance, may have one end in alignment with the stage left side of a fireplace and be separated from the wall by a distance equal to the depth of the sofa. Visual measurements of this type can be surprisingly accurate.

It is incumbent on the property master to make individual assignments for each member of the property crew. There may be some tendency to avoid this additional bit of planning by doing nothing about it other than assigning four members to handle all floor props. Under this type of blanket assignment there is a strong possibility that some vital prop will be overlooked in a shift simply because each crew member assumes that someone else is responsible. If each crew member knows which props she is responsible for, she soon becomes familiar with any peculiarities they may have, she knows when in the sequence of the shift it is safe to put them in place, knows the best way to carry each individual piece, exactly where to set it on stage, and where to put it in the storage area.

With a multiset production having numerous floor props, the property master is well advised to make a floor plan drawing of each setting with the position of each floor prop clearly indicated. These property plans should be drawn freehand on small cards so that they can be carried easily and consulted in a hurry as a means of checking all properties. Similar card drawings can spot the small hand props on top of a coffee table, a desk, a counter top, a dressing table, and so forth. These cards are especially helpful when an emergency makes it necessary to break in a person on a new assignment without benefit of prior rehearsal.

Property Table

Backstage space should, by all means, be found for a property table of some kind to use in keeping track of all hand props. The form of a prop table may range anywhere from a large rolling tablelike cabinet with several shelves and locking doors, to a conventional card table if space will not permit the use of anything better. The prop table should be placed offstage near the main entrance to a setting; but if this is not possible, then it should be placed in the lane of traffic used by actors as they enter or leave the stage. With the table stationed in such a position the actors can pick up their hand props just prior to their entrances and leave them after their exits. This simple plan does much to eliminate the frantic, last-minute confusion that results when a vital hand prop turns up missing. Very valuable, dangerous, or delicate hand props, such as binoculars, a handgun, or jewelry, are assigned as the special responsibility of a crew member in charge of the prop table. He can be charged with seeing to it that they are properly locked up in storage after each performance.

To anyone who is familiar with firearms it seems inconceivable that other people can be utterly ignorant about the handling, operation, and care of guns; but apparently many people are. Hence a word of caution about the use of firearms onstage may not be out of order in this discussion. The actor who uses a gun and the property man who cares for it must be instructed in how to handle the gun safely. They should know how the gun operates, whether it has a single or a double action, how to load and unload it, what caliber blanks to use, where the safety is located and how it operates, and, most importantly, at what distance from the muzzle one would be safe from powder burns. Such knowledge instills in those who must use the gun a sense of respect for what it can do and may possibly help to avoid an experience similar to one experienced by one of the authors. In an original play one of the scenes was laid in a western bunkhouse. The stage business called for one of the actors to thrust his arm through a window and shoot directly at another actor who was supposedly asleep on a bunk. The distance between the two was great enough to avoid any possibility of powder burns, but because of the position of the bunk relative to the window the alignment of the gun and the sleeping actor could not be faked. A last minute check of the revolver during one of the rehearsals revealed that it was loaded not with blanks, but with live ammunition! I grant this was an extreme case, but it stresses the need for a thorough training of those who are responsible for the use and care of firearms.

At the conclusion of each shift of scenery and properties the property master makes a quick check to assure himself of the presence and correct location of each prop, and he then notifies the stage manager: "Props are ready."

Assembly of Properties

Trying to bring order to any discussion of properties is extremely difficult for the simple reason that there is no end to the kind of properties that can be requested by a director or specified by a script. Beyond the usual array of more or less conventional floor and hand props are the exotic ones such as the disappearing cannon needed in Shaw's *Major Barbara*, the "machine" that is an essential part of Arzoomanian's *The Coop*, and the plant-that-talks and the stool-that-walks in Cocteau's *Knights of the Roundtable*. The list could go on and on. Some slight sense of order might be given to this topic if we were to begin with a discussion of the methods most often used in the procurement of floor properties. The designer and the director specify the period and list the number of items required and then give their list to the property master, whose job it is to procure the pieces. He has but five choices: he may buy them, rent them, borrow them, alter existing properties, or build them.

RENTING AND BORROWING FURNITURE

Should the theatre have a generous production budget and happen to be located in a city that has a property rental house, the problem of finding properties is simple indeed. The designer and the property master walk up and down the aisles of furniture, pointing to this or that piece; when the selection is complete they ask for delivery by a specified date. But few nonprofessional theatres are able to do this.

Some local furniture stores, shops specializing in secondhand furniture, or others dealing in so-called near antiques are sometimes willing to rent certain of their items for a small percentage of the selling price. Some shop owners are delighted to use the stage as a display case for their furniture, provided that they are given program credit. However, there is a logical desire on the part of the merchant for assurance that his furniture will not be damaged during a scene shift or while it is stored offstage. Whenever it is possible, one should mention the fact that once the furniture is placed onstage it will not again be moved until the end of the run, when it will be returned to the store. Keep to an absolute minimum the time that borrowed furniture is in the theatre; remember that while it is gone from a store the owners have lost it as a display and may therefore lose a sale. Any organization that embarks on a rental or borrowing program must be in a financial position to assure the owners that the theatre will pay for any repairs necessitated by damage or will be willing to buy the furniture outright.

Should the rental of furniture be out of the question for any reason, there is the possibility that needed items of furniture can be borrowed from stores, from the offices or lounges of the institution of which the theatre is a part, or directly from the homes of faculty members or friends of the theatre. No matter how, or from whom, the furniture is obtained, the property master must take every safety precaution she can think of to protect it from possible damage. If the furniture must be shifted, she makes certain that it suffers no damage by being carried through a doorway barely large enough to permit its passage—by removing from the setting a section of the wall to gain safe entry and exit. Store the furniture offstage in a place where it does not invite waiting actors or stagehands to lounge on it. Cover all stored furniture with dust covers. Notify the director and actors if upholstered furniture or any other borrowed piece can be permanently damaged by spilled drinks of any kind. Cover such pieces with a sheet of clear plastic during the technical and dress rehearsals after light levels have been established. The mere fact that furniture is covered with plastic is enough to remind actors to be careful in their handling of food and drinks.

ALTERATION OF FURNITURE

Altering or reupholstering furniture the theatre owns is not difficult. There is no given set of rules that can be applied with equal success to the alteration of all different types of furniture. Each item presents its own problem, and how successfully it can be altered will depend somewhat on the structural nature of the piece and a great deal on the ingenuity of the person doing the altering.

Excessive ornamentation can be removed or added to a piece of furniture; even the silhouette of such items as sofas, secretaries, and armchairs may be changed. Reupholstering can be done by removing the old covering and using it as a pattern to cut out the new covering. Follow the original tacking pattern in so far as it is possible. Blind tacking is a rapid method of concealing regular tack heads; where this is not feasible, the material may be hand sewn or decorative braid may be used to cover the tack heads. Braid of this type is applied with gimp tacks, which have very small heads that seem to get lost in the braid. Decorative upholsterer's tacks of brass, chrome, or other material are much larger and can be used if the style of furniture permits the tacks to be seen.

FURNITURE CONSTRUCTION

When the correct type or style of furniture cannot be borrowed or rented, it may become essential to build it. The problems involved in building furniture are actually much smaller than most people realize. There are several special considerations that should be noted prior to constructing furniture for stage use. Even though furniture for most productions will be used a short time, it generally receives much more abuse in that time than furniture in your home would receive in years. Home furniture is generally designed to be placed in one position in the home and not moved, or only moved occasionally for cleaning purposes, whereas furniture for stage use will usually be moved two or three times during each production or rehearsal day. For this reason it is essential that stage furniture be very solidly constructed. The exclusive use of costly hardwoods in furniture for the stage is not essential, as painting techniques can be employed to simulate different types of wood. Softwood pine, spruce, or fir can be used for the framing of upholstered pieces such as chairs of sofas and for many unupholstered pieces as well. Hardwoods should be used when the cross-sectional area of the wood becomes smaller than $3/4'' \times 1^{1}/4''$, as the hardwood is considerably stronger than a piece of softwood of the same size.

All of the above considerations directly affect the design and construction techniques used in making furniture for the stage.

Wood Joints

Stage furniture should be constructed employing the same wood joints as are used in better furniture fabrication. (See Plate 75.) These joints are quite strong and generally make the use of nails or screws extraneous. The doweled joint is the most prevalent method of joining wood in furniture construction. The closed or blind doweled joint, explained in Chapter 4, should be used whenever the dowel would be seen by the audience. The most frequently used method in joining stage furniture is the open dowel joint, where the dowel is inserted into a hole that has been drilled from the outside of the work after the pieces are correctly aligned. The closed mortise and tenon joint is extremely strong when used with hardwoods, but is difficult to fabricate rapidly and is not frequently used in the construction of stage furniture.

Very few joints are so strong that they could not use additional support. The use of a glue block will aid in bracing those joints that will receive an unusual amount of strain, such as the joints between the legs and top of a table. The glue block is a mitered piece of scrap hardwood that is snuggly fit into the

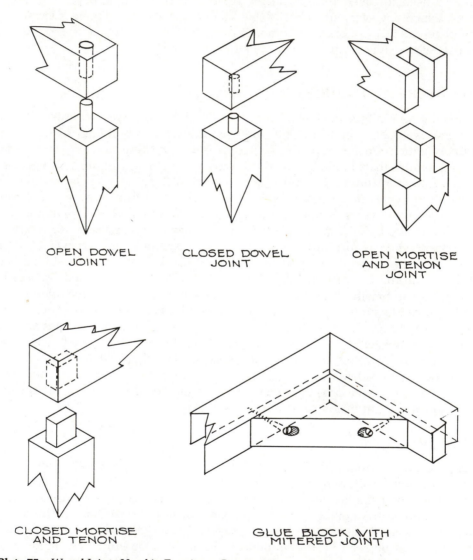

OPEN DOWEL
JOINT

CLOSED DOWEL
JOINT

OPEN MORTISE
AND TENON
JOINT

CLOSED MORTISE
AND TENON

GLUE BLOCK WITH
MITERED JOINT

Plate 75   Wood Joints Used in Furniture Construction

joint between the sides, legs, and top of the table. It is glued into position, and many times screws are used to increase the strength of the joint. Metal support braces are sometimes substituted for the glue block.

Adhesives

The primary adhesive used in stage furniture construction is white glue. This polyvinyl acetate glue is strong, dries with reasonable speed, and is readily available in most scene shops. Hot animal glue works well, but keeping it warm in the work area may be difficult. Hide glue, an animal glue that is not heat sensitive, is also an excellent glue for furniture construction. If the furniture will be subjected to extreme humidity, or if it will be used outside, then the waterproof resorcinal glues should be used.

Furniture Construction Techniques

After the appropriate design of the furniture is selected, construction can begin. It is very important that the construction of the piece follows the same techniques used in the fabrication of the original piece, as the structural integrity of the original design will not be maintained if the construction method is altered.

Plate 76 illustrates the use of open dowel joints to hold the leg of a small bench to the sides and top of the bench. Note that the dowels that are used to join adjacent stretchers (Detail B) are not in the same plane. If the dowels intersect with each other, the strength of both joints would be weakened. When preparing to drill the holes for the open dowel joint it is essential to align correctly the parts and clamp them into position. After the parts are properly aligned the holes for the open dowel joint can be drilled. The joint is then disassembled, glue applied to the holes and the dowel, the entire section is reassembled and the dowel is inserted into the holes, and the unit is clamped. Unless the audience is going to be in very close proximity to the stage, the open dowel joint can be used for almost all furniture construction as it can be hidden fairly well in the finishing process.

When working with upholstered furniture the period and design of the piece must be considered. It is generally much easier to build a tuxedo style sofa than a Victorian love seat. This is because the tuxedo sofa is relatively rectangular in form and generally does not have exposed wood. Unless one is an experienced furniture builder, it is much easier to recover an existing piece than attempt to construct a Victorian love seat or any other type of furniture that has a great deal of exposed, intricately turned and carved wood. However, the more mundane types of upholstered furniture called for in a large variety of scripts can be constructed with relative ease in the average scene shop.

The framework for the average sofa or upholstered chair can be constructed primarily from pine, spruce, or fir 1″ × 2″, 1″ × 3″, 1″ × 4″, and 2″ × 4″ using open dowel joints as shown in Plate 77. The traditional method of providing support for the seat and back cushions of upholstered furniture is the use of interwoven 4″ jute webbing tacked to the framework. It is possible to use this technique although a piece of 3/8″ or 1/2″ plywood will provide the necessary support and solidity. While the plywood will obviously not flex as much as the traditional woven webbing, it can be attached to the frame with ease and will be more than equal to the rugged use imposed on many stage sofas by the actors in

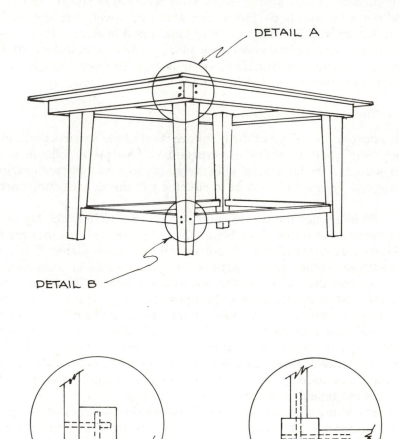

Plate 76   The Use of Open Dowel Joints

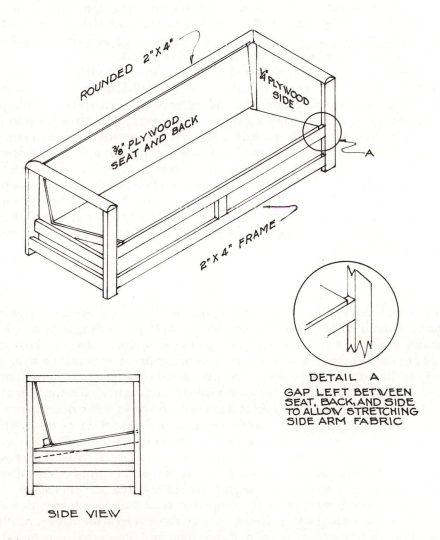

ROUNDED 2"X4"

¼" PLYWOOD SIDE

⅜" PLYWOOD SEAT AND BACK

2"X4" FRAME

A

DETAIL A
GAP LEFT BETWEEN
SEAT, BACK, AND SIDE
TO ALLOW STRETCHING
SIDE ARM FABRIC

SIDE VIEW

Plate 77   Sofa Framework

their stage business. After the framework is finished, any curved sections should be covered with cardboard or other stiffening material so the upholstery fabric will conform to the desired curve. Next the cushioning foam of an appropriate thickness is applied to the areas of the sofa that will not be covered by loose cushions. After all of the necessary foam is attached using glue, tacks, or staples, all of the exposed framework and foam is covered with muslin. The muslin covering of the foam and framework is extremely important and should not be omitted, as it provides a base over which the covering upholstery fabric can slide. If the muslin is omitted, then the heavy and sometimes rubber-backed upholstery cloth will catch and snag on the foam or wood with the result that the fabric will stretch out of shape and wrinkle very quickly.

When covering any upholstered piece care should be taken that the seat, back, and arms be covered separately and as individual units. A study of upholstered furniture will show that the material for each section of the piece must be attached and stretched separately. In general the seat is covered first, followed by the arms, with the back being the last section to be covered. The covering material is attached to the "seat-side" of the unit first, folded over the arm or back, and tacked or stapled to the bottom stringer on the outside. The covering scheme for each unit should be contemplated while drawing the plans for the piece, and can be perfected while covering the item with the muslin underlayment. Furniture glides should be attached to the legs of all stage furniture to prevent the ends of the legs from splintering as the unit is moved about the stage area.

Finishes for Furniture

Many techniques can be used in finishing furniture for stage use. The most traditional manner is to stain any exposed wood. When dealing with new wood probably the most economical type of stain to use is aniline dye. As most scene shops are already stocked with a wide assortment of colors of aniline dye, color selection should not be a problem. The dye can be dissolved in either alcohol or water. The use of alcohol as a vehicle for the dye results in a stain that dries very quickly and will not raise the grain of the wood. However it also necessitates that strong ventilation be provided while working with the stain as the resulting fumes from the alcohol are both explosive and toxic. Additionally, the use of alcohol as a vehicle for the dye necessitates that a sealer coat be applied to prevent the dye from bleeding through the finish coats of varnish. A good sealer can be made from a mixture of one part alcohol and one part shellac.

Most furniture manufacturing companies stain their furniture with aniline dye dissolved in boiling water. The use of water as a vehicle for the dye results in a stain that slightly raises the grain of the wood and does not dry as quickly as the alcohol stains. The general safety and ease of working with water-dissolved dyes makes this the preferable method of staining wood, as the slightly raised grain is not a significant factor. While a sealing coat is a good idea, it is not as essential when used with water stains as it is with the alcohol stains.

When working with water stains the work must be dampened prior to applying the stain. If possible it is preferable to apply the stain with a spray gun, but if this is not feasible then the stain can be applied with a brush. When using either alcohol or water stains it is necessary to work quickly and avoid runs or puddles, as the concentrated stain in the saturated areas will be darker when the stain dries.

Aniline dye stains can be used in refinishing previously stained or painted wood if all of the old paint or varnish is removed and the surface cleaned of any dirt or grease. As with previously unfinished wood, the surface of the piece must be dampened prior to applying the stain.

The commercially available oil or latex stains work well, but they are more expensive, take longer to dry, and are not available in as wide a range of colors as the aniline dye stains. Additionally, the resultant colors do not have the clarity and brilliance of the dye stains. The chief advantages of the oil or latex rubbing stains are that they do not penetrate the wood nearly as fast as the aniline stains and the technique used in applying the stain is not nearly as critical. The stain is applied to the wood with a brush or rag, allowed to set up, and the excess is removed with a clean rag. As with the aniline stains it is a good idea to cover the stain with a sealing coat of one part shellac and one part alcohol prior to applying the finishing coats of varnish.

To achieve a smooth, even finish coat that is evident on better furniture it is generally necessary to fill the grain of the wood with a paste filler coat. Filler coat is a commercially available paste which when used is thinned to the consistency of heavy cream. To apply the filler coat the paste is generously applied by rubbing it into the open grain of the wood, then the excess is removed with a clean rag. The filler coat can be tinted to match the stain using commercial universal colorants. The filler coat fills the open grains of softwoods such as spruce, fir, and pine to provide a smooth, uniformly hard surface for the finishing coats of varnish. The filler coat is generally followed by a coat of sealer or sanding sealer.

All stained wood should be finish coated with two coats of varnish or shellac after the sealer coat has dried. The desired sheen of the finish coat will help determine whether shellac or varnish should be used. Shellac dries to a glossy surface finish, but varnish is available in matte, satin, as well as glossy surface finishes. There are many types of natural and synthetic varnishes available, and all except spar varnish can be used to finish furniture. Spar varnish, intended for use on boats, is formulated to retain a slightly tacky surface to counteract the drying effects of the sun. The sticky surface makes spar varnish unsuitable for theatrical use.

Interesting textural effects can be made on the wood by using dry brush or graining techniques with casein paint after the stain and sealer coats have been applied to the wood. The use of a flat opaque paint to simulate graining results in an additional amount of apparent depth in the wood by increasing the contrast in the color as well as the texture of the wood itself. As the painted graining is applied prior to the application of the finishing coats of varnish, the two finish coats provide a uniform surface finish to the wood.

While painting wood to simulate a stained finish is not particularly effective, it can be done if necessary. To make this type of finish realistic the paint job should attempt to simulate some specific type of wood. After the simulation has been painted, the paint should be covered with slightly thinned shellac to seal the porous flexible surface of the paint. It may be necessary to use two sealer coats to coat the paint sufficiently. After the paint is sealed, the two finish coats of varnish should be applied. As the sealing and finish coats will deepen the hues and values of the paint, it will be necessary to lighten the paint by several shades over the desired finished color. If the final color and tone of the piece are critical, then a test board using the same type of wood, paints, sealers, and finish coats should be made prior to finishing the furniture.

It is not prudent to paint the exposed wood work of furniture with conventional scene paint. This type of paint is opaque, it covers completely any graining of the wood, and dries to a flat nonglossy finish. It gives an entirely different effect from the slightly glossy finish of most furniture.

SOLICITING PROPERTY DONATIONS

Every effort should be made to let the theatre-going public in your city or town know that your theatre would welcome any donation of old furniture, rugs, padding, pictures, china, or any other unwanted knickknacks. People are usually delighted to get rid of such items, especially if someone from the theatre will collect them. Accept almost anything in the way of donations; it's impossible to tell when that old battered birdcage or porch swing will be just the thing you'll need. Once this policy is established, it is surprising how rapidly the theatre's collection of furniture and properties will grow. Some of the things may need fixing; but in most cases repairs can be done well enough to make the articles suitable for stage purposes.

SPECIAL TOOLS NEEDED FOR
CONSTRUCTION OF PROPERTIES

Not all theatres have a special space reserved for the construction of properties. Such a place is of course ideal, as many properties, by their very nature, are small and may be damaged or lost if they are built and stored in the regular scene shop. If a separate property shop is planned, it should be on the same floor with, and adjacent to, the scene shop, because many of the larger power tools can be shared by members of both the property and the building crews. In lieu of a separate shop, steel lockers can be provided for storing props and the special tools used in their construction.

In addition to the hand and power tools found in a scene shop, the following tools are frequently needed for building properties:

Pop riveting tool	Wood-turning lathe
Staple gun	Set of wood-turning tools
Grommeting tools	Propane torch kit
Hollow chisel	Electric soldering gun
Punch	Electric glue gun
Anvil	Adjustable speed sabre saw
Upholsterer's hammer	Sewing awl
Tack puller	Hacksaw
Locking plier wrench	Coping saw
Duckbill tin snips	C-clamps
Regular nose slip joint	Bar clamps
pliers	Picture frame clamps
Spokeshave	Upholsterer's assorted straight
Wood rasps	and curved needles
Electric sander, orbital	Assorted paint brushes

PROPERTIES CONSTRUCTION

The frustrating and at the same time fascinating thing about property construction is that almost anything can be used to build a prop. By far the most important facet of property construction and design is that the property master have a very creative and imaginative mind. As previously mentioned, there are a tremendous range of requirements imposed on the designer-technician who works in properties. The property master and the technician who will be building the properties must have a thorough working knowledge of sculpting in all types of materials, woodworking, metalworking, fabric draping, upholstery, an understanding of the principles of electrical wiring, cake decorating, and a myriad other craft skills. Additionally she should have a solid knowledge of period furniture and furnishings, art, and architecture. The basic characteristics and methods of working with wood, metal, and plastics have been discussed in previous chapters. Below are listed several materials that are used quite frequently in properties construction.

Papier-mâché

Papier-mâché is a method of covering regular or irregular forms by soaking strips of newspaper in a wheatpaste mixture and applying it to the hardware cloth or chickenwire covered framework of the object. It is usually necessary to apply two or three layers of papier-mâché to make the surface strong enough for normal stage use. After the papier-mâché has dried, muslin is usually applied to the finished surface to give a good surface upon which the technician can paint.

There are some commercially available materials that are similar to papier-mâché. Generally they are sold as a powder or shredded paper premixed with dry paste, which, when mixed with water, forms a workable pulp the consistency of cottage cheese. The pulp can be formed in molds or applied to a previously prepared form.

Celastic

The working characteristics of Celastic have been described in Chapter 9. The use of Celastic is approximately the same as papier-mâché, except that the plastic impregnated cloth is much stronger and dries more rapidly than papier-mâché. It is a superior covering material for properties that are going to be handled by actors.

Fiberglass and Polyester Resin

Fiberglass or fiberglass reinforced plastics have been extensively discussed in Chapter 9. The uses of the fiberglass reinforced plastic are approximately the same as those of papier-mâché and Celastic. Of the three types of materials, fiberglass is by far the strongest. If the constructed property is to be subjected to unusually rough or harsh treatment, then the piece should be built with fiberglass. The polyester resin that is used in conjunction with the fiberglass cloth is a very versatile material in that any number of organic or inorganic materials can be added to the resin or sprinkled on the surface of the object to create a wide variety of surface treatments. Dry scenic pigment and bronzing powders can be added to the catalyzed resin to create many metallic types of finishes. More than any other single finishing material, the property master should fully explore the tremendous range of surface treatments and finishes that are available to him through the employment of polyester resin.

Fabric

The property master should be fully aware of the many types and styles of materials that are available. Not only is it essential that he have a thorough understanding of fabrics, but he must also know the types of trim, rope, and yarn that can be used to create shapes and designs or decorate the finished form of the prop. A trip to a well-supplied fabric store will acquaint the property master with the types and styles of materials and trims available in his locality.

ADDITIONAL CONSTRUCTION TECHNIQUES

In addition to the construction techniques presented elsewhere in this book, there are a number of methods of fabricating properties that are not often used in the other areas of scenic construction.

Casting

Casting is the process of fabricating an object by forming a material in a mold. Papier-mâché, plaster of Paris, Hydrocal (a stronger type of plaster), fiberglass, and Celastic are just a few of the many materials that can be formed by casting. Although the complete process of making molds is too extensive to be covered in this text, persons interested in the construction of properties should acquaint themselves with some of the excellent craft books on the subject.

The types of molds most frequently used in the theatre are those constructed of either plaster or latex. Plaster molds are rigid and cannot have any undercut areas that would prevent the casting from being removed from the mold. The latex mold is flexible and allows the form being cast to have a limited amount of undercutting, as the flexibility of the mold allows it to stretch around the casting after it has hardened.

The range of props that can be cast is extremely wide. Breakaway windows, glasses, and other forms can be cast using a boiled solution of supersaturated sugar and water. Sanolite MHP, a powdered plastic from the Monsanto Chemical Company, can be melted and cast into the appropriate mold. Molds can also be made of large stone statuary and the forms recast using fiberglass reinforced plastics. These fiberglass reproductions, while faithful copies of the heavy originals, are generally so light that weight must be added to the bottom to prevent them from tipping over.

Applique

An applique is a decorative trim that is applied to another object. In the case of stage properties appliques can be applied to almost anything: furniture, draperies, small boxes, dog collars, picture frames, and so on. The purpose of all appliques is to increase the visual interest of the basic form. Almost any type of material can be used to enhance or "glitz" a plain form. One of the most frequently used family of materials is the multitudinous types of decorative trims available in the notions section of a fabric store. More mundane items such as string, rope, nails, lace, and coffee grounds can be used to achieve a particular effect. When working with appliques one quickly becomes aware that the hot glue gun is an almost indispensable tool. Almost any type of material can be attached to anything else using the adhesive from a hot glue gun. The glue itself is also an extremely effective decorative device when one becomes proficient in its use. The glue is dispensed from the gun in a thin line, and very effective designs can be "drawn" on props with the glue. After the glue has hardened it can be painted or gilded to achieve the desired effect.

DRAPERIES

The most decorative features of many settings are the draperies of a window, door, or mantel. A designer may use them because they suggest a certain period, place, or style, or because they repeat a dominant line in the design, or because they introduce accent colors to her basic color scheme. In any event, draperies are classified as decorative properties, and procuring them becomes the responsibility of the property crew.

The usual parts of a window drapery ensemble are the window shade, glass curtains, overdrapes, and valance. According to circumstances, these parts may be used all together or in various combinations. The roller window shade is seldom used unless an actor must raise or lower it. Inexpensive roller curtains can be purchased from local variety stores. They become a part of the property room stock and can be reused many times. Their width can be reduced by removing the cap opposite the spring, cutting the roller and the curtain material to the desired width, and reassembling.

Glass curtains can be made from a variety of sheer materials such as marquisette, theatrical gauze, netting, chiffon, voile, or even very lightweight cheesecloth. If the top of the glass curtain is concealed in any way, you need not sew a typical pocket hem for the curtain rod; simply pleat the material and staple or tack it directly to a lightweight wooden batten. However, if the curtain top is not concealed or if the curtain must be opened or closed, it will be necessary to sew the curtain rod pocket, leaving the usual decorative hem above it. Inexpensive curtain rods whose lengths are adjustable can be found in most variety stores.

The overdrapes can be made from many different materials, but they are usually opaque and they must drape well. Needless to say, styles in draperies change as much as any other feature of interior decorating; hence the following suggestions can only be very general. The designer should indicate very definitely the exact style and draping pattern he desires. Many times overdrapes are concealed at the top by a decorative valance of some sort. This can be made from the same material as the drapes or from a contrasting material. If a solid, shaped valance is called for, it can be cut from Upson board or from 1/4" plywood that is reinforced by, and attached to, a framing box some 3" or 4" deep. The framing box holds the valance out from the wall and provides space for the fullness of the draperies. Normally overdrapes are rectangular panels pleated for fullness and allowed to fall in vertical folds or to be caught up by tiebacks to achieve more complicated draping. The amount of fullness depends, of course, on the designer's intent; but unless he has specified otherwise, 75 or 100 percent fullness will be right in most cases. When the tops of the drapes are concealed by a valance, the drapery material is pleated and tacked or stapled to a wooden batten that in turn is fastened permanently to the framing box. Wherever possible the entire drapery ensemble should be attached directly to the window flat and be shifted with the scenery. When this procedure is not possible, the draperies, valance, and framing box are attached to the scenery with picture hooks and eyes. The whole assembly can then be lifted off for the scene shift.

Draw Curtains

It is surprising how many times a play calls for a set of draperies that can be opened or closed as part of the stage business. If the budget will not allow the purchase of a conventional traverse rod track, there are three other methods of rigging that can be used. The first of these uses only one supporting rod, and therefore each section of the curtain must be moved independently. The supporting rod is a regulation drapery rod, about $1\frac{1}{8}''$ in diameter, obtainable from most lumber dealers. Spaced about 8" or 10" apart, large metal or wooden rings are sewn to the drapery tops. Rods and rings of this type are usually in full view, so that the supports for the rod can be quite decorative. A substitute drapery rod can be made from a length of $\frac{3}{4}'' \times 1\frac{1}{4}''$ stock lumber. After the rod has been stained or painted the proper color, it is lubricated with a liberal coating of paraffin. This allows the curtain rings to slide much more easily and with considerably less noise. One difficulty with this type of curtain rigging is that the draperies have a tendency to remain tented partly open after they have supposedly been closed. This is caused by both sections of the draperies being supported by a single curtain rod. The second and third rigging systems avoid this difficulty by employing a separate track for each section of the draperies, which permits the leading edges of the curtains to overlap. Either the second or the third system can be used when the top of the draperies is concealed by a valance or the lintel of a doorway. The second uses two small wooden curtain rods for tracks. These rods must be separated enough to permit the curtain rings to pass each other without fouling. The conventional draw-curtain rigging (see Plate 103) is used to permit operation of the curtains by a floor line. The third method achieves the same effect by using two tightly stretched piano wires for tracks. The wire can be stretched in the following manner: an eyebolt is used to anchor one end of each wire; the other end of the wire is served through one of the eyes of a small turnbuckle. Small metal rings or chromium-finished shower curtain rings are either sewn or pinned to the draperies and are threaded on to the piano wires before the wires are stretched. Although this type of track requires more time to rig, it has the advantage of being practically soundless in operation and it is much easier to operate because it has very little friction loss.

SPECIAL EFFECTS

There are a number of special effects that can fall within the area of responsibility of the property master. Many times realistic electrical campfires or fireplace effects are constructed by the property crew. The correct functioning and placement of wall sconces and table and floor lamps are similarly considered to be the province of properties. Breakaway furniture, glass, and crockery are made and rigged by the prop crew. Pyrotechnical effects such as explosions and smoke effects if not constructed in properties are often loaded and detonated by the property crew. While the majority of the special effects are electrically controlled or powered, there are still many effects that are solely mechanical. The following section will illustrate some of the methods by which these properties can be built and rigged.

Smoke

There are two principal methods by which lingering smoke can be produced onstage. (See Plate 78.) The first is through the use of commercially available oil smoke generators. These machines operate by forcing mineral oil vapor past a heater which turns the vapor into smoke. The resultant smoke has a somewhat objectionable odor, even if the available perfume is utilized. The smoke also tends to drift, takes a long time to dissipate, and generally leaves an oily residue on the scenery that it touches. The problem of drifting smoke can be solved if the stream of smoke is passed over dry ice which cools it and makes it cling to the floor area.

Another method of making smoke that will cover the stage floor is through the use of a dry ice fog machine. These units are available commercially, and they can also be built in the scene shop. The principle of operation for the dry ice fog machine is to plunge dry ice into heated water. This results in a dry ice fog which clings to the floor, dissipates fairly rapidly, and leaves no residue. The principal problem with the dry ice fogger is that once the fog has been generated, it takes a long time to heat the water again, and the amount of fog that is generated from one charge is not great. To effectively fog an entire stage area, two or more 55-gallon foggers are generally used.

Flash Effects

Although some of the following effects generate smoke, their principal effect is that of a brilliant flash of light. Many times these devices are used in conjunction with each other and with fog or smoke machines.

A flash pot is a device that uses an electrical current to set off a charge of flash powder. Flash pots can be either purchased or built in the shop. The simplest kind to build is a small metal or fireproof box with a removable screen lid as shown in Plate 79. In the bottom of the box two nails or screws are inserted into a piece of asbestos board which is insulated and electrically isolated from the metal box. One electrical power leg is attached to each nail or screw. A piece of copper wire—a single strand of wire from a piece of stranded 18 gauge household zip cord works well—is connected to both nails. A small charge of flash powder is poured over the wire. When the power is turned on the small strand of wire instantaneously heats to incandescence causing the powder to ignite.

Plate 79 illustrates a similar type of flash pot that can be made from low-amperage fuses. A three-amp or less fuse that has the transparent plastic top cut out is inserted into a socket that has been appropriately wired. A small amount of flash powder is poured into the fuse, and a wire guard screen is loosely placed over the top of the entire assembly. When the power is turned on the fuse link melts and ignites the powder.

Any time that flash powder or any similar explosive compound is used onstage there are a number of safety precautions that must be followed. The flash pots should never be placed near any flammable material such as drapes or a nonflameproofed substance. The flash powder should never be covered

OIL VAPOR SMOKE
MACHINE

DRY ICE FOG MACHINE

Plate 78   Special Effects Machines

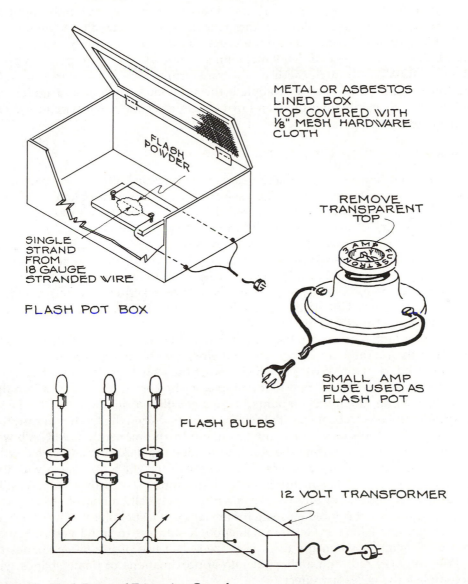

METAL OR ASBESTOS
LINED BOX
TOP COVERED WITH
⅛" MESH HARDWARE
CLOTH

FLASH
POWDER

SINGLE
STRAND
FROM
18 GAUGE
STRANDED WIRE

FLASH POT BOX

REMOVE
TRANSPARENT
TOP

SMALL AMP
FUSE USED AS
FLASH POT

FLASH BULBS

12 VOLT TRANSFORMER

Plate 79 Flash Pots and Triggering Console

with any material such as metal or asbestos board or even paper wadding. If the exploding powder is confined there is a great chance for an explosion, and if a real explosion does not occur, the covering material will be blown up into the air just like a mortar round. A piece of window screening should be placed in a tentlike configuration over the powder to prevent any pieces of powder or fuse wire from being blown clear of the flashpot.

If a flash without smoke is the desired effect, then a strobe light or flashbulbs can be used. Both of these devices are electrically triggered.

Plate 79 also illustrates a simple triggering device that can be used to fire flashbulbs in an irregular random manner. The 120 volt current is stepped down to 12 VAC through the use of a transformer. The momentary, or push button switches, are used to complete the individual circuits and ignite the flashbulbs. By eliminating the stepdown transformer the same type of system can be used to operate a series of flashpots.

Torches

It seems that almost every Shakespearean production calls for some type of torch, candle, or lantern light. The easiest solution to this problem is the use of actual torches, candles, and lanterns. However, open flames onstage are a violation of almost every fire code in the country. The only general exception to the code is the use of open flames on outdoor stages. Not only are the real flames dangerous, they have a tendency to be very distracting to the audience. The problem for the property master is to create a realistic flame without the intensity or danger of real fire. The flickering light of a torch as detailed by James Gill of the Old Globe Theatre in San Diego can be accomplished as indicated in Plate 80.

Three lamps are independently wired in the torch body. One is firmly wired in the traditional manner, and the other two bulbs are placed in loosely wound holders made of wire to which one of the power leads is attached. The second power lead is attached to the nipple on the base of the lamp. When the torch is moving, the loosely mounted lamps will flicker on and off as the lamp intermittently breaks contact with the wire holders. When the torch is at rest, the loosely wired lamps may or may not be on, but the permanently wired bulb will always be burning. By using the above technique the flickering associated with the moving flame will be apparent. The batteries and switch associated with the lamps can be concealed in the handle of the torch. To further enhance the realistic effect of this or any type of torch it is generally advisable to create a vertical transparent colored masking for the lamps. Plastic color medium such as Roscolene, Lee Filter, or Gelatran has enough stiffness to stand vertically and still move slightly when the torch is moved. The use of the flame shades of yellow, orange, red, and amber cut into approximations of flame shapes will accomplish the necessary effect.

The lanterns can be handled in two ways. Where fire codes permit the use of enclosed flames onstage, candles can be used inside of the lanterns. Oil-fed lamps should never be used onstage. The lamp can be broken or knocked over and the oil or kerosene spilled resulting in a disastrous fire. The light from this type of lantern is very steady, so that the use of a small electrical lamp substitute will not detract from the natural effect of the lamp. It is a simple matter to hide batteries somewhere within the lantern and wire the necessary switch and bulb to complete the circuit. If the lantern is to be

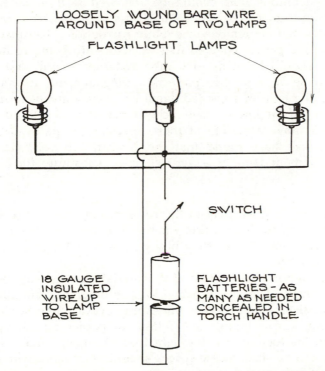

LOOSELY WOUND BARE WIRE
AROUND BASE OF TWO LAMPS

FLASHLIGHT LAMPS

SWITCH

18 GAUGE
INSULATED
WIRE UP
TO LAMP
BASE

FLASHLIGHT
BATTERIES - AS
MANY AS NEEDED
CONCEALED IN
TORCH HANDLE

WIRING DIAGRAM FOR FLICKERING TORCH

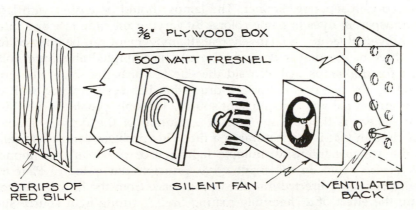

3/8" PLYWOOD BOX

500 WATT FRESNEL

STRIPS OF
RED SILK

SILENT FAN

VENTILATED
BACK

DANCING FIRELIGHT SPECIAL

Plate 80   Flickering Torch and Dancing Firelight Specials wall hung, then a 120 volt lamp can be placed in the lantern and connected to a dimmer.

Whether fire codes permit their use or not, candles are very frequently used onstage. While open flames should never be used, there are a number of safety considerations that should be followed if it is determined that candles are going to be employed. Candles should be placed in candleholders and set on tables that are removed from any surrounding flammable materials such as drapes and canvas-covered flats. If actors are going to hold candles, their costumes should be made of flame-resistant material, and the candles should have some type of drip protection to guard the actor's hands.

The flickering light of a gas-fed flame was very difficult to recreate until the development of the low-wattage flicker lamp. A well-stocked home lighting store should have a variety of these specialty lamps available for purchase. The authors have found that the 3 watt, 120 volt, clear-envelope, flame-shaped filament lamp is a very effective substitute for a gas lamp.

Fire Effects

Fire effects can add a great deal to the realism and mood of a scene. Many methods can be used to create a fire, whether it is the low smoldering glow of a peat fire in a hearth, a cheerfully blazing fire in a fireplace, or the dying embers of a campfire.

Of major importance is that the material that is supposedly being burned look realistic. The use of actual logs or other fuel should be considered. If for stylistic or other reasons this is impractical, then facsimiles can be constructed using carpet tubing and Celastic or papier-mâché. Space should be left between the logs so that the light from the lamps that will be placed under the logs can be seen. These spaces should be covered with color media gleaned from the lighting cabinet.

Three or more low-wattage lamps can be placed under the campfire and each wired to a separate dimmer. The lamps should be coated with lacquer-based transparent dyes in flame colors. By varying the fade rate and intensity of the individual lamps, a relatively realistic movement can be effected for the specific type of fire that is desired. The use of crumpled aluminum foil as a reflector for the lamps will also aid the effect. Much the same effect can be achieved by the use of a motorized drum that has been covered with crumpled aluminum foil and a single light source. The only problem with this type of arrangement is that the rhythmical revolution of the drum will set up a cyclical rhythm that is not natural in a fire. This problem can be alleviated by using the variable intensity multiple light source previously mentioned.

A device based on the shadow box principle illustrated in Plate 80 can be constructed and directed into the acting space from the hearth area to help simulate the effect of a cheerfully roaring fire. A strong light source such as an appropriately colored 500 watt fresnel spotlight is placed in back of a series of cut strips of red silk cloth. A small silent fan is directed at the strips, and when the light is turned on, the effect created is a very interesting dancing light that is quite similar to the irregular light emitted from a fire.

Rain and Snow

There are few effects that are more difficult to recreate in a realistic manner than those of rain and snow. But if they are done properly, the results are well worth the effort.

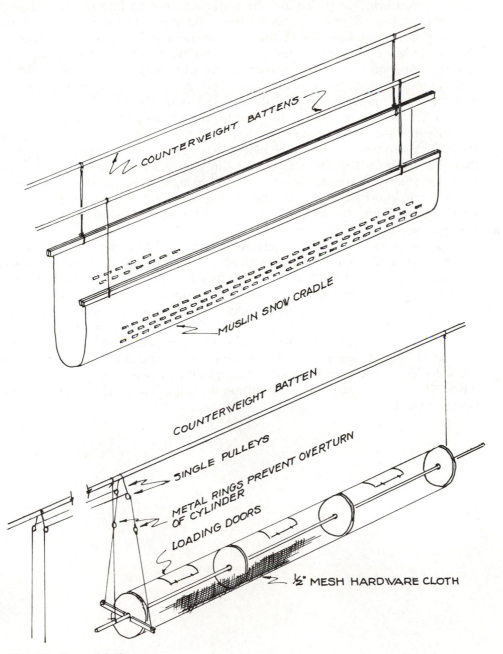

Plate 81 Snow Machines

Rain can be accomplished by feeding polyvinyl chloride (PVC) plastic pipe with hoses from a backstage faucet. The PVC pipe should have a series of $1/16''$ or smaller holes drilled on $1''$ centers to let the water out. When rigging the pipe it is advisable to place the holes so that they are pointing up rather than down. This will allow the water to shoot up into the air, fall back onto the pipe, and drip irregularly from the pipe. The irregularity of the falling water created in this manner will make a much more realistic effect than if the holes are pointed straight down so the water falls in evenly spaced streams. An equally important part of the rain effect is the sound that it makes when striking the ground. The usual method of catching the water is to have it fall into a trough and then be piped to a drain. If the effect is to play for any length of time, as in a production of *Rain*, the water can become an obtrusive sound that tends to overpower the actor's lines. To muffle the rain effect, window screen can be placed at an angle in the catching trough so that the water strikes the screen and the drops are broken into a smaller spray that flows down the screen into the trough. It is extremely important that the rain effect be back lit by the lighting designer. Unless there is quite a bit of light striking the dripping water from the upstage side of the effect, it will not be seen.

Snow effects are easier to create than rain. There have been few improvements on the traditional snow machine or snow cradle. Two versions of this device are shown in Plate 81. The material that is placed in the hopper of the snow machine will have a great deal to do with the final effect of the device. Probably the most realistic snow substitutes are cut tissue paper and shredded styrofoam. Both materials are very light and float in the lazy manner of real snow. The styrofoam has the added advantage that it sweeps up more easily than tissue paper. To heighten the realistic effect of the snow it is a good idea to use two rows of snow machines placed one upstage of the other. This will increase the apparent depth of the "howling blizzard" that is being created.

11

Scene Painting

ORGANIZATION OF THE PAINT CREW

Organizing the paint crew is done in essentially the same manner for an educational theatre or a community theatre. Most often the designer, who is responsible for painting the scenery, must work with inexperienced helpers. No small part of his work is the effort and time spent in teaching fundamentals to his crew members. Usually this time is well spent since some of his helpers, who show a marked aptitude for the job, will progress to a point where they are capable of executing increasingly difficult assignments.

In educational and community theatre organizations the designer heads the crew. In this capacity he either mixes all scene paint himself or closely supervises this critical step. He determines the order of painting procedure and instructs his crew in the various techniques required in the application of paint. If the paint job is very complicated or if the painting technique necessary is especially exacting, the designer may have to do much of the painting himself. If the number of experienced painters at his disposal will permit it, the work of scene painting can be divided as follows:

1. Designer or paint boss. He is responsible for supervising all phases of painting.
2. Layout men. These men (or women) work closely with the designer; their principal duty is assembling and assigning to the crew those areas designated by the designer to receive a given color or to be painted by a particular technique.
3. Fillers. The majority of the crew will serve as fillers whose duty is to do the priming, groundwork, and all large area covering.
4. Detail men. This is the most exacting work and it demands the most skill on the part of the painters.
5. Clean-up crews. Each member of the crew is responsible for clean-

217

ing his own brushes and paint containers. (The sooner this fact can be established, the happier all concerned will be!)

COLOR ELEVATIONS

If the designer is personally supervising the work of the paint crew there is little need for a paint guide other than that provided by the original water color sketch. Should the work of supervision and mixing of paint be turned over to a paint boss, it is advisable to supplement the information contained on the sketch with color elevations. These are large-scaled drawings, made on illustration board, which show the parts of a setting scheduled to receive a particular color applied in a particular manner. They are essentially nothing but samples of colors and painting techniques which have been made large enough for easy reading. Because of their similarity to scene paint, opaque water colors are frequently used in place of transparent pigments. Notes regarding the proportion of pigment used to obtain a particular hue should accompany these elevations.

GRAPHED ELEVATIONS

When the subject of a design is irregular in form, such as a drop for a woodland scene or a whimsical stylized street scene, the design is difficult to transfer from a scaled drawing to full-scale scenery by means of dimensions alone. This transfer can be made accurately by employment of graphed elevations. Since elevations are already drawn to scale, probably $1/2''$ or $3/4'' = 1'-0''$, it is an easy matter to divide the elevation into 2' squares (see Plate 82). Draw in the horizontal and vertical lines with a colored pencil and number the spaces consecutively for ready identification. After the drop or cutout has been built, it is also marked off, by a chalk line, into 2' squares; these squares, of course, correspond to those on the elevation. The outline of the design can now be transferred by noting the points of contact between the contour lines of the design and the graph lines on the elevations, finding the corresponding points on the scenery, and drawing in freehand the resulting enlargement of the design. It is gratifying and surprising to see how accurately and rapidly a design can be transferred by this method.

A slide and a projector can be used to transfer a design to scenery, but conditions must be almost perfect if the transfer is to be successful. The design must first be made into a slide which will produce a sharp, clear image. The lens of the projector must have the proper components to throw an image large enough to cover the desired area of scenery. Disadvantages of this technique are that no light other than that provided by the projector can be used without obliterating the image and that the designer must stand in her own shadow as she traces the outline of the design onto the scenery.

PAINT SHOP LAYOUT

It is not necessary to have an elaborately laid out scene shop or to make a large investment in painting equipment in order to do a good job of scene

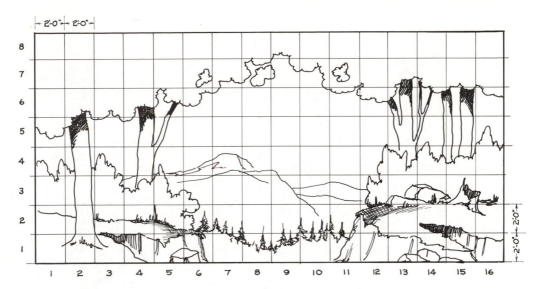

Plate 82 Graphed Elevation

painting. This statement has been amply proved by the work done in many colleges and community theatres where good shop facilities are lacking. Armed with nothing but a sound knowledge of scene painting, a few good brushes, some scene paint, and room enough to stand at least part of a set upright, these nonprofessional scene painters have turned out some remarkably well-executed settings. However, there is no denying that the same quality of work could have been done with greater speed and greater ease had the crew been working under better shop conditions.

The ideal paint shop for an educational or community theatre should be located at one end of the scene shop. Such an arrangement reduces the handling of scenery necessary to transport it from one shop to another. It also permits one person to supervise both painting and construction, a practice followed frequently in such theatres. The space allotted to painters within a scene shop should not be crowded or tucked back into a corner with a low ceiling. Ideally, there should be sufficient space along one wall of the shop to stand the walls of a full setting against it, placed end to end. There should be adequate floor space for all the three-dimensional free-standing units of a setting. There must be space reserved for mixing tables, sinks, paint bins, and paint containers. Adjacent to the painting area, there should be two small scene docks to be used for storing scenery that is waiting to be painted and that which is already finished.

BASIC EQUIPMENT

Counterbalanced Paint Frame

A device that completely eliminates any hazard caused by painting from ladders and one that is the greatest space saver in a paint shop is the counterbalanced paint frame (see Plate 83). It is a scaffolding made of 1¼″ ×

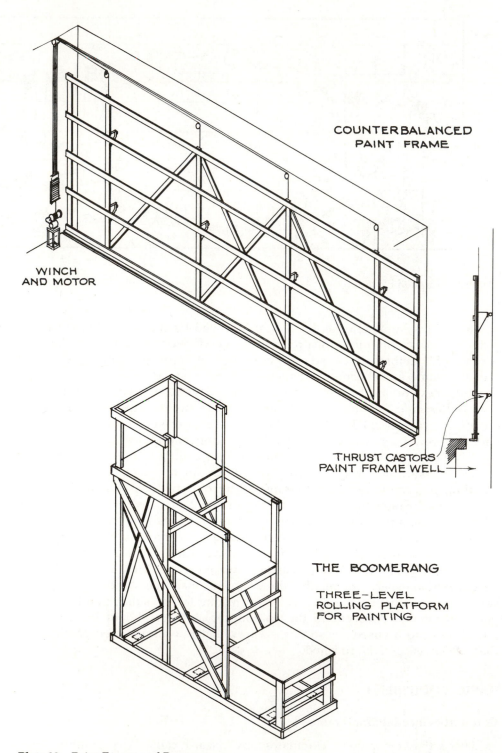

COUNTERBALANCED
PAINT FRAME

WINCH
AND MOTOR

THRUST CASTORS
PAINT FRAME WELL

THE BOOMERANG

THREE-LEVEL
ROLLING PLATFORM
FOR PAINTING

Plate 83 Paint Frame and Boomerang

6" white pine, about 16' to 18' high, and, ideally, long enough to accommodate the side walls and back wall of a setting. The scenery rests upon a projecting ledge at the bottom of the frame and is nailed to the vertical frame. The frame and its load of scenery is lowered through an 18" slot in the floor until the painters can reach the top of the flats while standing on the shop floor. The frame is supported by a series of ¼" wire ropes that run through loft blocks to a head block and are tied off to a counterweight arbor. The weight of the frame is permanently counterbalanced by weights placed in the arbor. The frame, and the additional weight of the scenery attached to it, is raised or lowered by a ⅜" steel cable attached to the bottom of the arbor and running to the drum of a motor-driven winch that is anchored to the shop floor. Automatic stop switches halt the movement of the frame at predetermined heights. Castors mounted on iron brackets are fastened to the back of the frame and roll against the wall to prevent the frame from swinging when painters are at work. If there are any windows in the wall against which the frame is installed, they should be covered by removable plugs or shutters to keep light from shining into the faces of the working crew members.

In both educational and community theatres the training of students and volunteer workers in all phases of theatre work is a primary goal. It is the authors' contention that the training given in scene painting can best be done by utilizing a vertical paint frame (Plate 83). Some of the advantages of such a paint frame are as follows:

1. It is easier for a beginner to learn to paint by using a conventional sized brush rather than one with a 4'-long handle extension.
2. Very little floor space is required for vertical painting. Both painting and construction work can be carried out simultaneously within the same general area.
3. It is much easier to keep the finished work clean and free of dust and footprints if it is mounted on a paint frame.
4. As the scenery is being painted there is no risk of its being damaged by the painters walking upon it. This occurs with frequency in horizontal painting.
5. Painted scenery dries faster on a paint frame because the air is free to circulate on both sides of the scenery.
6. Constant kneeling, stooping, or working on the hands and knees (as in stenciling) is greatly reduced when using a vertical paint frame.
7. It is much easier to check work in progress on a vertical frame by backing away from it and looking at it from a normal viewing position; that is, the line of sight is at a right angle to the plane of drawing. This checking can be done in horizontal painting only by using an overhead catwalk or viewing position.

Horizontal Painting

There are certain methods of scene painting that can best be done when the scenery is laid horizontally on the floor. (See Plate 84.) If the scenery is framed, painting it on the floor presents no special problem. One must of course be careful not to step too close to the framing members while painting. Since the painter is walking on the material inside the frame, the weight of his body can cause the covering material to be badly stretched or even torn.

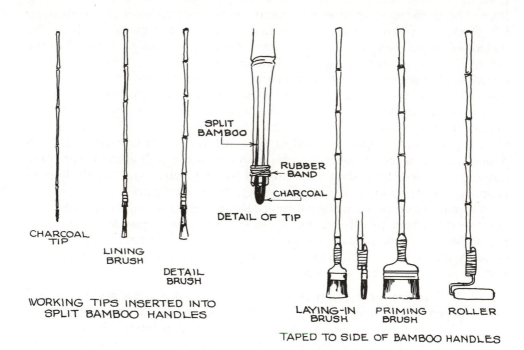

CHARCOAL
TIP

LINING
BRUSH

DETAIL
BRUSH

SPLIT
BAMBOO

RUBBER
BAND

CHARCOAL

DETAIL OF TIP

WORKING TIPS INSERTED INTO
SPLIT BAMBOO HANDLES

LAYING-IN
BRUSH

PRIMING
BRUSH

ROLLER

TAPED TO SIDE OF BAMBOO HANDLES

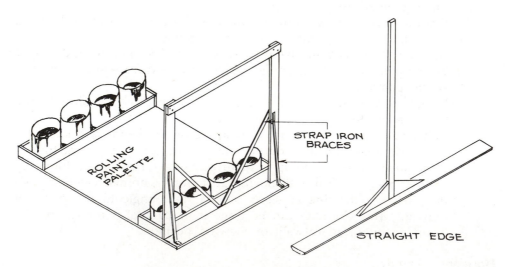

ROLLING
PAINT
PALETTE

STRAP IRON
BRACES

STRAIGHT EDGE

Plate 84   Brushes and Tools Used in Horizontal Painting

However, unframed scenery such as drops, gauzes, or borders must be carefully stapled on all sides to something stationary in order to prevent uneven shrinkage which occurs after the paint is applied. For this reason some scene shops are built with a wooden floor so that unframed scenery can be stapled directly to the flooring. Clearing a space in the construction area large enough to permit horizontal painting can be expedited by mounting castors on all the heavy power equipment and storage racks so that they may be rolled out of the way.

Shops with cement floors have been made suitable for horizontal painting by laying down a temporary wooden floor; such a floor can be formed from stock platforms of various sizes but of uniform heights. Other shops use some variant of the collapsible, adjustable, horizontal paint frame illustrated in Plate 168 (page 405).

There is no argument about the need for horizontal floor space in a scene shop; there are some operations that simply cannot be done except when the scenery is lying flat on the floor. An example would be applying the reinforcing netting to the back of a cutout drop. It is also true that while they can be done vertically, some painting techniques such as rolling, starching, wet blending, and stenciling are accomplished with more freedom and ease when done horizontally.

Stationary Wall Frame

For paint shops not equipped with a movable counterbalanced frame, a stationary frame will serve as a good substitute. A series of 2″ × 2″ horizontal wooden battens, placed 3′-6″ to 4′-0″ apart, are attached to an unobstructed wall area. The scenery is nailed to these battens in much the same manner as it is to the movable paint frame, but painting the upper parts of the set must be done from a boomerang or from ladders.

Boomerang

The boomerang is a two- or three-level rolling platform from which two or more workmen can paint at one time (see Plate 83). The upper working level is high enough so that a painter can easily reach the top of standard-height stock scenery. The remaining levels are spaced so as to permit the painters to overlap their work and to provide each with enough floor space to store his painting equipment and still move about safely.

Although the boomerang is a large piece of equipment and takes up valuable shop space, it provides a much faster and safer method of painting than working from ladders. Furthermore, its usefulness is not limited to painting alone. There is one at the University of Iowa that has been used to good advantage as a portable rigging platform, a multilevel light tower, and an impromptu offstage stairway.

Ladders

No matter how well equipped the paint shop may be, some painting will have to be done from ladders. The authors' experience has convinced them that the wide-based A-ladder is safest and most stable. Since both sides of this ladder are identical, two painters may use it at one time. Two A-ladders may be set at some distance apart and used with an extension plank for wide area painting. It is possible, though maybe not advisable, for a painter to lock one leg in back of the round rungs of an A-ladder in such a way as to free both his hands for painting. This cannot be done with the wide treads found on most step ladders. A gallon fruit or vegetable tin converted into a paint container can, by the addition of a hook made from heavy gauge wire, be attached to the rung of an A-ladder. The paint bucket rests solidly on one rung with the hook engaging the rung immediately above.

Mixing Tables and Sink

Indispensable parts of the paint shop's equipment are the mixing tables, hot and cold running water, and a sink. If possible, these should be located under a window to obtain the maximum amount of daylight for the critical job of mixing paint. The sink should be deep and large enough to permit a 3-gallon bucket to be placed beneath the faucet without tipping. Both hot and cold water should be vented through a pivoting mixing faucet. Since waste paint is disposed of by diluting it with hot water and allowing it to drain away, the sink trap should be large and accessible for cleaning. The mixing tables should be covered with copper or aluminum sheeting to protect their wooden tops. They should be placed on either side of the sink. Spilled paint and water will drain to the sink if the tops of the mixing tables slant toward it slightly. Beneath the table tops shelves should be built for the storage of buckets and cans used as paint containers.

Paint Bins

The kind of paint bin used for the storage of dry pigments depends to some extent on the space available for the purpose. The bins should be large enough to hold 25 or 30 pounds of pigment, and each bin should have a fitted top to keep out shop dust. If wall space is available near the mixing table area, permanent tilt-top bins can be constructed. These bins do not have fitted tops, but they fit smoothly into a rack and are dust free when closed. Each bin is hinged at the bottom so that it can be opened by pulling the top outward; the rack has a simple lock that prevents the bin from tipping all the way out and closes it automatically after use. The angle of the bottom of an open bin makes it easy to scoop up the last vestiges of paint. An alternate type of paint storage container can be made at less cost by constructing a rack that will hold at an angle several 20-gallon garbage cans (17" in diameter, 24" high) with fitted tops.

When wall space is not available for a rack in ￩ fixed position, the same rack can be built on a castored supporting frame and rolled out of the way when not in use (see Plate 85). Well-ventilated cupboards with doors that can be locked should be constructed above the paint bins; paint brushes can be hung to dry in the cupboards. Open shelves on both sides of the cupboards can be used for storage of dyes, bronzing powders, spray paint, and other small supplies.

Brushes

The most important single piece of equipment in the paint shop is a good paint brush. It is true that almost any old brush can be used to smear paint,

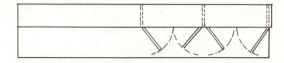

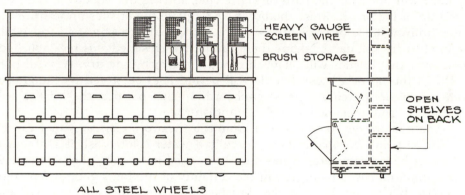

HEAVY GAUGE
SCREEN WIRE

BRUSH STORAGE

OPEN
SHELVES
ON BACK

ALL STEEL WHEELS

ROLLING PAINT BIN

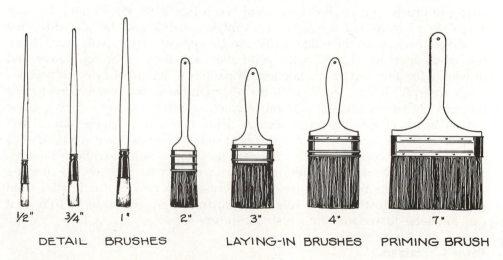

½"   ¾"   1"   2"   3"   4"   7"

DETAIL   BRUSHES   LAYING-IN BRUSHES   PRIMING BRUSH

Plate 85   Rolling Paint Bin and Brushes

but it is also true that about the same effect can be obtained with a mop or with rags tied around the end of a stick. However, good scene painting demands good brushes. The best scenic paint brushes, designed especially for use with water-soluble paint, are 100 percent bristle. Bristles are long and have a marked degree of spine or springiness. Such brushes are not handled by most local paint stores but must be bought direct from scenic supply houses. These brushes are expensive, but if given the care they deserve, they will outlast cheaper brushes many times.

Three cardinal rules to follow in keeping a scenic paint brush in good working condition are: clean thoroughly in water after each use, store properly, and avoid the use of oil paint. Water-soluble paint dries rapidly. Therefore, a brush should be cleaned immediately after it has been used or some pigment will dry near the base of the ferrule, forcing the bristles to flare out at the tip of the brush. Rinse the brush and agitate the bristles under running water until no trace of color can be seen. Shake out excess water, and while the bristles are still damp, shape them until a flat chisel edge is reestablished. Remember that bristles will retain the shape in which they dry. A small hole drilled in the tip of a brush handle will permit it to be stored by hanging it from a hook in a well-ventilated cupboard. In this position the bristles will dry rapidly and their shape will be undisturbed.

There is always some demand around a theatre for brushes that can be used in oil paint. No matter how carefully a water color brush is cleaned, it will never be the same after it has once been used in lacquer, shellac, enamel, or any other oil-based paint. Avoid the certainty of ruining a good water color brush by having on hand a few brushes that are especially marked and reserved for use in oil paint.

Three types of brushes are used in scenic work—the priming brush, the laying-in brush, and the lining or detail brush (see Plate 85). Priming brushes are 6″ to 8″ wide and are used for applying sizing and for all wide area coverage. Because of their size, paint can be applied very rapidly with them, but when they are charged with paint they are likely to be too heavy and unwieldy for anyone but an experienced painter to handle. Laying-in brushes range in width from 3″ to 5″, with the 4″ brush being the preference of most painters. By far the greatest amount of painting done in a scene shop is done with a brush of this type and size. A detail brush has a long handle and ranges in width from ¼″ to 3″. The best detail brushes have white bristles held in place by copper ferrules. They are used for painting architectural trim, all small detail work, and lettering. Great care must be exercised in cleaning and reshaping the bristles of these small brushes to prevent the bristles from gathering into clusters. Once this has occurred, there seems to be little that can be done to reclaim the brush for future use.

Paint Containers

It will sometimes seem that the greatest boon possible to a designer or a paint boss is having on hand enough vessels in which she can mix paints so that she does not have to clean from a bucket a paint that she may need again. There are a few simple requisites that such vessels must meet to be suitable for scenic work. Their bases should be wide enough so that the vessels will not tip over easily. The vessel should not have an overhanging inside rim, since the rim makes cleaning the vessel difficult. The mouth of the container should be wide enough to receive the largest of the laying-in brushes.

Large quantities of paint are best mixed in 2½- or 3-gallon buckets. One 3-gallon bucket, filled with paint, is usually enough to cover an average-sized interior with a single coat of paint. Large quantities of paint can be mixed in two or more buckets, but the paint must be thoroughly intermixed by pouring it from one bucket to another until the paint in all buckets is identical in hue. This process is called "boxing."

Most of the containers used for smaller quantities of paint can be obtained at little or no cost. Many restaurants receive their "fresh" fruits and vegetables in 1-gallon tin cans which make ideal paint containers. Providing each crew member with his own supply of paint in a gallon can will avoid the congestion, spilled paint, and delay that is likely to occur if all crew members are attempting to paint from a single large bucket. Fitted with a wire hook, the 1-gallon container is also just the right size to be used for ladder work. Wide-mouth coffee cans are useful for smaller measures of paint. Still smaller amounts of a variety of paints can be distributed in the different compartments of a muffin tin. Some scene painters fill the compartments of a muffin tin with different colored dry pigments and use it in much the same fashion as they would a box of dry pan colors—a brush is dipped in sizing water, touched to the dry pigment, and then mixed to painting consistency by working it on a palette made from a scrap of Upson board. A can of clear water is also needed to wash the brush between charges of paint.

Rolling Paint Palette

A great improvement over the scrap of Upson board and the muffin tin is the rolling paint palette (see Plate 86). It is used for the same purpose, but has the following advantages: it has a larger mixing surface, it carries a greater variety of colors, it is stable, it provides a worktable of convenient height, and it can be easily moved. It is a mixing table, mounted on swivel castors, that can be rolled to any position in the shop or on stage where detail or touch-up painting is to be done. The top, covered with copper or aluminum sheeting, is used as a mixing palette for small quantities of paint. At the back and along its length is a series of small covered compartments, each capable of holding about a quarter of a pound of dry scene paint. Beneath the top are two or three drawers for the temporary storage of brushes and other painting equipment. An open shelf beneath the drawers can carry large paint containers. The size of the table may vary, but one that stands 2'-6" from the floor, with a top measuring 4' × 2', will be adequate for most purposes and will not take up much floor space.

Straight Edge

The straight edge is to the scene painter what a T square it to a draftsman. All straight line work used in painting architectural trim is done with the aid of a straight edge. It may be purchased from a theatrical supply house or it can be made in the shop. The straight edge should be 6' long, about 2½" wide, and from ½" to ⅝" thick. A block of wood or a screen-door handle attached to the center makes a straight edge much easier to control. The

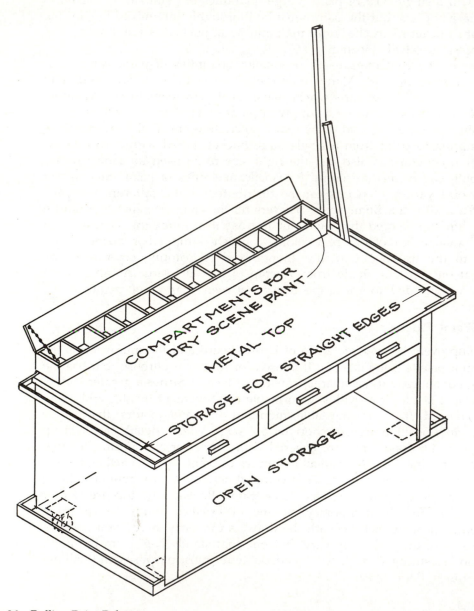

Plate 86 Rolling Paint Palette

underside of its length should be beveled to stop paint from running beneath it and being smeared on the face of the scenery. Be sure to sand the beveled edge to remove any rough spots or splinters that might snag one of the bristles of a lining brush, thus causing a blot or a variation in the width of a line. When the 6' straight edge is too long to be used, for example, when working in tight corners, shorter straight edges, 2' or 3' long, can be used. The secret of painting a perfectly straight line that does not vary in width is in holding the brush at a right angle to the canvas and in taking full advantage of the spine of the bristles by allowing only their tips to come in contact with the canvas as the brush is guided along the length of the straight edge.

Chalk Line

Long, perfectly straight lines can be marked off rapidly by the use of a chalk line. The chalk line is a twisted cotton line about 1/8" in diameter, charged with chalk, charcoal, or dry scene paint. The coloring agent is held in a small square of muslin and rubbed into the line. The line is placed against the scenery and stretched between two nails or pulled taut by two crew members. The center of the line is then pulled away from the scenery and allowed to snap back against it. This leaves a clear, sharp line imprint. Do not use the blue chalk normally used by carpenters for chalk lines, because it is difficult to paint over.

A variation of the chalk line, the bow snap line, is handy for use on small units of scenery or in confined spaces. A line is stretched between the ends of a resilient piece of wood, between 5' and 6' in length, forcing the wood to bow slightly. The line is charged with dry scene paint, placed against the scenery, and snapped.

Compass

A wooden compass with arms at least 2' in length is needed for drawing arcs and circles, for transferring measurements, and for division. The compass can be built from two 2' lengths of 1" × 2" wood, tapered as indicated in Plate 87. The two arms are bolted at the top with a single 1/4" carriage bolt, washer, and wing nut. In the tip of the marking arm drill a hole just large enough to receive a piece of chalk or charcoal. Make a saw kerf through the end of the arm to bisect the hole and to extend the full depth of the hole. A rubberband wrapped several times around the tip will exert enough pressure to hold the chalk in place. The pivot arm can be fitted with a nail or with a pointed pencil eraser, attached in the same manner as the chalk.

Larger circles and arcs can be drawn with a piece of wood, 3/4" wide by 1/4" thick, used in much the same fashion as a bar compass. A nail is driven through the 3/4" face of the slat at the desired radial distance from the pivot point. The slat is then rotated to mark the desired arc. A length of chalk line is sometimes used for the same purpose, but the tendency of the line to stretch makes it less accurate than the impromptu bar compass.

Charcoal and Chalk

Both charcoal and chalk are indispensable for blocking out designs, marking off areas to be painted, and indicating measurements. They are superior to

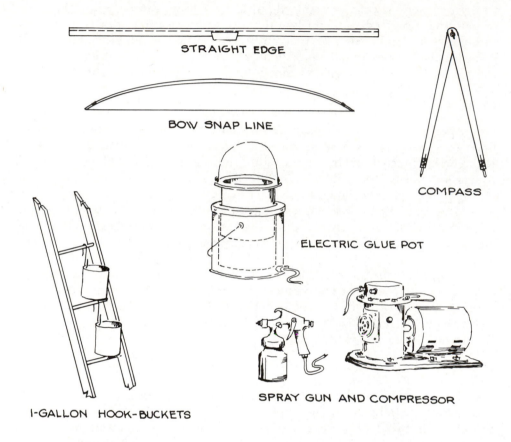

STRAIGHT EDGE

BOW SNAP LINE

COMPASS

ELECTRIC GLUE POT

I-GALLON HOOK-BUCKETS

SPRAY GUN AND COMPRESSOR

Plate 87   Miscellaneous Painting Tools

other marking media because they can be readily seen when used on painted surfaces and can easily be brushed off or overpainted.

Spray Guns

It is possible to get along in the paint shop without a spray gun and motor driven compressor, but they should be placed high on any list of desirable shop equipment. A motor driven compressor supplies the constant air pressure needed to make a spray gun operate. Certain types of painting techniques can be done much better with a spray gun and in a fraction of the time required to do them by brush painting.

An electrically driven, constant-pressure spray gun, with an assortment of different nozzles to control the shape of the spray, soon pays for its initial cost by the saving in work hours. It should be stressed that even the highest priced spray gun on the market will not give satisfactory results unless it is properly cleaned after each use. The paint container must be removed, thoroughly cleaned, partly filled with hot water, and reattached to the gun; the hot water is then sprayed through the gun to clean the inside of the paint duct, needle valve, and nozzle. The gun is then dismantled, wiped dry, and all working parts are lightly oiled to prevent pitting and rusting.

Inexpensive, hand-pumped spray guns have only limited use. They are hard to keep in working order, and it is very difficult to control the spray. Most of the work accomplished with them is, therefore, spotty.

Hand Powered Compressor Spray

Although originally designed for home garden work, the hand powered compressor spray, such as the Hudson Spray Gun, has been adapted for special work in scene painting. It is used for applying glazes, aniline dyes, starch, and liquid flameproofing to scenery. It is also quite satisfactory for doing various types of spatter work.

The Hudson Spray Compressor is available in 2-, 3-, or 4-gallon sizes. For most jobs the larger tank is preferred because it will hold a full 3½ gallons of liquid. The remaining space in the tank is required for air pressure. In this spray gun there is a built-in hand pump that must be given between 25 and 30 strokes to reach a good working pressure. Each tank is fitted with a short length of rubber or plastic hose that has a wandlike brass tube with an adjustable nozzle at the end. The nozzle is capable of producing sprays that vary from a fine mist to a solid stream. All liquids placed in the tank should be strained through a fine mesh screen, or better yet, through a screen formed from wet cheese cloth. This straining will catch all particles of undissolved paint or binder large enough to clog the nozzle.

Since most water-soluble scene paints dry rapidly, it is imperative that a spray gun be cleaned shortly after it has been used. Otherwise the paint dries in the tank, the hose, or the nozzle and makes the gun inoperative. The cleaning procedure is simple. Remove the pump and rinse out the tank with clear warm water. Refill the tank about one-quarter full with warm water to which has been added a little liquid detergent. Replace the pump and build up enough pressure to force the warm water through the nozzle. Continue to spray until all traces of paint have been removed. Remove the pump and store the tank bottom up so that it can drain.

The necessity of hand pumping a spray gun has been eliminated in some scene shops by inserting a tire valve fitting into the top of the tank. Air pressure is supplied from the large compressor used for other air tools. With the tank filled with 30 or 40 pounds of pressure, the air hose is removed allowing the painter to move about with the spray without the hindrance of a trailing hose. Judging the air pressure in a tank is easily done with a tire gauge.

Electric Glue Pot

Glue is prepared for mixing with scene paint by heating it in a double boiler. This may be done by placing glue and a little water in a bucket and inserting this into a second bucket partly filled with water which is then placed on a gas heater or an electric plate. Half of a brick placed between the bottoms of the two buckets will prevent their jamming together. The only difficulty with this method is the excellent chance that the water in the double boiler will boil away allowing the glue to burn. There aren't adequate words in the English language to describe how offensive the odor of burning glue can be. Speaking as an old and experienced glue-burner, one of the authors highly recommends the use of an electric glue pot. It is impossible to burn glue in an electric glue pot. Both of its vessels are made of copper, the heating elements are thermostatically controlled, and the glue is dissolved by heated air rather than by boiling water.

Scene Paint

Scene paint is sold in two forms, dry and wet. The dry pigments are in powdered form and will keep indefinitely without deterioration provided they are kept absolutely dry. The dry pigments are also the less expensive of the two. Wet paint is prepared in the form of a paste or pulp and is sold in gallon cans. Once a can has been opened, the paint may dry out and harden to such a degree that it cannot be used. However, some of the more unusual colors and the more saturated hues can be had only in pulp colors.

These pigments must be obtained through regular scenic supply houses; they should not be confused with packaged dry water colors sold at local paint stores. The two were developed for entirely different purposes. Scene paint is available in a much greater range of color, the hues are more saturated, and they were developed for the scenic artist who must paint over a variety of surfaces and with highly developed techniques of application. Household paints were developed for application over plaster walls or wood, the colors are more subdued, and they are usually packaged in small quantities. They are also more expensive than scene paint.

There are a number of excellent reasons why water-soluble paint is preferred to oil-based paint for scenic purposes.

1. It is less expensive.
2. It is noninflammable.
3. It dries much faster.
4. It is easier to mix.
5. It is much lighter in weight.
6. It is more easily cleaned from brushes and clothes.
7. It does not have a glossy finish when dry.
8. It may be washed from scenery to permit repainting.

BASIC COLORS

Name	Type	Characteristics
Light chrome yellow	Dry	Hue approximating primary yellow
Raw Italian sienna	Dry	Rich tan; used extensively mixed with other colors
French orange mineral	Dry	Saturated orange; heavy pigment requiring regular stirring
Turkey red lake	Dry	Hue approximating primary red; must be cut with alcohol before mixing with water
Venetian red	Dry	Exceptionally useful brick red; mixes well with chrome green to produce a good gray
Burnt sienna	Dry	Rich reddish brown
Raw turkey umber	Dry	Earth-colored brown
Burnt turkey umber	Dry	Rich, warm brown
Italian blue	Dry	Very saturated light blue-green; must be cut with alcohol before mixing with water; excellent for sky effects
Dark chrome green	Dry	Excellent dark green
French ultramarine blue	Dry	Intense color approximating primary blue
Cobalt blue	Dry	Extremely useful light blue
Hercules black	Dry	Jet black with excellent covering qualities
Danish whiting	Dry	White pigment; large quantities used in raising the brilliance of any hue

The catalogue of the Gothic Color Company of New York City offers a choice of colors from 46 different hues. This list includes both dry and wet colors. There is no need to keep in stock all, or even a majority, of the colors offered. A carefully selected list of basic colors will allow the scenic artist to meet the needs of all but the most elaborate paint jobs. Special colors should be ordered as needed. A basic list of preferred colors is given in the accompanying table.

The basic colors will, of course, be augmented by each designer's personal preference in colors and by the needs of a particular paint job. A selection of additional hues is also listed in table form.

ADDITIONAL HUES

Name	Type	Characteristics
Yellow		
Primrose yellow	Dry	Strong brilliant yellow
Milori yellow light	Dry	Similar to primrose yellow, but slightly darker
Milori yellow medium	Dry	Strong, saturated yellow
Hoyt's yellow lake	Wet	Saturated yellow, slightly transparent

ADDITIONAL HUES   *(Cont.)*

Name	Type	Characteristics
Orange		
Milori yellow orange	Dry	Saturated yellow-orange
Orange lake	Wet	Very rich, saturated orange
Tan or Buff		
French yellow ochre	Dry	Similar to raw sienna but more yellow and lighter
English Dutch pink	Dry	Rich, warm tan
Green		
Hanover green	Dry	Very light yellow-green
Emerald green	Dry	Saturated yellow-green with less yellow than Hanover green
Chrome green light	Dry	Good, inexpensive yellow-green
Medium chrome green	Dry	Very useful medium green
Malachite green	Wet	Saturated, very dark blue-green
Saphite green	Wet	Excellent foliage green
Royal green lake	Wet	Very strong, dark blue-green
Blue		
American ultramarine blue	Dry	Not as strong as French ultramarine blue; good primary blue
Celestial blue	Dry	Good, inexpensive, very dark blue
Prussian blue	Dry	Almost blue-black; very strong; must be cut with alcohol before mixing with water
Purple		
Violet lake	Wet	Slightly bluish purple; very powerful
Royal purple	Dry	Excellent purple with a slight red cast
Purple lake	Dry	Similar to violet lake but warmer in tone
Red		
English vermilion	Dry	Very saturated red-orange
Bulletin red	Dry	Similar to English vermilion but not as saturated
Solferino lake	Wet	Excellent magenta color, a hue difficult to mix
Magenta lake	Wet	Similar to Solferino lake but with less blue
Turkey lake	Wet	Rich, blood red
Light maroon	Wet	Yellowish red of low brilliance
Dark maroon	Wet	Very deep brick red

ADDITIONAL HUES *(Cont.)*

Name	Type	Characteristics
White		
Permanent white	Dry	Pure white with better covering qualities than Danish whiting
Black		
Ivory black	Dry	Slightly transparent but an intense black
Black lake	Wet	Jet black with good covering qualities

MIXING SCENE PAINT

Contrary to the belief of many students, mixing scene paint is not a mysterious rite nor a complex procedure if a few fundamental principles are understood and followed. Perhaps the most confusing feature is the fact that scene paint changes color and drops in brilliance when water is added to the dry pigment. This need not be disturbing when it is realized that the paint will resume its original tone after it has dried. (A few test samples will prove this statement.) For this reason all scene paint should be mixed and tested for accuracy of tone while the pigments are dry. It is advisable to mix all the hues to be used on a set at the same time. This provides an opportunity to compare the hues for harmony and degree of contrast and to check them against the colors indicated on the color guide or the sketch. In mixing pulp or wet colors there is no alternative to mixing the pigments wet and testing the dry samples for accuracy of tone. A small dab of scene paint can be placed on a scrap of muslin or Upson board and placed in the sun or held over a radiator where it will dry in a few minutes.

A second important fact that must be kept in mind is the painting consistency of the pigment. If it is too thin, it will not cover; if it is too thick, it is wasteful, difficult to apply, and has a tendency to flake off. No set rule can be given to govern how much water should be added to the pigment; the amount will vary somewhat according to the technique by which it is to be applied. For most purposes, however, it will be satisfactory if it has the consistency of thin cream or is similar to the viscosity of 20 grade oil.

Practically all scene paints are strikingly intense in color and are therefore seldom used in their saturated form. Usually, they are mixed with other pigments to alter their hue, to neutralize them, or to raise or lower their brilliance. Tints, obtained by adding whiting to the desired hue, are used with great frequency. Since whiting forms the base for so many hues used in scene painting, more of it is used than all the other pigments combined. It is advisable to keep this in mind when ordering a season's supply of paint.

Tints can also be made by mixing dry colors with casein paint. There are two major advantages to this combination of pigments; a tint mixed with casein has greater opacity and covering qualities than a tint mixed with whiting. When repainting an array of old flats of many different colors, one application of a casein mixture will suffice to produce an even coating over all flats. Two or more applications of a whiting mixed tint would be required to give the same effect. A second advantage of using casein is that it possesses its own binder. The adhesive quality of casein is enough to bind dry scene paint that has been added to the casein unless the amount of dry pigment far exceeds the amount of casein. If in doubt, paint a sample and test dry it to see if it has any tendency to rub off. Only if it does must more binder be added. Mixing dry colors with a paste form of casein must be done after both have had enough water added to bring them to painting consistency. Then while stirring the casein, add the colors a little at a time until the desired hue has been reached. As previously mentioned, it is advisable to test dry a sample and compare it to the color elevation or to the sketch before applying the paint to the scenery.

It cannot be said too often that one must mix a sufficient amount of paint to complete a given job. It is difficult enough for an experienced painter to match a short supply of paint, and it is most unlikely that any other person can do it successfully unless he has kept an accurate record of amounts and proportions originally used—a precautionary step that is seldom taken.

The Binder and Sizing Water

A binder must be added to all scene paints, dry or wet, to keep the paint from rubbing off. The binder is purchased as a dry glue in granulated, flake, or cake form, and must be heated with water in a double boiler to convert it into a hot, concentrated glue. Flake and cake glues should be soaked in water overnight before heating in a double boiler. Granulated glue can be covered with water and heated immediately, but stirring helps to speed up its conversion into a liquid state.

The hot glue is added directly to the mixture of pigment and water in the proportion of about ½ cup to 1 gallon of paint. Should there be any question about the strength of the glue, test dry a sample of paint; if the paint dusts off on a clean piece of muslin, add a little more glue. Too much glue added to the paint will force the paint to congeal in the bucket and to be glossy or brittle after it has been applied to the scenery.

Some scene painters prefer to work with a sizing water which is mixed in the proportion of 1 part hot glue to 16 parts water. The sizing water is then mixed with the dry pigments, no other water being added. One advantage of this method is that it is impossible to forget the addition of glue. It seems very easy to forget the concentrated hot glue when it is added separately. On the other hand, a prepared sizing water will deteriorate in time; and it always seems to be kept in the very buckets needed for mixing paint.

CASEIN PAINT

Casein paint may be looked upon as a rank newcomer when compared to the length of time that dry scene paint has been a staple in scenic paint shops. Casein paint is manufactured in an emulsified or paste form and can be obtained in quart, gallon, or 5-gallon containers. One of the advantages of casein paint is that it contains a protein resin binder which eliminates the need for adding an adhesive to mixed paint. This protein binder is more than adequate to insure that the pigments adhere to such covering materials as muslin, canvas, compositional boards, and primed lumber. Additional binding will be needed if the paints are to be used on nonporous materials such as plastics or metals.

Another of the advantages of casein paint is the ease with which it can be mixed. Place the desired amount of pigment paste in a container, add a little water, and stir until it is perfectly smooth. Add more water to this mixture, a little at a time, until it reaches the desired painting consistency and it is ready for use. Normal painting consistency for a coat of opaque paint is reached with the addition of two parts water to one part paint. With some brands of casein this dilution can be extended up to as much as 4 parts water to 1 part paste or even as high as 6 to 1 without noticeable loss of binder strength or purity of color.

In mixing casein paint, as indeed in mixing any other form of paint, when trying to match a particular color it is a good idea to mix small samples and test them before mixing a large quantity of paint. Samples can be mixed in one of two ways. A small amount of pure color can be lifted from a can on the tip of a flexible-bladed spatula and placed on an old white plate or other palette. Other pure colors are added and mixed with the first one until the desired hue is obtained. Then with a brush add enough water to this mixture to permit it to be painted on a scrap of material and test dried. Some people prefer to use a 1½" detail brush instead of a spatula for mixing samples. In this case the brush is dipped into a pure color and worked on a palette with a little water. Other pastes are added in the same manner until the desired color is obtained. With either method try to remember in what proportion one color was mixed with another in order to reach a given hue. Use this as a guide in mixing larger quantities of paint. Remember too that casein paint dries a little lighter than it is when wet.

Casein paint may be used either as a completely opaque paint or it may be thinned with additional water to form a transparent wash. When used as a wash, each successive coat builds up over washes previously applied, much in the same manner as in rendering a transparent water color sketch. A feature of casein paint that should be mentioned is its compatibility with other types of water-soluble paints. Aniline dye, dry colors, acrylics, vinyls, latex paint, and bronzing powders can be mixed with casein in order to obtain a particular color.

Casein paints can be stored on open shelves but care must be taken to see that the lids on all opened cans are replaced tightly. When pigment paste has been exposed to the air overnight, some of it will harden into an unusable mass. A good precaution to take after some of the paint has been removed from a can is to smooth out what paste remains and add just enough water to cover it. Replace the lid tightly and the paint will keep indefinitely. The small amount of water added does not perceptibly dilute the original color paste.

VINYL ACRYLIC PAINT

Another type of scene paint is available to the scenic artist in the form of vinyl acrylic paint. This paint is a product of the chemical industry and because the binder used in it is chemically similar to a wide variety of plastics, it will adhere to most of them. For instance, polyethylene sheeting is a plastic material that rejects most water-soluble paints, yet vinyl acrylic paint can be applied to it with no tendency for the paint to chip, flake, or dust off.

Vinyl acrylic is a water-soluble paint that dries in approximately 30 minutes. After it has dried long enough to cure thoroughly (24 to 48 hours), it becomes water resistant and as such is well adapted for scenery that will be used out of doors. Since it does become water resistant it is imperative that all brushes used in it should be washed as soon after use as possible. Brushes should be washed in warm water to which has been added a little liquid detergent.

The highly intense pigments of vinyl acrylic paint are manufactured as an emulsion and are available in 6-ounce, 12-ounce, and 1-quart containers. There are 15 colors obtainable plus two concentrated bases, a white and a clear. The pigments are designed to be diluted with water in the proportion of two parts water to one of pigment. This produces a mixture of a consistency to give a good one-coat coverage. If a tint of a particular color is desired the pigment is first mixed with water (2 parts water to 1 part pigment) then added to the concentrated white base until the proper value is reached. The clear base is mixed with the pigments when a saturated color is desired.

It is necessary to stir acrylic paint more thoroughly than casein or dry color paints because the pigment emulsions contain a small amount of mineral oil. After the paint has been allowed to stand for some time, the mineral oil forms a protective film across the top of the pigments which protects them from either drying out or spoiling. Although the initial cost of acrylic paint is high it becomes more competitive in price with other scene paints after it has been diluted to proper painting consistency.

ANILINE DYE

Water-soluble aniline dyes are completely transparent and should be one of the staple products found in a well equipped paint shop. They are used extensively in painting scrims and translucent drops. They may also be used in a variety of ways such as changing the color of a costume, an upholstered piece of furniture, a bedspread, or a set of draperies. The only requirement is that the fabric to be dyed must be of a lighter color than the dye to be used. Water-soluble aniline dyes are obtained from most scenic supply houses that handle scene paints. The dyes are sometimes sold by the ounce or, more generally, by the pound.

A very strong solution of any color dye can be made by adding a teaspoon of dye to a quart of boiling hot water. Lighter tints are obtained by adding more water. To prevent the dye from spreading or bleeding through other colors, add a little binder in the form of Dextrine, glue size, or clear vinyl. Dyes can also be used instead of dry pigments to tint white casein paint. Some hues, such as orchid, cerise, or chartreuse, are difficult to mix with scene paint, but they can be readily mixed with dyes.

SHELLAC: ORANGE OR WHITE

A standard supply item in any scene shop is shellac, both orange and white. Shellac is transparent and comes in a rather thick liquid form which, for general use, should be diluted with wood alcohol in the proportion of two parts shellac to one part alcohol. Because this results in an extremely fast-drying mixture, the brush or roller used in applying it should be washed in alcohol immediately after use.

Shellac is ideal for priming and sealing the surfaces of such materials as new wood, Masonite, and plywood. Shellac is frequently used to provide a glossy finish on stage furniture that has been painted with a flat finish scene paint. A protective coating of shellac can be given to such items as handrails, mantles, table tops, or any other parts of a setting that are likely to come in contact with the perspiring hands of actors or that are likely to have drinks spilled upon them. There is little danger of moisture-loosened scene paint rubbing off on the actors or their costumes if protected by a shield of clear shellac.

Shellac can be changed from a transparent to an opaque coat of any color by the addition of dry scene paint. Select either the orange or the white shellac, whichever is closest to the desired hue, and dilute it in the proper proportion with alcohol. Mix dry scene paint to the proper hue, but mix it with alcohol rather than water, then add the shellac. No binder other than the shellac will be needed. Transparent washes can be colored by using those dyes soluble in alcohol and mixing these with shellac.

Since shellac in any form will darken a surface painted with scene paint it is necessary to lighten the base paint sufficiently to make allowance for this change in value. Test dry a sample of the surface to be painted with shellac before applying it to a surface the audience will see.

SCENE PAINTING

The designer uses scene paint in much the same way and for the same reasons that an actor uses make-up. Through make-up an actor can accentuate certain features or make them less noticeable; he can materially alter his appearance to conform to the characteristics of a certain age level and, to a lesser degree, he can give some indication of the state of his character's mental and physical well-being. What he does with make-up is the final step in the development of his characterization.

The scene designer uses color in a somewhat broader, but just as meaningful, fashion. Color and its method of application are two important agents used to establish the age, period, and, in so far as possible, the country in which the setting is laid. It can be used to create a visual effect to parallel the mood of the play. The designer may use color to attract attention to some specific feature of the design or to add variety and interest. Color is one of the dominant parts of a setting; what it says to the eyes of an audience will be perceived even before the playwright's words are heard and comprehended. How paint is applied is almost as meaningful as the hue selected. If this truth could be instilled in those who design for the theatre, there would be a noticeable reduction in the number of flat, uninteresting, and lifeless paint jobs.

All scene painting is dictated by two principal requirements. First, it is necessary to exaggerate the manner of paint application if one is to achieve an effect that can be appreciated from a distance. Second, the effect of colored light on colored pigment must be considered in order to avoid some totally unexpected results. It can be easily understood that a spectator seated in the first row of the auditorium is separated from the back wall of a setting by the combined widths of the orchestra pit, the forestage, and the depth of the playing space. Small detail, fine lines, delicate hues, and subtle contrasts are lost to most of an audience simply because they are too far away. To overcome this problem scenic designers have resorted to an exaggeration of line, form, and color in the treatment of detail and in the techniques they have developed for the application of paint. A close inspection of these techniques reveals that the majority of them are characterized by a boldness of effect, a coarseness of application, and a sharpness of contrast that differ widely from methods used in any other field of painting. The most widely used painting techniques will be discussed in detail later in the chapter.

The best advise possible on how to find out what will happen to paint when it is seen under colored light is to test it. The variables that affect the results are so numerous that no accurate chart to predict the results can be constructed. There are no standard names for pigments of lighting color media; several spotlights, each with a different color medium, may be focused on the scenery in any number of combinations; some color media may have faded; the number of spotlights used and the intensity of their illumination will influence the color of the painted scenery. Add to these the almost limitless gradations that are possible through the mixture of color pigments, and it becomes clear why testing is the safest way to predict the effect of colored light on colored paint. Testing is done by viewing samples of a proposed color scheme under colored lights that duplicate those to be used on the stage. At this stage, corrections can be made either in the paints or the color media with a minimum of time and effort.

A few generalizations may be of value to those who have had little experience in judging the effect of colored light on painted surfaces. Very marked changes in the appearance of paint usually occur when both the pigment and the color medium are used in saturated form. If, for example, blue moonlight strikes the sides of a red barn, the barn appears to be purplish black in color. The more neutralized a paint becomes, that is, the closer it advances toward gray, the more accurately it reflects the colored light thrown upon it. Tints and deep shades of any hue are less likely to be changed by color lights than clear, saturated colors.

PREPARING SCENERY FOR PAINTING

In nonprofessional theatre organizations it is a common practice to reduce the expense and time of building by constructing new settings from scenery already on hand. The stock scenery is, of course, altered and reassembled, and the old pieces may be supplemented with one or two new flats or special units. This results in the use of a motley array of flats—some old, some new, some patched, and no two of the same color. It is difficult to paint such a collection of surfaces with any assurance that the finished job will not be disfigured by variations in surface textures or by underlying colors that bleed through. The precautionary steps listed below should be taken in order to overcome these difficulties and to facilitate an even application of paint over all the scenery.

1. Patch all holes in the canvas. Cover a piece of muslin about twice the size of the hole with canvas glue and place it over the hole on the

back of the flat. Pull the edges of the tear together on the face of the flat and smooth them down.

2. Paint over water or oil stains with a thin solution of shellac and alcohol. Serious oil stains should be cut out and the hole patched.

3. Tighten all loose canvas by painting the back of the flat with hot glue and water sizing to which a little cheap pigment has been added. (The pigment makes it easier to see which areas have been painted.)

4. In altering a window or door flat into a plain flat, try to find canvas or muslin that matches the condition of the covering material already on the flat. Otherwise, the difference between the surface textures of new canvas and old painted canvas may be discernible even after several coats of paint.

5. Apply dutchmen (strips of muslin covering the junction between hinged flats) with a paste composed of three parts cold water paste to one part hot glue. This mixture will not stain through the dutchman to darken the finish of the paint job. Select material for dutchmen to match the condition of the covering material used on adjacent flats.

6. Flats covered with new canvas or muslin should be given one or two coats of priming to reduce the difference in texture between the old and new flats.

Sizing

Sizing is a preparatory coat needed especially when flat frames are covered with new canvas or muslin. The application of sizing accomplishes two purposes. First, by shrinking, it tightens the new covering material on the frames of the flats; second, it lays the foundation for the coats of paint to follow. There are several ways in which sizing can be made. If all the flats are covered with new material, the sizing can consist of whiting, glue, hot water, and a little inexpensive pigment that makes the sizing easier to see during application. If the scenery is made from stock flats which vary in color, a little formaldehyde or alum (about 3/4 cup to 3 gallons of paint) can be added to the sizing to prevent the undercoats from bleeding through. Dye painting, used to achieve translucent effects, must be done on unpainted covering material with a special sizing made of starch. Laundry starch is cooked, then added to regular sizing water in the proportion of 1 cup of starch to 3 gallons of sizing water.

Priming

Priming is a preparatory coat of paint, needed especially when repainting old scenery, to provide a uniform surface for the succeeding coats of paint. It is normally made with a base of whiting to which has been added a cheap pigment which approximates the hue desired in the finished color. Priming also provides a good opportunity to use up all the old paint left over from a previous job. Assuming that the old paints have not spoiled and are not too saturated in hue, they may be mixed together and added to a base of whiting. Add to the resulting mixture enough of its complementary color to neutralize the hue and to produce a gray or brownish paint. Both colors are easily overpainted. Because of the greater covering quality of casein paint, the priming coat can be omitted if the succeeding coats are mixed with casein paint as a base rather than with whiting.

PAINTING TECHNIQUES

The basic techniques used in scene painting are simple in themselves, but they are as variable as the skill and ingenuity of the painter can make them. Even among experienced painters there is a noticeable difference in the results each will achieve, even when all are supposedly painting with the same technique. Somehow each painter manages to leave his own individual stamp on whatever techniques he happens to be using. The basic techniques are frequently combined to obtain a particular effect, and many of them are subjected to experiments and modifications that can lead to special innovations. How successfully a painter accomplishes this depends on how thoroughly he has mastered a technique and on his willingness to try for something new that may lead to a better, more expressive way of painting.

Base Coat

This coat of paint is the foundation. It establishes, as far as possible with a single application of paint, the hue and brilliance desired in the finished setting. This coat must be mixed and compared carefully with the color sketch or the color guide. Apply the paint carefully by working from the top of the scenery toward the bottom with brushes that are well charged with paint. Do not scrub or paint over the same area. This is particularly important when repainting old scenery; the underlying paint may become moist enough to work through and discolor the paint being applied. Paint with long, easy strokes and use the flat tip of the brush rather than its edge. Organize the work so as to avoid having to stop a day's work with an area of scenery only partly painted. Arrange to stop where a natural break of plane is reached, such as the junction of the side and back walls. This precaution will eliminate any slight difference of tonal effect caused by paints standing overnight and not being thoroughly stirred before reuse or by too obvious a junction between paint that has already dried and that which is applied afresh.

No matter how carefully the work is planned, there will, however, be occasions when it is necessary to stop painting an expanse of scenery before a natural break can be reached. Joining the dry and wet portions without too obvious a junction can be helped by "feathering out" an area before stopping. Rather than stopping with a sharp brush stroke, gradually work all pigment from the brush onto the unpainted canvas as the painted area is extended. To join a fresh area to one that is already dry, start on an adjacent unpainted area and repeat the above technique, working back to the dry area and allowing one feathered edge to overlap the other.

Shaded Base Coat

Effects such as the faded walls of a Victorian living room that has mellowed with age or the dark and dingy walls of a basement apartment can be made more realistic by gradually blending or shading the wall areas from one hue to another or by shading through different degrees of brilliance of a single hue. (See Plate 88.) The careful shading of wall areas from top to bottom, in the corners, and around fireplaces and architectural trim will also relieve the uninteresting effect produced by a flat, evenly applied base coat. Shading of this type is generally done with two, or possibly three, different degrees of brilliance of the same hue. The shading may be subtle or very distinct, depending on the degree of contrast between the paints being used. The secret of a smooth gradation is the speed with which the paint is applied; it must be graded on the scenery while the blending colors are still moist. Be sure to use a separate brush for each graduation color or the difference in brilliance will be lost by the paints being intermixed on the bristles of a single brush. Work a small area at a time and move progressively around those portions of the set to be shaded. It is much easier to shade or blend colors when one is working on new covering material, since it retains moisture longer than old, heavily painted scenery. Old coverings have a tendency to absorb fresh paint almost as rapidly as it can be applied.

Spattering

The appearance of uneven or poorly executed blending can be improved by spattering over it with the same paints used in blending (Plate 89). Interlace the spatters directly over the blended area by extending a dark spatter over a

Plate 88   Shading

Plate 89   Spattering

light painted area and carrying the light spatters over the dark. This should be done with a very fine spatter allowing it to fade off beyond the limits of the shaded area.

Spattering is one of the fastest methods of applying paint to scenery. It has, in addition to speed, a number of other advantages which make it one of the most valuable and versatile methods by which scenery can be painted. It is used extensively for shading parts of a setting by blending from one hue to another. It may be applied over any type of base coat without obliterating it. It is used to change the tonal effect of a paint job that may be off hue, too bright, or too dull. Wallpaper patterns or detail work which contrast too strongly with the base coat can be toned down by an application of spatter. Novelty scenery which is to change color under lights is usually painted by this method.

To apply spatter, dip the tip of the brush (about the last 1½" of the bristles) into paint and drain off most of the pigment. Stand about 4' from the scenery and strike the ferrule of the brush smartly against the heel of the left hand. This forces the bristles to snap forward throwing particles of paint toward the scenery. Constantly move the position of the hands and the body to assure an even distribution of paint. The size of the spatter particles depends upon the type of brush, the amount of paint carried by it, the distance of the painter from the scenery, and the force with which the brush is struck against the hand.

It is recommended that the inexperienced painter practice spattering on an old flat before attempting to work on a setting. In spite of the first few awkward attempts, spattering is not difficult to master if the suggestions above are followed. It will not be long before the painter discovers that she can lay an even spatter on a flat without getting most of the paint on herself.

Mask Spattering

Wide-striped wallpapers, festoons, large geometric figures, or wood paneling can be done by spattering over masks that are placed against the face of a piece of scenery. The masks can be made from lengths of stock lumber in varying widths, from pieces of rope temporarily tacked to the scenery in the proper position and shape, or from sections of building paper either pinned or taped to the canvas. Lines or forms produced in this fashion have the advantage of soft, indistinct edges that cannot be produced by a brush in contact with the painted surface. (See Plate 90.)

Scumbling

Scumbling provides an area with a multihued base. (See Plate 91.) It is a technique of painting similar to shading, but it differs from shading in that it produces an indistinct, all-over pattern rather than a progressive shading

Plate 90 Masked Spattering

Plate 91   Scumbling

from one area to another. It may be used to good advantage as a base for certain types of wallpapers, for timbering, for several kinds of stone work such as marble or stucco, or simply to give an area a more interesting texture.

The variety possible with this technique depends upon the number of hues being used, the degree of contrast between them, and the manner in which they are blended on the surface of the scenery. The effectiveness of scumbling depends upon blending the paints while they are still moist, and for this reason it is essential that scumbling, like shading, be done as rapidly as possible. Permit each color to blend partly with the next, but make sure that some of each color remains identifiable as itself. Excessive blending can result in each hue's losing all of its identity, thereby producing a flat, monochromatic effect as though the colors have been intermixed in a bucket before being applied to the scenery. As a precaution against overblending be sure to use separate brushes for each scumbling color.

Scumbling can be done with various types of brush strokes—large or small circular strokes, straight or angular strokes, crosshatching, or irregular patterned strokes. A little experimenting with different kinds of brush strokes will yield a great variety of effects offered by this method of painting.

Stippling

Stippling is another method of applying particles of paint over a base coat, but the effect is heavier and coarser than that produced by spattering (Plate

92). It is accomplished by touching the paint-charged bristles of a large brush against the surface of the scenery. Old brushes are best for this purpose since their bristles have a tendency to form clusters; each cluster leaves its own imprint on the painted surface. Change the position of the brush before each contact with the scenery in order to avoid a repeat pattern. Sponges or coarse woven materials can be used in place of a brush if a light effect is desired. If natural sponges are used, it is advisable to split them open to provide a wide, flat surface for contact with the scenery. If excessive pressure is used to apply paint, the covering material will be stretched beyond the point where it can shrink back tightly on the flat frames. When stippling with a sponge be particularly careful that too much pressure doesn't cause a heavy deposit of paint along the edges of the stiles and toggle bars. This concentration of paint will reveal an unattractive skeletal outline of the flat. An annoying repeat pattern can develop from the imprint of a sponge as easily as if from a brush. To avoid this, rotate the sponge slightly after each contact with the scenery and overlap one impression with another.

Dry Brushing

Dry brushing is a very useful method for shading, for producing striations needed in simulating the grain of wood or timbering, or for overpainting blended base coats. (See Plate 93.) To apply paint by the dry brush technique,

Plate 92 Stippling

Plate 93   Dry Brushing

partially charge the brush with paint and then remove most of it by wiping the brush against the sides of the bucket until the bristles cling together in small clusters. Draw just the tips of the bristles lightly over the scenery. A wide variety of effects is possible with this method of painting. For wood graining, it is recommended that some study be given to the patterns that are typical of the grains of different types of wood. These distinctive patterns can then be drawn in with the brush used in the manner described.

Rolling

Rolling is similar in effect to spattering and stippling, but it produces a much smoother distribution of paint (Plate 94). Rolling is used to simulate rough textured finishes such as stucco, adobe, or plaster, and it also can be used to good advantage in giving texture to a simple base coat.

Fray the edges of a piece of burlap, about 20″ square, by snapping it briskly in the air until it has a fringe at least 1½″ or 2″ long. Fold the material into a triangle and double over the two corners so that all the fringed edges are on the same side of the burlap. Roll the burlap toward the point of the triangle, keeping the fringe on the outside of the roll. Dip the roll in paint and wring it out until it no longer drips. Apply the roll to the face of the scenery with just enough pressure to leave an imprint of the fringe and to

Plate 94 Rolling

make sure the roll doesn't slip. Change the direction of the roll with each contact to prevent the development of a noticeable pattern. An even distribution of paint can be obtained by using the same direction pattern as that used in crosshatching. Use a separate roll for each color applied.

Crosshatching

Crosshatching is a method of painting accurately described by its name— brush strokes overlap each other at approximately 45° angles (Plate 95). Any irregularities of the subsurface or of individual brush strokes are less noticeable when paint is applied in this manner.

Puddling

A rich textural effect can be obtained by a method of blending two or more colors called puddling (Plate 96). Lay the scenery flat on the floor and, holding two well-charged brushes of paint about waist high, shake the paint from them onto the scenery. Two or more .colors may be blended in this manner but its success depends upon the nearly simultaneous application of all paints. This permits the paints to overlap, blend, and intermix while they are still in liquid form.

Plate 95   Crosshatching

Stenciling

The application of well-planned wallpaper to a setting will probably give it more character and atmosphere than any other single painting technique. Actual wallpaper patterns are usually too small and too intricate for stage purposes. Therefore, a desirable pattern is usually reworked to enlarge and simplify it (Plate 97). This can best be done on a scaled elevation of some part of the setting which is to receive the pattern. Be sure to use a large scale for this work, at least a 1″ or 1½″ = 1′-0″ scale. This large scale permits the designer to work out the details of the pattern, its exact dimensions, the number of repeats required, and the pattern relationship. With these factors known, the full-scale stencil can be cut.

Commercial stencil paper comes in sheets approximately 20″ × 24″, which is large enough for most designs. Stencil paper is a stiff but lightweight cardboard, impregnated with linseed oil to make it almost impervious to water. A substitute for stencil paper can be made from Bristol board which has been given several coats of shellac or lacquer after the stencil has been cut. When treating Bristol board in this manner, be sure to apply the shellac to both sides of the cardboard and especially to the exposed edges around the stencil cuts; if the cardboard is not completely covered, the water paints will soften it and the stencil will fall apart. Reinforce the stencil by tacking it to a

Plate 96   Puddling

wooden frame made of 1″ × 2″ stock that has been butt joined on edge (Plate 98).

Most wallpaper patterns are laid out on vertical, horizontal, or diagonal lines. If these basic lines are laid off on the scenery to serve as guide lines, the time required for spacing, locating, and aligning the stencil positions can be greatly reduced. A chalk line charged with dry scene paint the same hue as the base coat, but a little lighter or darker as an aid to visibility, is used to snap off the guide lines. The stencils are laid over the intersections of the guide lines. What remains of the guide lines can be removed from the scenery by brushing with a soft cloth or a dry paint brush.

The fastest method to apply a stencil is by using a power driven spray gun, but it can be done by using a brush or by very careful spattering. In all cases, to prevent the possibility of smearing and dripping, the scene paint is mixed to a consistency heavier than for most other purposes.

Wallpaper patterns calling for more than a single hue can be applied in one of two ways when a spray gun is used. A stencil can be masked for each color, that is, all areas to be one color are sprayed at the same time and then the stencil is remasked for each of the other colors. Or, the complete stencil can be sprayed with the dominant hue of the design, and the accent colors painted by hand over the sprayed design. The advantage of the second

Plate 97   Stenciling

technique is that the resulting design has enough variation in its repeat patterns so that it does not appear too mechanical.

Excessive contrast between stenciled patterns and the base coat should be avoided. Should this contrast appear too great, the patterns and the base can be toned together by spattering, rolling, or spraying over the designs with some of the base coat color. This breaks up the sharp lines of the stencil and reduces the contrast between it and the background.

Stamping with Paint or Dye

Repeating a distinctive shape in a random pattern is easily accomplished with a paint stamp. The stamp can be used to rapidly paint different sized leaves on a foliage background or to detail silhouettes of trees seen at a distance. Stamping may also be used in depicting clusters of flowers, irregular rock forms, or floor patterns such as tiles or flagstones. Depending upon the type of effect desired, the design can be cut from such materials as heavy pile carpeting, natural or artificial sponges, or from soft sponge rubber. Any material absorbent enough to take a charge of paint and yet sturdy enough to be cut into a distinctive shape can be used.

Constructing the stamp itself presents no problem. The cutout pattern of absorbent material is attached with contact cement to one face of a block of ³/₄″ plywood that is just slightly larger than the cutout design. The opposite face of the block is attached to a 30″ or 36″ wooden handle made from 1″ × 2″ stock. Any sort of low-lipped receptacle, such as a large cake pan, can be used to hold the paint. This type of painting is best done with the scenery lying flat on the floor. The floor provides the firm backing that is necessary for effective painting with the stamp.

It is usually a good idea to test the imprint left by the stamp before actually applying it to the surface to be painted. Select a scrap of material similar to that which is to receive the design, determine by experimentation how much paint the stamp will hold, how much pressure must be applied, and what happens if the pressure is applied unevenly by tipping the handle one way or the other. Sometimes experimentation can reveal a surprising effect that is more interesting than a regular repeat of the original shape. When this happens, happily accept the gift and incorporate it into your work.

Plate 98   Stencil on Frame

Appliqués

Rough stonework, irregular plaster, adobe, and novelty effects can be done
with appliqués. The scene paint is mixed with double-strength glue; to this
mixture is added shredded asbestos, ground cork, coarse sawdust, chopped
excelsior, or other similar material light enough to be held to the canvas by
the binder in the paint. Since the consistency of this paint is much heavier
than others, it may be necessary to apply it with a stiff, short-bristled brush
or even with a wide-bladed putty knife.

Spackle, or spackling plaster, is sometimes used for rough textured
surfaces, but it has the great disadvantage of adding a noticeable amount of
weight to the scenery. It also has a tendency to chip off during a scene shift
unless it has been applied over a solid surface such as plywood. Spackle can
be purchased in any local paint store in a dry or a paste form. The dry
powder is mixed with water and applied with a putty knife. It is pure white
in color, dries very rapidly, and receives scene paint well.

Backpainting

If new scenery, with only one or two coats of paint on it, is placed on stage
so as to receive strong back lighting, it becomes almost translucent so that the
audience can see the silhouette of the flat frames. This fault can be corrected
by backpainting. Do not use left-over paints that are saturated enough to
stain through the canvas and discolor a finished paint job. It is best to mix a
medium to dry gray paint by using whiting and black. Paint lightly and
rapidly over the back of the flats, being certain to work the paint close to the
edges of the frames. The moisture in the paint may darken the paint on the face
of the scenery temporarily, but there will be no perceptible change of brilliance or discoloration after the backpainting has dried.

Dipping

The rough texture typical of some types of stone, tree bark, or sunbaked earth
can be approximated by a method called dipping. The best covering material
for this purpose is heavy muslin. The muslin is cut into small sections, 18″ ×
24″ or 30″ dipped into paint, and applied to the flat one at a time. While the
paint is still wet, the muslin is pinched, twisted, and folded into the desired
shape and allowed to dry.

A variation of the dipping technique can sometimes be used to apply a
dutchman that may have been overlooked by the building crew. Dip into
scene paint strips of muslin, no wider than the combined widths of the two
stiles over which they will be placed. While they are soaking, paint the area
of the two flats where the dutchman is to be applied. Before this paint is dry,
squeeze out any excess paint from the dutchman, and then apply it to the
flats and smooth it down. There is sufficient glue in the paint to hold the
dutchman to the flat after it has dried. Dutchmen properly applied by this
method need not be tacked except at the top and bottom of the flat and
around each hinge.

Straight Edging

Painted architectural trim such as cornices, molding, and panels can be made
convincing only by the use of a straight edge and a lining brush (Plate 99). A

Plate 99   Straight Edging

perfectly straight line is practically impossible to paint freehand, even for a professional scene painter. Hence mastering the use of the lining brush and the straight edge is a basic requirement for the craftsman who paints scenery. The straight edge is held, firmly enough to prevent its slipping, against the face of the scenery and with its beveled edge tipped slightly away from the canvas. This will help keep the scene paint from seeping under the blade and smearing. To ensure a long unbroken line that does not vary in width, the lining brush must be well charged with paint and the tip of the bristles must be worked into a flat chisel edge. As stated before, the secret of painting a straight line that does not vary in width is holding the brush at a right angle to the canvas and taking full advantage of the spine of the bristles by allowing only their tips to come in contact with the canvas. In short, paint with the tip of the brush, not its side.

Stained-Glass Windows

Windows with simulated stained glass can be made in a number of different ways, but one of the easiest and quickest methods uses both opaque scene paint and transparent dyes painted directly on tightly stretched lightweight muslin. Windows done by this method are rugged enough so that they are not likely to be damaged in a scene shift. Such damage is almost invariably inflicted when color media are taped to a plywood cutout of the leading. Stretch the muslin tightly over the back of the window thickness. Outline the design in charcoal. Use a small detail brush and a dark gray opaque scene paint mixed with double-strength glue to paint in the leading; this must be a continuous line at least ½" wide to prevent the dye from spreading from one area to another. As soon as the scene paint has dried, the areas so enclosed can be filled in with the proper dye solution.

Glazing

Highly reflective painted surfaces are not usually found on painted scenery. The light they reflect is likely to prove distracting. There are occasions, however, when a slight gloss is desirable. An example might be the wood-work trim around doors, windows, and stairway of a supposedly smart interior. Such a gloss can be obtained by glazing, a process of covering a color with a thin, transparent wash which, when dry, will reflect more light than the uncovered color. Glazes can be made from clear shellac thinned with alcohol, from clear lacquer and lacquer thinner, from clear liquid wax, or from a solution of glue and water. As a precaution against getting too high a gloss, it is preferable to start with a weak solution and gradually to increase the gloss by waxing and polishing after the solution has dried. It is also advisable to test the solution on a sample of the color it is to cover, because a glaze may cause an objectionable change in hue or brilliance.

12

The Stage
and Its Equipment

The educational theatre is a fabulous creation. Its life began only within the present century, yet in that brief time it has succeeded in bringing live drama to countless audiences in every state of the Union. Considering the speed of its growth, it is not too surprising that the educational theatre should have made mistakes in planning the stages that were to house its productions, or that some of these mistakes and limitations should be perpetuated in yet other theatres by architects and building committees unfamiliar with the requirements of a stage or of the productions to be presented there.

THE DEVELOPMENT OF
THE EDUCATIONAL THEATRE PLANT

When drama was finding its place in the curriculum of our educational system, it had first to prove its worth to the administration and to a skeptical public. Men and women with vision and determination, who were convinced that drama should be a fully accredited part of our educational system, set about the gigantic task of finding a home for it. There was no idea of constructing a theatre building—there were simply no funds available for such a purpose. It became a problem of finding an unused space in some existing building, of convincing the administration that it could be put to good use, and then of converting it into something that resembled an auditorium and a stage. It was only natural that such makeshift theatres abounded in limitations of every conceivable nature.

257

Two such theatres, both in Iowa, will serve as examples. The first of these was on the third floor of the natural science building, which housed a 65'-0" square auditorium seating 1200. Appended to one of its four walls was a speaker's platform bounded by a semicircular plaster wall with a radius of just 18'-0". The platform became the so-called stage. Two doors of conventional size led from either side of the stage into the backstage space. This backstage area consisted of a semicircular passageway 6'-0" wide, whose outer wall was pierced by a continuous row of windows. On the floor directly above the passageway were the dressing rooms, without windows and without toilets. The scene shop was in an old wooden two-car garage located in an alley a block away and three floors down from the stage. The scene dock and storage room was in the basement of an old building across the river, a mile and a half from the shop! In spite of these limitations over 180 full-length plays were presented on this stage before the late Professor E. C. Mabie's dreams were realized with the construction of the University Theatre at Iowa in 1936.

The second theatre, in a basement under the library, possessed a modest auditorium seating about 220, with folding chairs placed on graduated levels. The proscenium opening was approximately 24'-0" wide. The depth of the stage was 25'-0", and there was perhaps 10'-0" of wing space on each side of the arch. But the grid, formed by the floor of the library above, was 9'-0" from the stage floor, and a supporting steel column was located slightly to one side of center stage not more than 10'-0" from the curtain line! This column was an unavoidable part of every setting, now disguised as a lamppost, now a tree, again as a newel post or a sewer pipe, but always there in some form. Somehow this organization managed to incorporate its supporting column into 40 productions before Coe College at Cedar Rapids built its new auditorium and stage in 1950.

These are not isolated examples, carefully selected to prove a point, but quite typical of the type of stage that most dramatic departments were forced to use until they had proved their right to better facilities. It was not until the late 1920s that the first theatre buildings were constructed for educational purposes. After the need for work in dramatics became evident and the pattern for building had been established, first one institution and then another followed the lead, until many of our colleges and universities are now either at work on the plans for, or possess, excellent theatre plants. This pattern of building has not been confined to the universities and colleges alone; it has been extended to many of our larger high schools, where both thought and money are being spent to provide stages for dramatic productions.

There is little similarity between these new theatres except that all possess an auditorium and a stage of some kind. This diversity in plan and form is a healthy condition, indicative of a vital and imaginative theatre, a theatre that is not wedded to a standardized method of production. The newer theatres fall roughly into three general classifications: (1) the conventional stage with a proscenium arch separating the auditorium from the stage, (2) the modified stage with some unusual treatment of the proscenium arch, and finally (3) the arena stage. Iowa, Indiana, and Wisconsin all have theatres of the conventional type. Baylor University in Texas has a modified stage with three proscenium arches and an auditorium equipped with swivel seats—a theatre capable of a remarkable degree of flexibility in production methods. The Ring Theatre at the University of Miami and the Penthouse Theatre at the University of Washington are good examples of the arena type.

It is not our intention to discuss the production methods that have led to variations in the form of theatre buildings, or to take up the problems of planning theatre buildings in general. This chapter will be devoted to a discussion of the various parts of the stage and to the equipment required to fit it for production work (Plate 100).

THE STRUCTURAL PARTS OF A STAGE

The Orchestra Pit

Traditionally the orchestra pit has been a characteristic feature of the American theatre; but for the sake of a closer relationship between audience and actor, some of the newer theatres have eliminated the pit entirely. The immediate goal of the actor-spectator relationship was achieved, but at the expense of productions requiring the services of an orchestra.

The old-fashioned brass-bordered moat that separates the audience from the stage apron is not necessary. A much more flexible and practical use of the space required for a pit can be made by following one of two schemes. The installation of an elevator that will lower a section of the auditorium floor to form a pit is quite successful. When there is no need for the orchestra pit, the elevator is raised to the auditorium floor level and fitted with additional rows of seats. By removing the temporary seats and raising the elevator to the level of the stage floor, additional playing space is added to the depth of the stage. An alternate scheme eliminates the considerable cost of the elevator. A pit is constructed to the depth of 3'-6" to 4'-0" below the level of the auditorium floor and its top is fitted with sections of flooring that slide out of the way under the apron of the stage. A temporary guard rail is erected around the edges of the pit, from which masking drapes are hung to shield the audience from the glare of the music-rack lights. When the services of the orchestra are not required the pit is covered, providing space for additional rows of temporary seats.

The Forestage

The forestage, or the apron as it is more commonly called, is that part of the stage floor extending beyond the curtain line into the auditorium. Whether or not the apron should be incorporated into the plans for new legitimate or community theatres has been the subject of many a heated debate. There are those who maintain that the forestage, like the orchestra pit, creates an unnecessary barrier between the audience and the actors, that it is nothing but a heritage from a by-gone period, and has long since lost its usefulness. The climax of the argument is usually reached by some such statement as, "Move the proscenium to the downstage side of the apron and gain that much more valuable space backstage where it is really needed." Others will argue just as heatedly in favor of the forestage, and they will point out its value as space for entr'acte entertainment, for announcements, for certain types of productions, and for helping to establish aesthetic distance. As far as the commercial and the community theatre is concerned, there seems to be no indication that the argument will be solved to everyone's satisfaction.

There is no argument between those responsible for planning educational theatres with respect to the desirability of the forestage. There seems to be universal agreement regarding its usefulness. Extensive use can be made of the

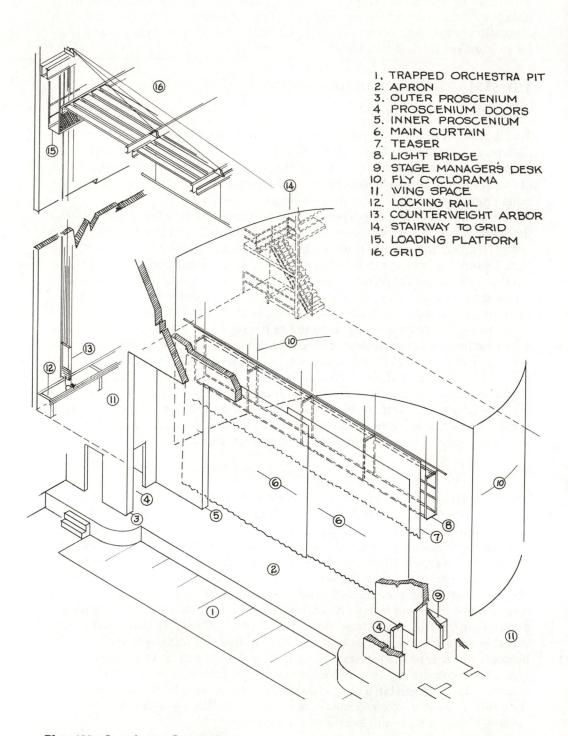

1. TRAPPED ORCHESTRA PIT
2. APRON
3. OUTER PROSCENIUM
4. PROSCENIUM DOORS
5. INNER PROSCENIUM
6. MAIN CURTAIN
7. TEASER
8. LIGHT BRIDGE
9. STAGE MANAGER'S DESK
10. FLY CYCLORAMA
11. WING SPACE
12. LOCKING RAIL
13. COUNTERWEIGHT ARBOR
14. STAIRWAY TO GRID
15. LOADING PLATFORM
16. GRID

Plate 100   Stagehouse Composite

auditorium for large classes when the stage is equipped with an apron that can serve as a speaker's platform. Readings, recitals, lectures, and similar activities can be held on the forestage against a background provided by the closed main curtain, without the need to dismantle or strike any scenery that might be in position onstage. With both the asbestos curtain and the main curtain closed, classroom exercises in acting and directing can be held on the apron while crew assignments are carried out on stage. Without the apron, certain types of period plays, so frequently found in the play programs of the educational theatre, cannot be done without incorporating a simulated forestage into the set design and taking the space for it from the valuable backstage area.

The forestage need not be an elaborate or extensive affair; if it has no more depth than 6'-0" to 8'-"0, it will meet the needs listed above. Some means of access to and from the apron should be provided other than that afforded by parting the front curtain. Unobtrusive doorways placed on either side of the apron, and connecting passageways leading from them to the backstage area and to the front of the house, provide a flexible and desirable arrangement.

The Proscenium Arch

In spite of its name, the proscenium arch is generally rectangular in shape. In theatres that possess an opening with an arched or rounded top in the proscenium wall, it is usually necessary to alter the opening into a rectangular shape by hanging expensive velour draperies just upstage of the proscenium opening. The reason for this is simple: most conventional stage settings are rectangular in shape, and unless the audience is to see the rigging that supports all of the flown scenery and stage lights, the top of the setting must be masked.

Although the proscenium arch can hardly be classified as a piece of stage equipment, its importance as it affects other stage equipment or the sight lines is so great that some mention of it here is in order. The size and shape of the arch are determined for a specific theatre by a study of its relation to the form and dimensions of the auditorium, and to the amount and distribution of available backstage space. The dimensions of the proscenium arch should not be selected at random; nor should it be assumed that because certain dimensions are satisfactory in one theatre they will be equally suitable in another theatre with an entirely different plan and arrangement. A few moments spent in a study of the plans for a proposed theatre will reveal that sight lines drawn from any position in the auditorium to the stage are governed by the limits of the proscenium arch. By testing the sightlines from the extreme seats in the auditorium—that is, from the highest seats in the balcony, from the extreme side seats in the orchestra, and from the seats closest to the proscenium—it is possible to determine how much or how little a spectator seated at those positions can see of the stage.

The desire of certain civic groups to possess the biggest and the best of everything has been carried over into the field of theatre architecture, and has occasionally resulted in the construction of a theatre that is literally too large for dramatic productions. Auditoriums seating 2000, 3000, or 4000 people, with proscenium arches 60'-0", 70'-0", or even 85'-0" wide, are not uncommon. These stages may be beautifully suited for spectacles, extravaganzas, and opera; but they are just too large for dramatic productions. The same fault could occur in the educational theatre should an administration decide that an all-purpose auditorium should be built to house the concert and lecture series as well as dramatic productions. Such an auditorium would of necessity be large enough to house most of the student body, and the stage would be fitted with a proscenium correspondingly wide.

For dramatic productions the acceptable width of the proscenium arch is from 32'-0" to possibly 36'-0" or 38'-0". When the arch is made much wider than this, there is an immediate increase in the problems affecting the movement of actors, the design of scenery, and the cost of production. The timing and pacing of actors' movements, without objectionable delays, increase in difficulty in direct proportion to the width of the stage. The action of most plays is laid in interior settings of some type, such as a living room, a den, a kitchen, or a bedroom. When the designer attempts to adapt the normal dimensions of such rooms to a stage that may be 45'-0" in width, he does so at the expense of any sense of reality. The wall areas have been so exaggerated and extended that the stage furniture and properties seem out of scale and isolated against them. More decorative properties and furniture are then added in an effort to make the setting seem more habitable. As the setting is extended in size, and as additional furniture is required to dress it, the cost of building scenery and renting properties increases.

STAGE EQUIPMENT

The Asbestos Curtain

State or city laws may require the installation of an asbestos fire curtain as part of the safety equipment of a theatre. Should a fire occur an asbestos curtain can be lowered to prevent the spread of fire from one part of the theatre to another. The composition of asbestos material is such that it cannot be pleated or folded and it must be rigged so that it hangs as a two-dimensional plane (Plate 101). The width of the asbestos must be greater than that of the proscenium opening, to provide at least a 1'-0" or 1'-6" overlap on each side of the arch. The outer edges of the asbestos are fitted with metal rings through which steel cables are stretched between the stage floor and the grid. This rigging prevents the asbestos from being sucked out of position by a heavy draft, and ensures a tight junction between the curtain and the proscenium wall. Just beyond the edges of the asbestos on each side are steel smoke pockets—vertical steel troughs bolted to the proscenium wall. They extend out and around the sides of the asbestos to form a protective shield. The asbestos is raised and lowered by a variation in the rigging of a conventional counterweight unit. The arbor, in this case, is mounted on the back of the proscenium wall in such a position that the operating line and its floor block are within a few feet of the asbestos. A special safety feature in the rigging of the asbestos is the cut-line that makes it possible to lower the curtain either automatically or manually from positions on either side of the arch. To achieve this, the balance between the asbestos and the counterweight is deliberately kept uneven so that the curtain is a little heavier than the weights in the arbor. This requires the use of a special ³/₈" rope, called the cut-line, to hold the curtain in position after it has been raised. At one side of the arch an end of the cut-line is attached to the floor. From this point it extends to the grid, over a block, across the grid to a second block, and then down to the stage floor and through a third block. The free end of the line is then tied to the operating line of the asbestos to hold it in place. At 10'-0" or 15'-0" intervals along the full length of the cut-line are inserted fusible links that are designed to separate when the

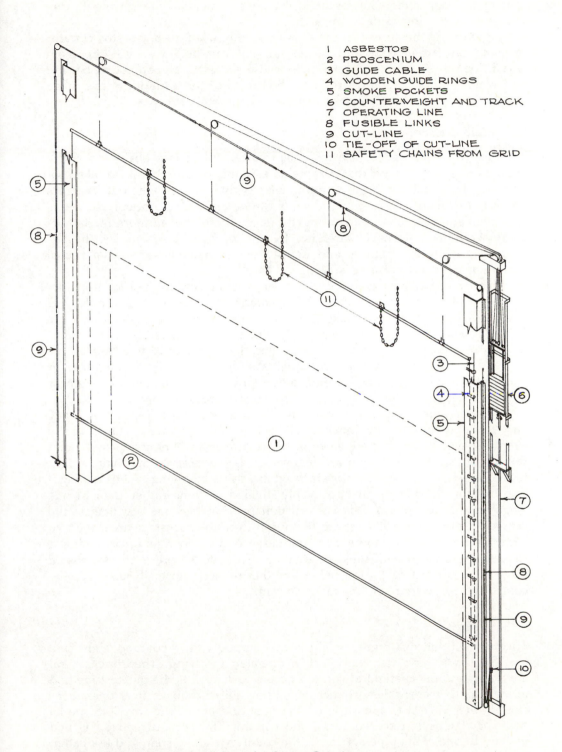

1 ASBESTOS
2 PROSCENIUM
3 GUIDE CABLE
4 WOODEN GUIDE RINGS
5 SMOKE POCKETS
6 COUNTERWEIGHT AND TRACK
7 OPERATING LINE
8 FUSIBLE LINKS
9 CUT-LINE
10 TIE-OFF OF CUT-LINE
11 SAFETY CHAINS FROM GRID

Plate 101   Rigging of Counterbalanced Asbestos Curtain

temperature reaches a given degree. The curtain would be lowered automatically by the separation of any of the fusible links, or manually by cutting the line with a knife on either side of the arch.

Preventing the spread of fire is not the only use for an asbestos curtain. It makes an excellent secondary curtain that can be lowered if the main curtain becomes fouled or inoperative. It also serves as a good sound barrier; and when it and the main curtain are both closed, the auditorium and stage can be used simultaneously for separate classroom purposes.

The Main Curtain

For theatres requiring the use of a main curtain there is probably no single piece of stage equipment that is quite so essential or one that is so taken for granted. It is not until the curtain fails to operate, or when it becomes necessary to replace it, that its full value can be realized. It not only serves as a convenient method of separating the stage from the auditorium, but its color serves as a focus of attention for the decorative scheme of the auditorium, while the fullness and density of its material serve as a partial barrier against the noise of shifting scenery.

The material best suited for use as a main curtain is a high-quality cotton velour. This is a heavyweight material that drapes beautifully and possesses a deep pile that looks well under lights. It is obtainable in a wide range of colors and in some patterns. Darker, plain colors are usually preferred to lighter hues, because they reflect less light and give less visible evidence of soilage. Whatever material is selected for the main curtain, it should be lined with a lightweight, tightly woven material such as sateen or twill in order to protect the main curtain and to increase its opacity.

The amount of fullness allowed for the draping of the front curtain may vary from 50 percent to as much as 100 percent. This fullness is taken up by evenly spaced pleats that are sewn to the reinforcing webbing attached along the top of the curtain. The lower hem serves as a pocket for the chain weight that is inserted to keep the curtain from excessive billowing or "fishtailing." The curtain is made up in two evenly divided sections rather than in one single continuous piece. This construction provides several advantages: the center opening provides access to the apron from the backstage area, the two sections are easier to handle than one large one when rigging or having it cleaned, and the curtain must be divided if it is to be operated as either a draw or a tab curtain. Listed below are the methods normally used for the control and operation of the main curtain.

The Fly Curtain

Theatres with adequate grid height and equipped with a counterweight system frequently have the main curtain operated by flying. There are several advantages to this method of controlling the curtain. It is the quietest method of operation; there is less chance of fouling the curtain as it is opened or closed; and when it is open it is off the floor and out of the way. No special track or rigging is required to fly the curtain. The curtain material is tied directly to one of the pipe battens of the counterweight system and the batten controlled from the locking rail (Plate 102).

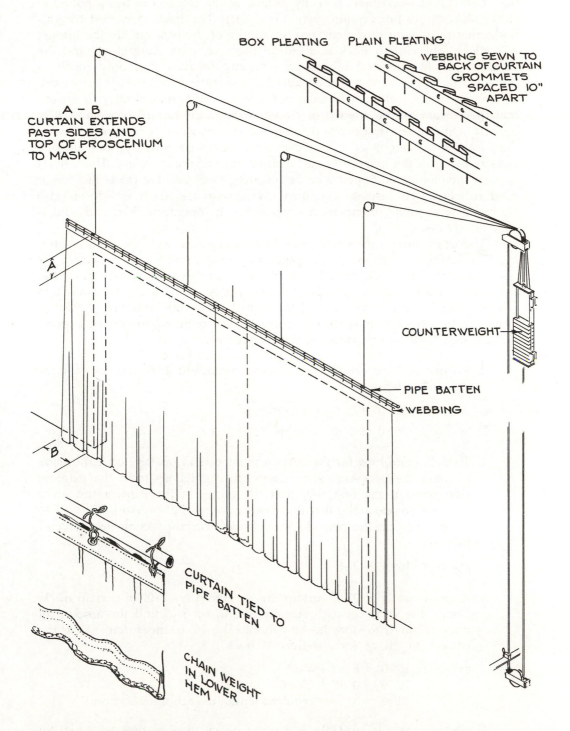

BOX PLEATING   PLAIN PLEATING

WEBBING SEWN TO
BACK OF CURTAIN
GROMMETS
SPACED 10"
APART

A – B
CURTAIN EXTENDS
PAST SIDES AND
TOP OF PROSCENIUM
TO MASK

A

COUNTERWEIGHT

B

PIPE BATTEN

WEBBING

CURTAIN TIED TO
PIPE BATTEN

CHAIN WEIGHT
IN LOWER
HEM

Plate 102   Fly Curtain

The Draw Curtain

Theatres with inadequate grid height for the operation of a fly curtain employ the draw curtain—one that opens by parting in the center and being pulled to either side of the proscenium arch (Plate 103). The tracks required for this horizontal movement of the curtains should be of the best quality the budget will allow. The curtain track is a critical piece of stage equipment, and the purchase of an inferior track as an economy measure can only result in dissatisfaction. The curtain tracks must be constructed to carry a heavy load, to operate easily without excessive noise, and, most importantly, to ensure that the curtain can be opened or closed without the hazard of fouling. The better-quality curtain tracks are of all-metal construction. It is also preferable that, for the full length of each section, the tracks be partially open on one side to allow for the inspection and maintenance of the travelers. The wheels of each traveler are equipped with ball-bearing races and are made of fiber or hard rubber as an insulation against excessive noise. Each traveler is also equipped with rubber bumpers, a support for the operating line, and adjustable tie chains.

The draw-curtain track is formed by two separate sections, each extending 1'-6" past the centerline of the stage in order to provide a 3'-0" overlap for the curtain material. If the full width of the arch is to be used, it is essential that the curtain tracks extend offstage past the edges of the arch far enough to permit gathering the curtain out of the sight lines of the audience. To determine the length of each section of curtain track required to service a proscenium arch 30'-0" wide, follow the steps listed below:

1. To one-half the width of the proscenium add 1'-6" required for the center overlap.

    EXAMPLE: 30'-0" ÷ 2   = 15'-0"
    15'-0" + 1'-6" = 16'-6"

2. To determine how far the curtain must extend offstage on either side to mask the backstage area, check the sight lines from the extreme side seats in the first row past the edges of the proscenium arch. Assume, for example, that this measurement is 3'-6". Add this 3'-6" to 16'-6" to obtain the overall width of each curtain section, exclusive of fullness.

    EXAMPLE: 16'-6" + 3'-6" = 20'-0"

3. Approximately 5'-0" of curtain can be stored on 1'-0" of curtain track. Divide the width of each curtain section by 5 to find the amount of track required to store it. Add this to the 16'-6" measurement for the correct length of each section of track.

    EXAMPLE: 20'-0" ÷ 5   = 4'-0"
    16'-6" + 4'-0" = 20'-6"
    20'-6"   = required length of each track section.

If offstage space is available, it is good policy to allow one extra foot for each section of track. Should the track be too long it can always be overlap-

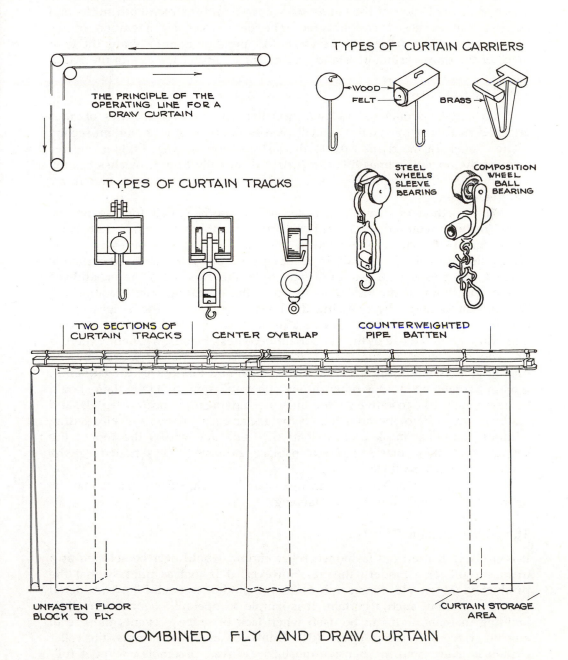

THE PRINCIPLE OF THE
OPERATING LINE FOR A
DRAW CURTAIN

TYPES OF CURTAIN CARRIERS

WOOD
FELT
BRASS

TYPES OF CURTAIN TRACKS

STEEL
WHEELS
SLEEVE
BEARING

COMPOSITION
WHEEL
BALL
BEARING

TWO SECTIONS OF
CURTAIN TRACKS

CENTER OVERLAP

COUNTERWEIGHTED
PIPE   BATTEN

UNFASTEN FLOOR
BLOCK TO FLY

CURTAIN STORAGE
AREA

COMBINED   FLY   AND   DRAW   CURTAIN

Plate 103   Types of Draw Curtain Carriers and Tracks

ped at the center, but if it is too short there is nothing that can be done to correct it.

In theatres possessing the proper facilities it is possible to have the front curtain so rigged that it can be converted to operate as either a fly or a draw curtain in a matter of minutes. In such cases the draw-curtain tracks are attached to the batten of the counterweight system by which both tracks and curtains can be raised and lowered. The only necessary alteration of the rigging required to change from draw to fly operation is unfastening the floor block of the draw-curtain lines and serving them around the end of the track.

The Tab Curtain

The tab curtain is operated by two lines that run through a series of rings attached to a webbing sewn diagonally across the back of each curtain section (Plate 104). Each line is tied off to the last and lowest ring. Pulling the free ends of the operating lines lifts the curtain diagonally until it reaches the full open position. This rigging drapes the curtain material into a decorative frame for the stage.

This method of controlling a curtain is poorly suited for use on the heavy material required for a front curtain. It is impossible to counterbalance the weight of the curtain operated in this manner, and it is necessary to tie off the lines to hold the curtain in an open position. The wider the curtain is opened, the greater becomes the weight to be lifted by the operator, and the greater the strain on the lock rings to which the operating lines are attached. The curtain is closed by releasing the lines and allowing the weight of the curtain to pull the operating lines back through the metal rings. Here another disadvantage to the use of the tab curtain becomes obvious: frequently there is not enough weight to the curtain to overcome the friction caused by the operating lines sliding through the metal rings, and this causes the curtain to remain partially open. One other disadvantage in using the tab curtain should be mentioned. Its decorative curved lines are suitable for concerts, recitals, and readings, but cannot be adjusted to the rectangular shape of a box setting without additional masking pieces at each side and across the top of the setting. With these masking pieces in place, however, the silhouette of the curtain is lost against them.

The main curtain of a few theatres has been rigged so that it may be operated by flying, drawing, or tabbing.

The Roller Curtain

It is unlikely that an old-fashioned roller curtain would ever be selected as a main curtain for a modern theatre. However, it is just as unlikely that the production of an old nineteenth-century melodrama would be considered complete without such a curtain. It is simple to operate, requires very little building material, and can be used when lack of space prevents the use of any other type of curtain (Plate 104). Unlike other front curtains, the roller curtain is made from inexpensive muslin or canvas, assembled without fullness of any kind, and then painted with some kind of decorative scene, usually bordered by advertisements of local merchants. The curtain material is supported by wooden battens in the same manner as for a regular drop. The lower hem is attached to a wooden cylinder, or roller, 8″ in diameter and about 3′-0″ longer than the required width of the curtain. The framework of

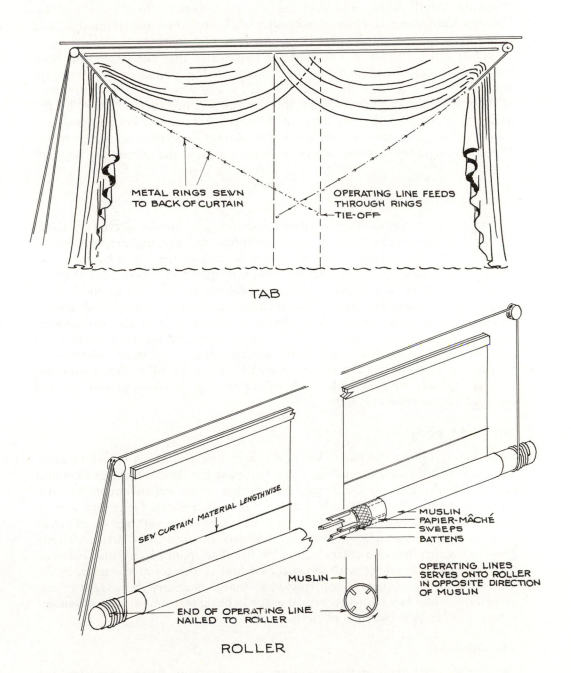

TAB

ROLLER

METAL RINGS SEWN
TO BACK OF CURTAIN

OPERATING LINE FEEDS
THROUGH RINGS
TIE-OFF

SEW CURTAIN MATERIAL LENGTHWISE

MUSLIN
PAPIER-MÂCHÉ
SWEEPS
BATTENS

MUSLIN

OPERATING LINES
SERVES ONTO ROLLER
IN OPPOSITE DIRECTION
OF MUSLIN

END OF OPERATING LINE
NAILED TO ROLLER

Plate 104 Tab and Roller Curtains

the roller is made from a series of wooden discs 8″ in diameter and four to six lengthwise battens. The discs are cut from 3/4″ 5-ply and the battens from 1″ × 3″ lumber. It is usually necessary to scarf-joint two pieces of 1″ × 3″ end to end to make one lengthwise batten. The discs are spaced at 3′-0″ to 4′-0″ intervals along the length of the roller and are notched to receive the 1″ × 3″ battens. The wooden frame is covered with chicken wire, then papier-mâché, and finally with strips of muslin glued over the dried papier-mâché.

The roller curtain is operated by two ropes that run from the floor through two overhead pulleys, then down to the points where they are attached at either end of the roller. The ropes are wrapped around the ends of the roller enough times to equal the vertical distance to be traveled by the roller. By pulling on the free ends of the rope, the roller is both turned and raised at the same time, which winds the curtain material around the roller. The operating lines must be tied off to a cleat to hold the curtain in the open position.

Teaser and Tormentors

Within certain limits the size of any proscenium arch can be altered by using a teaser and tormentors. The teaser is a horizontal masking border, usually made of the same material as the front curtain. It is attached to a batten of the counterweight system and suspended just upstage of the main curtain (Plate 105). The exposed area above settings of different heights can be masked by raising or lowering the teaser. The tormentors are vertical masking pieces, usually of plain flat construction, placed on either side of the proscenium opening just upstage of the teaser. They may be hinged together or arranged as a series of overlapping shutters that can either be shoved on stage to reduce the width of the arch or withdrawn to reveal its full width. Tormentor flats are usually covered with black velour or regular scene canvas painted black to avoid reflecting light.

The Light Bridge

Immediately upstage of the teaser is the light bridge. This is a metal framework about 2′-0″ wide extending a few feet past the limits of the proscenium arch on both sides of the stage. The bridge is an improvement of, and replacement for, the "first light border." It is suspended from two sets of counterweighted lines by which it may be adjusted to settings of different heights (Plate 106). It is raised and lowered by means of an electrically powered winch that also compensates for any discrepancy in balance between the weight of the bridge with its load and that of the counterweights in the arbor. Because the bridge is constructed so that it can carry the weight of one or two operators as well as the weight of the lighting instruments, its advantage over the older light batten is obvious.

The Gridiron

No matter what type of flying system a theatre may have—sandbags and rope-line rigging, counterweight system, multiple-speed counterweight system, or the Izenour electronic grid—it is essential that it be supported from some type of working platform that possesses great strength and provides a safe place on which crew members can work. Such a working platform is the gridiron, or grid

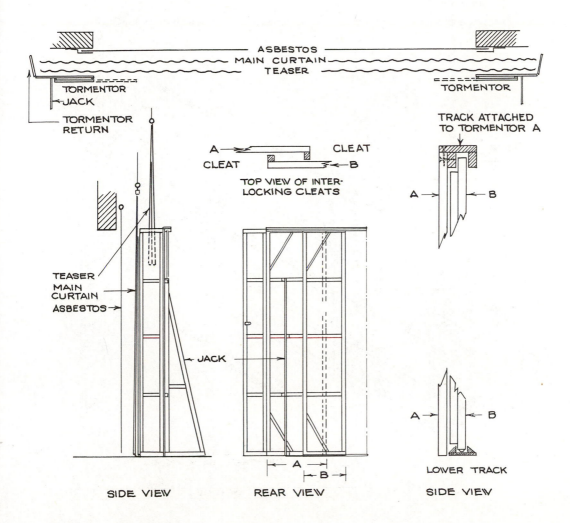

ASBESTOS
MAIN CURTAIN
TEASER

TORMENTOR
JACK
TORMENTOR
RETURN

TORMENTOR

TRACK ATTACHED
TO TORMENTOR A

A
CLEAT

CLEAT
B

TOP VIEW OF INTER-
LOCKING CLEATS

A
B

TEASER
MAIN
CURTAIN
ASBESTOS

JACK

A
B

A
B

LOWER TRACK

SIDE VIEW

REAR VIEW

SIDE VIEW

Plate 105   Adjustable Teaser and Tormentors

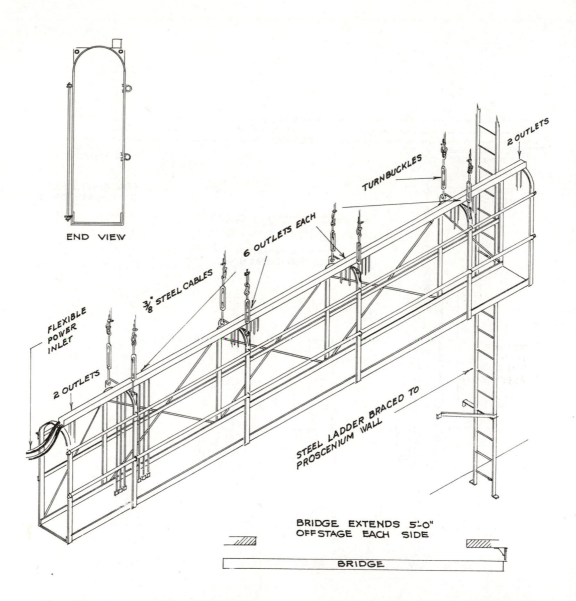

END VIEW

2 OUTLETS

TURNBUCKLES

6 OUTLETS EACH

3/8" STEEL CABLES

FLEXIBLE
POWER
INLET

2 OUTLETS

STEEL LADDER BRACED TO
PROSCENIUM WALL

BRIDGE EXTENDS 5'-0"
OFFSTAGE EACH SIDE

BRIDGE

Plate 106   Counterweighted Light Bridge

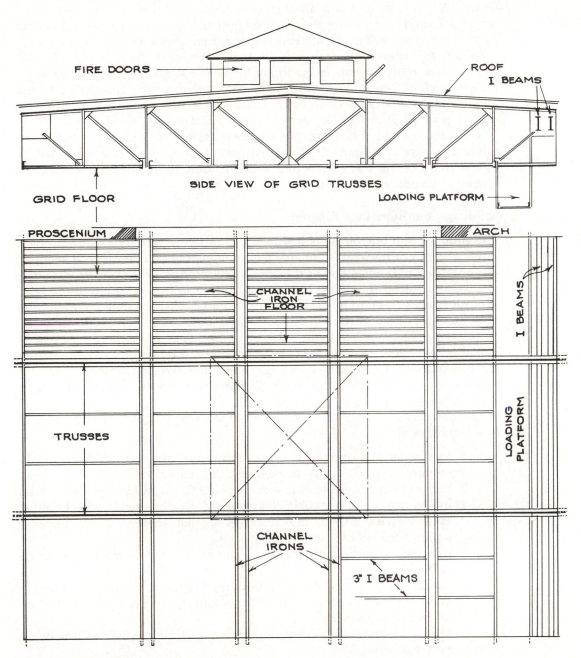

FIRE DOORS

ROOF
I BEAMS

SIDE VIEW OF GRID TRUSSES

GRID FLOOR

LOADING PLATFORM

PROSCENIUM

ARCH

CHANNEL
IRON
FLOOR

I BEAMS

TRUSSES

LOADING
PLATFORM

CHANNEL
IRONS

3" I BEAMS

Plate 107   Plan of Grid

(Plate 107). It is located at a distance of 5'-0" to 8'-0" beneath the roof of the stagehouse and extends over the entire stage area. The modern grid is formed by pairs of heavy supporting beams running at right angles to the proscenium wall, with each pair spaced approximately 10'-0" from the next. There is a space of 10" to 12" between each beam. To the top of the beams are bolted the loft blocks. A grilled floor is formed by bolting light channel irons at right angles to the supporting beams, spaced about 3" apart. These spaces form the necessary openings in the grid floor for special rigging effects; at the same time the irons provide a safe working floor for crew members. Access to the grid is provided by a stairway placed in one of the upstage corners of the stagehouse where it will be as much out of the way as possible. Open ladders to the grid are a senseless hazard in an educational theatre.

Sandbags and Rope-Line Rigging

The simplest and one of the oldest methods of flying scenery is lifting it by a series of ropes. If the load is too heavy for one man to handle easily, a sandbag can be added to the free end of the lines as counterbalance. Many of our older theatres are still so equipped. The ropes or lines run from a batten to the grid, over loft blocks, then to one side of the stagehouse, where they pass over the head blocks, and so down to the pinrail where they are tied off (Plate 108). The pinrail is a gallery attached to the sidewall of the stagehouse and usually placed 15'-0" to 20'-0" above the stage floor. There are two advantages to this location for the pinrail: (1) from this vantage point the flymen have a clear and unobstructed view of the stage floor; (2) the space beneath the pinrail can be used for storage of scenery and props.

However, the simplicity of this method of flying is more than offset by its disadvantages.

1. Expansion and shrinkage of the rope lines make it difficult to keep scenery in trim, that is, parallel with the stage floor.
2. Perfect balance between the scenery being flown and the sandbags used to balance it is impossible, because the weight of the scenery must always exceed that of the sandbags so that scenery can be lowered without the aid of special rigging lines.
3. Constant inspections must be made of rope lines and sandbags to ensure safety.
4. Scenery must be raised to high trim (the highest point to which scenery must be raised to get it out of sight) before the sandbag can be attached to counterbalance the load.
5. There is nothing to prevent the sidesway of the sandbag as it is being raised or levered.

This type of flying system is not recommended for the educational theatre. Students simply do not have the opportunity of working with it long enough to become proficient in its use or to guarantee safety.

The Counterweight System

The counterweight system is a much safer and better method of flying scenery and it has succeeded in overcoming all of the major disadvantages of rope-line rigging. In this system the rope lines have been replaced by steel cables, which

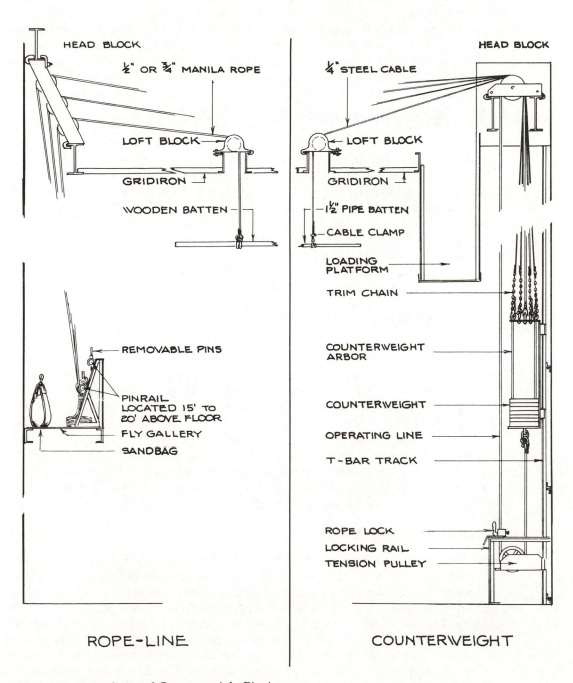

HEAD BLOCK

½" OR ¾" MANILA ROPE

LOFT BLOCK

GRIDIRON

WOODEN BATTEN

REMOVABLE PINS

PINRAIL
LOCATED 15' TO
20' ABOVE FLOOR

FLY GALLERY

SANDBAG

HEAD BLOCK

¼" STEEL CABLE

LOFT BLOCK

GRIDIRON

1½" PIPE BATTEN

CABLE CLAMP

LOADING
PLATFORM

TRIM CHAIN

COUNTERWEIGHT
ARBOR

COUNTERWEIGHT

OPERATING LINE

T-BAR TRACK

ROPE LOCK

LOCKING RAIL

TENSION PULLEY

ROPE-LINE

COUNTERWEIGHT

Plate 108   Rope-line and Counterweight Rigging

run from a pipe batten to the grid, over the loft blocks to one side of the stage where they pass over the head block, and are fastened off to a movable metal frame called the arbor (Plate 108). The cables are of such length that when the batten can be reached from the floor, the arbor is at the top of the stagehouse opposite the grid. Attached to the grid is the loading platform, from which the counterweights can be loaded into or removed from the arbor. Sidesway of the arbor is controlled by guide wires stretched between the grid and the floor, or by a vertical T-bar track secured to the side of the stagehouse. The batten and the arbor can be moved vertically by a ³/₄" manila rope called the purchase line or operating line. One end of this line is tied off to the bottom of the arbor. The other end then feeds down through a special tension pulley, passes up through the rope lock to the grid, then over the head block, and is tied off to the top of the arbor. The operating line might be considered as an endless loop, with the arbor forming a connecting link between the two ends of the line. Pulling down on the part of the purchase line that passes through the rope lock raises the arbor and lowers the scenery. Pulling down on the offstage line, or the part of the operating line attached to the bottom of the arbor, reverses the process. The rope locks are mounted on a metal framework called the locking rail that extends along the sidewall the full depth of the stagehouse. One great advantage of the counterweight system is that almost perfect balance can be obtained between the weight of the flown scenery and the counterweights.

The Multiple-Speed Counterweight System

The multiple-speed counterweight system employs a mechanical advantage of 2 to 1 in its rigging. The pipe batten moves twice as far and twice as fast as the arbor by which it is balanced. This system is especially suitable in remodeled theatres where the distance from the pinrail to the grid is less than that of the grid to the floor and in theatres where the stage floor area extends beyond the limits of the fly loft. This rigging permits the locking rail to be installed above the stage floor. The manufacturers of this system say it is the only rigging of this type that can be so perfectly counterbalanced that it requires no more effort to operate than a conventional counterweight set. Because of the special rigging arrangement used with this system, it is necessary to double the amount of counterweight normally required to balance the weight of the scenery.

Electrified Hoisting System

Enterprising engineers and theatre technicians are always seeking new methods of improving existing stage machinery. One of the earliest efforts to couple electrical power with the counterweight system resulted in the use of a motor-driven windlass and a heavy rope; variations of this principle are still used today. A loaded batten can be raised by attaching a rope to the underside of an arbor and serving the rope several times around the windlass; with the power turned on and tension kept on the rope the arbor can be brought to the stage floor, thus raising the batten. Perhaps the most sophisticated method of electrifying the counterweight system was introduced by George Izenour. He substituted electrical power and winches for counterweights and movable swivel loft blocks for fixed loft blocks and conventional pipe battens. Each winch was fitted with a ¹/₈" steel cable called a liftline that could be spotted at any desired position over the stage. The motors could be used separately or in combination. Controls for the motors were housed in a rolling console located backstage where it could be easily moved to meet the needs of a particular production. The latest refinement of the Izenour system has the motors located on the stage floor at the locking rail rather than at the grid, and the winches have been replaced by a gear reduction box and a sprocket over which runs a link chain that is attached to an operating cable and an arbor. The flexibility afforded by the movable swivel loft blocks is retained as is the movable control console.

CYCLORAMAS

The problem of providing the bit of sky seen through the windows of a setting is easily solved with a conventional backing, but the need for a wide expanse of sky required in many exterior settings has plagued dozens of designers. The problem has been solved in various ways. Where the budget is limited and the back wall of the stagehouse is unadorned by radiators, pipes, and other permanent equipment, a coat of plaster and sky-blue paint has often sufficed. The dependable though old-fashioned sky drop is also still used extensively. But these devices provide only a partial solution—the problem of masking the sides of the stage still remains. A step forward from the use of the sky drop was the introduction of the arm cyclorama. This was literally three sky drops—one across the back of the stage and one on each side extending obliquely toward offstage left and right. However, this arrangement presented an angular junction at the point where the side arms met the rear drop, a junction both unsightly and difficult to light. Continued experimentation has led to the development of the various types of cloth cycloramas that have proved highly satisfactory.

The Fly Cyc

The modern cyclorama is an unbroken expanse of canvas, either dyed or painted a sky blue, suspended from a U-shaped pipe batten, and enclosing the acting area on three sides. A second pipe batten is laced to the bottom of the cyc to hold the material free of wrinkles and prevent it from blowing. The cyc is raised and lowered by means of the counterweight system. Eight steel cables, from two arbors bolted together, are passed around muling blocks (blocks mounted in a horizontal position on the grid to change the direction of the cables), over special loft blocks, and then down to the top curved pipe batten, where they are clamped off. When the cyc is in its lowered position onstage there must be 18'-0" to 24'-0" of loft space above the top batten to permit the cyc to be raised above the stage floor by this distance. This provides the necessary clearance for the movement of scenery and reduces the likelihood of damage to the cyc.

The size of the cyc is determined by testing the horizontal and vertical sight lines from the extreme side seats in the front row against both the height and depth of the cyc. For example, when the proscenium arch is used at its full height and width, a person seated in one of these front seats should not be able to see the top of the cyc, or beyond the downstage limits of the side arms.

The placement of the cyc onstage in relation to the acting area and to the offstage area is very important. The side arms must be placed far enough offstage to allow adequate clearance for free movement of the counterweight battens, and enough floor space beyond the normal wall limits of a setting for placing backings. But, if the side arms are placed too far offstage, this could seriously reduce the space saved for storage of scenery and properties. Enough space should be left upstage of the cyc (3'-0" or 4'-0") for a crossover for actors and crew members.

The Trip Cyc

A variation of the fly cyc is the trip, or folding, cyc, which can be used in theatres with too little grid height for a regular fly cyc (Plate 109). The size and shape of a trip cyc may be identical with that of a regular fly cyc, but it differs in three respects: (1) The top batten of the trip cyc is permanently chained to the grid. (2) This cyc is fitted with a third curve pipe batten (the trip batten) that is laced to the back of the cyc material at a distance of 20'-0" or 24'-0" above the bottom batten. (3) The third difference lies in the rigging. The cables of the counter-weight sets are attached to the trip batten, and as these are raised the lower section of the cyc is lifted vertically while the upper section is folded to half its height by the same movement.

The trip cyc has two minor disadvantages: (1) Only the part of the cyc beneath the trip batten can be perfectly counterbalanced; as the cyc is raised the batten also lifts some of the weight of the material of the upper section. This increases the weight that must be manually lifted by the lineman operating the cyc. This is not too serious, as the weight does not become too heavy for one stagehand to lift it. (2) Wrinkles may appear around the trip batten after the cyc material has stretched. This can be easily corrected by retrimming the top batten through adjustment of the anchor chains holding it to the grid.

The Linnebach Cyc

Adolph Linnebach of Munich perfected a cloth cyclorama that operates on an entirely new principle. Like the trip cyc, it is suitable for theatres with insufficient grid height to permit the use of the conventional fly cyclorama. In shape the Linnebach cyc is similar to that of the fly cyc, but instead of being lifted vertically it moves horizontally and is stored by serving around a cone. The cyc is suspended from a hollow curved track which has an open slot on the bottom extending its full length. Feeding through the track is a rope of large diameter to which is attached a heavy canvas sleeve that drops through the slot in the track. The main body of the cyc is laced to the sleeve. Plate 110 illustrates this method of operation.

The Plaster Dome

A few theatres are equipped with plaster domes instead of cloth cycloramas. The back and sides of the dome are similar in shape to those of the cyclorama, but the dome also has an enclosing top that curves in overhead toward the proscenium arch. About the only advantage offered by this dome is its superior reflecting surface and the durability of the plaster, but its disadvantages are numerous. Its initial cost far exceeds the cost of a cloth cyclorama; the curved overhead extension precludes the possibility of using any extensive system of flying scenery; and, probably most serious of all, the permanent sidewalls force the movement of all actors, crew members, scenery, and props through restricted channels between the ends of the side arms and the proscenium wall, resulting in time-consuming traffic jams during scene shifts. In an effort to overcome the disadvantage of a dome built in a fixed position, the Germans developed a dome that could be rolled backward from the proscenium arch to clear the stage area. This scheme, while eliminating one disadvantage, introduces two others: it

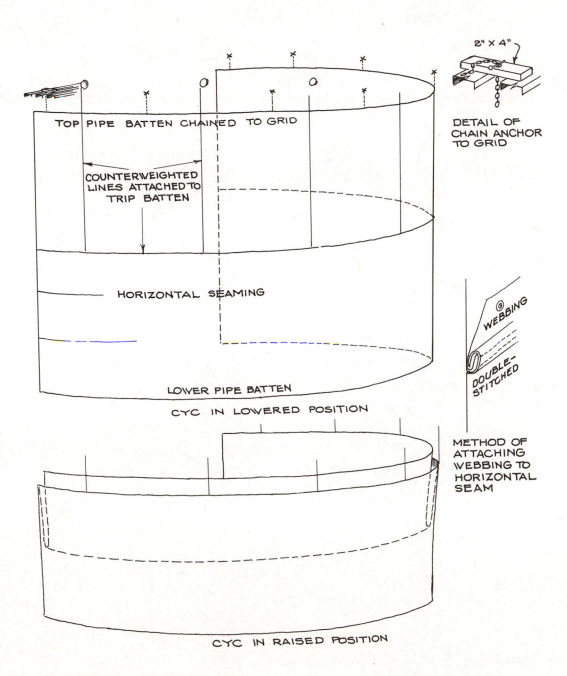

2" X 4"

DETAIL OF
CHAIN ANCHOR
TO GRID

TOP PIPE BATTEN CHAINED TO GRID

COUNTERWEIGHTED
LINES ATTACHED TO
TRIP BATTEN

HORIZONTAL SEAMING

LOWER PIPE BATTEN

CYC IN LOWERED POSITION

WEBBING

DOUBLE-
STITCHED

METHOD OF
ATTACHING
WEBBING TO
HORIZONTAL
SEAM

CYC IN RAISED POSITION

Plate 109   Diagram of Trip Cyc Rigging

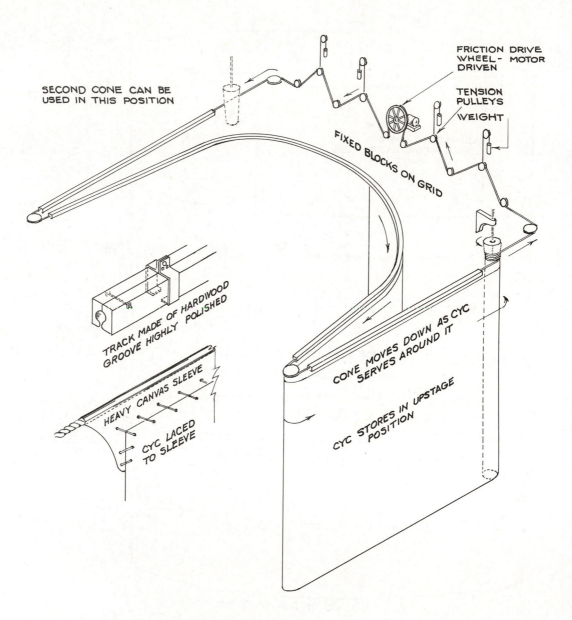

SECOND CONE CAN BE USED IN THIS POSITION

FRICTION DRIVE WHEEL- MOTOR DRIVEN

TENSION PULLEYS

WEIGHT

FIXED BLOCKS ON GRID

TRACK MADE OF HARDWOOD GROOVE HIGHLY POLISHED

HEAVY CANVAS SLEEVE

CYC LACED TO SLEEVE

CONE MOVES DOWN AS CYC SERVES AROUND IT

CYC STORES IN UPSTAGE POSITION

Plate 110   Operating Principle of Continental Cyc

requires an almost prohibitive amount of floor space to store it, and its construction cost is beyond the limit of most educational theatre budgets.

The Floor Cloth

The principal acting areas of the stage are covered with a heavy canvas cloth stretched over felt or jute padding. This floor cloth is usually dark brown, tan, or gray-green. It is laid with its downstage edge even with the curtain line. It extends about 4'-0" or 5'-0" beyond the proscenium arch on each side and upstage to a point beyond the average depth of a setting. It is usually tacked directly to the stage floor. Holding the floor cloth in place by fastening grommets over projecting screwheads driven into the floor is unsatisfactory. The heads of the projecting screws are hard to see and easy to trip over and they are soon bent and battered by rolling scenery. The floor cloth not only improves the appearance of settings that cannot make use of carpeting, but it also serves to muffle the noise created by shifting scenery and props and to deaden the sound of the footsteps of actors and crews.

13

Handling, Joining, and Shifting Scenery

As we have seen in Chapters 6 and 7, a set of scenery consists of a series of individual parts or units made separately and joined together by various methods to form the finished setting. Because these individual pieces of scenery will be handled many times during the process of shifting, whatever methods are used in joining them together onstage must be governed by the ease and quietness of assembly and by the degree of compactness and portability. This chapter is concerned with how individual pieces of scenery can be handled, joined, and shifted.

HANDLING SCENERY

Two-dimensional framed scenery is comparatively light in weight, but its width and height can make it very awkward for an inexperienced person to move (Plate 111). Furthermore, time spent in building and painting scenery can be lost and the scenery damaged seriously in any number of ways by improper handling. Careless stacking or handling methods can result in ruined paint jobs, stretched or snagged or torn covering material, and in extreme cases even warped or broken framing members. Damage of this type can usually be avoided by following the suggestions given below for handling scenery.

Raising a Flat

All but the largest and heaviest flats can be raised to a vertical position by a single person. Move to the center of the flat and lift it so that it rests on one stile.

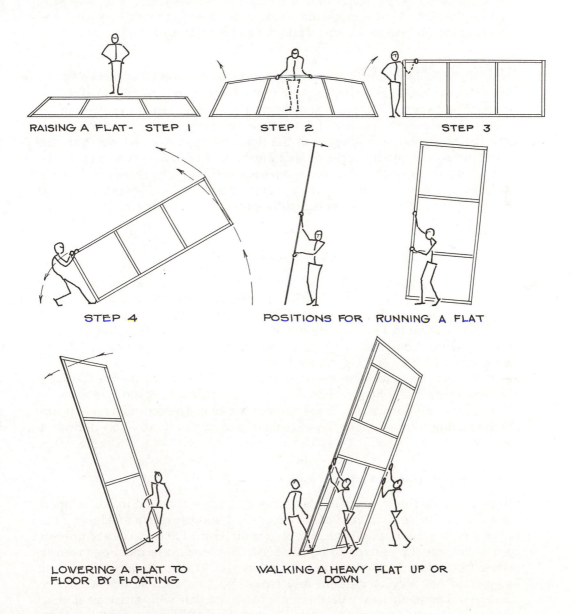

RAISING A FLAT- STEP 1

STEP 2

STEP 3

STEP 4

POSITIONS FOR RUNNING A FLAT

LOWERING A FLAT TO
FLOOR BY FLOATING

WALKING A HEAVY FLAT UP OR
DOWN

Plate 111 Suggestions for Handling Flats

Balance it in this position and move toward its base. Place one foot against the lower corner and with both hands gripping the upper corner pull sharply downward and out. As the flat reaches the vertical position move to one side of it and grasp the stile with one hand placed a little above head level. The other arm crosses the body at the waist with the hand gripping the stile from this level. The lower arm is kept rigidly in this position while the upper arm is used to balance the flat. A few moments spent experimenting with this grip and balancing the flat will reveal how easily it can be controlled.

Walking or Running a Flat

The above method of gripping a flat forces the stagehand to face in the direction he proposes to move. The flat is at one side of him and in such a position that it will not interfere with his view. Lifting the leading edge of the flat a few inches from the floor, and with the top of the flat leaning in slightly over him, the stagehand moves rapidly in the desired direction. The trailing corner of the flat skids along on the floor and serves as a partial stabilizer. The more rapidly a flat is moved, the greater is the air pressure exerted against its side surfaces—a fact that can be used to good advantage in helping to balance any wide flat that is being moved.

Raising a Heavy Flat or a Series of Hinged Flats

Oversized flats or several flats that have been joined together require two or more stagehands to raise them. The lower rails must be blocked to prevent their slipping; the upper rails are lifted until the stagehands can reach the stiles. They then raise the unit to a vertical position by "walking" hand over hand along the stiles. Care must be taken not to push against the unsupported canvas during this process or the covering material will be badly stretched. Large flats and folded flats are best moved by two crew members. The lead man grips the flat in the same manner as if he were handling it alone, while the second man grips the trailing edge and pushes as well as helps to balance it. The second man must not lift the trailing corner from the floor, as this makes the unit extremely difficult to balance.

Lowering Flats from a Vertical Position

Single-plane flats or a series of plane flats that are not folded into a compact stack can be "floated" to the floor by blocking the lower rails and allowing the flats to fall face down; the air cushion caught under the flat surfaces will prevent their falling rapidly enough to be damaged. However, care must be taken to release both sides of the unit to fall together; otherwise the air cushion will escape and one side of the unit may strike the floor with sufficient force to damage it. Extremely heavy flats, narrow flats, and flats with extensive door or window openings in them are best lowered to the floor by "walking them down."

Stacking Scenery

Units of scenery will be moved and stored temporarily any number of times in the process of building and during the run of a production. A little care in stacking can avoid possible damage.

1. The more nearly vertical the scenery can be stacked, the less risk there will be of warping the stiles and the less floor space will be required.
2. On the back of each unit should be painted act and scene identification numbers. Stack the units in the order in which they will be used.
3. Stack the scenery on stage as close as possible to the position where it will be used.
4. Protect the paint job by stacking with painted surfaces placed face to face.

JOINING SCENERY

The fact that scenery must be portable and easily joined is one of the conditions governing its construction and shifting. The technician will have determined by her analysis of the production how the individual parts of the setting will be made, how they are to be joined to form units, and how these units will be assembled into the completed setting. Her decisions on these matters are governed by two considerations: the ease and convenience of handling the part during construction, and the rapidity and quietness of assembling it during a scene shift. Scenery is assembled by being permanently joined, by hinging, or by lashing.

Permanent Joining

Within the limits of portability, any part of the setting that can be handled as a unit is permanently joined by means of bolts, screws, or nails. The various parts of such units as a fireplace, a door, or a window will be so assembled. A stairway and its backings may be permanently joined by mounting them on a wagon and shifting them by rolling. Individual flats may be permanently joined to each other by hinging. Permanent joining is used except when it will interfere with the fast and easy assembly of units during a scene shift.

Hinging

Hinging scenery can provide either a permanent or a temporary method of joining (Plate 112). Permanent junctions are formed by the use of tight-pin back-flap hinges, temporary junctions by pin hinges with removable pins. By using a loose-pin hinge any two units can be quietly and quickly locked together or taken apart.

It is an unusual setting that does not have a wall area greater than the maximum width of any individual flat. Such expanses of wall are usually formed by permanently hinging a series of flats edge to edge and covering both the junction and the hinges with a strip of canvas called a dutchman. For flats that are to fold face to face one hinge is placed on the face of the flat a foot down from the top, the second a foot up from the bottom, and the third midway between. Hinges should not be separated by a greater distance than 4'-0" or 5'-0", as this may result in irregularities in alignment of the stiles that will in turn cause the dutchman to buckle or wrinkle. Only when the scenery is too light in color and subjected to strong side lighting is it necessary to countersink the hinges, because the shadow of hinges may then prove objectionable. The diagrams in Plate 112 illustrate some of the problems that must be met in hinging two or more flats together. Two flats of any widths can be hinged together and will fold without complications. Three flats of varying widths can be hinged together,

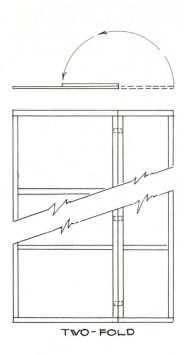

TWO-FOLD

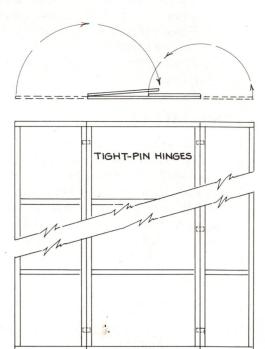

TIGHT-PIN HINGES

THREE-FOLD   PLACE WIDE FLAT IN
THE CENTER

TUMBLER

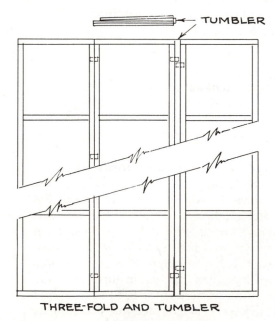

THREE-FOLD AND TUMBLER

LOOSE-PIN
HINGES

FLATS HINGED ON BACK

Plate 112   Joining Flats by Hinging

provided that the widest flat can be placed in the center. This permits the two outer flats to fold over each other without binding. Three flats of almost identical widths cannot be folded together without the stile of one binding against that of another. This problem can be overcome by inserting a vertical 1″ × 3″, called a tumbler, between two of the flats and hinging it to both. This will provide the necessary clearance for folding the flats into a compact unit.

If a hinged unit is to be shifted by running, it is well to avoid joining more than three large flats or four small ones together. A standard plain flat 5′-9″ × 14′-0″ that has been painted two or three times will weigh about 35 to 40 pounds; four such flats would make a top-heavy unit of 160 pounds! Hinging flats together has the following advantages:

1. It reduces the number of individual flats to be handled.
2. It reduces the number of required lashings.
3. It reduces the time required for shifting.
4. It eliminates the visible junction between flats that are joined edge to edge.
5. It holds flats more rigidly in place than lashing does.
6. The paint job is automatically protected when flats fold face to face.

Joining Scenery by Lashing

Even when a setting does not have to be shifted it is rare to find one that does not have some of its units joined by lashing. If for no other reason than convenience in assembling and striking, it is worth the little time required to fit the units with lashing hardware. There is a strong possibility too, if the various parts of the setting have been permanently joined by nails or screws, that some will be damaged during the process of dismantling. Student crews seem to work much harder and with more abandon in striking a set than at any other time. One or two misdirected blows with a hammer, or an energetic yank on the lower part of a stile that is still nailed to another unit at the top, can result in damaged stock.

Lashing is the process of joining two flats by lacing them together with ¼″ cotton sash cord that engages cleats placed alternately at graduated heights on both flats. As one faces the rear of two flats that are to be joined by this method, the lash line is always attached to the upper right-hand corner of the left flat. It can be attached to a conventional lash-line eye that is screwed in place on the inner edge of the stile just beneath the upper corner block; or a ³⁄₈″ hole drilled through the corner block can be substituted for a lash-line eye. In either case the lash line is inserted in the hole, knotted, drawn tight, and trimmed so that the free end will just touch the floor. This leaves an adequate length for the tie-off knot, and yet is not long enough to be stepped on when the flat is being shifted, or to get caught under a stack of scenery.

Placement of Lashing Hardware (Plate 113). There are three standard measurements governing the placing of lash cleats. The highest cleat should be placed about 1′-6″ below the top of the flat. If it is placed closer to the anchor point of the lash line, it is hard to throw the lash line around it. For the same reason no lash cleat should be placed closer to a toggle bar than 6″ or 8″ unless the cleat can be reached from the floor. The third fixed measurement is the height of the two tie-off cleats. These should be placed exactly opposite each

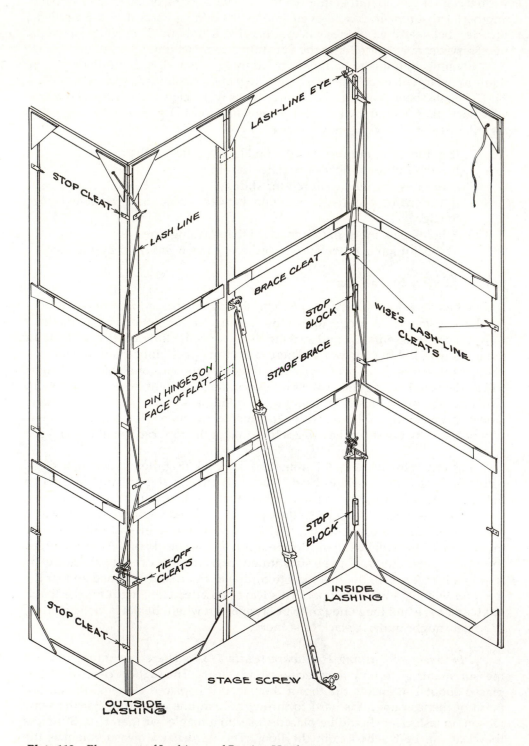

Plate 113   Placement of Lashing and Bracing Hardware

other 3'-0" from the floor. If they are placed lower than this, they are awkward for the stagehand to reach while tying off the lash line. Furthermore, unless the lash line is left longer than the flat, there is not enough of it below the cleats with which to make a tie-off knot, and the disadvantage of having the lash line longer than the flat has already been mentioned. The number of lash cleats in addition to the highest and tie-off cleats is determined by the height of the flat. These cleats are placed alternately on the two flats about 3'-0" apart.

Throwing the Lash Line.   Throwing the lash line around the cleats requires a little skill and a great deal of practice. An experienced stagehand can do it with great speed and practically no noise. A novice, on the other hand, may add several long minutes to a scene shift, and sound as though he were beating a rug while he is at it. Lashing two flats together is accomplished in the following manner: First place the two edges of the flats in position, align them, and hold them in place with the left hand. Grasp the lash line with the right hand, pull it taut, and hold it a second or two in this position until it has stopped all movement. Now make a sharp semicircular movement to the right which will give a partial loop to the line. At the same instant allow a little slack in the line by raising the right arm so that the loop can travel the full length of the lash line. Since the uppermost cleat is on the right-hand flat, the right-handed loop has a good chance of engaging it. The next lower cleat will be on the left-hand flat so that a loop thrown to the left will engage it. Repeat this process with each cleat until the two tie-off cleats are reached. Pass the line under both these cleats, form a loop with the end of the line, and pass it under that part of the line just above the cleats. Pull down sharply on the loop; this will draw the lash line tight and ensure a close junction between the flats. Complete the tie-off knot by passing a second loop through the first and pulling it tight. This knot is illustrated on Plate 113. The sound effect of beating a rug is usually caused by holding the lash line too tight and snapping it violently against the back of the canvas. Not only is this an objectionable noise, but there is an excellent chance of chipping the paint off the face of the flat.

Types of Lashing Joints.   There are three types of possible lashings: outside lashing; edge-to-edge, or 180° lashing; and inside lashing. If the technician has any choice in the matter, she will select units that can be joined by using the outside lashing, as this is by far the easiest to make. Any junction formed by two flats whose backs are separated by an angle greater than 180° is considered an outside lashing. The edge-to-edge lashing is used only when the junction between the flats can be concealed by architectural trim placed over the face of the flats, or when the junction will be out of sight of the audience. It is practically impossible to lash the edges of two flats tightly enough together to keep the junction from being visible or to keep a backstage light from spilling through. The inside lashing is formed when the backs of the flats are placed at an angle of less than 180°. This type of lashing is avoided whenever possible, because the more acute the angle between the flats becomes the less room there is for handling the lash line. Furthermore, because of the change in the direction of the lash line's pull on the cleats, there is a risk that the cleats will be torn loose from the stiles when the line is pulled tight.

The butt joints formed by the edges of flats joined by lashing should be placed as nearly parallel to the proscenium opening as is possible. This makes the junction a little less obvious; more importantly, it destroys the possibility of seeing a backstage light from out front.

The Use of Stop Cleats and Stop Blocks.   A set of either stop cleats or stop blocks is placed on one of any two flats that are to be joined by lashing. Stop cleats are an aid in aligning the edges of the flats and are used only on outside and edge-to-edge lashings. The stop cleat is a 3″ length of strap iron ³/₄″ wide, with one end drilled to receive two screws. The cleat is attached to the stile with its free end projecting ³/₄″ beyond the outer edge of the stile. Three cleats usually make up the set employed on each lashing—one placed near the top of the flat, one near the bottom, and the third midway between the two.

An inside lashing requires the use of stop blocks to prevent one flat from slipping past the edge of the other. These stop blocks are made from scrap lumber by cutting strips of wood 1″ wide and 6″ to 8″ long and drilling each strip to receive two No. 9 1¹/₂″ screws. The blocks are screwed to the back side of the stile ³/₄″ from the outer edge in approximately the same positions as the stop cleats: one near the top, one near the bottom, and the other halfway between these two.

Substitute Lashing Hardware.   If the budget will not permit the purchase of conventional lashing hardware, it is possible to make acceptable substitute lash cleats and stop cleats. Probably the best lash cleat is made from ¹/₄″ plywood, 2″ wide by 4¹/₂″ long. Shape one end of the cleat into a rounded point and attach the other end to the flat by screws or clout nails. A stronger lash cleat can be made from strap iron ¹/₈″ thick by ³/₄″ wide. Cut this into 4¹/₂″ lengths, drill one end to receive two roundheaded screws, and round off the other end with an emery wheel. Still another and less expensive lash cleat can be made from a 6″ length of 1″ × 3″. This block is nailed or screwed to the back of the stile and a heavy roundheaded screw is driven into its inner edge and left projecting by 1″ or so. The line can be lashed around this projecting screw. Projecting nails or screws driven directly into the inner edges of stiles are not satisfactory because the lack of clearance between them and the canvas makes them hard to engage with the lash line. Use of the block as just described gives an added ³/₄″ in clearance.

An unorthodox, but highly effective, method of joining scenery is the use of either C-clamps or adjustable wooden clamps. Occasionally two or more wagons (platforms mounted on castors) may be joined into a single unit while onstage and locked by clamps fitted around adjoining framing members. Sometimes the clamps can be used to good advantage for joining edge to edge two flats that cannot be drawn tightly enough together by lashing.

BRACING SCENERY

There are few things quite so shattering to the illusion created by a well-constructed and well-painted setting as to have the setting shake and wobble when an actor touches it or a door is closed. Since scenery must necessarily be light in weight, it must also be solidly braced to eliminate this possibility of shaking. At the same time, the bracing of scenery must be governed by the same factors that dictate its construction: namely, that the bracing be light and portable, strong, and capable of fast and quiet joining and disassembly.

The temporary bracing of scenery is normally accomplished by one of several methods: (1) by use of a standard adjustable stage brace, cleat, and stage screw; (2) by use of rigid or folding jacks; (3) by use of stiffening battens; and (4) by bracing one unit against another that can be placed at an angle to it. When a setting does not have to be shifted, the bracing can be of a permanent type—supported by diagonal braces, jacks, or guy wires that may be nailed, screwed, or bolted into place.

The Stage Brace

The most common method of bracing scenery is by the use of a standard adjustable stage brace. This brace consists of two overlapping lengths of hardwood that can be extended or contracted and held at the desired length by tightening a thumbscrew. One end of the brace is equipped with a double-pronged curved hook that is designed to engage the eye of a brace cleat. The lower end of the brace is equipped with either an angular or a curved rigid foot iron through which a stage screw can be driven into the floor to lock the brace into position. The cleat is attached to the rear of the stile at a point a little above half the height of the flat. Scenery, of course, can be braced at any point where there is need for it, but under normal circumstances it is usually braced on the back of flats that have been joined by hinging. There is usually little need of bracing at a point where two flats are joined by lashing. Those flats are generally at an angle to each other and so brace themselves.

There are exceptional cases where, for one reason or another, stage screws cannot be driven into the stage floor—floors of linoleum-covered concrete or highly polished hardwood are examples. In such situations one of the following alternatives can be used: (1) rigid or folding jacks can be attached to the scenery with their bases weighted down by sandbags; (2) regular stage braces can be used, provided that special wooden bases are constructed to receive the stage screws. A base of this type is made of 2″ stock; it is about 20″ square, with a rubber bathmat glued to its undersurface to prevent its slipping. Additional stability can be given to the bases by weighting them down with sandbags.

Rigid and Folding Jacks

In situations where the shape or size of scenery prevents the use of standard braces, or when the scenery is subjected to violent action, bracing is usually accomplished by a homemade brace called a jack. The jack is a three-cornered frame made of 1″ × 3″ or 1″ × 4″ stock, and consists of a vertical member, a base, and a diagonal (Plate 114). The three parts are joined to each other by corner blocks and keystones held by clout nails. The vertical member must be extended at least two-thirds the height of the unit for adequate support. A rigid foot iron or a stage-brace cleat bent at right angles and attached to the base of the jack will provide a means of screwing the jack to the floor. The jack is fastened to the flat by hinging it either to a stile or to two or more cross battens. By placing the hinges on alternate sides of the vertical the jack is held rigidly at right angles to the flat. On flats that must be shifted, the jack can be folded flush against the flat by placing all the hinges on the same side of the vertical. For lightweight cutouts such as bushes or hedges, a small sandbag weighing about 10 pounds is thrown over the base of the jack as a substitute for foot irons and stage screws. Irregularly shaped units can be both supported and braced by jacks that are constructed to fit the desired form. See illustration on Plate 114.

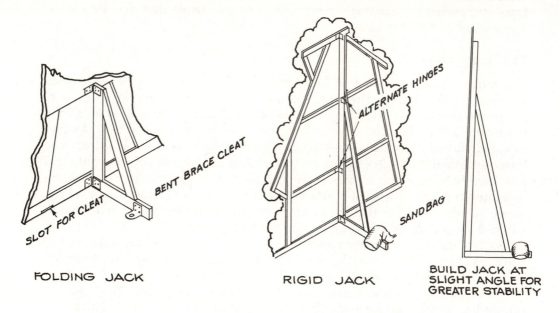

FOLDING JACK

RIGID JACK

BUILD JACK AT
SLIGHT ANGLE FOR
GREATER STABILITY

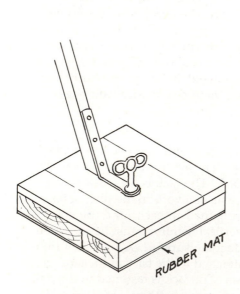

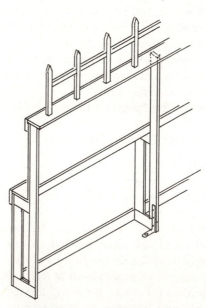

PROTECTIVE FLOOR BLOCK

RIGID JACK ADAPTED TO
IRREGULAR SHAPE

Plate 114   Jacks

Stiffening Battens

When standard 1″ × 3″ or 1″ × 4″ stock is fastened to a series of hinged flats with the width of the lumber at right angles to the direction of the fold, it will hold the flats in a rigid position (Plate 115). Stock lumber used in this manner is known as a stiffening batten. There are several types of these battens, or stiffeners, in common use: permanent, detachable, and swivel stiffeners.

Permanent Stiffener A permanent stiffener is attached to units of scenery that must be held in a rigid position both during the playing of a scene and while the scenery is being shifted. (The back wall of a setting that is to be shifted by flying, or a section of wall that is to be handled on a tip jack, are good examples.) The stiffener is made as long as the unit is wide and is attached to the back of the flats by hinging it on alternate side to the stiles. Usually one stiffener placed at a height about two-thirds that of the flats is adequate. On exceptionally tall flats (18′-0″ or over) it may be necessary to use two. The stiffener, like the jack, may be shaped to conform with any irregularly formed unit and can be used in a vertical as well as horizontal position.

Detachable Stiffener. The detachable stiffener is used on units that require additional bracing during the time they are used but must be folded into a compact stack for the shift or for storage. A series of S-hooks is made of ¼″ × ¾″ strap iron; one end of each hook is shaped to fit over the toggle bars, and the other end is shaped to receive the stiffening batten. It is important that the hooks be tightly fitted to both toggles and batten; otherwise it will allow too much free movement to the flats it is supposedly bracing. To prevent the S-hooks from tearing the covering material or poking holes in it when the flats are folded, the hooks are generally screwed permanently to the stiffening batten and shifted with it. The use of this type of stiffener requires that all of the toggle bars be at the same height from the lower rails.

Swivel Stiffener. The swivel stiffener serves the same purpose as the detachable stiffener, but it can be used only on flats that when folded are no wider than half the length of the stiffener. Two pieces of 1″ × 3″ are cut as long as the combined widths of the flats to which they will be attached. The stiffener is made by joining the two along their length by butting the edge of one against the width of the other. The stiffener is then bolted to one of the center stiles by a single carriage bolt and wing nut so that it is free to pivot. When the stiffener is pivoted to the horizontal position, its ends engage the S-hooks that are permanently attached to the toggle bars of the flats.

SHIFTING SCENERY

Despite the tremendous diversity in plans and equipment of theatres, and despite the variety in form and shape of stage settings, there are but four recognized methods by which scenery can be shifted. It can be propelled about the stage manually by running it, as was described earlier in this chapter; it can be raised above the stage floor by flying it; it can be rolled in any number of ways; and it can be lowered through the floor to the basement by means of elevators. However, as far as the educational theatre is concerned, the last method of

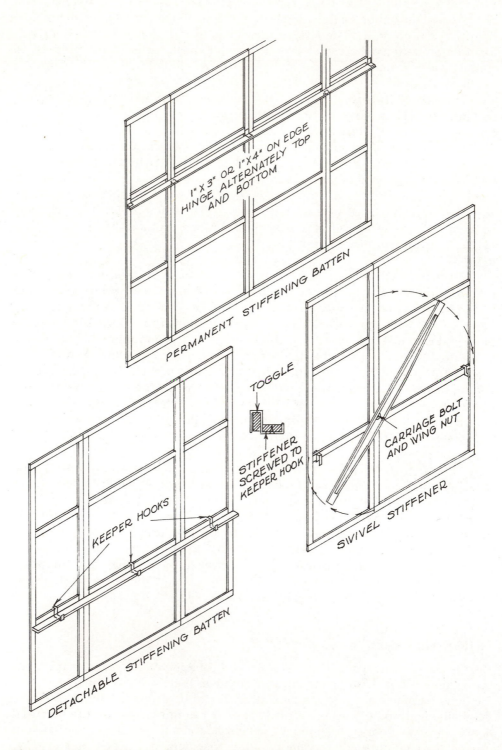

Plate 115   Three Methods of Attaching Stiffener Battens

shifting is best disregarded—the cost of the elevators and their installation is usually prohibitive.

Running Scenery

Running scenery is the simplest and the most commonly used method of shifting scenery. It requires no special equipment and on very small stages is frequently the only way that it can be shifted at all. No matter how elaborately a stage may be equipped or how much floor space there may be, some parts of each setting are usually shifted by running.

Flying Scenery

Flying is the fastest and quietest method of shifting. Moreover, it has the advantage of keeping scenery off the stage floor and out of the way when not in use, and it automatically stores it where there is little likelihood of its being damaged. It has already been pointed out that there are four systems used in flying scenery: rope-line rigging and sandbag balance, counterweight system, multiple-speed counterweight system, and the Izenour electronic grid. Of these the counterweight system is most frequently found in educational theatres, and hence a detailed account of its use is given here. To suspend a unit of scenery from a counterweight batten proceed as follows:

1. Select and lower to within a few feet of the floor a batten that is at the desired distance from the arch.
2. Establish the correct position for the flown unit in respect to the center line of the stage and mark it on the stage floor.
3. Place the unit face down on these marks with the upper rails or batten directly beneath the pipe batten from which it will be suspended.
4. Attach the scenery to the batten with chain, rope, wire, or batten clamps. (The permanent hardware, such as hanger irons, hook hanger irons, ceiling plates, and so forth, was bolted to the scenery while it was still in the shop.)
5. Balance the weight of the scenery with counterweights placed in the arbor.
6. Raise the scenery to a vertical position and make final adjustments in both counterbalance and snatch lines to obtain perfect balance and trim.
7. Place identification card on the locking rail to identify the unit with the operating line controlling its movement.
8. Reverse the procedure to remove scenery from a counterbalanced batten.

Safety Precautions for Use with the Counterweight System. There is nothing complicated about the use of the counterweight system. By exercising a little common sense, and by following the precautions listed below, it is possible to avoid unnecessary risks.

1. Clear the stage of all personnel when crew members are working on the grid. Clear the area under the loading platform when counterweights are being loaded or unloaded.
2. When crew members are working on the grid or loading platform, do not permit them to carry extra tools or objects that might fall from their pockets to the floor below.

3. Do not stack counterweights above the lip of the loading platform where they might be knocked off.
4. In the process of rigging scenery to fly, attach the scenery to the batten first and then add the counterweights to the arbor.
5. In striking scenery (dismantling the production), unload the counterweights from the arbor first and then unfasten the scenery.
6. Heavy units of scenery should be flown with the snatch lines attached to the bottom member of the piece, to place all joints under compression.
7. Inspect and eliminate all faulty materials used in attaching scenery to the batten.
8. All hardware used in supporting a flown unit should be bolted in place. Screws used alone may pull loose from soft wood if subjected to a sudden strain.
9. The rope lock must not be used to secure an imbalanced load. The lock is intended solely to prevent any possible creeping of a set of lines that is only slightly out of balance.

Safety Precautions for Use with Rope Line Rigging System. Some theatres are still equipped with the old rope line and sandbag rigging system or they have a combination of both rope line and counterweight systems. For those who are unfamiliar with rope lines, the following precautions are offered:

1. Regular periodic inspection of rope lines is essential.
2. Check sandbags for possible leaks. A serious accident can occur if sand has leaked from a sandbag after it has been used to balance a load of scenery.
3. Inspect the wooden battens for possible weakness. These battens are usually 2″ thick by 4″ wide and are made from lengths of 1″ × 4″ screwed face to face with staggered butt joints and with the outer edges rounded to prevent damage to the lines.
4. Estimate the weight of the scenery that is to be flown. Make sure sandbags of a comparable weight are available and in the proper position along the pin rail.
5. In attaching light weight scenery to a set of lines follow this procedure: lower empty batten to the floor and attach scenery with trim chains. Two or three flymen pull scenery to its high trim and snub the lines around a pin in the pin rail to hold the scenery in this position temporarily. Now attach a clew plate to the lines above the pin rail and a sandbag to the clew plate. Release lines from the pin rail and test the balance.
6. Flown scenery must be heavier than the sandbags that are used partially to balance the scenery; otherwise the scenery cannot be lowered to the stage floor without a special rigging line.
7. Heavy scenery is usually raised to high trim by means of a tackle rigging. Before attaching scenery to a batten raise the empty batten to high trim, attach a clew plate to the lines, and the moving block of a tackle to the clew plate. Lower the batten while at the same time paying out line of the tackle. Attach scenery to the batten and raise to high trim by the mechanical advantage of this tackle. Sandbags of the proper weight are snapped on or chained to the clew plate. The tackle rigging can now be removed.

8. A set of lines from which the wooden batten has been removed must be looped together and a sandbag of sufficient weight attached to pull the lines back to the stage floor once the empty lines have been taken to high trim.

9. When control of a unit of scenery depends upon a flyman's grip on a rope, a safe working load is a relatively low 45 to 50 pounds. This figure is highly variable since it depends upon the diameter of the rope being handled and on the individual flyman's strength. It is better to underestimate this figure than to run the risk of having an accident.

10. When removing scenery from a set of lines, just reverse the procedure by which it was initially rigged.

Rolling Scenery

Three-dimensional, heavy, or irregularly shaped scenery is most easily shifted by mounting it on castors and rolling it. This method of shifting is not only the easiest, but also one of the most adaptable techniques for moving scenery. It can be employed for moving the smaller individual parts of a setting or adapted to handle whole wall sections; or it can be used to shift an entire setting, including all of the decorative and practical properties. Rolling units can be powered by one of three methods: they can be moved manually by being pulled or shoved, they can be moved mechanically by the aid of winches or tackle rigging, or they can be so rigged that they are driven electrically.

Wagon Stages. One of the advantages of the rigid over the parallel platform is the ease with which it can be converted into a small wagon. Plate 116 illustrates the method of attaching castors to the underside of the platform tops to convert them into either single-step wagons or wagons of greater height. Probably the most commonly used wagon height is the single-step unit with an elevation of about 7″ from the stage floor. This size can be used in a raised alcove, at the base of a stairway, or in a raised entranceway. Wagons of this height must be equipped with castors of the proper size and capacity. Those illustrated are rubber-tired swivel castors that measure 4½″ from the bottom of the wheel to the top of the plate; they are fitted with wheels 3″ in diameter. These castors are rated as a medium-heavy-duty type with a maximum capacity of 400 pounds. Castors of this height can be so mounted that the finished wagon is only 6¾″ high. To attach them, turn the platform upside down and measure the distance between the 2″ × 4″ supporting members. Cut four lengths of 2″ × 6″ and test-fit them into the four corners of the platform. These will form the plates to which the castors will be bolted. Since they will remain permanently attached to the platforms after the castors have been removed, be sure that they are held back 4 or 5″ from the end frames so that they will not take up the space required for bolting legs to the same platform. Mark the position of the castors on the 2″ × 6″ plates and drill holes for ⅜″ × 2½″ carriage bolts. Be sure to countersink the bolt heads so that the top of the plates will fit flush against the underside of the flooring. Bolt the castors into place, fit the 2″ × 6″ plates into position on the platform, and drive 12-penny nails through the 2″ × 4″ framework into the ends of each plate. Additional support can be given to the assembly by screwing the floor boards directly above the castors to the 2″ × 4″ framing. This type of assembly has proved satisfactory for all normal wagon loads. Under exceptional weight loads, brackets made from ¼″ or ⁵⁄₁₆″ × 2½″ strap iron are made to fit

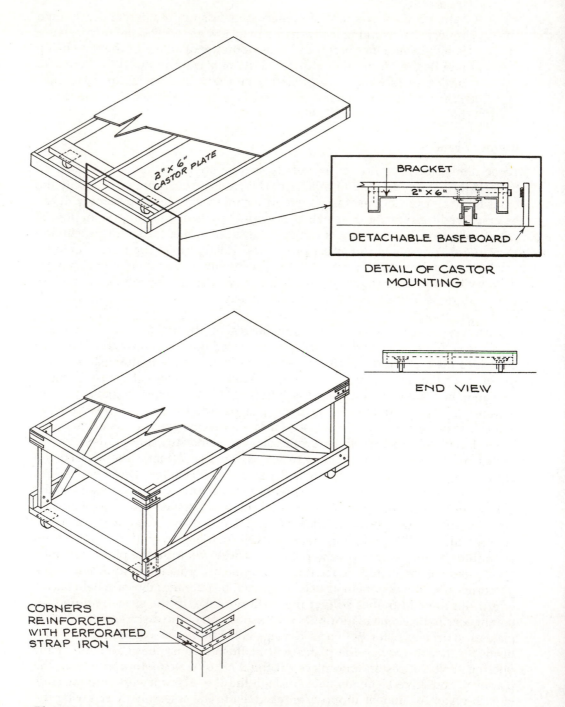

2" X 6"
CASTOR PLATE

BRACKET

2" X 6"

DETACHABLE BASEBOARD

DETAIL OF CASTOR
MOUNTING

END VIEW

CORNERS
REINFORCED
WITH PERFORATED
STRAP IRON

Plate 116   Converting Rigid Platforms into Wagon Stages under the 2″ × 4″ frames and to the underside of the castor plate. Bolting the brackets to the 2″ × 6″'s greatly increases the strength of the wagon.

Attaching castors to platforms higher than a single step is comparatively simple. In this case the 2″ × 6″ castor plate is cut as long as the platform is wide, and the castors are bolted to its face 3″ in from each end. Legs made of 2″ × 4″ are used in addition to the castors and castor plates to raise the platform top to the desired height; these legs are bolted to the framework of the platform. Fastened to the side of the legs and flush with their bottoms are additional 2″ × 4″ frames, to which the castor plates are bolted. This assembly eliminates any danger of the castor plates twisting off, which can happen if the plates are joined to the frame by nailing.

It is necessary to lock wagon stages in place onstage to stop any tendency they may have to roll as a result of the movements of the actors. This can be done by forcing wedges between the floor and the underside of the wagon, so that the weight of the wagon rests on the wedges rather than on the castors. This locking method is successful when the wedges can be placed on opposite sides of the platform; otherwise the wagons may slip off the wedges. Another and more reliable job of locking is done by bolting hinged foot irons to the sides of a wagon and stage-screwing them into place. Before the wagon is moved be sure that the free end of the foot iron is folded up out of the way so that it will not gouge into the floor or tear the floor cloth. A turn button can be used to hold it out of the way, or the axle of the hinge can be tightened by a few blows of a hammer to increase the friction and eliminate the free movement of the hinge.

Heavily loaded wagons are best moved manually by pull ropes or pull bars on each corner. Pull ropes are tied to ceiling plates or hanger irons that are bolted to the sides or top of the wagon. The free ends of the ropes are knotted to provide a handhold to pull and guide the wagon. Pull bars are detachable and are made of ³/₈″ iron rods with a handle shaped at one end and a sharp right-angle hook at the other. By engaging the hooks into holes drilled in the platform tops, the movement of the wagon can be easily controlled.

Slip Stages. The only difference between a wagon stage and a slip stage is that the latter is much larger and rolls on rigid castors or flanged wheels and a track (Plate 117). Small wagons are mounted on four or six swivel castors and so may be moved about in any direction with ease, because the castors will pivot to follow the direction of pull. A large wagon requires many castors to support it, and this increases the difficulty of getting all of them properly aligned. Unless the castors are all pivoted to approximately the same angle, it becomes almost impossible to move the wagon without much pulling and prying. For this reason the large slip stage is mounted on rigid castors or on flanged wheels that will limit its movement to two directions. When the offstage space left and right is equal in length to the width of the proscenium arch, two slip stages can be employed. Slip stages large enough to carry a full setting are generally mounted on flanged wheels that roll on tracks embedded in the stage floor. For stages lacking this type of permanent equipment, temporary tracks made of 1″ × 2¹/₂″ oak strips can be pegged or screwed to the face of the stage floor. Construction details for a slip stage 8¹/₂″ high, 36′-0″ long, and 16′-0″ wide are shown in Plate 117. This slip stage has been in use for 30 years at the University of Iowa.

The Jackknife Stage. Like the slip stage, the jackknife stage is designed to shift an entire setting as a single unit. Two space requirements must be met if

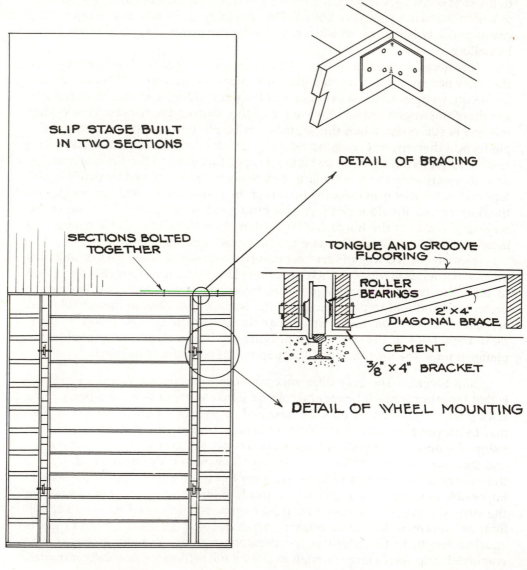

SLIP STAGE BUILT
IN TWO SECTIONS

SECTIONS BOLTED
TOGETHER

DETAIL OF BRACING

TONGUE AND GROOVE
FLOORING

ROLLER
BEARINGS

2" X 4"
DIAGONAL BRACE

CEMENT

⅜" X 4" BRACKET

DETAIL OF WHEEL MOUNTING

TOP VIEW

Plate 117   Slip Stage

this device is to be used. The depth of the stage from the tormentor line to the back wall of the stagehouse must be greater than the width of the proscenium opening; and the amount of offstage space left and right must be greater than the depth (or width) of the wagon (Plate 118). Two jackknife wagons are generally used. In offstage position each is stored at right angles to the proscenium arch, with the corner nearest the arch anchored by a pivot pin. The stages are brought into service by rolling them in a quarter arc; this brings them into position parallel with the arch.

The construction of this type of oversized wagon is identical with that of the slip stage. The difficulty and expense of getting curved tracks eliminates the use of flanged wheels. Instead rigid rubber-tired castors are used. The ease with which the stage will pivot depends upon accuracy in aligning the wheel of each castor to ensure a true right angle between it and a line representing the radius taken from the pivot pin. The anchor or pivot pin can be made by dropping a heavy machine bolt through holes drilled in the wagon and stage floor and reinforcing the holes with metal collars.

Tip Jacks.   When a unit of scenery such as a side wall of a setting is too heavy to run, cannot be folded, or cannot be flown—in short, when it seems impossible to shift it by any means—there is a good possibility that it can be fitted with tip jacks and moved easily. The tip jack is similar to the rigid jack except that it is fitted with castors, and the vertical member is at an angle of less than 90 degrees to its base. Two jacks are required on each unit that is to be so shifted. They are attached to the scenery by pin-hinging them to the cross members of the flats and to the stiffening battens, as illustrated in Plate 119. Note that when the scenery is in an upright position none of its weight rests on the jacks. Only when the scenery is unlashed and tipped backward, ready to be shifted, is its weight transferred to the jacks.

The angle at which the scenery rests against the jacks as it is being shifted is critical. The more nearly perpendicular it is to the stage floor, the less offstage space will be required for its movement and storage; yet this angle must be great enough to insure stability to the unit as it rests upon the jacks. Obviously scenery with heavy architectural trim near its base will require a greater angle to keep it from tipping forward than a unit with a heavy cornice attached to its top. The procedure for finding the proper angle for the construction of the jacks is both simple and effective. Stand the scenery upright and then gradually tip it backward until there is no tendency for it to fall forward. Measure this angle and build the jacks accordingly.

Wide sections of scenery mounted on tip jacks should be rolled in a line parallel with the width in order to keep air pressure against the face of the flats from tipping over the whole unit.

Lift Jacks.   The principle of the fulcrum and lever is used in the operation of the lift jack. In its simplest form it is a lever, with castors bolted to its lower face, hinged by one end to a unit of scenery (Plate 120). By applying pressure to the free end of the lever the lead castor is made to serve as a fulcrum, and the scenery can easily be lifted until its weight is supported entirely by the castors. The lever is then locked in position and the scenery rolled. This type of jack is used on heavy three-dimensional scenery that must stand solidly on its own base during the playing of a scene, but can best be shifted by rolling.

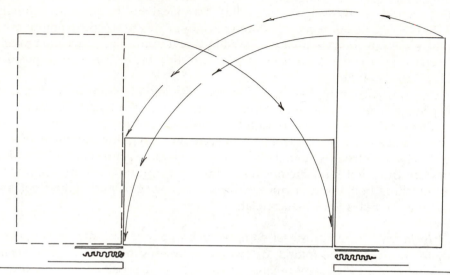

PLAN OF JACKKNIFE STAGE

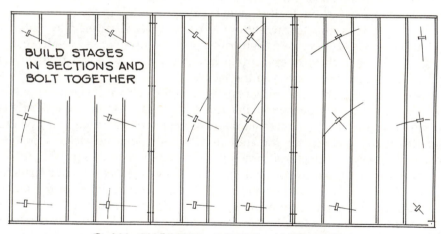

BUILD STAGES
IN SECTIONS AND
BOLT TOGETHER

PLAN SHOWING WHEEL ALIGNMENT

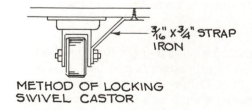

$\frac{3}{16}$" X $\frac{3}{4}$" STRAP
IRON

METHOD OF LOCKING
SWIVEL CASTOR

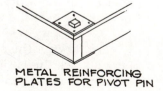

METAL REINFORCING
PLATES FOR PIVOT PIN

Plate 118   Jackknife Stage

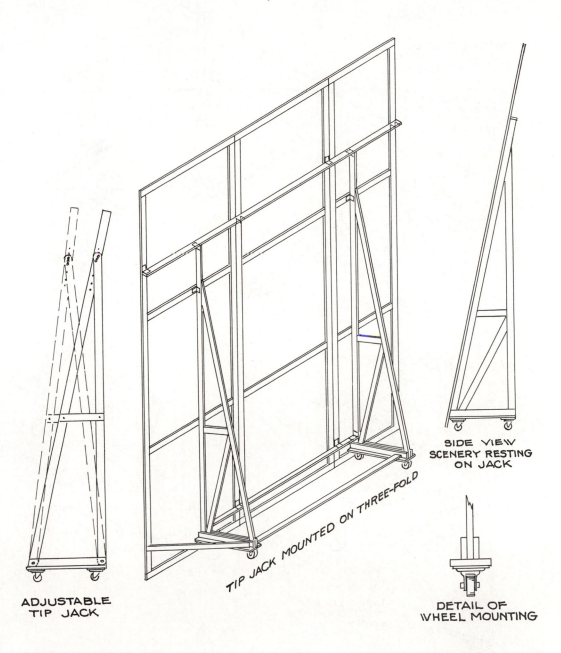

ADJUSTABLE
TIP JACK

TIP JACK MOUNTED ON THREE-FOLD

SIDE VIEW
SCENERY RESTING
ON JACK

DETAIL OF
WHEEL MOUNTING

Plate 119   The Tip Jack

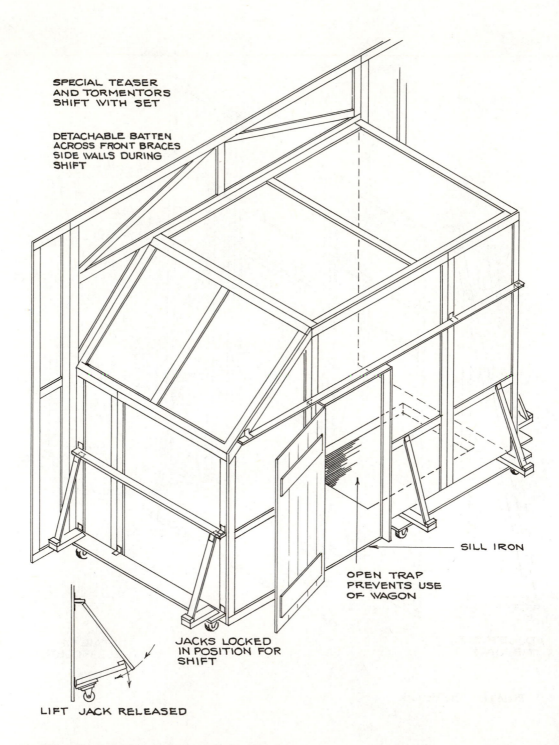

SPECIAL TEASER
AND TORMENTORS
SHIFT WITH SET

DETACHABLE BATTEN
ACROSS FRONT BRACES
SIDE WALLS DURING
SHIFT

SILL IRON

OPEN TRAP
PREVENTS USE
OF WAGON

JACKS LOCKED
IN POSITION FOR
SHIFT

LIFT JACK RELEASED

Plate 120   Lift Jacks Used to Shift Small Setting

The principle of the lever and fulcrum is so simple that the jacks can be built in any number of ways and adapted to many different forms of scenery. Few shifting devices, in fact, are capable of such varied uses as lift jacks. They can, for instance, be made in a very compact form, and because of this can be fitted inside such stage units as a stairway, a bar, a fireplace, or even an irregular-shaped practical rock. Plate 120 illustrates how lift jacks were attached to shift a small setting. Several other examples, including a detachable lift jack, are illustrated in Chapter 15, Plates 138, 139, and 140.

Outriggers. Occasionally a piece of scenery is of such an odd shape or size that it seems to defy all methods of shifting. For example, a semicircular concave window alcove would certainly be too heavy to run, its shape would prevent the use of tip or lift jacks, the design of the settting could prevent placing it on a wagon, and it would be extremely difficult to rig for flying, assuming that adequate lines and space could be spared for the purpose. Here is where the outrigger is useful. This is a skeletonized wagon constructed to conform to the desired shape and attached to the back of the unit (Plate 121). Unlike the tip jack or lift jack that supports the scenery only when it is shifted, the outrigger carries the weight of the unit at all times. In order to conserve offstage space, its depth extends not more than 3'-0" or 3'-6" beyond the unit it is supporting. Stability is obtained by loading the outrigger with sandbags and locking it in position onstage with wedges or hinged foot irons and stage screws.

Segment Stages. The segment stage is a large pie-shaped wagon pivoted at the apex of the wedge on the upstage side to allow the curved area to rotate from side to side past the proscenium arch (Plate 122). Two or three sets can be mounted side by side on the segment and brought into position with a minimum of time and effort. This principle of shifting is well suited to such episodic plays as *Sweet Mystery of Life*. In an elaborate production of this play designed by Donald Oenslager, a second level was provided by supporting a second segment immediately above the first. Two sets were placed on the second level directly above two settings of identical size mounted on the first level. Double-masking shutters guided by vertical tracks were either lowered to reveal a particular setting on the upper level, or raised to disclose one on the lower level.

Revolving Stage. The principle of the revolving stage has been used in one form or another since the time of the early Greeks. There are two types of revolves in common use: a temporary circular disc designed and built for use in a particular production; and much larger, permanently installed, revolving units embedded flush with the stage floor (Plate 123). Depending upon their size and the type of installation, the revolves can be turned manually or mechanically by use of winches and cables. The larger revolves are driven electrically, either with a rack and pinion or with cables serving around a curved channel iron attached to the underside of the revolve.

When used for shifting realistic settings, the revolve is not without its disadvantages. Its very shape restricts the form of settings placed on it to some variation of a segment; its circular shape makes it impossible to have side walls of a conventional sort without extending them past the revolve onto the stationary part of the stage floor; but perhaps the most serious disadvantage is the difficulty of placing both interior and exterior settings on it at the same time.

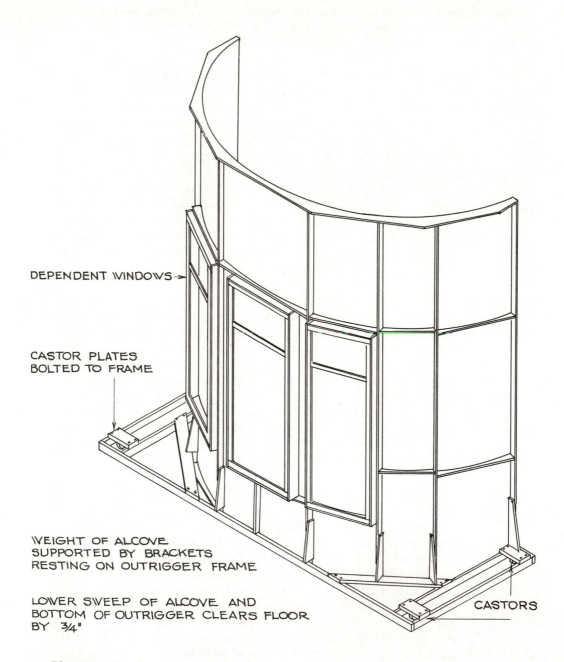

DEPENDENT WINDOWS

CASTOR PLATES
BOLTED TO FRAME

WEIGHT OF ALCOVE
SUPPORTED BY BRACKETS
RESTING ON OUTRIGGER FRAME

LOWER SWEEP OF ALCOVE AND
BOTTOM OF OUTRIGGER CLEARS FLOOR
BY 3/4"

CASTORS

Plate 121 Outrigger

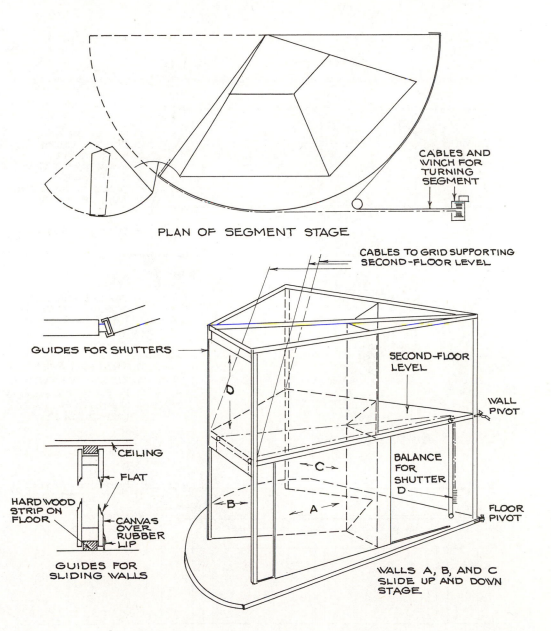

PLAN OF SEGMENT STAGE

CABLES AND
WINCH FOR
TURNING
SEGMENT

CABLES TO GRID SUPPORTING
SECOND-FLOOR LEVEL

GUIDES FOR SHUTTERS

SECOND-FLOOR
LEVEL

WALL
PIVOT

D

CEILING

FLAT

HARDWOOD
STRIP ON
FLOOR

CANVAS
OVER
RUBBER
LIP

BALANCE
FOR
SHUTTER
D

C

B

A

FLOOR
PIVOT

GUIDES FOR
SLIDING WALLS

WALLS A, B, AND C
SLIDE UP AND DOWN
STAGE

Plate 122   Plan and Diagram of Double-Decked Segment Stage

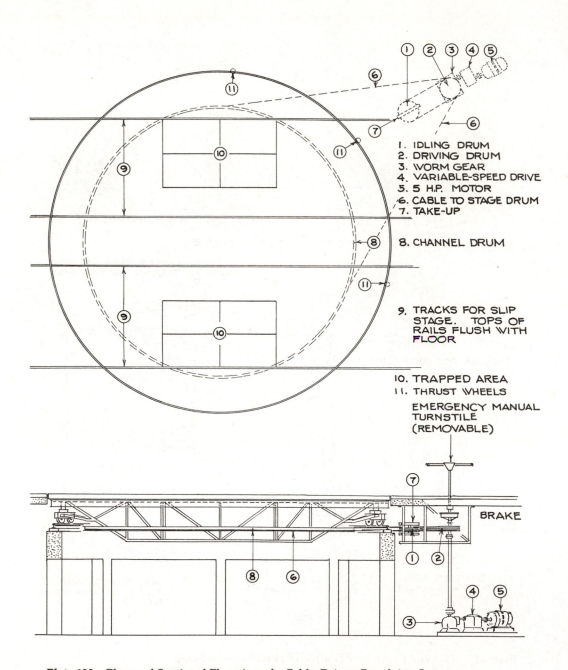

1. IDLING DRUM
2. DRIVING DRUM
3. WORM GEAR
4. VARIABLE-SPEED DRIVE
5. 5 H.P. MOTOR
6. CABLE TO STAGE DRUM
7. TAKE-UP

8. CHANNEL DRUM

9. TRACKS FOR SLIP
   STAGE. TOPS OF
   RAILS FLUSH WITH
   FLOOR

10. TRAPPED AREA
11. THRUST WHEELS

EMERGENCY MANUAL
TURNSTILE
(REMOVABLE)

BRAKE

Plate 123   Plan and Sectional Elevation of a Cable-Driven Revolving Stage

This can only be done when it is possible to build the exterior up over the top of the interiors, or when the exterior is of such a nature that buildings or dense shrubbery and trees can be used to mask the interiors. It should not be concluded, however, that the permanent revolve is a needless expense and almost useless as a shifting device. It is beautifully adapted to formalized or stylized structures that can be permanently mounted on it and revolved in full view of the audience to bring different facets of the design into focus. It is equally successful when used in conjunction with fragmentary settings mounted against black draperies. The draperies are suspended from a batten parallel with the proscenium and at a point where they will divide the revolve in half. Two settings can be in place on the revolve at one time, one in back of the proscenium, the other upstage of the blacks ready to be revolved into playing position. The shift consists of raising the blacks, making a half turn of the revolve, and then lowering the blacks. The first setting can then be struck and a third scene assembled while the action is taking place in the second.

The temporary revolve is capable of great variety both in size and in the manner in which it is used. Since this type of revolve is a disc superimposed on the stage floor, it is sometimes considered necessary to conceal its height and form by building up the surrounding floor areas to the same level. More frequently, however, no effort is made to conceal its circular shape. The use of the revolve is not confined to a single disc large enough to carry several settings. Two or three much smaller revolves are sometimes employed to shift different parts of the same setting. A revolve placed on either side of the stage can carry two side walls placed back to back and at the same time provide adequate floor space for the furniture required for two settings. A production of *Talent and Its Admirers* at the Simonov theatre in Moscow made excellent use of three small discs to handle the numerous settings required by the play. One small disc was placed downstage left and another downstage right. Each was divided into thirds by a vertical framework covered with black draperies. Against these draperies and supported by the framework were placed parts of three settings. The third and largest of the discs was placed upstage center. The supporting framework on this unit divided it in half, and parts of two settings were placed on it. Against the background of black draperies the fragmentary set pieces stood out in bold relief, and the discs were turned in plain view of the audience by stagehands concealed behind the units.

14

The Rigging of Scenery

Specifically the word "rigging" applies to the assembly, joining, and adjustment of the parts of a setting that are to be shifted by flying. However, common acceptance and usage have broadened the meaning to include all of the activities associated with the initial assembly of a setting when it is first taken to the stage. Both the time required for rigging and the ease with which it can be accomplished depend upon how thoroughly the technician has analyzed the production in respect to the sequence of construction. This is especially important because the period immediately preceding the technical and dress rehearsals invariably finds extensive use being made of the stage space by director, actors, and members of the lighting, property, and sound crews. If the order of construction has been properly planned, the various parts of the setting requiring extensive rigging can be taken to the stage in advance of others, thus allowing plenty of time for rigging without interfering with other uses of the stage.

RIGGING SEQUENCE

The varied nature of stage settings, coupled with the diversity of equipment by which it will be handled, makes it impossible to establish an order of procedure for rigging that can be applied with equal success to all productions. Each production will present problems that are peculiar to itself and that demand some unusual variation in the manner by which the rigging is accomplished.

However, under average circumstances, the sequence of rigging operations follows the outline given below.

1. The ground plan of each setting is chalked or taped off on the stage floor.
2. Scenery is moved from shop to stage in the order required for its rigging.
3. Units of scenery or special pieces of lighting equipment that will be shifted by flying are rigged first.
4. All practical, weight-bearing, three-dimensional units are tested in place for proper fit and alignment.
5. All two-dimensional units are placed in position and joined.
6. All three-dimensional pieces that fit into or against the two-dimensional units are tested in place for proper fit and alignment.
7. All flown units are lowered into position and adjusted.
8. All backings, groundrows, cutouts, and set pieces are placed in position and marked.
9. All lashing and bracing hardware is checked for proper placement and ease of operation.
10. After final adjustments are made the position of the setting is marked on the stage floor with identifying colored scene paint, colored chalk, or tape.
11. The setting is struck and its various parts stored in predetermined spaces nearest their point of use.
12. The back of each unit is marked with act and scene number for ready identification.

RIGGING MATERIALS

The principal tools and materials required for the rigging of scenery are essentially the same as those required in its construction. In addition there will be need for such joining materials as rope, wire, cables, chains, and occasionally clamps.

Rope

Rope is one of the technician's most useful tools and joining materials. His uses for it are many and varied: scenery is joined, flown, pulled, guided, and restrained by it; actors can be lifted, lowered, and pulled by it. The smooth functioning of a complicated rigging can be completely dependent upon rope. Through its use in tackle rigging, manual power can be increased. Perhaps its greatest value lies in the safety and protection afforded to the backstage personnel by the proper use of good quality, well-preserved rope. It is therefore only sensible that the technician take every step possible to inform himself of the nature, limitations, and maintenance of such a vital material as rope.

Judging the condition of a rope by its appearance is difficult; to an untrained person an old piece of rope looks very much like any other. A general rule for judging the condition of manila rope is the following: if the rope feels slightly oily, if it is a little stiff and awkward to handle, and if one gets more than the average number of rope splinters from it, it is likely to be in good condition. But if it seems dry, soft, pliable, and a pleasure to handle, look out! It is probably old and unsafe for heavy use. More specifically, when inspecting a rope, look for worn or frayed areas where it might have been damaged by abrasive action. Look for broken strands, cuts that could weaken it, or discolored spots that might indicate chemical damage. If but one area is damaged in an otherwise sound length of rope, cut out the damaged spot and splice. Sometimes after a rope has been used it will develop a tendency to kink; it is then said to be out of balance. This is caused by additional twisting imparted to the rope by the rigging and can be corrected by twisting the rope in the opposite direction. An easy way to do this is to tie one end of the line to a batten of the counterweight system and raise it until the rope hangs free of the floor. Usually it will then spin of its own accord until it is free of kinks; if not, it is easy to give it the necessary countertwist while it is hanging in this position.

Rope is made from four different materials: vegetable, animal, mineral, and synthetics. Rope used on stage is generally made from vegetable matter. Our best hard-fiber ropes are made from a plant called manila, grown in the Philippines. The stalks of this plant, which contain the fibers, are stripped and either hand- or machine-whipped to remove all foreign matter. After being washed, dried, and graded, the fibers are lubricated and formed into hanks called "roping." The roping is twisted from left to right to form the yarn, and the yarns are twisted in the opposite direction, from right to left, to make the strands. The strands are finally twisted from left to right to "lay" the rope.

Rope Sizes and Strengths. The following specifications are for three-strand rope with standard lay. In selecting a rope that would be safe to use for a given load, allow a 10 to 1 safety factor; that is, if the weight to be raised is 50 pounds, select a rope that has a working load of 500 pounds or better. A higher working load may be selected only with expert knowledge of conditions and professional estimates of risk—if the rope has not been subjected to dynamic loading or other excessive use, has been inspected and found to be in good condition, and is to be used in the recommended manner; and the application does not involve elevated temperatures, extended periods under load, or obvious dynamic loading such as sudden drops, snubs, or pick-ups. For all such applications, for applications involving more severe exposure conditions, or for recommendations on special applications, consult the technical department of The Cordage Group.

MANILA ROPE
REGULAR CONSTRUCTION

Size (Inches)		Pounds/ 100 feet	Feet/ Pound	New Rope Tensile Strength (Lb)	Working Load (Lb)*
Diameter	Circumference				
3/16	5/8	1.5	66.60	405	41
1/4	3/4	2.0	50.00	540	54
5/16	1	2.9	34.50	900	90
3/8	1 1/8	4.1	24.40	1215	122
7/16	1 1/4	5.3	19.00	1575	176
1/2	1 1/2	7.5	13.33	2385	264
9/16	1 3/4	10.4	9.61	3105	388

MANILA ROPE
REGULAR CONSTRUCTION *(Cont.)*

Size (Inches)		Pounds/ 100 feet	Feet/ Pound	New Rope Tensile Strength (Lb)	Working Load (Lb)*
Diameter	Circumference				
5/8	2	13.3	7.50	3960	496
3/4	2 1/4	16.7	6.00	4860	695
13/16	2 1/2	19.5	5.13	5850	835
7/8	2 3/4	22.5	4.45	6930	995
1	3	27.0	3.71	8100	1160

*CAUTION: Use of Working Loads. Because of the wide range of rope use, rope condition, exposure to the several factors affecting rope behavior, and the degree of risk to life and property involved, it is impossible to make blanket recommendations as to working loads. However, to provide guidelines, working loads are tabulated for rope in good condition with appropriate splices in noncritical applications and under normal service conditions.

Many uses of rope involve serious risk of injury to personnel or damage to valuable property. This danger is often obvious, as when a heavy load is supported above one or more workmen. An equally dangerous situation occurs if personnel are in line with a rope under excessive tension. Should the rope fail, it may recoil with considerable force—especially if the rope is nylon. Persons should be warned against standing in line with the rope. In all cases where any such risks are present, or there is any question about the loads involved or the conditions of use, the working load should be substantially reduced and the rope properly inspected.

Inspection. The most common error in using rope is ignoring signs of excessive wear or damage incurred on the job. Any rope should be inspected frequently, especially if it is used in applications involving a risk of personal injury or property damage. When inspecting rope, look for the following:

1. Cuts, gouges, badly abraded spots.
2. Seriously worn surface yarns.
3. Considerable filament or fiber breakage along the line where adjacent strands meet. (Light fuzzing is acceptable.)
4. Particles of broken filaments or fibers inside the rope between the strands. (Check inside the rope.)
5. Discoloration or harshness that may mean chemical damage or excessive exposure to sunlight. Check filaments or fibers for weakness or brittleness.
6. Kinks or twists.

If any of the above signs of possible damage appear, the rope may be unsafe.

Recommended Procedure for Using Rope. You can best utilize the strength of your rope and promote on-the-job safety by following these rules:

1. Use eye splices at points of attachment. Avoid knots in rope.
2. Avoid running rope over sharp corners or edges, or around diameters less than eight times the diameter of the rope.

3. Protect from damage such as cutting, wedging, and severe abrasion.
4. Store away from exposure to sun and rain, and avoid such exposure as much as possible.
5. To dry wet rope, hang it loosely in coils.
6. Keep rope away from chemicals harmful to your specific type of rope. (With nylon rope, avoid strong acids; polyester rope: strong alkalis; polypropylene rope: hot petroleum-based oils and solvents; manila rope: acids, alkalis, detergents, and most other chemical agents.)

Before Loading. Inspect the rope. Be sure the rope is in satisfactory condition and that you are using it in the recommended manner. Be sure that the load weight is accurately estimated, and that the rope selected is correct for that working load. You must determine if your application involves shock loading, long-term sustained loading, or elevated temperatures. If knots must be used for attachment or along the rope, or if the rope must be used around sharp bends or small radii, you must reduce by 40 percent the acceptable working load on the rope being used. You should also be fully familiar with the tables of knot and splice strengths.*

KNOT OR HITCH EFFICIENCIES

Knot or Hitch	Percent of Retained Strength
Anchor Bend	
Over 5/8" diameter ring	55–65%
Over 4" diameter post	80–90%
Two Half Hitches	
Over 5/8" diameter ring	60–70%
Over 4" diameter post	65–75%
Square Knot	43–47%
Sheet Bend	48–58%
Fisherman's Knot	50–58%
Carrick Bend	55–60%
Bowline	65–75%

3-STRAND ROPE SPLICE EFFICIENCIES

Type of Splice	Rope Strength Retained	Increase in Diameter of Splice
Eye	100%	60%
Short	95–100%	60%
Long	85–90%	25%
Long Blind	50–60%	0%

Rope Knots

When a rope is used it is generally necessary to employ a knot of some type to fasten it to an object or to another rope. To support, guide, pull, or lift an object

*The material on manila rope sizes, strengths, and recommended inspection procedure, and the table for knot and splice efficiencies, are by courtesy of The Cordage Group, Division of Columbian Rope Co., Auburn, N.Y.

safely and efficiently by means of rope demands a knowledge of basic knot types (Plate 124). The terms used in describing a knot are as follows: the end is the part of the rope used in forming the knot; the standing part is the portion between the knot and the opposite end; the bight is the loop, or bend, usually formed between the end and the standing part (it forms the basis of many knots); the knot itself is the interlacing of the end of a rope with itself or with another rope, or to an object, to form a temporary union.

The Overhand Knot.   This is the simplest of all knots, and forms the basis for many more complicated knots. Pass the end over the standing part to form a loop; then pass the end through the loop from under the standing part and pull it tight.

The Figure-Eight Knot.   Larger than the overhand and much easier to untie, this knot is used on the end of a rope to keep it from unserving or to prevent the end of a rope from slipping through a block or pulley. Form a loop by passing the end under the standing part. Bring the end up over the standing part, then down under and up through the loop.

The Square Knot.   Although the square knot is probably the most commonly used all-purpose knot, it jams easily when tied with small cord or rope, and will sometimes slip when tied with ropes of unequal diameters. Basically it consists of two interlocking loops. Form a loop by bringing the end around against the standing part. Pass the other end of the rope up through the loop then down under and around the base of the first loop. Bring the end up over and down through the loop. Draw the knot tight.

The Slip Knot.   Easily tied and untied, this knot is used for light lifting or pulling jobs and where speed of operation is a prime consideration. Pass the end of the rope around the object, then over in front and around in back of the standing part. Tuck a loop through the overhand knot thus formed and pull the knot tight. The knot is untied by pulling on the free end of the rope.

The Lash-Line Knot.   This is the tie-off knot used to join two flats together by lashing. (This process is described on page 289.) Pass the line under the two tie-off cleats; form a loop with the end of the line and pass it under the standing part just above the cleats. Pull down sharply on the loop. Pass a second loop through the first and tighten the knot. Like the slip knot, this knot unties quickly by pulling on the free end of the rope.

The Bowline.   When properly tied, the bowline forms a loop that will not slip or jam and can be easily untied even after it has been subjected to heavy strain. Form a loop by passing the end over the standing part. Pass the end up through the loop, then up and around the standing part and down through the loop again. Adjust and draw tight.

The Tarbuck.   The tarbuck is similar to the bowline but has the advantage of forming a loop that is adjustable in size and will not slip when pressure is applied to it or to the standing part. Form a loop and pass the end of the line four times around the standing part. Bring the end up over the loop, and form a half

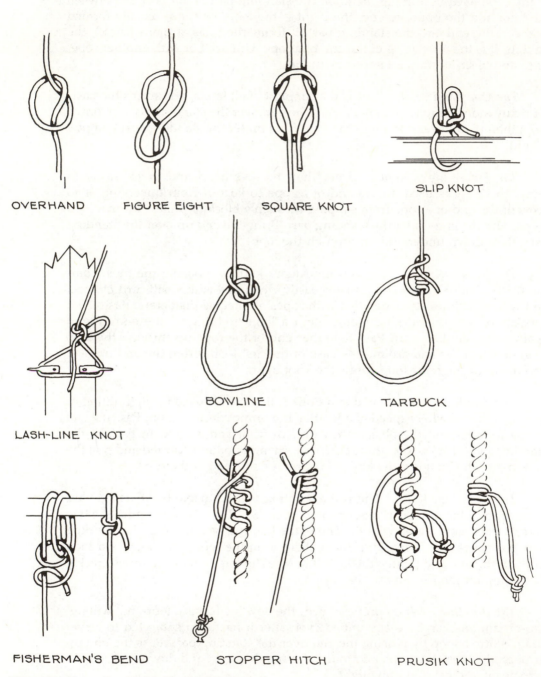

OVERHAND   FIGURE EIGHT   SQUARE KNOT   SLIP KNOT

LASH-LINE KNOT   BOWLINE   TARBUCK

FISHERMAN'S BEND   STOPPER HITCH   PRUSIK KNOT

Plate 124   Knots Frequently Used in Rigging

hitch around the standing part. Adjust and tighten all loops to bring maximum contact with the standing part of the knot.

The Fisherman's Bend.   This knot is used extensively for attaching snatch lines or ropes to a pipe batten preparatory to flying scenery. Form two loops around the batten. Pass the end around the standing part and through both loops. Draw the knot tight. Make a second half hitch around the standing part and pull tight.

The Stopper Hitch.   This is a pressure knot—the greater the pull, the greater the pressure exerted by the knot. One end of a short length of line is anchored to the locking rail by an eyebolt. The stopper hitch is used as a safety feature by tying it around the operating line of a counterweight unit that is temporarily out of balance. Pass the free end of the rope around in back of the operating line, then over the standing part. Make four or more turns with the end around the operating line below the first turn. Tighten the knot by adjusting the turns and sliding them up until they jam against the first turn.

The Prusik Knot.   Like the stopper hitch, the prusik is a pressure knot that can be tied around a line or set of lines that is already under load. It is used as a substitute for a clew plate or as a means of attaching a second line. Form an endless loop by tying together, with an overhand knot, the two ends of a short length of rope. Place the loop in back of the operating line. Pass one end of the loop two or more times around the operating line and under the other half of the loop. Pull tight and adjust the loops for maximum contact.

Sheet Bend.   Two ropes of different diameters can be easily joined by using this simple knot. Form a loop at the end of one line; pass the end of the second line through the loop from back to front, then around in back of loop and under the standing part of the second line. Adjust and pull the knot tight; this knot is easily untied after pressure is released.

Carrick Bend.   This knot offers the perfect solution to the problem of joining two ropes of large diameter together with a knot that can be easily untied. The Carrick Bend is basically two interlocking loops formed at one end of two separate lines. A cross-over loop is formed with one line; the second line feeds into the loop from in back, then over the top of the next two sections of loop, under the next two, and finally out and over the top to finish the knot.

Timber Hitch.   This is an excellent knot for fastening a line to a pole, a plank, or a pipe which can be tied very quickly. Throw the end of a line over a pole; bring the free end of the line up in front of the pole and then pass the end around the standing part of the line. Two or three turns of the end around the near side of the loop completes the knot.

Sheepshank.   The sheepshank provides a method of shortening a line without cutting it. Grasp the standing part of the line at some points between the two ends and double it two or more times until the excess line is taken up. Be sure to keep the loops even. Pass a half hitch over one end of the

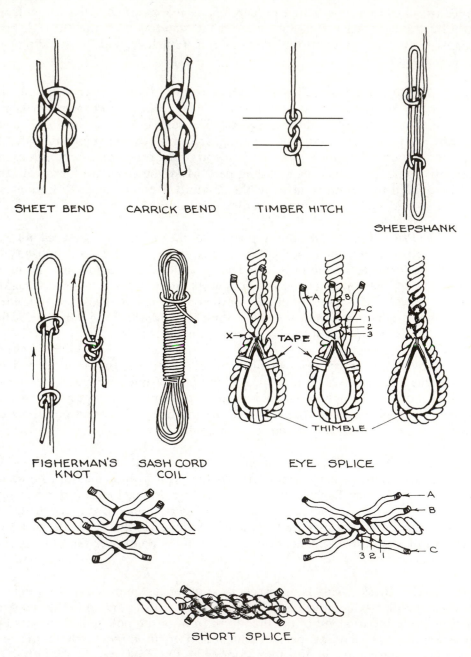

SHEET BEND   CARRICK BEND   TIMBER HITCH

SHEEPSHANK

FISHERMAN'S   SASH CORD   EYE SPLICE
KNOT   COIL

SHORT SPLICE

Plate 125   Knots and Splices

loops; a second half hitch is thrown around the opposite loops. Pull both ends of the line until the two hitches firmly grasp the doubled loops.

Fisherman's Knot. Because the surface texture of nylon rope is extremely slick and smooth many knots cannot be used on it; they will slip or come untied. The fisherman's knot will do neither. For this reason it is a very good knot to use when forming a loop in a nylon line or for joining two lengths of nylon line end to end. To form a loop make an overhand knot near one end of the line, pass the free end of the line through the knot and make a second overhand knot around the standing part. Pull the loop until the two knots are forced together. To join two lengths of nylon end to end make a loose overhand knot near the end of one length of line; pass the second line through this overhand knot and form a second overhand knot around the standing part of the first line. Pull both lines until the two overhand knots are forced together.

Sash Cord Coil. An effective way of preventing a length of rope from becoming entangled is to form it into coils that can be stored easily by hanging them up or placing them in drawers. Starting at one end of the rope begin doubling the line into 10" or 12" lengths until there remains 5' or 6' of free line. Try to keep the loops even at each end of the doubling. With the free line form a half hitch around the doubled loops about 3" from one end. Now serve the line around the body of the doubled section until it is within 3" of the other end. Form a loop with the remaining free line; pass this loop through the combined loops of the hank, bring it forward, and adjust it until it is snug against the servings around the hank.

Eye Splice or Side Splice. Start the splice by unlaying the strands, about 6" to 1' or more, or 6 to 10 turns of lay, depending on the size of rope you are splicing. Now whip the end of each strand to prevent its unlaying while being handled. If working with synthetic rope, it is sometimes helpful to use masking tape wrapped around the unlaid strands every 4 to 6" to help hold the "turn" in the strand. The ends may be fused with flame or whipped.

Next form a loop in the rope by laying the end back along the standing part. Hold the standing part away from you in the left hand, loop toward you. The stranded end can be worked with the right hand.

The size of loop is determined by the point at which the opened strands are first tucked under the standing part of the rope. If the splice is being made around a thimble, the rope is laid snugly in the thimble groove and point X will be at the tapered end of the thimble. The thimble may be temporarily taped or tied in place until the job is finished.

Now lay the three opened strands across the standing part as shown so that the center strand B lies over and directly along the standing part. Left-hand strand A leads off to the left; right-hand strand C to the right of the standing part.

Tucking of strand ends A, B and C under the strands of the standing part is the next step. Get this right and the rest is easy.

Start with the center strand B. Select the topmost strand (2) of the standing part near point X and tuck B under it. Haul it up snug but not so tight as to distort the natural lay of all strands. Note that the tuck is made from right to left, against the lay of the standing part.

Now take left-hand strand A and tuck under strand 1, which lies to the left of strand 2. Similarly take strand C and tuck under strand 3, which lies to the right of strand 2. Be sure to tuck from right to left in every case.

The greatest risk of starting wrong is the first tuck of strand C. It should go under 3, from right to left. Of course, strands 1, 2, and 3 are arranged symmetrically around the rope. If the first tuck of each of strands A, B, and C is correctly made, the splice at this point will look as shown.

The splice is completed by making at least two additional tucks in manila rope or four full tucks in synthetic rope with each of strands A, B, and C. As each added tuck is made, be sure it passes over one strand of the standing part, then under the strand next above it, and so on, the tucked strand running against the lay of the strands of the standing part.

The splice can be made neater by tapering. This is done by cutting out part of the yarns from the tucking strands, before the finishing tucks. In any case, the first three tucks in manila or four tucks in synthetics are made with the full strands. (Synthetics are slippery and stretchy and thus require at least one extra tuck.) After that, some prefer to cut out one-third of the yarns, make a tuck, then cut out another third of the yarn, and make the last tuck. This produces an even taper. After the splice is finished, roll it on deck under foot to smooth it up. Then put a strain on it and finally cut off the projecting ends of the strands. Do not cut off the "tails" of synthetic rope too short. If possible seat the splice in use or whip down the ends before cutting. The loose fibers may be fused with a match or candle to finish off, but be careful not to melt the rope.

How to Make a Short Splice. A short splice is used where two ropes are to be permanently joined, provided they do not have to pass through the sheave hole, swallow or throat, of a block. The splice will be much stronger than any knot. The short splice enlarges the rope's diameter at the splice, so in cases where the spliced rope must pass through a sheave hole, a long splice should be used.

To start the short splice, unlay the strands of both rope ends for a short distance as described for the eye splice. Whip the six strand ends, or fuse or tape them, to prevent unplaying. A seizing should also be made around each of the ropes to prevent strands from unlaying too far. These seizings can be cut as the splice is completed.

Next "marry" the ends so that the strands of each rope lie alternately between strands of the other as shown. Now tie all three strands of one rope temporarily to the other. (Some omit this step; it is not absolutely essential.)

Working with the three free strands, remove temporary seizing from around the other rope and splice them into the other rope by tucking strands exactly as described for the eye splice, working over and under successive strands from right to left against the lay of the rope. When first tucks have been made, snug down all three strands. Then tuck two or three more times on that side. Next cut the temporary seizing of the other strands of the rope and repeat, splicing those three remaining strands into the opposite rope.*

*Copyright 1978 by the Hearst Corporation; *Piloting, Seamanship and Small Boat Handling* by Charles F. Chapman.

Wire

Several types of wire are used for various stage purposes.

Stovepipe Wire. This is an annealed lightweight iron wire. It has no great strength and should not be used for rigging. It is used primarily in the construction of properties and for hanging wall decorations.

Galvanized Iron Wire. Wire of this type is sold in various gauges or diameters. Like stovepipe wire, it is comparatively easy to work but should not be used to suspend heavy scenery. One of its most frequent uses is as a substitute for misplaced pins from pin hinges.

Piano Wire. This wire is made from spring steel and has remarkable tensile strength for its diameter. It is frequently used for suspending scenery when the means of support must be as unobtrusive as possible. Every precaution should be taken to prevent the wire from kinking, as this reduces tensile strength.

CABLE BREAKING STRENGTH

6 × 19 Fibre Core Cable

Size	Breaking Strength in Tons
$1/4''$	2.74
$5/16''$	4.26
$3/8''$	6.10
$7/16''$	8.27
$1/2''$	10.70

6 × 37 Fibre Core Cable

$1/4''$	2.59
$5/16''$	4.03
$3/8''$	5.77
$7/16''$	7.83
$1/2''$	10.20

7 × 19 Galvanized Aircraft Cable

$1/8''$	1.0
$3/16''$	2.1
$1/4''$	3.5
$5/16''$	4.9

The above descriptive data courtesy of Tech Theatre Incorporated, 4724 Main Street, Lisle, Ill. 60532.

RIGGING PRINCIPLES

Tackle Rigging

Tackle is described by Webster as "an assemblage of ropes and pulleys arranged for hoisting or pulling." In stage terminology tackle rigging applies to the use of rope and pulleys to fly scenery or to obtain special effects. In its simplest form a tackle rigging may consist of a rope passing over a single pulley to change the direction of pull or of an applied force. More complicated arrangements of ropes and pulleys can increase the mechanical advantage by 2, 3, 4 and so forth, depending upon the type of rigging employed (Plate 126). This means that, if the rigging being used has an advantage of 2 to 1, 100 pounds disregarding the friction loss could be lifted by applying a 50-pound pull on the fall. (The fall is the part of the rope handled by the operator, on which the initial force is applied.)

The ordinary tackle used in moving or lifting heavy objects consists of two blocks and a rope. One block, the stationary block, is mounted in a fixed position; the other block, to which the load will be attached, is a movable block. These blocks may house one, two, three, or four grooved wheels, called sheaves, mounted on a common axle. The number of sheaves in the blocks and the way the rope is reeved (the manner of passing a rope through the blocks) will determine the mechanical advantage offered by a particular rigging.

Just why rope passing around a series of grooved wheels should increase the lifting power at the movable block over that exerted on the fall is perplexing to some. However, the principle is not difficult to understand if the tensions exerted on the movable block are counted. As an example, look at the rigging of a single whip shown in Plate 126. A single-sheaved block is mounted in a fixed position. Over this sheave passes a rope. As one end of the rope is pulled, the other moves up at the same rate of speed. There is no mechanical advantage with this rigging, just a change of direction. But now suppose that an object too heavy to be lifted by a direct pull must be raised to a gallery. Exactly the same equipment can be employed, but by changing the manner of rigging its lifting power can be increased 100 percent. Tie one end of the line to the gallery, pass the other end of the rope through the block, attach the load to the block, and pull up on the fall. With this rig, called the running block, two tensions are exerted on the moving block, one by the force applied to the fall, and the other by the part of the line tied off to the gallery. Hence the mechanical advantage is 2 to 1.

Some friction loss always occurs with the use of any tackle rigging, and due allowance should be made for it in determining the actual force required to lift a given load. This is done by allowing a 10 percent friction loss for each sheave over which the rope must pass. As an example, assume that a load of 200 pounds is to be raised by a double luff (Plate 126). Since the rope passes over four sheaves in this rigging, the total friction loss is 40 percent. Add the friction loss to the total to be lifted, and divide by the mechanical advantage, thus

$$40\% \text{ of } 200 \text{ lbs.} = 80 \text{ lbs.}$$
$$200 + 80 = 280$$
$$280 \div 4 = 70\text{-pound pull required to lift this load.}$$

It should be kept in mind that, as the mechanical advantage increases, the speed with which the moving block travels is reduced. The moving block of a double whip travels but half the distance and at half the speed that the fall is taken up; with a double luff the moving block moves but a quarter of the distance and at one-quarter the speed of the fall.

Spotlining

Spotlining is employed when it is necessary to fly some piece of equipment or scenery located onstage where it cannot be serviced by either counterweight

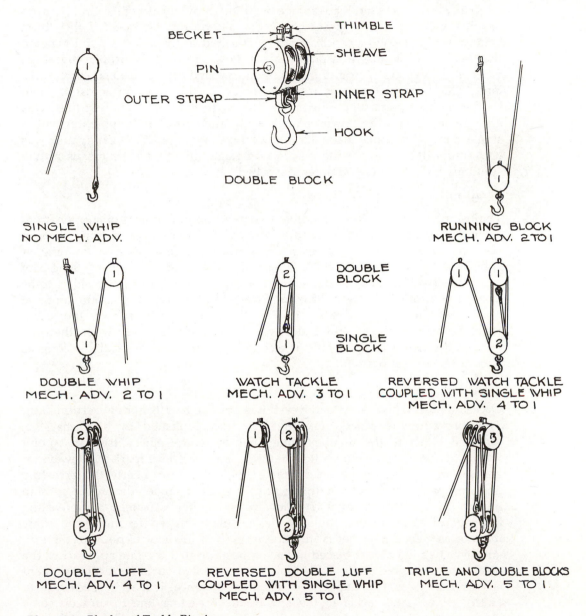

BECKET — THIMBLE
PIN — SHEAVE
OUTER STRAP — INNER STRAP
— HOOK

DOUBLE BLOCK

SINGLE WHIP
NO MECH. ADV.

RUNNING BLOCK
MECH. ADV. 2 TO 1

DOUBLE WHIP
MECH. ADV. 2 TO 1

DOUBLE
BLOCK

SINGLE
BLOCK

WATCH TACKLE
MECH. ADV. 3 TO 1

REVERSED WATCH TACKLE
COUPLED WITH SINGLE WHIP
MECH. ADV. 4 TO 1

DOUBLE LUFF
MECH. ADV. 4 TO 1

REVERSED DOUBLE LUFF
COUPLED WITH SINGLE WHIP
MECH. ADV. 5 TO 1

TRIPLE AND DOUBLE BLOCKS
MECH. ADV. 5 TO 1

Plate 126   Block and Tackle Rigging

or sandbag equipment. Spotlining is one of the simplest and most frequently used of all special stage riggings. It consists of a rope that runs from the controlling point at the locking rail or pinrail, to the grid, over a loft block or pulley, across the grid, and over a second block that has been placed in such a position that the line falls to the floor on the desired spot (Plate 127). Normally no mechanical advantage is offered by this rigging, but it does provide a change in the point of location of the pulling force. If the object being raised is heavy, a sandbag can be attached to the fall at a point beneath the first block. Because it is impossible to keep an object in proper alignment when it is suspended from a single line, a second line is used to correct this fault. This second rope runs from the object to the grid and across its own loft blocks to a point where it can be tied off to the fall of the first line. This arrangement keeps the flown object in trim, and provides the operator with a single controlling line. Place 127 shows how an impractical gangplank was both supported in its playing position on stage, and shifted by means of two spotlines rigged in the manner described above.

Saddling

The use of saddles makes it possible to obtain multiple points of support from a single line (Plate 128). A saddle is generally used when a long piece of scenery, such as a drop or a set of draperies, must be flown by spotlining. A spotline is attached at the center point of a short (14'-0" to 18'-0") length of rope. The two free ends of the short rope are then tied off on the object to be lifted; this forms the saddle. It is important to remember that as the angle at the top of the saddle increases in size, the strain on the rope is increased. Since the full strength of the saddle rope can be utilized only when the rope is submitted to a straight pull, it is advisable to make a saddle as long as circumstances will permit.

Breasting

Occasionally it is necessary to move a flown object out of its normal vertical path. This procedure is called breasting. It is accomplished by a special line attached either to the regular flying lines or to the object itself at a point where, if force is applied to the breasting line, it will impart a sideways or angular movement to the object (Plate 129). The more nearly the breasting line approaches the vertical flying line at a right angle, the easier it is to impart the desired diagonal or sideways movement. To keep the breasting line out of sight of the audience, it is usually rigged in much the same manner as a spotline—that is, the line runs from the control point to the grid and over two loft blocks placed in such a position that the line approaches the object at the desired angle. If the object being pulled out of vertical alignment is very heavy, or if it must move any great distance, it may be necessary to attach a block and tackle to the end of the breasting line to provide some mechanical advantage. Obviously, the farther an object is pulled out of vertical alignment, the more its weight is transferred to the breasting line. Notice the rigging used on the bucket in *High Tor* to move it upstage, where it appeared to be overhanging the cliff (Plate 129).

Tripping

Flying scenery in theatres with unusually low grids presents the problem of raising the scenery high enough to get it out of sight. Tripping is a method of

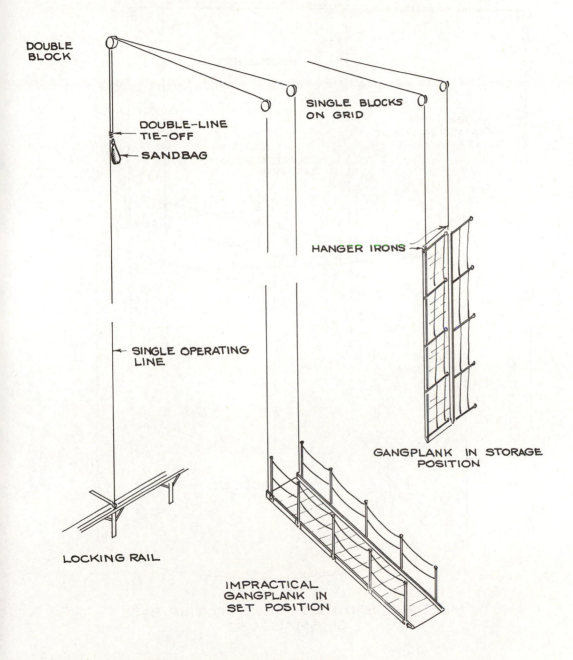

DOUBLE
BLOCK

DOUBLE-LINE
TIE-OFF

SANDBAG

SINGLE BLOCKS
ON GRID

HANGER IRONS

SINGLE OPERATING
LINE

GANGPLANK IN STORAGE
POSITION

LOCKING RAIL

IMPRACTICAL
GANGPLANK IN
SET POSITION

Plate 127   Diagram for Rigging a Double Spotline

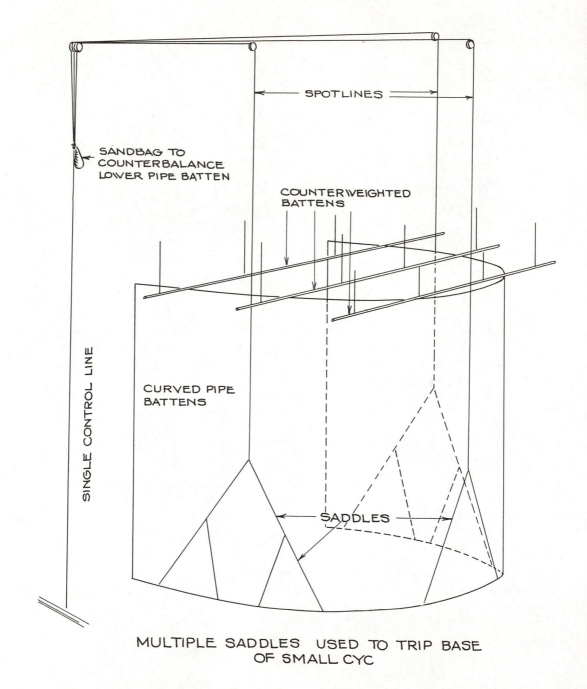

SPOTLINES

SANDBAG TO
COUNTERBALANCE
LOWER PIPE BATTEN

COUNTERWEIGHTED
BATTENS

SINGLE CONTROL LINE

CURVED PIPE
BATTENS

SADDLES

MULTIPLE SADDLES USED TO TRIP BASE
OF SMALL CYC

Plate 128   Saddling Technique

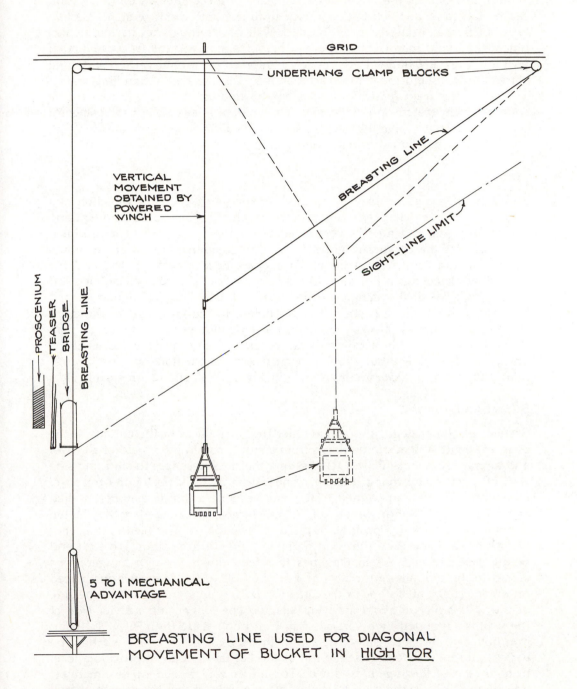

GRID

UNDERHANG CLAMP BLOCKS

BREASTING LINE

SIGHT-LINE LIMIT

VERTICAL
MOVEMENT
OBTAINED BY
POWERED
WINCH

PROSCENIUM

TEASER

BRIDGE

BREASTING LINE

5 TO I MECHANICAL
ADVANTAGE

BREASTING LINE USED FOR DIAGONAL
MOVEMENT OF BUCKET IN HIGH TOR

Plate 129   Breasting Technique

rigging that can sometimes be used to solve this particular problem. Tripping is accomplished by a set of lines placed upstage of the flown unit and attached either at the bottom of the units or to a special trip batten located at about mid-height of the flown unit. By means of these lines an unframed unit can be folded or doubled back on itself until it is raised out of sight. Certain types of framed units, such as the back wall of a setting, can be handled in much the same manner by tipping them from a vertical to a horizontal position. Such a wall must be properly reinforced by several vertical stiffening battens to withstand the strain placed on it by this method of handling.

The lines used for tripping can be attached to an empty batten of the counterweight system, provided that a free batten is available just upstage of the flown unit; or it may be necessary to rig a special set of spotlines that can be used for the same purpose. See Plate 128.

Muling

Through the use of loft blocks mounted on special brackets the direction of a rigging line can be changed. This process is called muling. Since the working space above the grid may be obstructed by trusses, supports, light conduits, and cables of the counterweight system, it is frequently necessary to guide special rigging lines around them. To avoid excessive wear, noise, and the possibility of fouling, ropes or steel cables must feed into the sheave of a loft block parallel with the flange on the sheaves (Plate 130). Triangular-shaped brackets made of $3/8''$ x $2''$ strap iron are bolted to the grid, and to these are clamped standard loft blocks mounted in a horizontal position. By adjustment of the brackets a line or set of lines can be guided into their loft blocks at the proper angle and without rubbing against any obstruction. The muling required for a flown cyclorama as shown in Plate 130 illustrates this principle.

Swivel and Hook

Scenery placed onstage at an angle other than parallel with the battens of the counterweight system can be flown from a single batten by the aid of a swivel and a strap-iron hook (Plate 131). Assume that it is desirable to shift one side wall of a setting by flying, but only one batten is available for the purpose. Horizontal stiffeners are added to the wall section so that it may be handled as a rigid unit. A short length of $1/4''$ steel cable is clamped to the batten directly above the stage position of the wall. The cable is fastened to the cener of a short section of $1^1/2''$ pipe and clamped tightly into position. To each end of the pipe are tied $3/8''$ snatch lines that feed down through hanger irons bolted to the top rails of the flats and are tied off to foot hanger irons placed on the lower flat rails. Pipe bridle and snatch lines must be placed to one side of the wall center to avoid an even balance. The longer and heavier side of the wall is supported by a vertical strap-iron hook made from $1/4'' \times 3/4''$ strap iron bolted to the outer stile. The top of the hook is bent to fit over the pipe batten, and must extend past the top of the flat far enough to provide a level trim for the wall when it is flown. To shift a wall rigged in this manner, unlash and unbrace the unit, raise the batten a little so that the section of wall supported by the snatch lines will clear the floor by 6″ or 8″, lift the free end of the wall, walk it around until it is parallel with the batten, engage the hook over the batten, and raise the unit to high trim. Because both the hook and

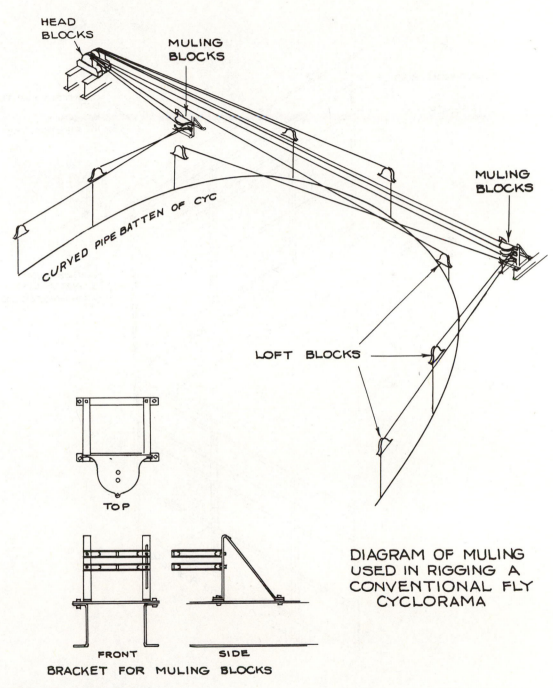

HEAD BLOCKS

MULING BLOCKS

MULING BLOCKS

CURVED PIPE BATTEN OF CYC

LOFT BLOCKS

TOP

FRONT

SIDE

BRACKET FOR MULING BLOCKS

DIAGRAM OF MULING USED IN RIGGING A CONVENTIONAL FLY CYCLORAMA

Plate 130 Muling Technique

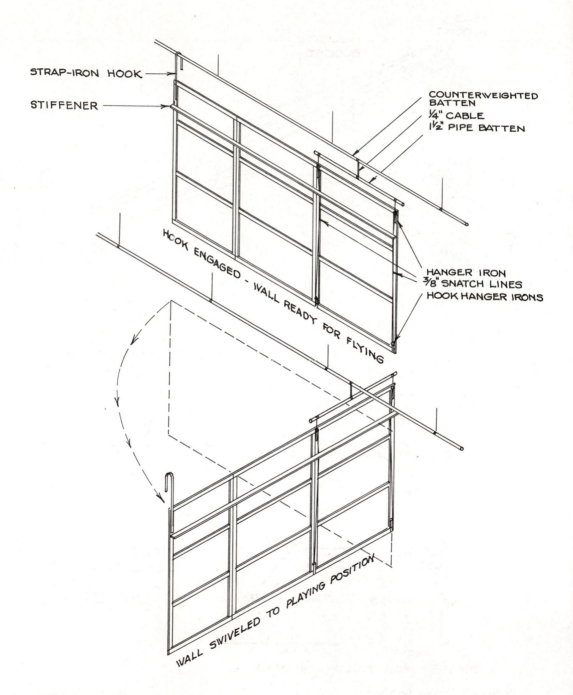

STRAP-IRON HOOK

STIFFENER

COUNTERWEIGHTED BATTEN
¼" CABLE
1½" PIPE BATTEN

HOOK ENGAGED - WALL READY FOR FLYING

HANGER IRON
⅜" SNATCH LINES
HOOK HANGER IRONS

WALL SWIVELED TO PLAYING POSITION

Plate 131   The Swivel and Hook

the swivel extend above the top of the flats, this type of rigging cannot be used on settings fitted with ceilings. It is especially suitable for shifting heavy backings or fragmentary units intended for use without a ceiling.

Control of the Unbalanced Arbor

During some scene shifts it may be necessary to unfasten a flown unit of scenery from the counterweighted batten that supported it. This creates the special problem of what to do with the counterweight left unbalanced high above the stage floor. The brief time allowed for shifting scenery precludes the possibility of sending a crew member to the grid to unload the arbor, even if the matter of safety were ignored. Four methods of rigging have been developed to solve this type of problem.

The Substitution of Counterbalance for the Weight of the Scenery.   If the scenery is not excessively heavy, a sandbag of equal weight can be snapped onto the lowered batten before the scenery is unfastened (Plate 132). The process can be expedited by attaching a special ³/₄″ snatch line to the pipe batten. The free end of the snatch line is fitted with a heavy metal ring and adjusted in height so that the hook of a sandbag can be snapped to it without lifting the bag. Heavy sandbags can be rolled into position by hauling them on small dollies built for the purpose.

Controlling the Unbalanced Arbor with a Tackle and Choker.   The choker is a loop made from a 3'-0″ length of ¹/₄″ steel cable or from ³/₈″ manila rope. The loop is passed around the onstage side of the operating line of the counterweight unit at a point just above the rope lock. Since this will not foul either the rope lock or the head block, it can be taped to the operating line and left in position even when not in use. The hook of the moving block can be quickly and easily engaged or disengaged from the choker. The stationary block of the tackle is permanently attached to an eyebolt mounted through the top of the locking rail. Before the scenery is removed from the batten, the hook of the moving block is engaged in the choker, and tension is exerted on the tackle. The scenery is then unfastened, and the unbalanced counterweight lowered by controlling it with the mechanical advantage offered by the block and tackle. When the scenery is to be reengaged, the empty batten is lowered to the floor by raising the arbor with the tackle. Details of this rigging are shown in Plate 132.

The Carpet Hoist.   The carpet hoist provides another way of solving the problem of the unbalanced arbor (Plate 133). This is rigged through the use of two arbors and a set of brackets. Stated simply, what is involved is the transfer of weight from one arbor to another. Two adjacent arbors must be employed for this rigging. To the bottom of the first arbor are bolted two heavy brackets that extend out to one side just far enough to prevent the second arbor from passing it. The scenery is fastened to the batten controlled by the first arbor. The weight required to balance the scenery is placed in the second arbor; the two arbors are then moved in unison. Since the arbor and the operating line are the only parts of the second counterweight set used in this rigging, the cables and the pipe batten are removed.

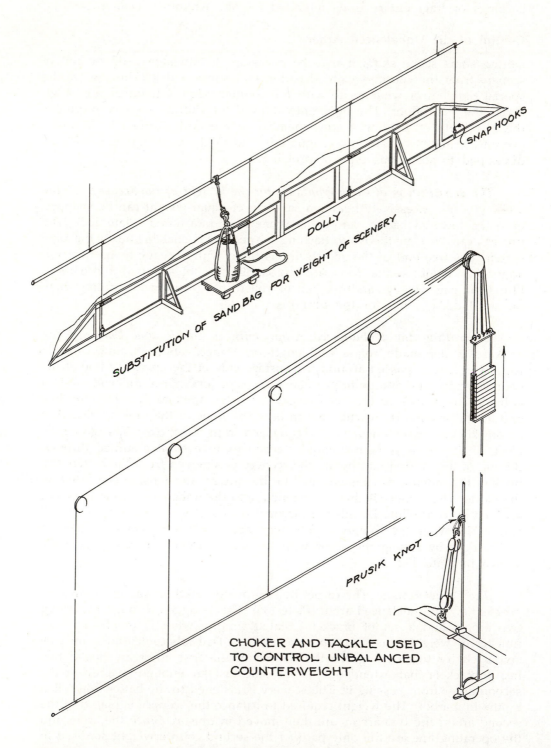

Plate 132   Two Methods Used to Control Unbalanced Counterweight

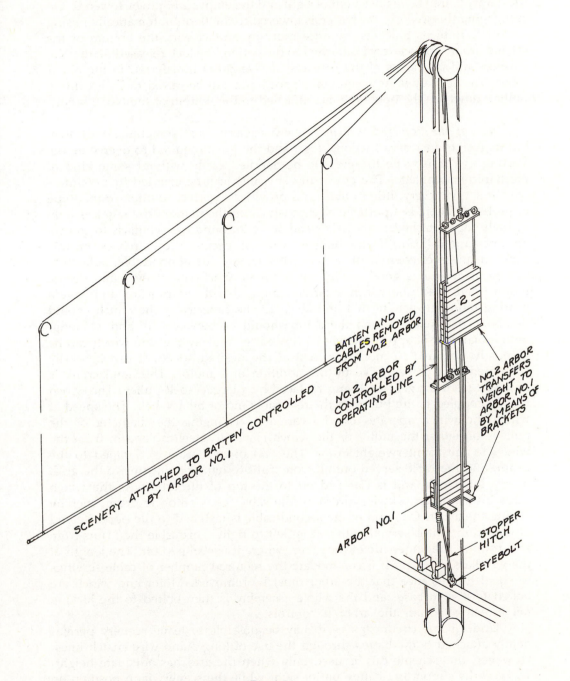

BATTEN AND CABLES REMOVED FROM NO.2 ARBOR

NO.2 ARBOR CONTROLLED BY OPERATING LINE

NO.2 ARBOR TRANSFERS WEIGHT TO ARBOR NO.1 BY MEANS OF BRACKETS

SCENERY ATTACHED TO BATTEN CONTROLLED BY ARBOR NO.1

ARBOR NO.1

STOPPER HITCH

EYEBOLT

Plate 133   Diagram of Carpet-Hoist Rigging

When the scenery is at floor level and ready to be disengaged from the batten, both arbors will be high above the floor. The second arbor, carrying the counterweight, is tied off in this position by use of the rope lock and a stopper hitch tied around the operating line. The scenery is then unfastened, permitting the empty batten to be raised out of sight and the empty arbor to be lowered. On reengaging the scenery, the batten is lowered to the floor, automatically raising the arbor until its brackets are once more in contact with the bottom of the second arbor. The scenery is attached to the batten, the lock released on the No. 2 arbor, and by means of the brackets the weight is transferred to the No. 1 arbor. The scenery is now counterbalanced and can be raised to high trim by pulling down on the operating line attached to the bottom of the No. 2 arbor.

Use of the Powered Winch. Heavy scenery must sometimes be flown; but its weight increases frictional loss, and the force required to overcome the starting inertia may be too great to be handled easily without some kind of mechanical advantage. The power-driven winch can be coupled to a counterweight set with very little trouble, and provides a perfect solution to this type of problem. There is a portable electric winch on the market that requires only a single rope attached to the arbor and served around the windlass to control an unbalanced load. If the budget will not permit the purchase of this excellent piece of equipment, a very satisfactory, but nonportable, substitute can be made from a good quality hand-driven winch and a reversible electric motor (Plate 134). The winch must be equipped with worm gears and have a gearing ratio between 18 to 1 and 25 to 1. The capacity of the winch should be about 1000 pounds, and the drum should be between 10" and 14" long, with a diameter of approximately 6". Since it is unlikely that the winch can be manually operated to move the load at the desired speed, it can be easily converted to a power drive by the addition of a motor. The hand crank is removed from the gear shaft and replaced by a large V-belt pulley. The winch is then coupled to the pulley of the reversible motor by a V-belt. The speed at which the winch operates can be varied by changing the diameter of the pulleys on either the motor or the winch. Two ¼" steel cables run from the winch to the counterweight arbor. The end of one cable is clamped to the drum, and the cable served onto it from right to left. It then runs to the grid, over a loft block, and is clamped off to the top of the arbor. As the winch turns in a counterclockwise direction, the cable feeds onto the drum, thereby raising the arbor. One end of the second cable is fastened to the opposite end of the drum, but is served onto it from left to right. This cable then runs from the drum to the underside of the arbor, where it is clamped off. The length of the windlass drum must accommodate the required number of cable servings to equal the distance that the arbor must be removed. Motor and winch are bolted to a solid base, and the whole assembly is then bolted to the locking rail directly beneath the arbor it controls.

Under some circumstances it may be possible to leave scenery permanently attached to the batten through the use of long piano wire snatch lines. However, this scheme can be used only when the grid has adequate height. To keep the supporting batten out of sight while the scenery is in position on stage demands the use of long snatch lines. It also means that when the batten has been raised to its highest point there must be sufficient height to

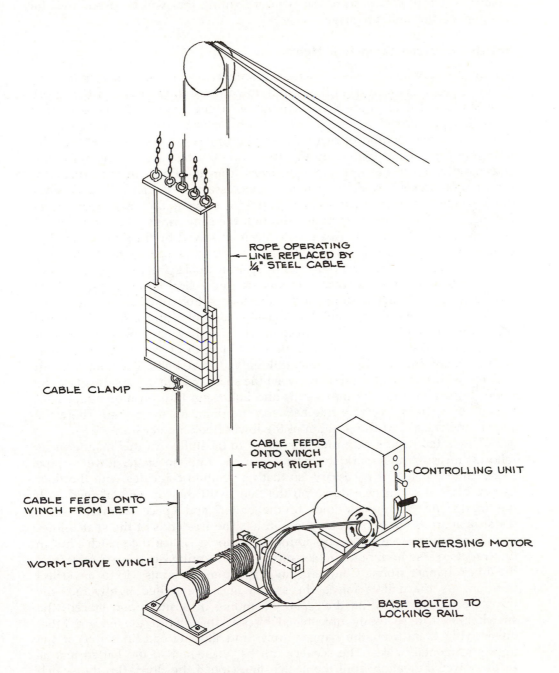

ROPE OPERATING
LINE REPLACED BY
¼" STEEL CABLE

CABLE CLAMP

CABLE FEEDS
ONTO WINCH
FROM RIGHT

CONTROLLING UNIT

CABLE FEEDS ONTO
WINCH FROM LEFT

REVERSING MOTOR

WORM-DRIVE WINCH

BASE BOLTED TO
LOCKING RAIL

Plate 134   Power-Driven Winch Adapted to Counterweight System the stagehouse to prevent the audience from seeing the flown unit. Unfortunately, this simple scheme of avoiding an unbalanced arbor cannot be used as frequently as one would like. In addition to low grid, other deterring factors may prevent its use: the nature of the object to be flown, the type of backing against which it will be seen, the type of lighting that will be used, and the position of the unit on stage.

Snatch Lines and Strap-Iron Hooks

All but the very lightest pieces of framed scenery are flown by snatch lines of $^3/_8"$ or $^1/_2"$ rope that run from the batten down through the rings of the upper hanger irons. The lines are then snapped off to the rings of the hook hanger irons that are located on the lower rails of the flats. An awkward problem arises when this method of rigging is used on pieces of scenery that must be unfastened from the batten during the shift, or that are too high for the stagehand to reach the upper hanger irons from the floor. In the process of unfastening scenery from the batten it is necessary to guide the snatch lines out through the rings on the hanger irons to prevent the snap hooks from fouling; and they must be threaded through the same rings when the scenery is reengaged to the batten. This problem can be solved by the use of a ladder, by tipping the scenery forward until the hanger irons can be reached, or by the substitution of special horizontal strap-iron hooks for the upper hanger irons (Plate 135). The first two solutions are impractical because they require too much time during a shift; but by the use of horizontal hooks the same result can be achieved as rapidly as lashing or unlashing a flat. Strap-iron hooks are easily made, they are inexpensive, and they have proved remarkably effective. Each hook is made from a 2'-0" length of $^1/_4" \times ^3/_4"$ strap iron, with the shaft drilled to receive at least three $^3/_{16}"$ stove bolts. The hook is about 8" deep, with a space of about 2" between the shaft and the inner side. Place the hooks horizontally on the upper rails and bolt them into position about 1'-6" outside of a straight vertical line between the point on the batten where the snatch line is tied and the position of the lower hook hanger iron.

The initial rigging of a unit of scenery to be shifted in this manner is as follows: measure and mark the position of the unit on stage; lower a pipe batten and adjust it, if necessary, so that its position coincides with the floor marks; place the unit face down on the floor with the top rails aligned with the marks; tie two snatch lines to the batten and space them the same distance apart as the two hook hanger irons. The free ends of the snatch lines should be equipped with strong spring snap hooks. Place the snatch lines in the throats of the horizontal hooks and snap the spring hooks to the rings of the hook hanger irons. Counterbalance the unit and raise it to a vertical position. As the unit is raised the snatch lines are pulled tightly into the throats of the hooks. With the scenery standing in position and braced, the snatch lines can be easily unfastened by slacking off on the lines a little, unsnapping them from the hanger irons, and flipping the lines free of the upper horizontal hooks. The scenery can be refastened to the batten just as easily: lower the batten until the snatch lines touch the floor, flip the snatch lines to engage the horizontal hooks, and snap the lines into the rings of the hook hanger irons. Raise the batten enough to put some tension on the lines

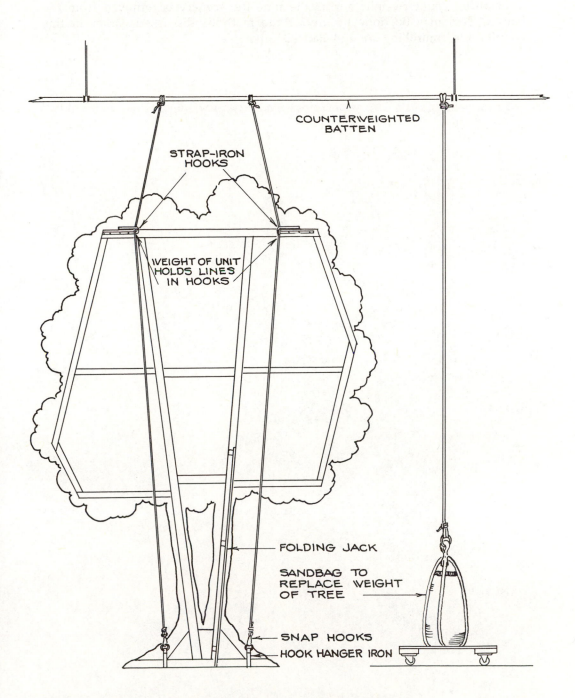

COUNTERWEIGHTED
BATTEN

STRAP-IRON
HOOKS

WEIGHT OF UNIT
HOLDS LINES
IN HOOKS

FOLDING JACK

SANDBAG TO
REPLACE WEIGHT
OF TREE

SNAP HOOKS
HOOK HANGER IRON

Plate 135 Substitution of Strap-Iron Hooks for Upper Hangar Irons to keep them from falling free of the horizontal hooks. The scenery can now be unbraced and flown.

When this method of·rigging is employed, it is necessary to control the unbalanced counterweight during the time the scenery is removed from the batten. This may be done by any of the methods discussed earlier in this chapter for controlling an unbalanced arbor.

15

Special Construction and Rigging Problems

As we have remarked before, each theatre production may present new problems involving construction principles and methods of rigging. As these problems and their solutions will vary from one production to another, so will they vary as they are adapted to different stages. There will be differences in stage plans and dimensions, in physical equipment of shops and stages, and in the operating budgets of each organization. These differences make it unlikely that the solution to any special problem can be used without modification to solve a similar problem controlled by a different set of circumstances. The ability to improvise, to "make do" with what is available, and to adapt established principles of construction or rigging to the solution of a new problem is one of the most important traits of a first-class technician. The technician should have a flair for invention and a willingness to experiment with new methods of doing things, even if this often means additional work and occasionally failure. Only in this way is he or she likely to develop a technique or invent a device that will contribute substantially to the fund of knowledge that helps raise the general standard of stage productions.

The examples of construction and rigging found in this chapter are not the result of paper projects. They have been given the most rigorous testing by actual use on stage during the run of a production. They are given here, not with the idea that they can or should be copied, but to illustrate how a principle can be adapted or modified to solve a particular problem. These examples may give you a suggestion or an idea that can be shaped to your own use.

CONSTRUCTION AND BRACING
OF FRAGMENTARY SETTINGS

The suggestive or fragmentary setting is one possible answer to the problems presented by a play that requires several settings. Such a partial setting reduces the time required for construction, is less expensive, and is easier to shift and store than a complete setting. At the same time it is likely to present unusual problems in both construction and bracing.

The drawings of the railway coach in Plate 136, one of the six settings needed in producing *Point of No Return,* present a good example of problems met in constructing and bracing fragmentary scenery. Without the benefit of the side walls that would normally be used to help support the curved ceiling, some other scheme of bracing had to be devised. The double-faced seats would be too heavy and bulky to shift easily, and the number of windows in the back wall would make this unit awkward to handle. All of these problems were solved by mounting the setting on a wagon and by using modified jacks.

Two rigid platforms taken from stock, one 5'-0" × 10'-0" and the other 5'-0" × 5'-0", were bolted together end to end to form a wagon 5'-0" wide, 15'-0" long, and 7" high. The back wall was constructed as an oversized window flat. Each window was made as a separate unit and attached to the window openings by means of its 4" thickness pieces. Galvanized wire screen was stretched across the back of each window as a substitute for glass. The wall was braced by four rigid jacks screwed to 2" × 4" blocks attached to the wagon tops. Each jack had been modified by attaching a concave sweep to its top. The concave shape of the car roof was obtained by nailing sheets of corrugated cardboard to the supporting sweeps of the jacks.

The back-to-back car seats were supported by two frames made from 1" × 3" stock, and were covered on the downstage side by a single sheet of ¼" plywood. The seats themselves were made as individual units from 1" × 4" stock on edge, covered with ¼" plywood, and screwed between the two supporting frames at the proper height and angle. The backs were formed by nailing single sheets of ¼" plywood to the edges of the supporting frames. Both seats and backs were padded with moss and cotton batting and covered with dark-green rep. The assembled seats were placed on the platform with their upstage faces flush against the back wall and screwed into position. Their weight, stability, and height helped them to serve as additional bracing for the back wall.

OUTRIGGER AND MODIFIED RIGID JACKS

Scenic designers are constantly on the lookout for architectural features that will give added interest and atmosphere to their settings. Such features as cornices, beams, slanting roof lines, and dormer windows add interest to settings where their use can be justified. However, these features complicate the problem of construction and shifting to such a degree that in some cases the designer may be forced to forego their use.

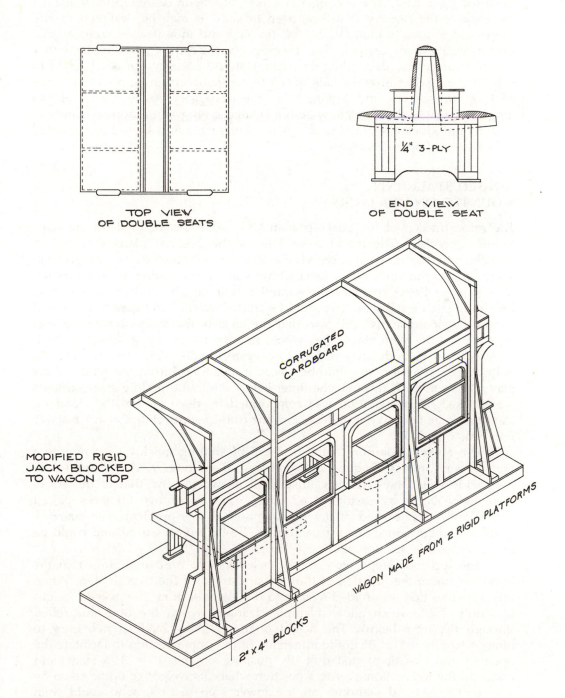

TOP VIEW
OF DOUBLE SEATS

END VIEW
OF DOUBLE SEAT

¼" 3-PLY

CORRUGATED
CARDBOARD

MODIFIED RIGID
JACK BLOCKED
TO WAGON TOP

WAGON MADE FROM 2 RIGID PLATFORMS

2" X 4" BLOCKS

Plate 136 Construction and Bracing of a Fragmentary Set

Where adequate stage space is available for rolling units, a possible solution to some of those problems may be found in the use of outriggers and modified rigid jacks. The outrigger is a skeletal wagon designed to fit against the back of the scenery it will be used to shift. It may be designed to any shape and is usually made of 2" × 4" framing and mounted on conventional rubber-tired swivel castors. The flooring on the outrigger may be either complete or partial, depending on circumstances. Scenery can be attached to it by screwing it against the side of the frame or by attaching a batten to the back of the scenery and locking it to the outrigger top by means of pin hinges. Plate 137 illustrates how both a slanted ceiling and a dormer window, used in a production of *The Crucible*, were constructed and shifted by means of jacks mounted on an outrigger.

HINGED STAIR UNIT
MOUNTED ON LIFT JACKS

The reconstruction of the Shakespearian Old Globe theatre used on the stage at the University Theatre at Iowa follows the original plans closely and consequently has no permanent visible stairway by which actors can go from stage level to the inner-above level within view of the audience. In a production of *Julius Caesar* the director wanted a stairway the audience could see. Providing such a stairway that could be shifted quickly and quietly presented several major problems. One was that the level of the inner-above floor was 10'-0" above the main stage. This would require a stairway at least 9'-4" high which would be both awkward and heavy to handle. Another was that the only way such a stairway could be placed in position during the action of the play was to move it through the inner-below while the middle stage curtains were closed. This operation was complicated by the fact that the clearance from the stage floor to the underside of the trusses supporting the inner-above floor was only 8'-2".

The obvious solution to the problem of shifting quickly was mounting the stairway on castors; but a unit that was 18'-6" long, 9'-4" high, and only 3'-0" wide would be extremely unstable if its weight and that of the actors were to be borne by castors at all times. The use of two lift jacks placed within and at either end of the stairway solved this problem. The stairway could rest solidly on its own base during the time it was used and could be raised onto the jack for shifting (Plate 138).

The top four steps were made as a separate unit and hinged to the lower section at the junction of the riser and tread of the twelfth step. When this upper section was folded over onto the lower section, the over-all height was only 7'-0", which allowed ample clearance when the unit was rolled through the inner-below. The height of the stairway made it necessary to hinge a length of 1" × 3" to the underside of the upper section to facilitate the opening and closing of that unit. By pushing on this 1" × 3" a stagehand could tip the top section over to a position where its weight could be taken by a second stagehand standing on the lower step section, who could then "walk it down." By reversing this procedure the top could be placed in position for action.

Notice that the lower section of the stairway, while made as a single rigid unit, is so planned and constructed that sawing through the horizontal

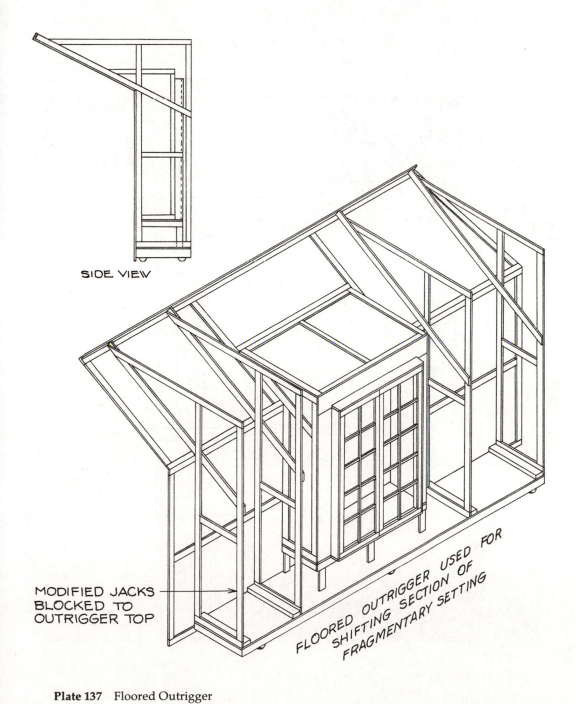

SIDE VIEW

MODIFIED JACKS
BLOCKED TO
OUTRIGGER TOP

FLOORED OUTRIGGER USED FOR
SHIFTING SECTION OF
FRAGMENTARY SETTING

Plate 137   Floored Outrigger

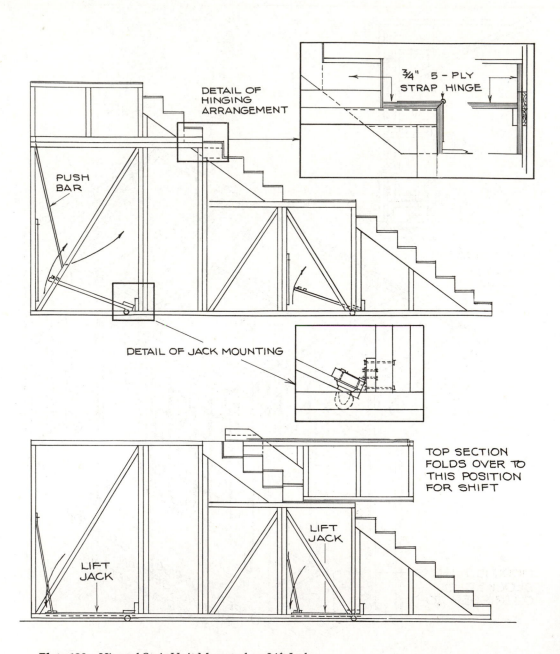

Plate 138   Hinged Stair Unit Mounted on Lift Jacks

members will reduce the structure to five separate step-and-landing sections for independent use. Although this was the original intention, it has never been done because so many uses were found for the unit as it stood that it was decided to keep it as it was. It has been variously used as an offstage stairway, a rolling tower stand for lights, a rigging platform, and a paint boomerang.

Reversible Unit Mounted on Lift Jacks

In Obey's play, *Noah*, three of the five scenes take place on the deck of the ark. The limitations placed on the size of the ark by the stage dimensions resulted in a setting that noticeably restricted the action of the actors and made it difficult for the director to obtain the variety in stage movements he felt the play demanded.

In an effort to overcome these problems the designer and the director planned to change the position of the ark between scenes. By reversing the direction in which the ark was apparently sailing, the major acting areas would also be changed, and at the same time the compositional arrangement of the setting would be altered. Such a scheme could be accomplished in several ways: (1) Two separate arks could be constructed; each would be a duplication of the other as far as design was concerned, but one would be a reverse of the other. (2) A single double-faced setting could be built and mounted on the revolve. (3) A single reversible unit could be built and mounted on lift jacks. Because cost, available storage space, and length of scene shifts had to be considered, it was decided that the reversible unit would be the most logical choice. The use of the revolve as a shifting device was thereby eliminated—an important consideration because the stage had to be cleared for the opening and closing scenes.

Plate 139 illustrates the general principle of construction and the placement of the two lift jacks used in shifting it. Since the roof of the deckhouse had to support the capering of both "animals" and humans, and since there was to be much running up and down both stairways, the lift jacks were employed instead of mounting the whole structure on a wagon. The jacks permitted the cabin to be lowered to rest on its own base during the playing of the scenes, thus eliminating any tendency the unit might have had to creep or roll.

The framing of the sidewalls and the base of the cabin were made from 2" × 4" fir. A much lighter structure could have been built by using 1¼" × 3" white pine, but this would have doubled its cost. In this particular case the weight of the heavier lumber was not a factor for consideration because the cabin was to be shifted by rolling. The two stairways, one on each side of the cabin, were built as separate units and bolted to the slanting sidewalls of the cabin; they were shifted as an integral part of the cabin.

The mast of the ark was an independent structure and was placed along the deck 12'-0" forward of the cabin. The mast, a tapered, three-dimensional column 16'-0" high, was given a broad stable base by having it anchored in a most unnautical fashion, to the center of a 4'-0" × 6'-0" hatch. The mast and hatch were the only other elements of the design, besides the cabin, that were too large and awkward to be shifted by running. Two small lift jacks mounted inside the hatch converted it into a rolling unit that was easily shifted. The

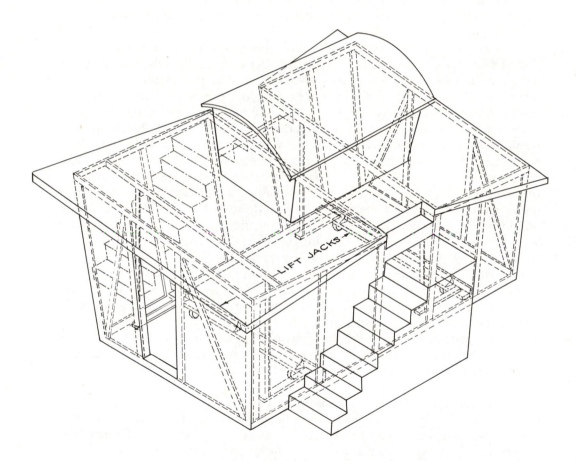

Plate 139   Reversible Deck Cabin for *Noah*, Mounted on Lift Jacks

gunwales of the ark were two-dimensional cutouts made as reverse duplicates to be shifted by running.

Detachable Lift Jacks

The conventional lift jack is one of the most useful of the scene-shifting devices at the disposal of the technician. By means of it units of scenery that are too heavy, too irregular in shape, or too awkward to shift manually can be lifted onto castors and easily moved by rolling. Under normal circumstances the lift jacks are concealed from the audience by placing them within or behind the unit they are designed to shift.

A variation that makes the lift jack even more useful is the detachable jack. This jack was designed to meet an unusual problem that arose in connection with a production of *The Grass Harp*. One of the settings required in this play is a tree house supported between two trunks of a divided tree. The floor level of the tree house was 9'-0" above the stage floor, and it had to be large enough and strong enough to support the weight and movement of six actors. As it was designed, the tree had a spread of 23'-0" between the outermost branches and stood 19'-0" high. The base that locked the two trunks together was comparatively small—only 7'-0" wide and 11'-0" long. Standard lift jacks could not be used because the base was too small to conceal them. Even mounting the base on a heavy wagon seemed ill-advised, since the rubber-tired castors would have compressed under the weight of tree and actors, possibly causing an objectionable swaying of the whole tree form. The problem of moving the finished tree from the shop to the stage, a distance of 120'-0", and of shifting it during performances, was met by designing a lift jack that could be attached and detached from the tree base (Plate 140).

Four sets of heavyweight brackets were made from $3/8" \times 4"$ strap iron. Each set consisted of two hooks, one to be bolted to the base of the tree frame, the other to be bolted to the jack dolly. Two dollies, each 8'-0" long and 3'-0" wide, were made of $2" \times 4"$ framing and mounted on four swivel castors with 3" rubber-tired wheels. An upright hand bar mounted on the back of the dolly made it easy for a stagehand to operate. The mounting position of the hooks on both the tree base and the dolly was critical. It was necessary to place them in such a position that they could be engaged only when the offstage side of the dolly was raised. Using the forward set of castors as a fulcrum and the dolly as a lever, the base of the tree frame could be raised about one inch from the stage floor when the dolly was lowered to rest on its four castors. The two dollies were rolled into position on either side of the tree base, the brackets engaged, and both dollies were lowered. The entire weight of the tree was thereby transferred to the castors. Although the hand bar on each dolly was made long enough for two stagehands to use it, it was discovered that only one operator on each dolly was required to shift the tree.

APPARITION EFFECT

The apparition scene, in which an apparently solid substance disappears to reveal objects beyond it, is an old trick in the theatre. That it can still prove

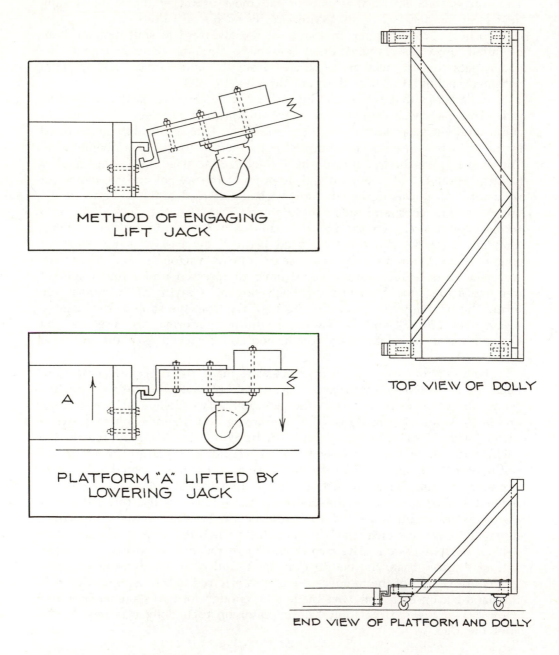

METHOD OF ENGAGING
LIFT JACK

PLATFORM "A" LIFTED BY
LOWERING JACK

TOP VIEW OF DOLLY

END VIEW OF PLATFORM AND DOLLY

Plate 140 Detachable Lift Jack

effective was demonstrated convincingly in an experimental production of a script entitled *Black Blizzard* by Sherwood Collins.

The play, in the mid-1930s, centers about the struggles of a Kansas farmer and his family against the ravages of prolonged drought and dust storms. Although the main action of the play was treated realistically, a poetic quality was introduced through the medium of flashbacks. These spoke of man's ravishing the land and retold much of the romantic pioneer history of the area. They made use of ten historical figures such as the Buffalo Hunter, the Homesteader, the Cowboy, the Quitter, and so forth. Each appeared out of darkness to give his short monologue and then disappeared into darkness. Since none of these flashback scenes was longer than two or three minutes, it became imperative to devise some scheme of integration that would reduce to a minimum the interruption of the main theme of the play. Several different schemes were proposed; what was finally selected was an adaptation of the old apparition or disappearance scene.

The setting was designed as a composite interior-exterior of the old farm. The interior revealed the living room and a corner of the dining room; the exterior showed the front porch, the second story, and a general outline of the whole house. The second story was used for the apparition scenes. The silhouette of the second floor was made of two-dimensional framing; the center section, through which the historical figures were seen, was covered with sharkstooth scrim. The areas on either side were covered with canvas and were therefore opaque (Plate 141).

Immediately behind the scrim section was placed a 7'-0" by 11'-0" platform with its floor 10'-0" from the stage floor. On this platform small backing flats formed a three-sided booth with the open face against the scrim. A baffle entranceway with black draperies at either end and a small ceiling over the top made this booth completely light-proof.

The success of the apparition effect depends upon how well the light can be controlled. During the playing of all scenes within the living room or on the front porch, and when the sky cyc lights were up, it was necessary to prevent any of this light from striking the back of the scrim and making this part of the second story transparent. It was equally important, during the playing of the apparition scenes, when all other lights were out, to control any spill or reflected light emanating from the booth spot, as this would cause disturbing patches of light to appear on the cyclorama. As a further precaution against light spills, therefore, a set of black draw curtains was rigged within the booth just upstage of the scrim, which could be closed while the actor was taking his position within the booth. This arrangement eliminated the risk of having spill-light filtering through the scrim and revealing the actor's presence. The curtains were opened just before the booth light was raised to its proper reading. The transition from the realistic scenes on the lower acting levels to the apparition scenes of the historical figures on the upper level required only the few seconds needed to lower one set of stage lights, open the black draw curtains, and dim up the booth spot.

THE DISAPPEARANCE TRAP AND ELEVATOR

Well-equipped theatres have all or part of the stage floor trapped. The trapped areas consist of sections of the flooring that can be removed sepa-

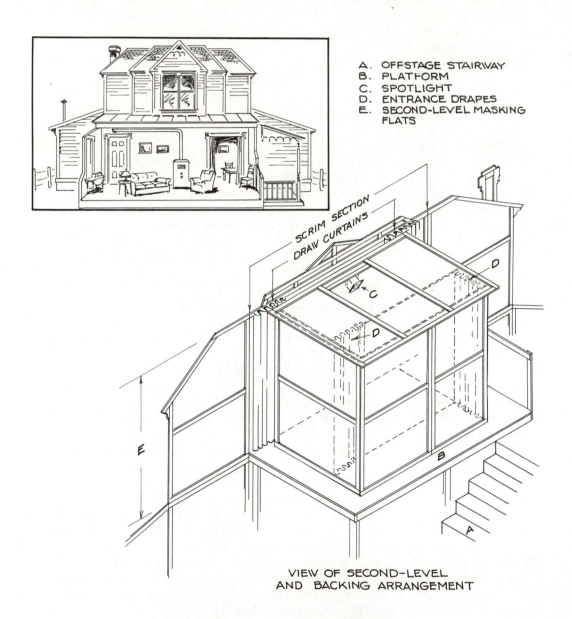

A. OFFSTAGE STAIRWAY
B. PLATFORM
C. SPOTLIGHT
D. ENTRANCE DRAPES
E. SECOND-LEVEL MASKING
   FLATS

SCRIM SECTION
DRAW CURTAINS

VIEW OF SECOND-LEVEL
AND BACKING ARRANGEMENT

Plate 141   Rigging Used for Apparition Scenes in *Black Blizzard* rately or in combination to form various-sized openings and make possible the vertical movement of actors or properties through the stage floor. Stairways are normally used for this purpose, but in some instances, as in *Don Juan*, the play may call for the sudden disappearance of an actor.

The elevator illustrated in Plate 142 is a fast-acting type. Its use was coupled with a flash of fire, smoke, and thunder when Don Juan disappeared from the center of the stage. An opening 3'-0" × 2'-8" was made in the floor by removing one of the traps and reflooring all but the desired opening. An elevator with a floor area slightly less than that of the trap opening was constructed of 1¼" × 3" stock. This unit was diagonally braced, and all joints were either screwed or bolted for greater strength. The elevator was 3'-6" high and had as its basic members two vertical 2" × 6"s centered on either side. To the outer face of each 2" × 6" was bolted a length of 2" × 2" that formed a projecting tongue; these tongues fitted into grooves on the vertical tracks and served as guides for the movement of the elevator. The grooves on each track were formed by bolting two 2" × 2"s to the face of the 2" × 6" just far enough apart to permit the tongues to fit between them. Each vertical track was carefully centered on either side of the trap opening and lag-screwed to the supporting beams of the stage floor. It was necessary to have the tracks solidly braced to hold them equidistant from each other and to prevent their springing apart. This bracing eliminated any chance of the elevator's binding between the tracks or of its becoming disengaged from the guiding grooves. (For the sake of clarity the diagonal bracing is omitted from the drawing.)

Power for the operation of the elevator was provided by a double-whip tackle rigging and a sandbag counterbalance. Two separate lines of ½" manila rope ran from a pipe yoke up over two single blocks attached to the floor beams, passed down under two additional blocks on the bottom of the elevator and up again to the floor beams, where they were tied off. This rigging provides a 2 to 1 mechanical advantage and reduces by about half the weight required to counterbalance the elevator and its load. This weight was sufficient to hold the top of the empty elevator flush with the stage floor. Until it was time for its use, the elevator rested upon a 2" × 4" lock bar, one end of which was pivoted from one track and supported on the other by a 2" × 4" hinged trigger attached to the opposite track. A length of ¼" sash cord was attached to the free end of the trigger, passed over a pulley, and then down to within reach of the operator. When the actor stepped to the center of the elevator top, the trigger was released on a given cue. The additional weight of the actor forced the elevator to fall rapidly until the angle of the supporting lines became more acute. The more nearly these lines paralleled the elevator's line of travel, the greater became their upward thrust, thus gradually slowing the elevator's speed. By the time the elevator had fallen about 8 feet it had slowed sufficiently to permit the actor to step off onto a landing platform. The weight of the sandbag then propelled the empty elevator back to stage level. Since the upward movement of the empty elevator was rapid, a snubbing line was attached to the bottom to prevent its projecting above the stage floor, the lock bar was pivoted into position and the trigger engaged. Plate 142 illustrates the moment when the elevator has been freed of its load and is starting upward to its stage position.

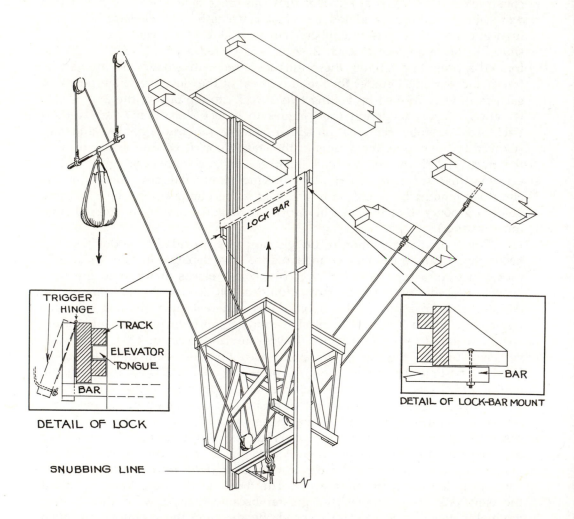

TRIGGER
HINGE
TRACK
ELEVATOR
TONGUE
BAR

DETAIL OF LOCK

LOCK BAR

DETAIL OF LOCK-BAR MOUNT

BAR

SNUBBING LINE

Plate 142   Disappearance Trap

The Power-Driven Elevator

The elevator needed in the production of *The Faithful Shepherdess* served an entirely different purpose than that employed in *Don Juan*. Here the figure of the god Neptune had to rise in a slow and stately fashion from the depths of a well—and just to make the problem more interesting, he carried in his arms the body 'of the shepherdess Amaryllis. (Neptune weighed 255 pounds, Amaryllis 110, the elevator 86 pounds—a total of 471 pounds.) Since it was necessary for these actors to move from the elevator to the stage floor, there would be a shifting of weight and of the points of strain on both the elevator and its guiding tracks. This necessitated a different method of construction, rigging, and guiding than that used for a disappearance trap.

The size of the trap opening and of the elevator was determined by the length of the reclining figure of Amaryllis as she was held in the arms of Neptune. This resulted in an elevator 5'-0" long, 3'-0" wide, and 3'-6" high. To keep its weight at a minimum, the elevator was built of 1" × 4" lumber with diagonal bracing of 1" × 3" white pine stock. On the four corners of both top and bottom the lengthwise pieces were joined to the cross members by notched joints, the ends extending past the corners by 1½" and 3½". This is shown in the detail drawings in Plate 143. This method of joining formed a right-angle extension on each of the eight corners. Into these extensions fitted the four vertical 2" × 4" guideposts. These posts were lag-screwed to the heavy supporting beams of the stage floor; they served both to guide and to steady the elevator from its four corners. Diagonal and cross bracing placed on the outside of the 2" × 4" guideposts held them firmly in place and yet did not interfere with the vertical movement of the elevator. The lower horizontal cross bracing was extended to one side of the guideposts far enough to form the supporting members for the platform required for mounting the winch and motor.

Along each side and on the underside of the elevator was fastened a length of 2" × 4". Four steel loft blocks were aligned with each other and bolted to the 2" × 4"s. These blocks were placed as close as possible to the outer corners of the elevator. Through these blocks ran the rigging lines that gave support on all four corners of the elevator. The rigging lines were made from ¼" steel cable, not because its strength was needed, but to avoid both the stretching and the creaking that would accompany the use of rope lines for a load of this weight. Each cable ran from its anchor point on the overhead floor beam down and under both loft blocks on each side of the elevator, up and over a third block fastened to the floor beam; there it was clamped off to a short length of 1½" pipe. An inverted saddle of ¼" cable was clamped to the pipe yoke, from which ran a cable that served onto the drum of an electrically driven winch. The methods of coupling the winch to the motor and of mounting them are described in the discussion of the powered winch in the preceding chapter. In case of either motor or electrical failure, the elevator could still be operated manually by removing the V-belt pulley from the winch and substituting the hand crank—an operation that required only a few seconds.

THE CLOUD MACHINE

Much of the fun associated with a production of Aristophanes' play, *The Birds*, came from the use of a modern version of the old Greek *mechane* or

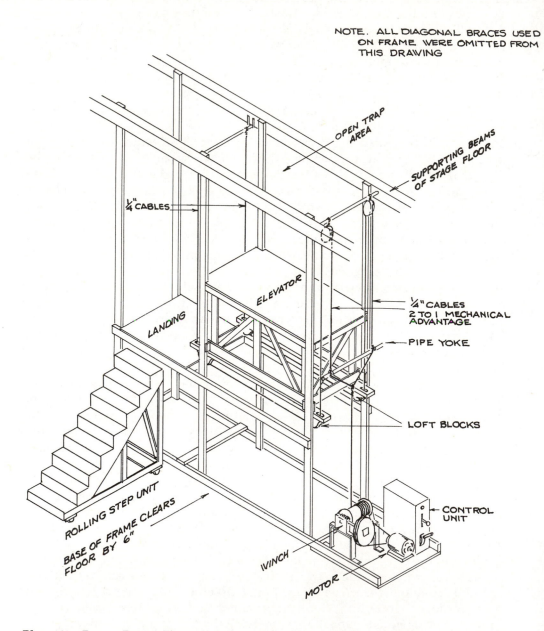

NOTE. ALL DIAGONAL BRACES USED
ON FRAME WERE OMITTED FROM
THIS DRAWING

OPEN TRAP AREA

SUPPORTING BEAMS OF STAGE FLOOR

¼" CABLES

ELEVATOR

¼" CABLES
2 TO 1 MECHANICAL ADVANTAGE

PIPE YOKE

LANDING

LOFT BLOCKS

ROLLING STEP UNIT

BASE OF FRAME CLEARS FLOOR BY 6"

CONTROL UNIT

WINCH

MOTOR

Plate 143 Power-Driven Elevator, Suspended from Underside of Revolve suspension machine. Three ambassadors of the gods, riding upon a cloud, descend to inspect the newly created city of Nephelococcugia. The cloud first appears from directly overhead, with the ambassadors leaning over the edge discussing the general state of affairs as the cloud descends. After reaching the stage floor the ambassadors leave the cloud, which rises until it is out of sight. Later in the play, when they are ready to leave, the cloud reappears and settles gently to the ground. The three ambassadors mount and after they are lifted a few feet from the floor one of them decides to stay. The cloud returns to earth once more and the ambassador leaves, but his place on the cloud is taken by two mortals. Here then is a problem involving not only an unbalanced arbor, but a load that is variable in weight as well.

Three adjacent arbors were used in this rigging (Plate 144). The No. 1 and No. 2 arbors were clamped together, and from the battens controlled by them were supported the cloud and the concealed platform on which the actors stood. A conventional carpet-hoist rig was used between the No. 2 and No. 3 arbors. A weight equal to that of the cloud and the platform, 120 pounds, was evenly divided between the first two arbors. The No. 3 arbor was loaded with counterbalance to equal the combined weights of the three heavyweight ambassadors—in this case 215, 205, and 170 pounds. Had the problem remained simply that of the actors leaving and entering the platform, the standard carpet hoist would have proved adequate. But the exchange of one actor for two others, as passengers aboard the cloud, meant that an additional 80 pounds had to be lifted on the last trip aloft. To handle this difference in weight, as well as to compensate for the frictional loss of such a heavy load, the old reliable winch and motor was coupled by cable to the top and bottom of the combined first two arbors.

An additional safety precaution was used in locking off the No. 3 arbor at its high position when the empty cloud platform was raised. To the top of the arbor was attached a steel cable that ran to the grid, over a special loft block and back down to the stage floor. A heavy welded ring was clamped to the free end of this cable. The hook of the moving block, used in a double luff, was slipped into the ring, and tension was exerted on the tackle. The fall of the tackle was then tied off to an eyebolt on the locking rail. This rig, coupled with the rope lock and a stopper hitch tied to the operating line, safely held the 590 pounds in place.

The cloud platform was made as two units, the weight-bearing platform and the cloud silhouette. As the diagram shows, the platform was constructed like any standard rigid platform, except that to its sides were bolted 2″ × 4″ uprights that formed the supports for the protective guard rails and the hinged gate. In order that the weight of both the platform and the actors could be flown under compression, two U-shaped strap-iron brackets were bolted in place around each end of the platform. Four steel cables ran from the brackets to the two pipe battens from which the platform was suspended. The cloud silhouette was made as a canvas-covered, two-dimensional framed cutout screwed to the downstage side of the platform. The part of the canvas cloud which extended below the base of the platform was left unframed so that it would not interfere when the platform rested on the stage floor. No effort was made to conceal the supporting steel cables. The stylized designs used in this production seemed to justify decorating the cables with knotted ropes liberally entwined with flowers and vines.

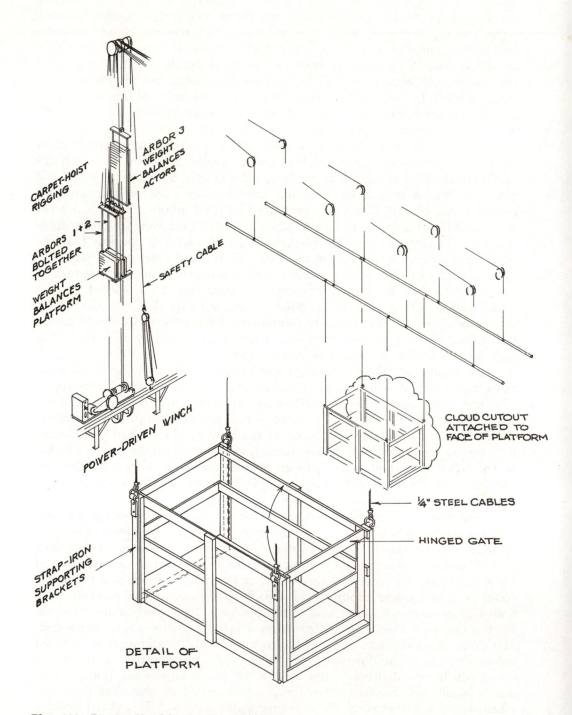

CARPET-HOIST RIGGING

ARBOR 3 WEIGHT BALANCES ACTORS

ARBORS 1 + 2 BOLTED TOGETHER

WEIGHT BALANCES PLATFORM

SAFETY CABLE

POWER-DRIVEN WINCH

CLOUD CUTOUT ATTACHED TO FACE OF PLATFORM

STRAP-IRON SUPPORTING BRACKETS

¼" STEEL CABLES

HINGED GATE

DETAIL OF PLATFORM

Plate 144   Rigging Used for the Cloud Machine

THE CARPET HOIST USED WITH A
DOUBLE-WHIP TACKLE RIGGING

A variation of the cloud machine just described was the swing used in the same play by the god's messenger, Iris (Plate 145). Unlike the slow and leisurely entrance of the ambassadors, the director wanted the entrance of Iris to be breathtaking and swift. In addition, he wanted Iris to appear first in her swing in the upper right-hand corner of the proscenium arch, swing diagonally across the stage, and, in a series of diminishing arcs, come to rest on a prescribed spot on the stage floor. She was then to dismount, and the empty swing would be raised out of sight, to return for her later in the play.

Occasionally some particular stage effect cannot be obtained by any one rigging technique, and a combination of rigging principles is required in order to achieve it. This was the case with Iris's swing, which employed a spotline, breasting line, tackle rigging, rope-line carpet hoist, a metal yoke, and saddles.

On the grid directly above the spot where Iris was to land, which was almost center stage, was placed one of the two loft blocks required for the rigging of a spotline. The second block was located on the grid above the locking rail so that the operator could see past the end of the lowered cyclorama and observe the movement of the swing. The spotline was rigged as a double whip to give the operator a 2 to 1 mechanical advantage. Notice in the diagram that one end of the line, A, is attached to the grid; the line then passes through a single movable block, up over the center loft block, over the head block, and down to the stage floor at the locking rail. A single cable runs from the movable block to a connecting link, to which is centered and clamped a short cable saddle. This saddle is fastened to both ends of a short iron bar yoke fitted with two heavy welded rings at each end. From the second set of rings on the yoke two cables run down to the small chain saddles on each side of the swing. These saddles made it easy to adjust the angle of the chair seat and eliminated any tendency for the swing to tip. As an additional precaution the swing was fitted with a back, arms, and a safety belt—making it impossible for Iris to fall out even had she fainted.

A breasting line, B, was run from the locking rail over a pulley, fastened to the stagehouse wall 25'-0" from the floor, and tied off to one of the rings on the yoke. This kept the swing facing the audience and provided the means of moving it from side to side.

A special line, S, was required to lower the empty swing to the stage floor. The failure of the empty swing to return without help to the floor was due in part to the friction loss caused by the operating line's passing over three blocks but principally to the weight of the operating line between the stage floor and the point where it passed over the head block. This special line ran from the locking rail to the grid, over a block, then back down to where it was tied off to the operating line at X. Pulling on the special line lifted the weight of the operating line, and the swing could then be lowered as rapidly as was needed.

Although Iris in this production weighed only 105 pounds, the friction loss from the tackle rigging used amounted to approximately $30\frac{1}{2}$ pounds. This meant that the operator was lifting about 67 pounds, even with the 2 to 1 mechanical advantage offered by the double whip. Since he could not

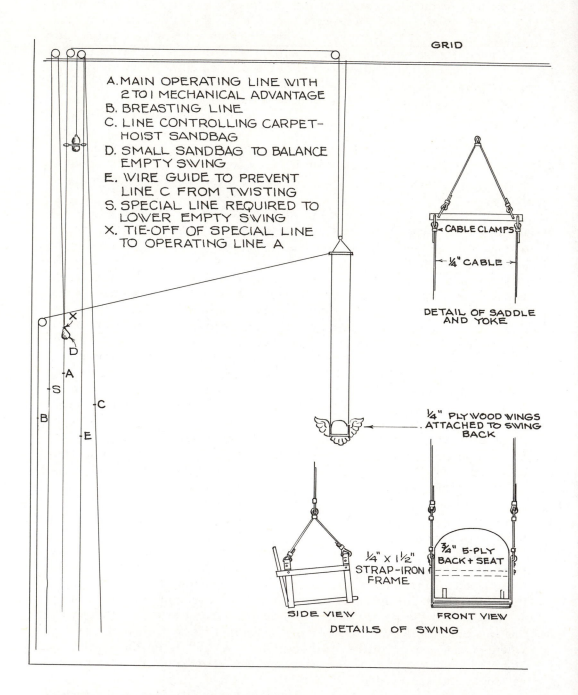

GRID

A. MAIN OPERATING LINE WITH 2 TO 1 MECHANICAL ADVANTAGE
B. BREASTING LINE
C. LINE CONTROLLING CARPET-HOIST SANDBAG
D. SMALL SANDBAG TO BALANCE EMPTY SWING
E. WIRE GUIDE TO PREVENT LINE C FROM TWISTING
S. SPECIAL LINE REQUIRED TO LOWER EMPTY SWING
X. TIE-OFF OF SPECIAL LINE TO OPERATING LINE A

CABLE CLAMPS
¼" CABLE

DETAIL OF SADDLE AND YOKE

¼" PLYWOOD WINGS ATTACHED TO SWING BACK

¼" x 1½" STRAP-IRON FRAME

¾" 5-PLY BACK + SEAT

SIDE VIEW   FRONT VIEW

DETAILS OF SWING

Plate 145   A Combination of Rigging Principles

control this much weight safely, or move it at the speed asked by the director, a 40-pound sandbag carpet hoist was coupled to the operating line of the double whip. A separate line, C, was used to control the sandbag and to tie it off at its high position when the empty swing was to be raised. A metal ring was tied to each side of the sandbag. Through one passed the operating line of the double whip; through the other passed a wire guide that kept the bag from swinging or pivoting around the other lines and fouling them. Notice that the special line was tied off to the operating line at a point below the metal ring on the sandbag. By raising the operating line until the tie-off at X came in contact with the ring, it was possible to transfer the 40-pound weight to the double-whip rigging.

The crew members who were to operate the swing were carefully trained, and the rigging of the swing was tested repeatedly before it was used in rehearsal. A sandbag that equaled the weight of Iris was strapped into the swing and put through a series of tests that were much more severe in all respects than anything required in the performance routine. Frequent inspections of the rigging were maintained for possible signs of wear or strain. Only after the crew had been thoroughly trained and the rigging repeatedly tested did the actress try out the swing for the first time. She became accustomed to the feel of the swing gradually; she was raised, lowered, and swung from side to side at increasing heights and speed until the performance routine was achieved.

SUPPORTING TRUSSES

Educational theatres may differ radically from each other in many ways, but in one respect there is a great similarity—they all produce Shakespeare. If their productions of the bard have progressed beyond the "drapery background" type of setting, there is a good possibility that their thinking has been focused upon the problems involved in building a setting that is representative of an Elizabethan playhouse. Foremost among these is the problem of how to support a wide inner-above stage and leave the inner-below area directly beneath free of supporting columns or posts. Coupled with this are the problems of keeping the cost down and of devising a platform arrangement that will be easy to assemble, strike, and store. A modified reconstruction of the Old Globe Playhouse, built from the plans shown here, was used at the University Theatre at Iowa for about 20 years (Plate 146).

The weight-bearing and bracing units used in this particular reconstruction consist of the following: diagonal-bracing stairways, offstage landing platforms, weight-bearing supports, trusses, and the inner-above platform flooring.

The bracing stairways are made as dependent step units. They not only provide access to the landing platform, but when locked to both platform and stage floor they also serve as diagonal bracing. This eliminates any possible sidesway of the assembled platform structure.

Each of the offstage landings is 5'-0" wide and 7'-0" long. The top of each is made as a rigid platform with 2" × 4" frames covered with tongue and groove flooring. To each lengthwise side of the platform top is bolted a set of preassembled legs that raise the platform top 10'-0" from the floor. Each set of legs carries identification marks that correspond with similar marks on the

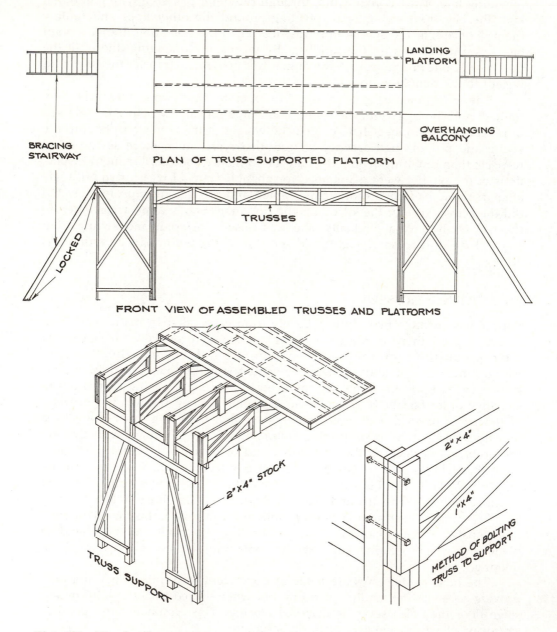

LANDING PLATFORM

OVERHANGING BALCONY

BRACING STAIRWAY

PLAN OF TRUSS—SUPPORTED PLATFORM

LOCKED

TRUSSES

FRONT VIEW OF ASSEMBLED TRUSSES AND PLATFORMS

2"×4" STOCK

TRUSS SUPPORT

2"×4"

1"×4"

METHOD OF BOLTING TRUSS TO SUPPORT

Plate 146   Wooden Trusses

platform—a precaution that avoids assembly by the trial-and-error method. Temporary cross bracing between each set of legs is made by nailing 1″ × 3″ members into place.

Bolted to the onstage side of each landing are the supporting frames for the joists. These are made of doubled 2″ × 4″ stock. As can be seen in Plate 146, this provides a frame with four 4″ × 4″ supporting legs diagonally braced on either side of a doorway and joined together by three horizontal cross members. One of the 2″ × 4″s from each leg extends 1′-6″ above the top horizontal 2″ × 4″ and serves as a support to which a truss is bolted.

The four trusses make it possible to span a distance of 20′-0″ without central supports. A truss can be described as an assemblage of members or beams so combined and reinforced by triangular bracing as to form a rigid framework. In this case each truss is 21′-0″ long and 1′-6″ wide, or more accurately, 1′-6″ from top to bottom. Two 21′-0″ lengths of 2″ × 4″ were laid out parallel with each other and separated by cross members of the same-sized stock. These were joined by battening 1″ × 4″ stock over each of the butt joints formed by the 2″ × 4″s. Fitting tightly against the edges of the 1″ × 4″ cross members are diagonal braces of 1″ × 4″. Both sides of each truss are treated in the same manner.

The flooring that rests on top of the trusses consists of five rigid platforms, each 4′-2³/₁₆″ wide and 10′-0″ long. With the trusses in place, the flooring sections are raised on end and skidded into position on top of the trusses. The first section is bolted to the side of the landing platform, the second is then bolted to the first, the third to the second, and so on, until all flooring sections are not only bolted together but bolted to the side landings as well. This method of joining the various parts of the structure gives it surprising rigidity. Since the flooring sections extend 3′-0″ past the downstage truss, they form an overhanging balcony for the inner-above. As an additional lock to prevent their tipping up at the back, the upstage end of each section is cleated to the side of the upstage truss.

Assembly of the platforms onstage moves rapidly if the operational steps listed here are followed. (1) Measure and mark the exact position of the landing platform on the stage floor. (2) Rig a double-luff tackle from a pipe batten that is directly above the center of the inner-above area. This can be used to help right the landing platforms as well as to lift the trusses into place. (3) Turn the landing platform upside down and bolt the leg sections into place, reinforcing them by nailing on cross-bracing members. (4) Turn the platforms right side up and position them on their marks, attach the bracing stairways, and bolt the supporting frames of the onstage sides of the landing platforms. (5) Rig a saddle on the double luff, and raise the trusses into place. (6) Next, skid the floor sections into place and bolt them. (7) Remove the tackle rigging from the pipe batten. The platform structure is now completely assembled and ready to receive the masking flats that will complete the setting.

Occasionally, when the nature of the design calls for the use of a second-floor level, good use is made of this platform structure in other productions. Both the captain's bridge in a production of *Mr. Roberts* and the second floor of the Hilliard home in *Desperate Hours* used these platforms to advantage in Iowa productions.

RIGGING FOR HORIZONTAL
MOVEMENT OF DRAPERY TREES

In a production of *Emperor Jones,* designed by Ricahrd Knaub, trees were constructed from 30'-0" lengths of black drapery material that had been given three-dimensional form by attaching them at top and bottom to circular wooden sweeps and suspending them from the pipe battens of the counterweight system (Plate 147). These drapery trees were supplemented by back projections of jungle forms thrown on a translucent muslin drop. The combination formed a convincing imaginative jungle in which Jones finds himself hopelessly lost. The director asked if it would be possible, at the climax of one scene, to have several of these drapery trees move horizontally and actually converge on the cowering figure of Jones.

The construction and rigging for this effect were fairly simple. A dolly was made for each tree that was to move, consisting of a 3'-0" length of 2" × 4" suspended from one of the counterweight pipe battens by means fo two wooden sheaves attached to the 2" × 4" by brackets made of 3/16" × 3/4" strap iron. The sheaves were turned by lathe to fit the contour of the pipe batten and were made from wood to reduce any sound that might be heard as the dolly rolled along the batten. The top circular sweep of each tree was bolted to the underside of the dolly. This kept the tree sweeps parallel with the floor and prevented their tipping. An operating line of 1/4" sash cord ran from a floor block over a double pulley and a single pulley placed at opposite ends of the batten; the free ends of the operating line were attached to each end of the dolly. This rigging gave the dolly and the tree freedom for a horizontal movement of about 10'-0", which was the distance between the cable supports of the pipe batten.

It was thought at first that it might be necessary to use guy lines from the battens to the stage floor to keep the operating lines from moving or swinging the pipe battens, but they were not needed when care was used in placing the floor block directly beneath the double block mounted on the batten. The straight-down pull on the operating line needed to move the trees had no tendency to impart a swinging motion to the batten.

GEAR-DRIVEN REVOLVING DISC

Sidney Howard's play *Yellow Jack* calls for the use of a small revolving disc to be mounted on top of a platform and to turn in full view of the audience. Ordinary means of turning the revolve could not be used in this instance. A cable drive was impractical because of the elevated position, and walking the revolve around with pull rods was out of the question with the curtain open. Two gears and a hand crank gleaned from the local junkyard made highly satisfactory equipment for accomplishing this effect (Plate 148).

The cost of the materials for the disc, which was to be 8'-0" in diameter, was held to a minimum by using one of the rigid platforms taken from stock. By building 2" × 4" triangular frames that fell within the desired circumference of the disc and covering them with 3/4" fir 5-ply flooring cut to a circular shape, it was possible to bolt them to four sides of the 4'-0" × 7'-0" platform and complete its circular shape. Four rigid castors, one to each of the triangular frames, were placed an equal distance in from the circumference, with

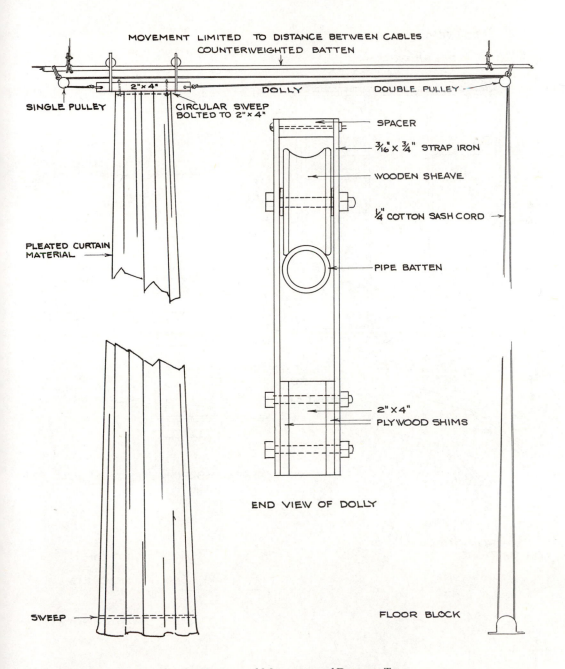

MOVEMENT LIMITED TO DISTANCE BETWEEN CABLES

COUNTERWEIGHTED BATTEN

2" × 4"

DOLLY

DOUBLE PULLEY

SINGLE PULLEY

CIRCULAR SWEEP
BOLTED TO 2" × 4"

SPACER

$\frac{3}{16}$" × $\frac{3}{4}$" STRAP IRON

WOODEN SHEAVE

$\frac{1}{4}$" COTTON SASH CORD

PLEATED CURTAIN
MATERIAL

PIPE BATTEN

2" × 4"

PLYWOOD SHIMS

END VIEW OF DOLLY

SWEEP

FLOOR BLOCK

Plate 147   Rigging for the Horizontal Movement of Drapery Trees

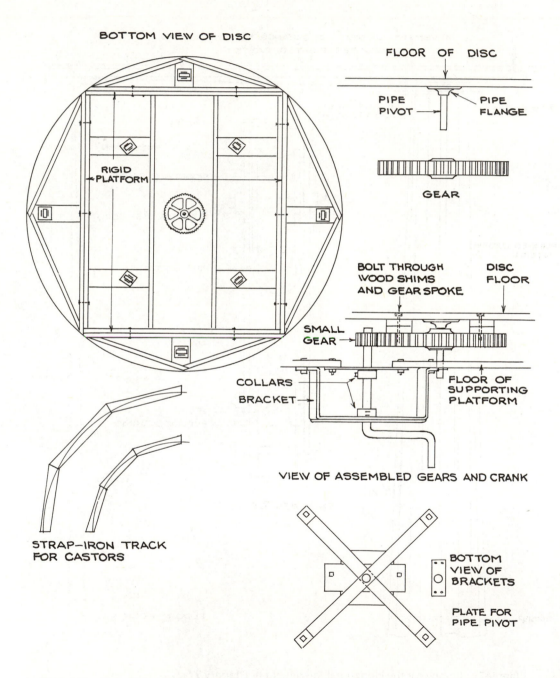

BOTTOM VIEW OF DISC

FLOOR OF DISC

PIPE
PIVOT →

PIPE
FLANGE

GEAR

RIGID
←PLATFORM

BOLT THROUGH
WOOD SHIMS
AND GEAR SPOKE

DISC
FLOOR

SMALL
GEAR →

COLLARS

BRACKET →

FLOOR OF
SUPPORTING
PLATFORM

VIEW OF ASSEMBLED GEARS AND CRANK

STRAP—IRON TRACK
FOR CASTORS

BOTTOM
VIEW OF
BRACKETS

PLATE FOR
PIPE PIVOT

Plate 148   Gear Drive for Small Disc

their wheels at a right angle to a radius line. Four additional castors were mounted in the same manner to the rigid platform. Since the flooring on the platform on which the disc was to turn was not too smooth, two sets of sheet-iron tracks were made, from short straight sections of $\frac{1}{8}$" × 4" strap iron with mitered ends, drilled so that they could be screwed to the platform top.

The axle, or pivot, was made from a pipe flange and a short length of 1" pipe securely fastened to the exact center of the disc on the underside. The pipe extended through a hole drilled in the top of the supporting platform. This prevented the disc from creeping out of position as it was turned.

The larger of the two gears (12" in diameter) was shimmed up and bolted to the underside of the disc, with the pivot pipe projecting through the arbor in the gear. An 8" square hole was cut in the flooring of the supporting platform at a point where the small gear and crank could be positioned to engage the larger gear. After the disc had been placed in position on the platform, the smaller gear and the crank were put into place. Two sets of strap-iron brackets that fitted around the crankshaft had been designed so that they could be screwed into position from the underside of the platform. Horizontal adjustment of the two gears was made by proper placing of the brackets, and two adjustable collars around the shaft and between the brackets made the vertical adjustment of the gears easy.

Variations in Castor-Mounting for a Revolving Disc

In some settings the design may necessitate an entirely new solution for a problem that is normally solved in a much simpler fashion. This was the case with the revolving gun turret required in the production of a script called *Flowers of Victory* by Richard Smith. Most of the action of this play involved the crew of a tank destroyer who had taken up its position in the wreckage of a French village. The only way the crew had of entering the destroyer was through the hatch in the top of the 37 MM gun turret. This, of course, meant that the turret could not be constructed as a regular revolving disc with a solid base and a central pivot point; the base of the turret had to be open, allowing the crew to drop through into the body of the destroyer.

Although the gun turret was only 3'-0" in diameter, eight rigid castors were used to obtain the desired effect. Four of them served to carry the weight of the turret and gun, and on them the gun turret revolved. The other four were needed to hold the turret centered within the circular opening cut in the top of the tank destroyer (Plate 149).

This assembly consisted basically of but two parts: the supporting table mounted inside the body of the destroyer on which both sets of castors were bolted, and the turret and gun itself. The 3'-0" square tabletop was open in the center and was literally nothing but a frame of 1" × 6" with halved jointed corners. It was supported by 1" × 4" legs diagonally braced for stability; the base of each leg was blocked and screwed to the floor of the destroyer. The castors on which the turret revolved were placed upside down and bolted to the 1" × 6" in the center of each table side. The wheel of each castor was placed at a right angle to a line from the center of the table. In the corners of the table were placed the four guiding castors. Because they had to be mounted in a horizontal position so

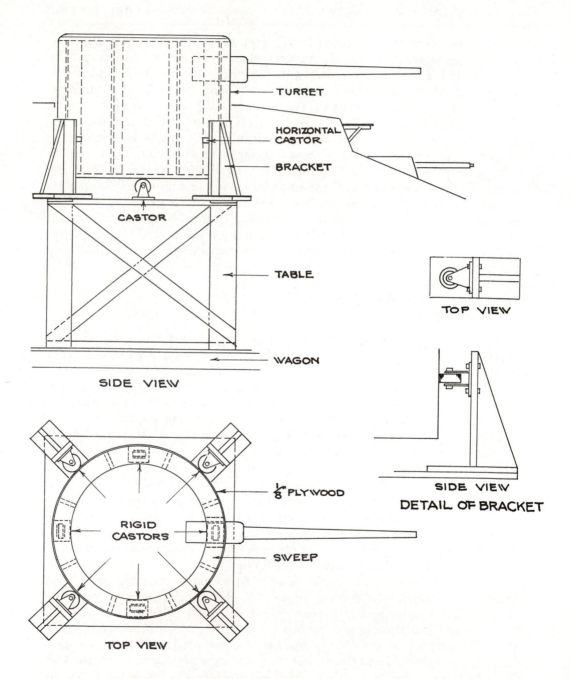

Plate 149   Variations in Castor Mounting

that the wheels would bear against the sides of the turret, they were bolted to wooden brackets made of $1'' \times 6''$. The brackets could be easily adjusted and then screwed into position on the top of the supporting table corners.

The turret was made on the same principle as a three-dimensional column. Two completely circular sweeps were cut from $^3/_4''$ 5-ply fir, the outside diameter of each was $3'-0''$, the width $3^1/_2''$. The two sweeps were separated by vertical $1'' \times 4''$s spaced about $1'-6''$ apart around their circumferences. The side of the turret was covered with $^1/_8''$ thick fir plywood. Although the turret extended only $1'-6''$ above the deck of the destroyer, it was made $2'-6''$ high, to allow its circular sides to drop far enough below the deck to permit the guiding castors to bear against it.

The only fault of this rigging was that the turret turned too easily. This was corrected in part by changing the position of the weight-bearing castors slightly in order to force the rubber-tired wheels to skid against the movement of the disc. A few counterweights placed between the vertical spacers and strapped to the top of the lower sweep gave the turret the much needed weight and noticeably reduced the speed and ease with which it turned.

FLYING HARNESS AND RIGGING

Few plays have as much appeal for both youngsters and oldsters as Barrie's *Peter Pan*. Almost everybody has a desire to fly, and certainly a part of the fun and appeal of this play comes from the vicarious pleasure people receive from watching others fly.

The actual tackle rigging used for flying Peter and the children is neither complicated nor difficult to rig. But if this type of rigging is to be employed, it is important to understand in advance that there are three basic requirements for its successful operation: there must be adequate grid height, at least $55'-0''$ to $60'-0''$; the flying harness worn by the actor must be comfortable and safe; and both crew members and actors must be perfectly trained in movements and timing.

The tackle rigging illustrated in Plate 150 shows how very simple this rig can be. Basically it is nothing but a spotline with a 2 to 1 mechanical advantage. This part of the rig served only one purpose: it provided the vertical movement of the actor. The horizontal movement, the direction of swing, and the speed of her flight were controlled by the actor. Literally she became merely a weight on the free end of a line, a weight capable of movement in any direction and at whatever speed was desired.

There was one such rig for each of the four characters who were to fly. The loft blocks for these rigs were clustered on the grid within $4'-0''$ of each other and were placed directly over center stage. The operating lines ran across the grid, over the head blocks and down to a double-decked tower. The tower was placed downstage right out of sight of the audience but in a position where the two operators on each of the decks could see past the ends of the lowered cyclorama and had an unobstructed view of the stage.

The harness was made of heavy canvas reinforced by webbing and leather. It was designed as a one-piece garment to be laced down the side; the two adjustable shoulder straps then laced to the front of the jacket, as did the two crotch straps. The padded and chamois-covered crotch straps were placed in much the same position as the crotch straps of a parachute harness.

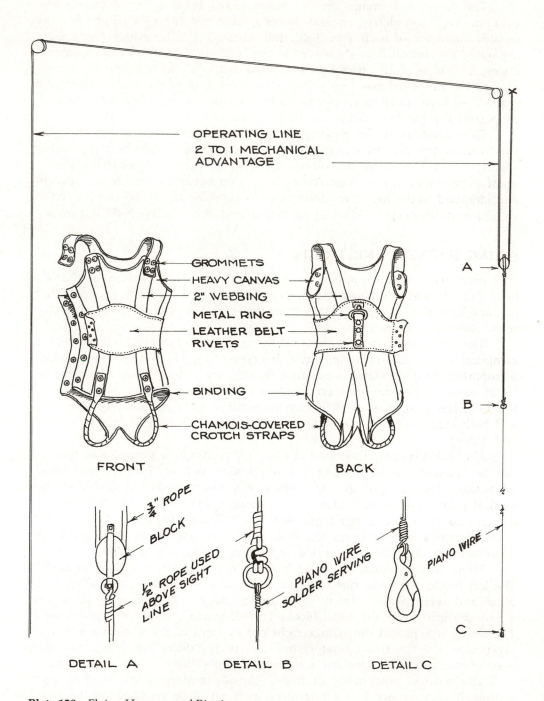

OPERATING LINE
2 TO I MECHANICAL
ADVANTAGE

GROMMETS
HEAVY CANVAS
2" WEBBING
METAL RING
LEATHER BELT
RIVETS

BINDING

CHAMOIS-COVERED
CROTCH STRAPS

FRONT   BACK

A

B

¾" ROPE
BLOCK
½" ROPE USED
ABOVE SIGHT
LINE

PIANO WIRE
SOLDER SERVING

PIANO WIRE

PIANO WIRE

C

DETAIL A   DETAIL B   DETAIL C

Plate 150   Flying Harness and Rigging

There was no chafing or rubbing from any part of the harness, and it proved to be surprisingly comfortable to wear in spite of its formidable appearance. Encircling this basic garment was a wide band of leather that was riveted and sewn in place. This too was laced together at the side. A welded metal ring, located about 2½″ below the shoulder blades, was fastened to the belt by means of a strap that was riveted to the leather belt and to the webbing and canvas. The exact location of the ring on the harness was quite important: if it was placed too high, the actor was forced to fly in a near-vertical position; if it was too low, the actor had difficulty in swinging her legs back under her for her landings.

The training of crew members and actors in the operation of the rigging and harness began on an empty stage. Each actor was assigned his own operator, and the two worked together as a team. For the actor the first lesson consisted of trying out the harness, getting accustomed to the feel of it as he was lifted off the floor a foot or two, and discovering how to keep his balance while flying. The operators learned how to lift the actors without jerking them and how to lower them easily, and began to understand the importance of timing their movements with those of the actors. As both members of a team built up confidence in each other, the "flight plan" for each rehearsal gradually increased in complexity. Each routine was carefully planned, then rehearsed until it could be performed perfectly. Soon the actors were taking off from a bed at stage left, flying the full width of the stage and landing on the mantel of a fireplace at stage right. This final act was not accomplished, of course, without some hilarious backward flights that resulted when an actor failed to take off with enough speed, or when an operator failed to lower the actor at that split second when his feet touched the mantel.

THE BOATSWAIN'S SEAT

There will be times during the process of rigging when it will be essential to work at a height from the stage floor that cannot be reached even with the use of an extension ladder. The boatswain's seat provides the answer to this problem. This device consists of a short board seat slung from two saddles and supported by the moving lower block of a watch tackle (Plate 151). The workman, seated in the chair, raises and lowers himself by operating the fall. When he reaches his working level, he ties the fall to the hook of the movable block, thus freeing both his hands.

The watch tackle gives a mechanical advantage of 3 to 1 and is rigged with one single and one double block. As shown in Plate 151, the upper or double block is tied off at the grid, and the single block provides the hook for support of the seat. In reeving this tackle, pass one end of the line over a sheave of the double block, down and through the sheave of the single block, over the second sheave of the double block, and tie or splice the end of the rope to the becket on the movable block.

The seat of the chair can be made from 1″ stock lumber, with reinforcing cleats placed at right angles on the underside as a precaution against splitting of the board. A stronger seat can be made by using ¾″ fir 5-ply reinforced in the same manner. The length of the seat is usually about 22″ or 24″ and its width about 10″. The saddles can be made of either rope or 3/16″ steel cables.

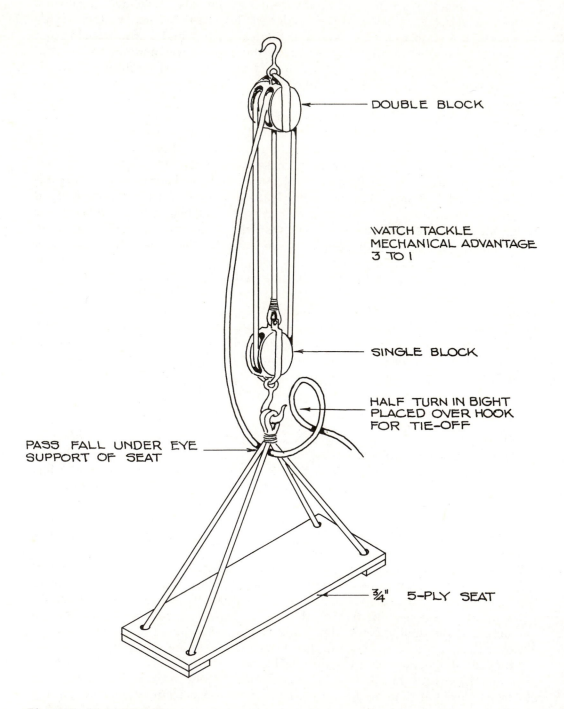

DOUBLE BLOCK

WATCH TACKLE
MECHANICAL ADVANTAGE
3 TO I

SINGLE BLOCK

HALF TURN IN BIGHT
PLACED OVER HOOK
FOR TIE-OFF

PASS FALL UNDER EYE
SUPPORT OF SEAT

¾" 5-PLY SEAT

Plate 151   Boatswain's Seat

If rope is used, two holes are bored near each end of the seat. A single rope is then threaded through the holes and the two ends either tied or spliced together. A double loop is formed at the top and center of the saddle by serving them in place with cord. If the saddles are formed of cables, one length of cable will be needed for each saddle. The free ends of each cable are clamped to eyebolts located in the four corners of the seat board. The two cable saddles are caught together at the top center, where two loops are formed, by using a large cable clamp or serving them together with wire and tape. The advantages of cables for saddles are that they make a stronger rigging, and the seat board thus rigged cannot slip out of horizontal adjustment.

The boatswain's seat is tied off at the desired working level by forming an underhand loop in the fall (an operation that can be done with one hand), passing this between the sides of the saddle, and dropping it over the projecting hook of the movable block.

WOODEN WINCH

For an Iowa production of *Thurber Carnival* three small 8'-0" revolving stages were to be powered by hand winches capable of completing a 180° turn in a matter of seconds. To obtain this speed we needed a winch drum 1'-0" in diameter; 3'-1½" of steel cable could be served onto a drum of this size with each revolution of the winch handle. Four revolutions of the winch could move the 8'-0" revolve the desired 180°. Since a winch with a drum this size could not be found in any catalogue, we decided to build our own.

The winch drum (the cylinder around which the cable is served) was made of two discs of ¾" 5-ply fir and a series of 2" × 4"s beveled to provide a roughly circular cylinder when assembled. With this type of joining for the 2" × 4"s, the tighter the cable was pulled the more pressure was exerted on the beveled joints. Each 2" × 4" was joined to the top and bottom discs by 2" flathead screws.

The major problem was to devise a method of attaching a metal axle and crank handle to the wooden drum. The axle was formed by a 1'-0" length of 1¼" I.D. (inside diameter) pipe. One end of a 12" length of ⅜" × 1½" strap iron was welded to the upper end of the pipe. At the opposite end of the strap iron a handle was attached by placing a 6" length of ¾" galvanized pipe over a locked machine bolt, thus forming a rotating sleeve around the bolt (Plate 152). An 8" × 8" × 3/16" piece of plate iron was drilled in the center to fit the pipe axle and also drilled and countersunk in eight places around the outer edges to receive 1¼" No. 9 flathead screws. This plate iron collar was welded at a true right angle to the pipe axle 4½" down from its top. Center holes were drilled in the discs at the top and bottom of the drum to accommodate the pipe axle. The pipe was inserted into the holes until the plate iron collar rested on the top disc; it was then fastened solidly in place with 1¼" wood screws.

Both the top and bottom supporting frames were made from pieces of 5-ply joined by three 1'-6" lengths of 2" × 6". Holes were drilled in these two pieces to accommodate the pipe axle. The assembled pipe axle could not be inserted into the axle hole of the upper supporting frame because of the crank handle and arm. To offset this difficulty a length of 2" × 6" was placed under

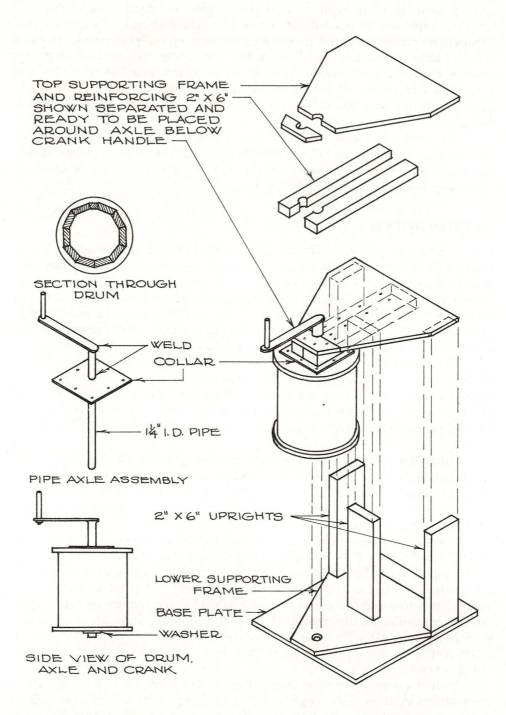

TOP SUPPORTING FRAME
AND REINFORCING 2" X 6"
SHOWN SEPARATED AND
READY TO BE PLACED
AROUND AXLE BELOW
CRANK HANDLE

SECTION THROUGH
DRUM

WELD

COLLAR

1¼" I. D. PIPE

PIPE AXLE ASSEMBLY

2" X 6" UPRIGHTS

LOWER SUPPORTING
FRAME

BASE PLATE

WASHER

SIDE VIEW OF DRUM,
AXLE AND CRANK

Plate 152   Wooden Winch

the top frame and a hole drilled in it that was in alignment with the other two. The 2″ × 6″ was then ripped down the center, with the saw kerf bisecting the actual hole. This arrangement permitted the two sections of the 2″ × 6″ to be placed on either side of the axle while the same could be done with the two parts of the plywood top. The lap joint thus formed by the two sections of 2″ × 6″ and the two sections of the plywood top were then firmly stove-bolted together. This wooden bearing, like the one in the lower supporting frame, was liberally coated with grease. (See Plate 152).

A final step in the completion of the winch was the addition of a baseplate. This was a piece of 5-ply 1′-10″ wide by 2′-2″ long screwed to the bottom side of the lower supporting frame. This baseplate served three purposes: it prevented the grease from the lower axle hole from staining the floor cloth, it provided a method of screwing the base to the stage floor, and it also provided a very easy method of adjusting the tension exerted by the winch on the steel cables. When it became necessary to tighten the cables, the screws were removed from the base and the whole winch assembly was pulled away from the revolve until the cables were taut; then the base was once more screwed to the stage floor.

To assemble a pipe axle, collar, arm, and handle cost approximately $8 for materials. The wooden parts of the winches were made from scene-shop scrap materials. These three winches became a part of our permanent stage equipment and have been used in many other productions since *Thurber Carnival*.

SMALL CABLE-DRIVEN WOODEN REVOLVES

One of the delightful features of *Thurber Carnival* is the speed with which it moves from one episode to another. Scene after scene appears with amazing rapidity—all accomplished by the aid of three small revolves, each carrying a typical Thurber cartoon painted on a sliding screen that divides the revolve in half. It is difficult to conceive of a scheme that is better suited for use in this type of episodic play. It takes only two or three seconds to make a half revolution of one of these revolves, or for that matter, of all three. Since the supports for the sliding screen are mounted on the revolve, it is quite possible to have a second screen on the upstage side of the exposed one. Hence both the background and what few props are required can be preset for each following scene. It is truly a rapid-fire method of shifting.

The effectiveness of the three revolves can be enhanced if a false stage floor is built up to the level of the revolve floor. (See description of false stage floor, Plate 158). This false floor conceals the castors and the cable rigging needed to turn the revolve. It also provides the actors with an unbroken acting area and one that is free of entangling cables.

The placement of the revolves was determined by the sight-line limits of our theatre. The center revolve was farther upstage than the two flanking revolves. Each of the two was as far to the side as sight lines would permit. All three revolves were backed by sets of black drapery legs on the sides and with a continuous run of draperies upstage. The latter hung in three sections, the two side pieces on one batten and the center section on another batten farther upstage. This arrangement of draperies made it possible for the actors to enter or leave the acting area between any set of drapery wings. There was also adequate space between the three revolves for the free movement of actors.

Each revolve was 8'-0" in diameter, with the flooring made from two sheets of ³/₄" thick 4'-0" × 8'-0" plywood (Plate 153). Two sheets of plywood were butted edge to edge and marked with a trammel bar on a 4'-0" radius. The two halves of the revolve were then placed on sawhorses and cut with a sabre saw. The scrap material was saved to be used in building up the false stage floor around each revolve. Six radiating spokes of 2" × 6" were spaced evenly on the underside of the revolve. All were used as mounting plates for rubber-tired castors, each with wheels 3" in diameter; two of them were also used to form a batten to which the halves of the revolve were screwed. (See Plate 153.) Notice that the spokes did not meet in the center, but projected 2" into a 1'-0" square removable trap that was used as a mount for the pivoting axle. The outer end of each spoke failed to meet the lip of the revolve by a matter of 2". Between each spoke, cut on a radius of 3'-10", were sections of 2" × 8". These, together with the end of each spoke, formed a circular sweep that was solidly screwed to the underside of the revolve and formed the surface around which the driving cables were served. To stop the cables from slipping off the 1¹/₂" sweep, a second sweep made from scrap ¹/₄" plywood was cut on a 1" larger diameter and was nailed to each 2" × 8" sweep in such a manner as to form a 1" projecting lip.

The castors were spaced as shown in the drawing, with two supplementary castors mounted near the center to prevent any strain from transferring to the battened butt joint holding the two halves of the revolve together. The castors were necessarily placed with their wheels at right angles to a line representing the radius. All castors had to be rigid or locked swivel castors.

The pivot axle was made from two pipe flanges and two short lengths of pipe, with one pipe small enough to fit inside the other. The large pipe and its flange was screwed to the stage floor; the smaller flange and its pipe was screwed to the center of the removable 1'-0" trap in the center of the revolve. This scheme simplified the problem of engaging both pipes when the revolve was taken from the shop and placed in position onstage. The revolve was turned on edge and wheeled from the shop to the stage, the large flange and pipe was secured to the floor in its proper position, and the revolve placed on its castors. After the exact center of the 1'-0" trap was located by means of strings stretched diagonally across the trap opening, the revolve then could be moved over the floor flange until it reached the point where the intersecting diagonal strings were exactly over the center of the pipe. The trap cover and its pipe flange were fitted into position and the cover screwed to the 2" projecting ends of the 2" × 6" spokes (Plate 153).

The fast-acting wooden winch previously described was used to turn the revolves. One long length of ³/₁₆" steel cable, a double floor block, and a winch were needed in this rigging. One end of the cable was fastened to the winch drum by stapling it in place, then several servings of the cable were made around the drum. The free end of the cable was passed through the floor block, and three servings were made around the revolve cable disc. Now the cable could be fed back through the floor block and served onto the drum in the opposite direction and locked. The cable was prevented from slipping on the revolve by stapling it to the cable disc at a point where it would not interfere with the 180° turning of the revolve (Plate 154).

The supporting frame for the sliding screens was mounted as an integral part of the revolve. Slots ³/₄" × 3¹/₂" were cut through the revolve and

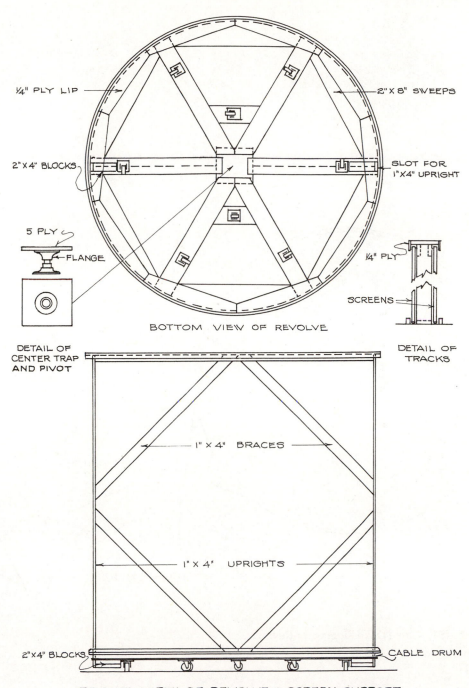

¼" PLY LIP

2" X 8" SWEEPS

2" X 4" BLOCKS

SLOT FOR
1" X 4" UPRIGHT

5 PLY

FLANGE

¼" PLY

SCREENS

BOTTOM VIEW OF REVOLVE

DETAIL OF
CENTER TRAP
AND PIVOT

DETAIL OF
TRACKS

1" X 4" BRACES

1" X 4" UPRIGHTS

2"X 4" BLOCKS

CABLE DRUM

FRONT VIEW OF REVOLVE & SCREEN SUPPORT

Plate 153 Revolve and Screen Support

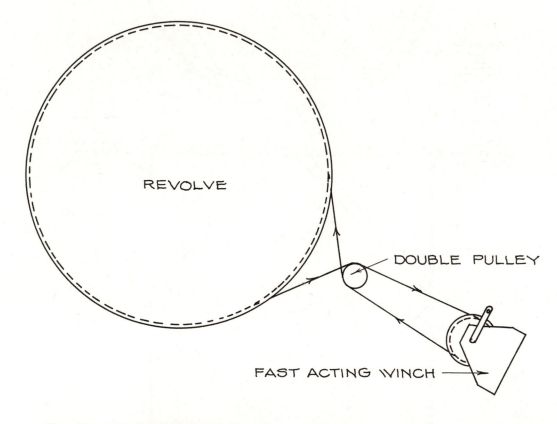

Plate 154 Cable Drive Rigging for Revolve

notched into the ends of the two spokes that battened the halves of the revolve together. Two 2″ × 4″s 1′-0″ long were added to the underside at the ends of these two spokes for an additional surface to which the 1″ × 4″ uprights could be screwed. The uprights extended 8′-1″ above the floor level of the revolve and were fastened together at the top by two 1″ × 3″s screwed flush with the outer edges of the uprights. Across the top was laid a 1″ × 6″ that projected 1″ beyond the edges of the uprights, and strips of ¼″ ply 2″ wide were nailed to the outer edges of the 1″ × 6″. These helped to form the upper track for the sliding screens. The lower track was made in much the same manner, except that the retaining strips were ¾″ wide and 1″ high and were nailed directly to the floor of the revolve. Four 1″ × 4″ diagonal braces kept the framework in square.

The sliding screens were made 8′-0″ × 8′-0″ with double stiles in the center and with all joints halved. This made it possible to cover both sides of the frames with muslin and to separate each screen into 4′-0″ × 8′-0″ standard stock flats after the production had closed. The bottom rail of each screen was fitted with three chromium furniture skids to reduce the friction of sliding them in the tracks.

PERIAKTOI

Modern designers have not hesitated to reach back into the history of theatre to capitalize on a staging convention of another time; for example, note the frequent use of old sliding wings and shutters. Frequently these historical stage machines have been adapted for, and used to good effect in, contemporary plays or in plays of another period and country. So it was when *periaktoi*, stage machines of the Greek theatre, were effectively used in an Iowa production of *The Imaginary Invalid* directed by David Schaal and designed by Jerry Collins.

The *periactus* is a three-sided column capable of being revolved to expose a different scene painted on each of its three faces. Scholars seem a bit uncertain of the exact manner in which the periaktoi were used, but it is generally believed that one of these prisms stood at each side of the skene and that they were turned to indicate a change of locale. In any event it has been proved through the years to be a very effective device and has been used in many ways for modern productions.

The design for *The Imaginary Invalid* used two periaktoi on each side of the stage placed in much the same positions as a series of wings. Across the back of the settings were two additional periaktoi aligned in one plane and positioned so that the edges of one almost touched the edges of the·other. The two together formed the design for the back wall, yet each periactus could be turned independently. A unifying element of the design was a "wrought-iron," open-work frieze that extended over the tops of all periaktoi. This frieze extended from downstage right to the back wall, across this to the stage left wall, and from there to the downstage left tormentor. A set of black draperies surrounded the entire design.

Three settings are called for by the script of *The Imaginary Invalid*: a garden, a street scene, and an interior. A part of the design for each of these was painted on one of the faces of each periactus. Shifting from one scene to another required only a second or two when each periactus was turned to expose another vista. Rather than using regular stagehands for this purpose, the director used a group of gymnasts who incorporated the turning of each prism into the business of their entr'acte entertainment (Plate 155).

Each periactus was 4'-6" wide by 10'-0" high. The base of each was cut from two pieces of ³/₄" plywood butted edge to edge down the center line and cleated together. Around the outer edges of each base were screwed 1" × 4"s placed on their sides to help reinforce the base as well as to provide a surface to which the sides of the periactus were attached. The underside of the base was fitted with a pipe flange pivot in the center and with three rigid rubber-tired castors mounted near each point of the triangle. The sides of each periactus were made from flats taken from stock. Rather than bevel the stiles where the flats met at each corner, a sharp edge was provided by nailing two beveled strips of wood to the edges of each flat and covering these in turn with a muslin dutchman. The castors and pivots were concealed by the flats, which were allowed to extend to within ³/₄" of the floor. Screws driven through the stiles into the edges of the 1" × 4" cleats on the base held the flats in position. A top of ¹/₄" plywood was nailed to the exposed rail edges of all three flats. The solid base, the plywood top, and the triangular shape of the structure itself made unnecessary any further bracing to hold the prisms rigid.

Each periactus turned on a 4'-0" disc that was made of ¹/₄" plywood and that served two purposes. To provide a pivot point for the pipe flange that was mounted on the periactus base, the mating flange was centered on the disc; the disc also provided a perfectly smooth raceway for the castors, thus eliminating the slight wobble caused by the castors' rolling over uneven padding or seaming in the floor cloth. The edges of the two periaktoi forming the back wall were kept in perfect vertical alignment by adding to the top of each a pivot that engaged corresponding sockets attached to the overhead decorative frieze.

BARRELL-LIFTING RIG
FOR *DARK OF THE MOON*

One of the scenes in the delightful fantasy *Dark of the Moon* occurs in a little country store and concerns itself with a contest of strength between the Town Bully and the Witch Boy. Both boys are interested in the young lady for whom they are performing. The Bully picks up a full barrel of apples and struts around the store with it before putting it back on its stand against a wall. Not to be outdone, the Witch Boy approaches the barrel and with a wave of his hand forces the barrel to rise from the floor a distance of about 5'-0", where it stays suspended until he once more waves it back to its place (Plate 156).

The possibility of suspending the barrel by a wire from a spotline was ruled out as a means of support, not only because the wire would have been too easily seen, but also because it would have been difficult to keep the line attached while the barrel was moved around the stage. We decided to raise the barrel by means of a supporting arm that was placed beneath it and controlled by a double-whip tackle rigging concealed behind the upstage wall.

Concealing the slot through which the supporting arm projected into the scenery proved no great problem. The walls of the general store were painted to resemble random width vertical planking. One of the junctions between

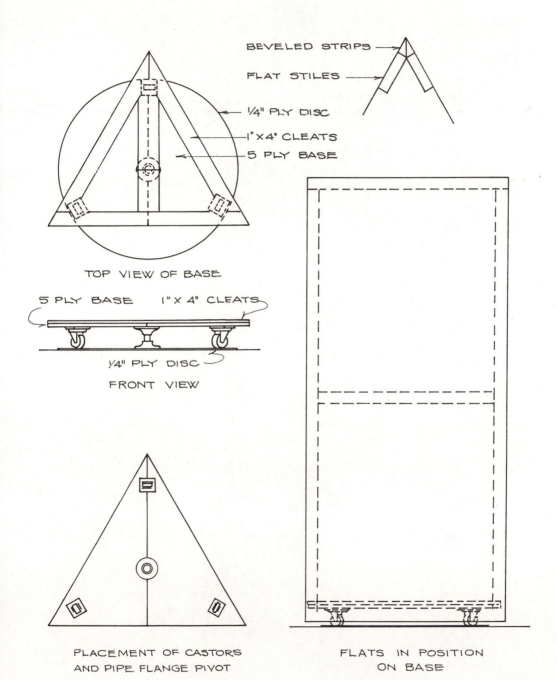

BEVELED STRIPS
FLAT STILES
¼" PLY DISC
1" X 4" CLEATS
5 PLY BASE

TOP VIEW OF BASE

5 PLY BASE   1" X 4" CLEATS
¼" PLY DISC
FRONT VIEW

PLACEMENT OF CASTORS
AND PIPE FLANGE PIVOT

FLATS IN POSITION
ON BASE

Plate 155 Periaktoi

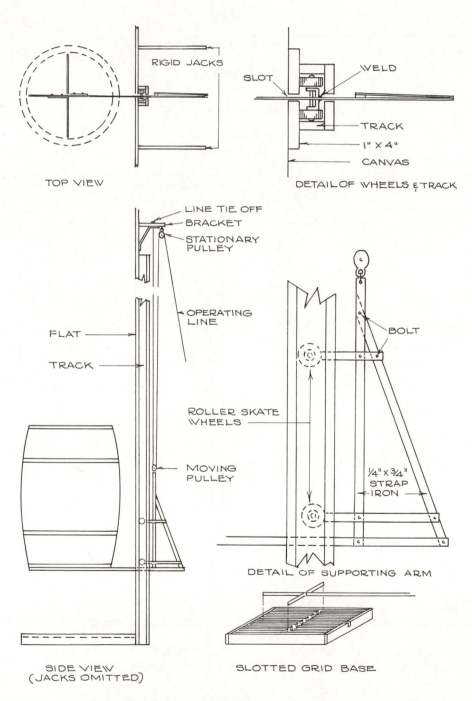

RIGID JACKS

SLOT

WELD

TRACK

1" X 4"

CANVAS

TOP VIEW

DETAIL OF WHEELS & TRACK

LINE TIE OFF

BRACKET

STATIONARY PULLEY

OPERATING LINE

FLAT

TRACK

BOLT

ROLLER SKATE WHEELS

MOVING PULLEY

¼" x ¾" STRAP IRON

DETAIL OF SUPPORTING ARM

SIDE VIEW (JACKS OMITTED)

SLOTTED GRID BASE

Plate 156 Barrel Lifting Rig for *Dark of the Moon*

the planks was made as a $^1/_2''$ wide slot that ran the full height of the fragmentary wall. The covering material of the flat was glued and stapled to the vertical members forming the slot. Rather than cutting off the canvas even with the edges of the slot, it was allowed to extend over the full width of the slot before it was trimmed. In this manner the free edge of the covering material on one flat overlapped the edge of the material from the other flat and thus concealed the slot. It did, however, make it possible for the supporting arms to move freely in a vertical path.

The supporting arm was made of $^1/_4'' \times {}^3/_4''$ strap iron. The section of the arm that held the barrel was made in the form of a plus sign by riveting two L-shaped arms to either side of the main beam. The main beam projected through the wall and extended 12" offstage. To that offstage section of the main beam were attached both a vertical and a diagonal strap-iron member. Near the top and the bottom of the vertical member a pair of roller-skate wheels were attached and were spaced so as to ride against the faces of the 1" $\times$ 4"s that formed the slot. The diagonal held the other two pieces of strap iron at a true right angle. To keep the lower set of wheels directly below the upper set, a track was made from two L-shaped lengths of wood which were screwed in place on either side of the slot.

The moving block of a double whip was attached just above the upper set of wheels to the vertical strap-iron member. The stationary block was attached to the top of the scenery in alignment with the slot. The operating line ran up and over the stationary pulley, down and through the moving pulley, and back to the top of the scenery, where it was tied off. By pulling on the free end of the operating line, the supporting arm and its load could be raised with a 2 to 1 mechanical advantage.

The onstage section of the supporting arm was concealed in the gridded top of a small platform that served as a stand for the apple barrel. The bottom of most barrels is recessed about $^3/_4''$ or 1" from the lower metal reinforcing ring. In this case it was important to fill this recessed area until it was flush with the lip of the reinforcing band in order to keep the barrel from teetering on the supporting arm.

A PIVOTING WALL FOR A
PRODUCTION OF *THE AMOROUS FLEA*

It is not necessary that one travel to New York or to Chicago to see ingenious scenic effects. At the Cedar Rapids Community Theatre in Iowa, I witnessed a production of *The Amorous Flea*, directed by Don Tescher and designed by F. L. Brinkman, that amply proved the truth of my introductory statement.

The script of this spirited musical, by Jerry Devine and Bruce Montgomery, called for two scenes: a street scene and a walled garden of Arnolphe's home. The action of the play moves from one setting to the other many times, making it mandatory that the time required for the scene shifts be kept to an absolute minimum. This has usually been accomplished by using a double-faced wall that pivots from an upstage point. The actors simply push the wall to expose either the garden or the street scene. But not in Mr. Brinkman's scheme of things. When it came time for the first shift in this production, the wall pivoted smartly from one position to another without an actor's coming anywhere near it! A backstage tour after the performance revealed how the problem of the pivoting wall had been solved (Plate 157).

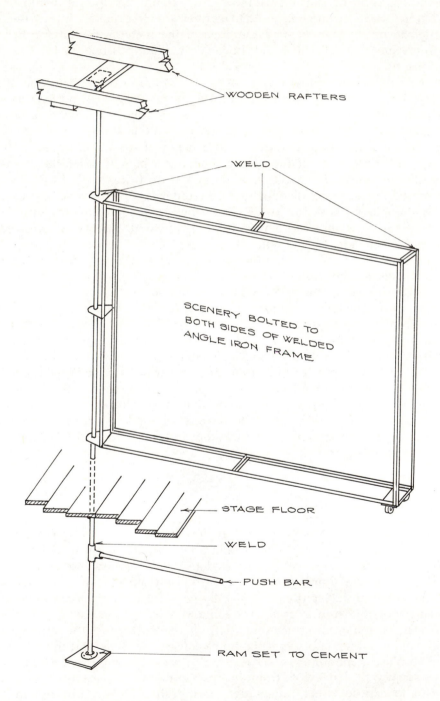

WOODEN RAFTERS

WELD

SCENERY BOLTED TO
BOTH SIDES OF WELDED
ANGLE IRON FRAME

STAGE FLOOR

WELD

PUSH BAR

RAM SET TO CEMENT

Plate 157   Pivoting Wall for *Amorous Flea*

At the pivot point of the wall a hole had been drilled in the stage floor to accept a 1¼″ inside diameter pipe. The pipe extended below the floor 8′ to the basement floor. A baseplate with a collar in which the pipe could turn was ramset to the cement floor. Four feet above the baseplate was welded an oversized T-pipe fitting from which projected a 5′-0″ length of pipe that was used as a push bar. Above the stage floor the vertical pipe extended 18′-0″ to a second collar that was fastened to the wooden beams of the grid. Three triangular plates of sheet iron were welded to the pipe at three points. The first was just a few inches above the stage floor, the second was level with the top of the wall, and the third was located midway between these two. A hole was drilled in each plate to receive the pipe. At two corners of these triangular plates, vertical angle irons were welded. Extending out at right angles from the vertical iron frame were two rectangular frames made from reinforced angle irons. The double-faced wall for the garden and the street scene was bolted to these horizontal frames. A set of rigid castors was bolted beneath the free end of the pivoting wall to support its weight. Further stabilization of the wall was provided by castors in the base of a bench that was attached to the garden side and by castors under the base of a fountain on the street side of the wall. Stagehands waiting in the basement at the push bar took their cue for pivoting the wall from directions given them over a telephone headset by the stage manager. The leverage offered by the push bar made it easy for them to move the entire pivoting structure.

WINCH-DRIVEN WAGONS
AND FALSE STAGE FLOOR

Small wagon stages (4′ × 8′, 5′ × 10′, etc.) that must be shifted in view of an audience can be propelled into, or retracted from, their onstage positions by using a fast-acting winch and a false stage floor; the floor is required to form a guiding track for the wagons, and to conceal the floor blocks and operating cables.

Such a scheme at first glance may seem to be beyond the scenery budget of many theatres, but it can be achieved at very little cost if the theatre has enough different-sized 2″ × 4″ rigid platforms to cover the desired acting area. The platforms are shimmed up to a height of 6″ or 7″ by ripping scrap 2″ × 4″ to the desired shim height, cutting these into 1′-6″ lengths, and nailing them to the lengthwise supporting members of the rigid platforms. The shims need not run the full length of the supporting members, but can be placed wherever they are needed to eliminate any possible springing of the platforms. The platform frames are not damaged in any way by this shimming method, and the shims can be removed easily with a rip hammer or a crowbar (Plate 158).

Perhaps the most common pattern for the movement of these wagons is parallel with the proscenium. This plan does away with any masking problem when the wagons are in an offstage position. However, the path of movement can be placed at any desired angle to the proscenium, even at such an extreme angle as having the wagons move directly upstage and downstage. Once the direction of movement has been determined, the layout of the rigid platforms can be planned. A guiding track is formed by a row of platforms on either side of a center line representing the desired line of movement. A

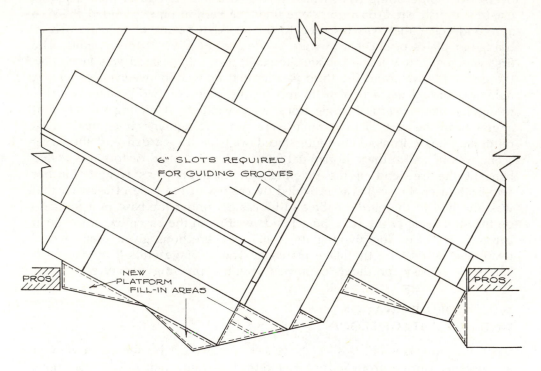

6" SLOTS REQUIRED
FOR GUIDING GROOVES

PROS

NEW
PLATFORM
FILL-IN AREAS

PROS

EXAMPLE OF RANDOM SIZED PLATFORMS USED TO BUILD
FALSE STAGE FLOOR FOR A PRODUCTION OF UBU ROI

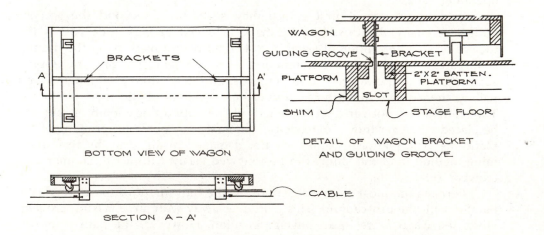

BRACKETS

A

A'

BOTTOM VIEW OF WAGON

WAGON

GUIDING GROOVE

BRACKET

PLATFORM

2"X 2" BATTEN.
PLATFORM

SLOT

SHIM

STAGE FLOOR

DETAIL OF WAGON BRACKET
AND GUIDING GROOVE

CABLE

SECTION A – A'

Plate 158   Winch-Driven Wagon to Be Operated on False Stage Floor space of 6″ is needed between the two rows to provide room for the floor block, the operating cable, the 2″ × 2″ supporting battens, and the floor strips. This is a remarkably simple plan, as can be seen in the illustrations. The 2″ × 2″ battens are nailed to the sides of the platforms ³/₄″ below the platform top, and a series of 1″ × 3″s are laid on their sides to be nailed to the batten tops. A space of ¹/₂″ is left between the opposing edges of the 1″ × 3″s to form the guiding grooves for the wagons. Once the guiding grooves have been established, the remaining sections of the acting area are filled in with shimmed platforms. Occasionally it may be necessary to fill in a small area that is not covered by the existing stock platforms. In this case, 2″ × 4″ battens are nailed to the side of the rigid platform top, and a series of 1″ × 3″ are laid on their sides to be nailed to the side of the rigid platforms, and the flooring is nailed to the top of these battens.

It is unnecessary to bolt one platform to the next in forming a false stage floor. Usually the weight of the platforms is sufficient to prevent their creeping. A certain amount of interlocking automatically occurs when the 2″ × 2″ battens forming a part of the guiding groove are attached to the platforms and when the canvas dutchmen are glued and stapled over the junctions between platforms. If the offstage platforms are small, it is advantageous to block them to the stage floor to prevent their creeping. This blocking also helps to hold in their proper positions all the other platforms that are placed inside them.

Because their movement is restricted to only two directions, the wagons should be fitted with rigid or locked swivel castors. If the floor surface of the rigid platforms turns out to be uneven, a 4″ wide track made of ¹/₈″ Masonite or ¹/₄″ plywood strips is nailed to the false floor in alignment with the castors. The castors riding on this track will get rid of any slight jarring caused when the wheels strike the platform junctions. The finished false floor is given a coat of rubber-based paint that will not "dust off" under heavy wear as will regular scene paint.

Rolling wagons may be constructed from any rigid platforms of appropriate size. In addition to the necessary castors two 10″ lengths of ¹/₈″ × 4″ wide strap iron are bolted to the center lengthwise supporting member of the wagon to form brackets and are placed approximately one foot from each end of the wagon. These strap-iron brackets project through the guiding slot of the false stage floor and serve not only as a place to which the operating cables are made fast but as guides to steer the wagon along a desired path.

The rigging materials needed to propel a wagon along its tracks are two lengths of ³/₁₆″ steel cable, one single block, one double block, and a winch. The single block is lag-screwed to the regular stage floor at the onstage end of the guiding groove. It is desirable to have a small section of the false floor directly above the floor block so that the section can be easily removed if it becomes necessary to service the block. One end of a cable is clamped to the leading strap-iron wagon bracket. The free end of this cable is fed through the floor block back to the double block, located on the floor just ahead of the winch, and it is then served several times around the winch drum before it is clamped off. A second cable is locked to the winch drum and served onto it in the opposite direction from the first cable. (The number of servings must supply a length of cable that equals the distance the wagon is expected to move.) The free end of the second cable is then fed through the double block and is clamped to the offstage strap-iron wagon bracket. The winch is pulled offstage until both cables are tight and then is locked to the stage floor.

Plywood Skids

A variation of this general plan for rolling wagons and a false stage floor is obtained by substituting 4′ × 8′ or 4′ × 10′ sheets of ³/₄″ thick 5-plywood for the more conventional rigid wagons. The advantage of the plywood skids lies in the fact that they are only 1″ or 1¹/₄″ high. This low silhouette is obtained by substituting large-sized chromium furniture glides for regulation castors. These glides must be aligned so that they ride on Masonite tracks that have been heavily rubbed with paraffin as a lubricant. Furniture glides that are secured by a bolt or a screw shaft are better than glides that are just attached with several small pointed teeth. The latter have a tendency to pull loose if they happen to strike an obstruction. The wagon cable brackets are of the same material (strap iron) that was used on the rigid wagon, but now they must be L-shaped in order to bolt them to the bottom of the plywood. In all other respects the rigging for these plywood skids is identical with that used on the more conventional rolling wagons.

TRACKS FOR WINGS AND SHUTTERS

Despite electrically powered stage machinery and the many technical advances of the twentieth century, there are few that match for speed the surprisingly swift scene changes provided by the old wings and shutters sliding smoothly in their tracks. This was proved convincingly by an Iowa production of Wycherly's *The Country Wife,* designed by John Kasarda and directed by David Knauf.

The design presented a typical and colorful forestage flanked 'on either side by proscenium doors. Overhead was a decorative ceiling that joined the proscenium door units to provide a portal 20′-0″ wide and low enough to remove any need for masking borders. Upstage and on either side of the portal were two sets of wings, and farther upstage were a series of shutters to complete the design for each of the four settings required in the play (Plate 159).

Each of the wings was 7′-0″ wide and 14′-0″ high and each was made from two stock flats joined edge to edge and hinged on the front as well as the back to prevent their folding. The shutters were fashioned in the same manner from stock flats but were 12′-0″ wide, and when one was butted against its mate they formed a solid painted wall 24′-0″ wide by 14′-0″ high.

The lower tracks were made from strips of ¹/₄″ plywood 8³/₄″ wide by 14′-0″ long. Five strips of ³/₄″ × 1¹/₂″ white pine were set on edge and nailed to the plywood to supply four slots, each 1¹/₂″ wide. Once the tracks had been fastened in position they were painted to match the specially painted ground cloth. The bottom rail of each wing and shutter was fitted with chromium furniture glides, and the track slots were heavily waxed with paraffin to reduce friction. The upper tracks were made on the same principle, but a length of 1″ × 9³/₄″ stock was substituted for the plywood strip, and strips ³/₄″

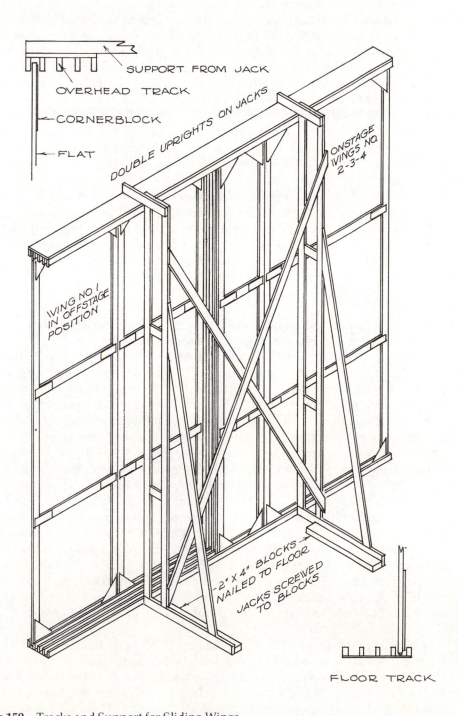

SUPPORT FROM JACK

OVERHEAD TRACK

CORNERBLOCK

FLAT

DOUBLE UPRIGHTS ON JACKS

ONSTAGE WINGS NO. 2-3-4

WING NO 1 IN OFFSTAGE POSITION

2" X 4" BLOCKS NAILED TO FLOOR

JACKS SCREWED TO BLOCKS

FLOOR TRACK

Plate 159   Tracks and Support for Sliding Wings

× 2³/₄″ rather than ³/₄″ × 1¹/₂″ were used to form the slots. The overhead tracks were supported by rigid jacks solidly fastened and braced to the stage floor. Both upper and lower tracks were placed far enough onstage to accept the wings when they were being viewed by an audience. The remainder of each track extended onstage half its length to support the wings when they were in the offstage position. Because of the close spacing of the wings, two extension arms were attached about shoulder-high to the offstage stiles of the two center wings. This made it possible to push these two wings onstage or to withdraw them without interference from the wings on either side of them.

The downstage wing of each set of wings was painted for the first scene of the play. As they were withdrawn, they revealed the second scene, the withdrawal of the second set revealed the third, and so on. The shutters were arranged in the same manner. If a scene was repeated, the appropriate set of wings and shutters was shoved onstage to conceal those of the previous scene.

This production was unique in another and quite unexpected way. It brought complaints from the audience that they couldn't enjoy the scene shifts because they were executed so quickly! Literally, the shifts required no more time than it took for a well-trained stagehand to slide one piece of scenery onstage or offstage a distance of 7'-0" or 12'-0".

A CIRCUS WAGON

On a stage devoid of all scenery except a set of black masking draperies, a troupe of traveling players maneuvered a gaudily decorated circus wagon into center stage. Amid the usual frantic business of setting up any traveling circus, the players went about their assigned tasks to prepare their wagon for a production of Carlo Goldoni's *The Servant of Two Masters*. Bright red sawhorses and brilliantly painted boxes of costumes and properties were handed out through a small door in one end of the wagon. By elaborate measurements and much squinting to make sure the sawhorses were properly aligned, they were placed a few feet downstage of the wagon. Finally, accompanied by many shouted directions, the whole side of the wagon from front to back began to swing away from the top, and the actors gradually lowered it until it formed a sloping stage floor.

Barbara Reynolds, the designer, had made no effort to create a realistic circus wagon. Rather, she had chosen to emphasize by both line and color a stylized version of a circus wagon that was pictorially intriguing in itself and very much in harmony with the antics of such zany Commedia characters as Brighella, Pantalone, Truffaldino, and company. The inventive mind of James Gouseff, the director, made brilliant use not only of the setting but of his array of Commedia characters to fashion a delightful evening of slapstick comedy (Plate 160).

The base of the wagon was 6'-0" wide by 12'-0" long, but it tapered out at both ends to yield a total length of 16'-0" when measured at the top. The roof line of the wagon was broken at each end by a projecting booth that rose 2'-0" higher than the center span. These booths provided the additional height needed for the inclusion of the stationary blocks by which the side of the wagon was raised and lowered. Just beneath the booths on the front face of the wagon, the side

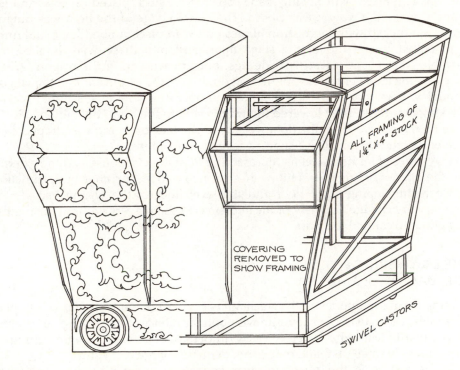

WAGON WITH SIDE CLOSED

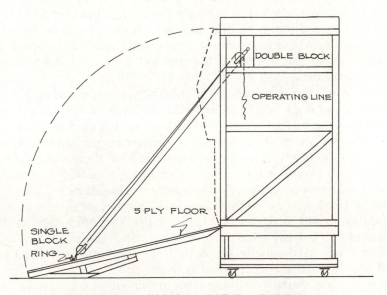

WAGON WITH SIDE OPEN

Plate 160   Circus Wagon

projected outward to form triangular supports for the acting area once the side of the wagon had been lowered to the stage floor.

The movable side of the wagon was made of sheets of 3/4" thick fir plywood that was reinforced with ribbing made of 1¼" × 3" stock placed on edge and left exposed when the wagon was closed. The bottom edge of the floor was hinged to the wagon bed with large strap hinges bolted in place. Imbedded metal rings were bolted to the top of the stage floor, and into these were hooked the movable blocks of two watch-tackle rigs, one at each end of the wagon. When the cue came to lower the side of the wagon, two of the actors entered the wagon through a rear door and each manned the operating line of his watch tackle. Working in unison, they lowered the wagon side to the floor; the moving blocks were then removed from the floor rings, and the tackle rigging was draped over each end of the wagon. The "stage" was ready for action.

A series of folding screens representing Pantalone's House and the exterior and the interior of Brighella's Inn were stationed two feet upstage of the junction between the sloping stage floor and the level floor of the wagon bed. These screens were changed in view of the audience by the players without raising the stage floor to conceal the shift.

THE DRAWBRIDGE STAIRS
FOR *MAN OF LA MANCHA*

Judging by the frequency with which *Man of La Mancha* appears on yearly play schedules, this musical is a favorite with both audiences and producing groups. Its popularity with the latter is easily understood: it has a single setting, a comparatively small cast, and it does not demand a large orchestra.

The setting is the prisoner's common room in an old dungeon. From outside, the only access to this pit is by a run of stairs that is lowered and raised as a drawbridge. When lowered, it reaches from the upper level of the prison to the floor of the pit. There is no question that a high point in the play's action is reached when these chain-supported heavy stairs gradually appear out of the darkness overhead and are slowly lowered to the floor for the first entrance of Miguel de Cervantes.

An easy way to rig these stairs so that they can be raised and lowered is to place them center stage and head-on to the audience, that is, at a right angle to the proscenium arch. This means that both of the lifting chains are perfectly in line with the customary placement of the counterweight battens. Although the rigging can be simpler with the stairs in this position, there are disadvantages in what it does to the composition of the setting and, dramatically speaking, what it does to the movements of the actors who must use the stairs.

Man of La Mancha as produced at the University of Iowa was directed by Cosmo Catalano and designed by Michael Griffith. Griffith felt that the center placement of the stairway which divided the setting into halves was an effect he wanted to avoid. Accordingly he located the stairs so that when they were lowered they formed an acute angle with the proscenium arch. This was not only more pleasing visually than the other arrangement would have been, but it made the exits and entrances of the actors more dynamic because the actors could more easily relate to the audience.

Griffith's setting was composed of a two-level raked stage floor extending past the proscenium out over the apron. Five huge stone columns, their tops disappearing in darkness, were evenly spaced around the perimeter of the acting area. One was placed center stage just beyond the raked floor; on either side of it were two columns that followed the roughly circular contour of the acting platform; the two columns closest to the audience concealed the actual limits of the proscenium arch. The point at which the stairs were hinged was at the second level of the dungeon wall 16'-0" up from the stage floor and just stage right of the center column. When the stairs were lowered they formed an acute angle of 65° with the proscenium. (See Plate 161.)

With the stairs mounted in this position one of the lift chains was farther downstage than the other; this necessitated the use of a yoke overhead to keep the chains parallel with each other. The yoke also served as a swivel, so that both chains could be supported from a single batten. The counterweight batten was reinforced by enclosing it in two channel-shaped irons that were bolted in place at the point where the swivel was attached to the batten. This kept the batten from bending under the weight of the stairs.

To increase the apparent length of the stairs and the height at which they were hinged, the width of the treads and the heights of the risers diminished gradually from bottom to top. Each carriage was formed by two 2" × 12" fir planks that were butted and that overlapped enough to produce the required length of 21'-8". They were further reinforced by two No. 260 Dexion angle irons butted together and then bolted between the two inner faces of each carriage.

Because the combined weights of the stairway and the supporting chain exceeded the counterweight capacity of the arbor, the remaining overload was handled by a two-man winch connected to the bottom of the arbor by ¼" steel cable. The winch was solidly bolted to the stage floor and to the locking rail.

A CIRCULAR AND RAMPED
FALSE STAGE FLOOR

The increasing desire of some directors and designers to use ramped stage floors of unusual shape presents the technician with an interesting problem. To build such a structure entirely of new materials would in most cases be excessively expensive. However, the major part of it can often be built by adapting regular 2" × 4" framed rigid platforms. On all of them the supporting frames are made of 2" × 4"s and the tops of ¾" thick plywood or some other type of flooring. Except for this, almost nothing about such platforms is standardized. Certainly there is likely to be an enormous variety in the width and length of them.

One of the fastest methods of determining the most advantageous placement of these multisized platforms within a desired over-all shape begins at the drafting board. Assume that a completely circular form is called for. It is to be 32'-0" in diameter and to project 6'-0" past the proscenium arch out onto the apron of the stage. Using a scale at least as large as ½" to 1'-0", lay out a ground plan of the proposed circular shape reaching to the proscenium arch and to the apron of the stage. Refer now to your card index of stock platforms. Make scaled paper models, showing the width and length of each platform you hope to use in assembling the major floor area. These slips of paper can be shuffled about in numerous groupings until you find the particular scheme that most nearly fulfills the intended shape. When this point in the planning has been reached, it is prudent to transfer the platform pattern to the ground plan, being sure to show the exact position of each individual platform as well as to identify it by its

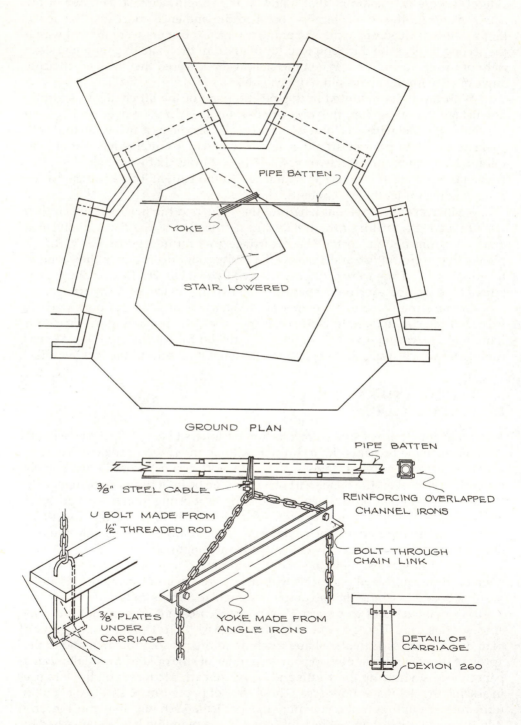

Plate 161 Drawbridge Stairs for *Man of La Mancha*

dimensions and catalogue number. The ground plan will now show a highly irregular perimeter left between the platforms and boundary line of the circle. The framing and the flooring of these areas are left until all platforms are properly legged up and joined (Plate 162).

It is difficult for actors to move with any sense of freedom and grace on a stage floor that has been ramped at too steep an angle. Rather than selecting an angle at random, it is suggested that the designer and technician should give the director an opportunity to see and to try out the proposed angle. This can be done with very little trouble. Place one end of a large platform on the shop floor and temporarily leg up the opposite end until the top is at, for instance, a 15° angle. The director, with some of his actors, should now try moving about on it. Keep varying the height of the legs until the actors feel at home on the ramp, and the director is satisfied with the way they move. Chances are that the 15° angle will seem too steep, and that one of 11° will be more satisfactory.

Once the angle has been chosen, the process of legging up each platform can begin. The legs can be cut in pairs and so bolted to the platforms. This is made much simpler if each platform is set with its length at a right angle to the proscenium arch. Should the platforms be placed at any other angle to the proscenium, the length of each individual leg would have to be figured separately. A side view of the ramp will show the length of any leg no matter where a platform is placed within the ramped area. In practically all cases the legs should be made of 2″ × 4″ lumber, and the top of each cut on the same angle as that chosen for the ramp—in this case probably 11°. These are bolted to the supporting frame of the rigid platform with ³/₈″ × 4″ carriage bolts. Each leg should be individually braced to the platform with short lengths of 1″ × 3″ nailed into place. When the platforms are assembled in position onstage they are joined together by either bolting or clamping their outside framing members one to another.

When the platform assembly is completed the remaining unfloored outer edges of the circle can be filled in. Short lengths of 2″ × 4″ are cleated to the outside framing members ³/₄″ below the ramp floor top. Where necessary, diagonal 2″ × 4″ supports are nailed to the ends of the cleats and additional legs can be affixed to these supporting members as needed. Flooring material is cut to fit and nailed to the top of the cleats. Allow the flooring material to project slightly beyond the circular boundary line. Using a steel tape that is attached to a nail placed at the center point of the circle, prescribe an arc laid out on a 16′-0″ radius. Cut off the projecting flooring material with a sabre saw to produce a circle with a 32′-0″ diameter. All junctions between platforms should be covered with muslin or canvas dutchmen before they are painted.

WINCH-POWERED TRAP
IN FALSE STAGE FLOOR

A production of *King Lear*, designed by Richard Pick and directed by Cosmo Catalano, used for the principal acting area a false stage floor that was ramped and circular. In the center of this disc was a hinged trapdoor the director wanted to use in two partially opened positions. When the trap was opened only enough for it to be parallel with the regular stage floor, it was used as a base for the king's throne, and in this position it had to bear the weight of three actors—a matter of some 410 pounds. At another time, when the trap was opened wider,

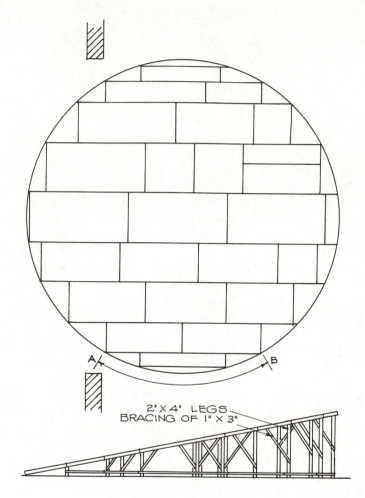

2' X 4" LEGS
BRACING OF 1" X 3"

PLAN AND SIDE VIEW OF DISC

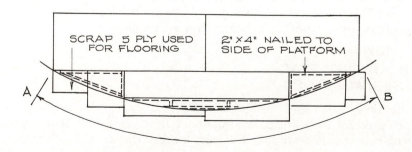

SCRAP 5 PLY USED
FOR FLOORING

2" X 4" NAILED TO
SIDE OF PLATFORM

Plate 162   A Circular and Ramped False Stage Floor

it became the cave where Poor Tom found shelter. The time allotted for opening and closing the trap between scenes was limited to six seconds.

This trapdoor was 4'-0" × 5'-6", with the longer dimension parallel with the proscenium (Plate 163). The upstage side of the trap was hinged to the permanent section of the ramp with four heavy butt hinges countersunk and bolted in place. A 3'-10" leg made of 2" × 4" lumber was bolted to the inside face of each of the two side framing members of the trap. Use of a single ³/₈" × 4" carriage bolt permitted the legs to pivot at the point where they were fastened to the trap floor. The bottom of the 2" × 4" legs rested on the face of a 2" × 6" castor plate 5'-6" long, and bolted in place with short sections of angle iron. On the lower face of the 2" × 6" two 3" rubber-tired rigid castors were bolted. Hinged to the upright edge of the 2" × 6" castor plate was a diagonally braced 2" × 4" tongue, its free end capable of sliding in and out of a wooden housing. The tongue and housing provided a means of locking the legs and castors in the desired vertical positions. The lock was a short length of pipe that engaged matching holes in the tongue and the housing.

The mechanism that opened and closed the trapdoor consisted of two hanger irons, two ³/₁₆" wire cable yokes, two lengths of the same ³/₁₆" sized cable, a floor block, a guiding block, and a fast-acting winch with a large 1'-0" drum. The two hanger irons were bolted to the underside of the castor plate just inside the positions of the castors. The cable yokes were clipped to the hanger irons, thus providing a yoke on both the upstage and the downstage side of the castor plate. A cable was attached to the downstage yoke, then fed through a floor block that was bolted to the stage floor at a point located about 3'-0" downstage of the trap opening. The cable, after passing through the floor block, changed direction, ran upstage, and was served around the winch drum several times and locked off. The second cable was locked to the drum, then wrapped several times around the drum in the opposite direction from the first. It then passed through the guiding block, and its free end was clipped to the upstage yoke on the castor plate. The cables and yokes were tightened by pulling the winch upstage until both were taut, and at that spot the winch was screwed to the stage floor to lock it in position. When the winch turned in one direction the trapdoor opened; turning the winch in the opposite direction closed the trap.

Because of the acute angle assumed by the castored legs when the trapdoor was in a horizontal position, two supplementary legs were required to stabilize the door under the weight and movement of the actors. These legs were hinged to the underside of the trapdoor and were joined together by a horizontal cross member placed at a point below the ramp surface. Slightly to one side of center on the cross member a 6'-0" length of 1" × 3" was hinged. It served as a manual adjustment and release lever. These two supplementary legs kept the trapdoor from sagging or rocking under the weight of the three actors when it was used in the throne scene. The underside of the door and both sets of legs were painted black. This so successfully camouflaged the method of supporting the trap that the presence of the legs was not objectionable.

AN ELEVATOR FIREPLACE

An old mystery play, *The Bat,* has one scene taking place in a secret room. Within the room is a wall safe that is further concealed by placing it in a small compartment hidden behind a fireplace which at times functions as a door.

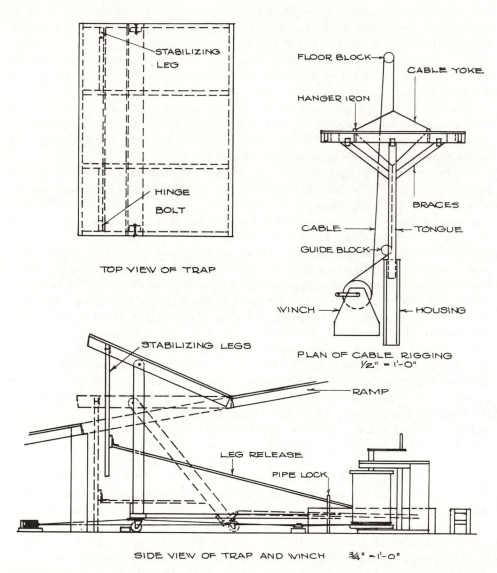

STABILIZING
LEG

HINGE
BOLT

TOP VIEW OF TRAP

FLOOR BLOCK

CABLE YOKE

HANGER IRON

BRACES

CABLE

TONGUE

GUIDE BLOCK

WINCH

HOUSING

PLAN OF CABLE RIGGING
½" = 1'-0"

STABILIZING LEGS

RAMP

LEG RELEASE

PIPE LOCK

SIDE VIEW OF TRAP AND WINCH   ¾" = 1'-0"

Plate 163   Winch-Operated Trap

Rather than having the fireplace swing to one side or the other, as a door normally would, the director asked if the fireplace could be rasied vertically. He felt that this might add another element of surprise to the production. Since the setting was covered with a ceiling piece that precluded the possibility of lifting the fireplace by flying it with lines from the counterweight system, it was decided that the fireplace would be lifted by a double-whip rigging system mounted within the framework of the fireplace. The system was to be operated from a position upstage of the concealed compartment (Plate 164).

The fireplace was located in the center of the back wall facing the audience. This position presented the best sight lines into the small compartment and also made it possible to mask the guide tracks on which the fireplace was to ride. The flat backing the fireplace was constructed with stiles made from 1" × 4"s rather than the conventional 1" × 3"s. The additional width of the stiles provided space for cutting a mortise into each and fitting a window sash pulley into each mortise. The edges of the stiles were left exposed to form the track tongue that was to guide the vertical movement of the fireplace.

The fireplace itself was kept as light as possible by building it of canvas-covered 1" × 2" frames. It was designed as a brick structure with a slanting partial hood resting on top of the mantel. The hood provided the height required for the tie-off point for the double whip as well as for masking the window sash pulleys mounted in the stiles of the flat. At the bottom of the fireplace a single pulley was mounted on each side. The operating lines were ¼" braided cotton sash cord tied off at the top within the fireplace hood; they ran from the tie-off point down through the lower pulleys, then up to where they passed over the stile pulleys. These lines then ran upstage over the top of the compartment to a second set of pulleys, and were finally tied off to a pipe yoke. The rigging system was activated by pulling down on the pipe yoke, thus raising the fireplace. This method of rigging made it possible to raise the bottom of the fireplace as high as the bottom of the stile pulleys.

The outer side frames of the fireplace were made with halved joints. This avoided the problem that would have been presented by the ¼" thickness of the plywood corner blocks and keystones ordinarily used on joints. To the inside face of each side frame a piece of 1" × 2" was screwed, and this formed one side of a groove running the full height of the fireplace. The opposite side of the groove was formed by two horizontal 1" × 4"s, one placed near the top, the other at the bottom of the fireplace. Chromium-finished furniture glides were placed on these 1" × 4"s at points where they would slide on the stiles of the fireplace flat. This kept the paint on the flat from being scraped off when the fireplace was raised and lowered.

AN ELEVATOR COUCH

Luigi Pirandello's *Six Characters in Search of an Author* is a play normally thought of as not requiring scenery. The play concerns itself with a troupe of actors who have gathered on an empty stage and are preparing to rehearse; the empty stage is essentially the only setting required. Although it is true that the major portion of the play requires no scenic effects, there is one point in the action that demands the use of fragmentary scenery. The stage manager directs several of the actor "stagehands" to bring a section of wall in to represent a room and to place against it a studio couch that is covered with a decorative afghan. Once this

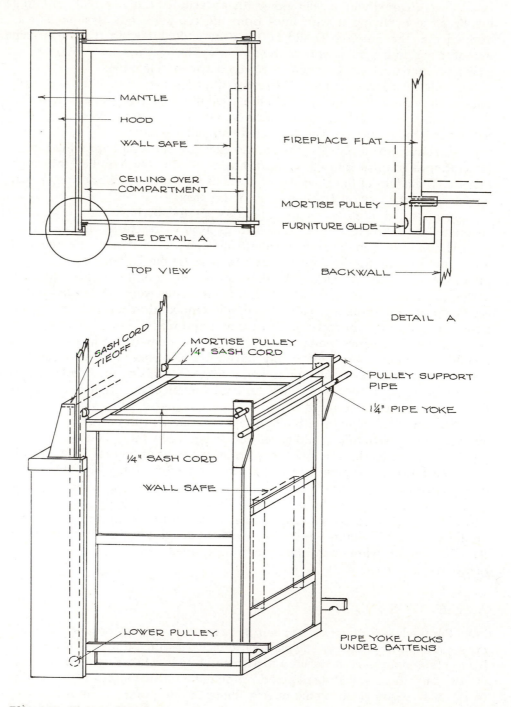

MANTLE

HOOD

WALL SAFE

CEILING OVER
COMPARTMENT

SEE DETAIL A

TOP VIEW

FIREPLACE FLAT

MORTISE PULLEY

FURNITURE GLIDE

BACKWALL

DETAIL A

SASH CORD
TIEOFF

MORTISE PULLEY
¼" SASH CORD

PULLEY SUPPORT
PIPE

1¼" PIPE YOKE

¼" SASH CORD

WALL SAFE

LOWER PULLEY

PIPE YOKE LOCKS
UNDER BATTENS

Plate 164   Elevator Fireplace

business has been carried out, the play's action continues elsewhere on the stage for a while before moving back to the "room with the studio couch." Then for the first time the audience becomes aware that the couch now bears the reclining figure of an actress—and there was certainly no one lying on the couch when it was first rolled into place against the wall! Actually, the audience is correct. There was no one lying on it when it was brought to the stage; the actress was inside the couch. While their attention was elsewhere on the stage, she was very slowly raised by means of a crank-operated elevator until she appeared to be lying on top of the couch. The decorative afghan had been draped across the couch in a way that concealed the opening when the elevator was out of sight (Plate 165).

The body of the couch was constructed as a hollow framework mounted on castors with its center section filled by an elevator large enough to hold the reclining actress. The elevator was guided at its four corners by vertical tracks and was lifted by two $\frac{1}{8}$" steel cables activated by a winch. Each of the cables ran parallel to the elevator's length and each was rigged in a fashion identical with the other. One end of each cable was permanently tied off to the underside of the outer framework. It then passed through a pulley that was mounted on one end of the elevator to a second pulley that was mounted on the opposite end; from there the cable fed through a pulley attached to the underside of the supporting framework and was finally served around the drum of a $1\frac{1}{4}$" pipe winch where it was again tied off. The pipe forming the drum of the winch projected 8 inches beyond the upstage side of the couch and through a matching hole cut in the scenery wall. Because a hole in the canvas might be noticed during the setup, the canvas was split in the form of a T and its corners were temporarily held together with scotch tape. When the couch was placed against the wall the tape was removed and the protruding pipe inserted in the hole. Once the stagehands had put the couch in its proper place, a detachable crank handle was made fast to the protruding pipe. One of the stagehands remained concealed behind the wall to operate the winch. A wire loop engaged the crank handle and held the elevator in the "up" position.

SEMICIRCLE REVOLVE

When the major portion of a design structure cannot be disturbed, yet it is necessary to indicate some change of locale, it may be beneficial to consider the use of a semicircle revolve for that purpose. The semicircle revolve is just what its name implies. It is exactly a half circle in shape, is mounted on rigid castors, and pivots around a fixed floor axle. Usually along the straight side of the semicircle there is a double-faced wall used as a masking device. When the semicircle is in the closed, or upstage, position, that section of the exposed wall is designed to become an integral part of the major design structure; the design on this side of the wall usually does not change during the play. The semicircular side is most frequently used to designate locales other than those depicted in the basic design (Plate 166).

The construction of the semicircle can make use of existing stock platforms; this not only reduces the cost of the unit but requires much less shop time for completion of it. To construct a semicircle use the largest platform that can be fitted into the semicircular shape. Add 2" × 4" framing members to the rigid platform to fill in the unfloored area. These can be floored over with $\frac{3}{4}$" ply or

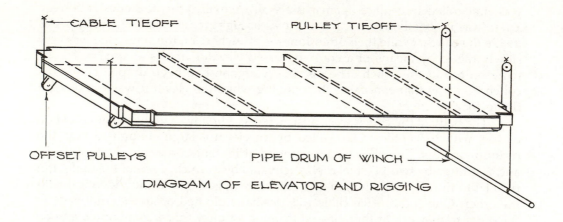

CABLE TIEOFF   PULLEY TIEOFF

OFFSET PULLEYS   PIPE DRUM OF WINCH

DIAGRAM OF ELEVATOR AND RIGGING

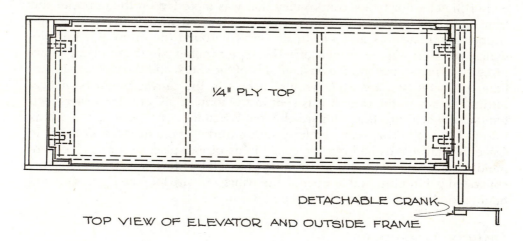

¼" PLY TOP

DETACHABLE CRANK

TOP VIEW OF ELEVATOR AND OUTSIDE FRAME

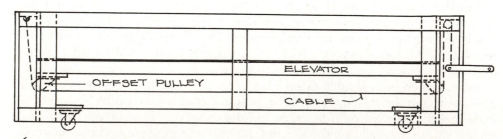

ELEVATOR

OFFSET PULLEY

CABLE

(COVER OUTSIDE FRAME WITH ¼" PLY AND UPHOLSTERING)

FRONT VIEW OF OUTSIDE FRAME WITH ELEVATOR LOWERED

Plate 165   Elevator Couch

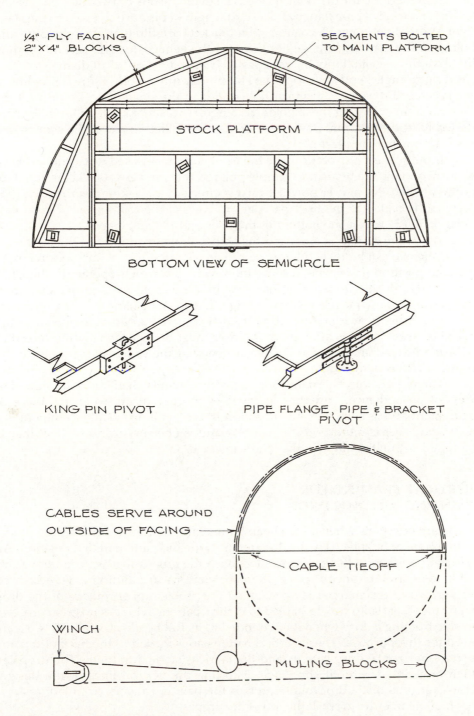

¼" PLY FACING
2"x4" BLOCKS

SEGMENTS BOLTED
TO MAIN PLATFORM

STOCK PLATFORM

BOTTOM VIEW OF SEMICIRCLE

KING PIN PIVOT

PIPE FLANGE, PIPE & BRACKET
PIVOT

CABLES SERVE AROUND
OUTSIDE OF FACING

CABLE TIEOFF

WINCH

MULING BLOCKS

Plate 166 A Semicircle Revolve

other flooring material. Allow the flooring to extend beyond the circular boundary, mark the desired radius and cut off the excess flooring with a sabre saw. A pivot point for the semicircle can be made by one of two methods. Using the first method, a pipe flange and a short length of pipe are screwed to the stage floor at the pivot point. Two strap-iron brackets are fitted around the pipe and bolted to the center of the straight side of the semicircle. The second method involves the use of a kingpin, which is an iron rod $1/2''$ or $5/8''$ in diameter with a short right-angle bend at its top. The kingpin fits into a hole on the center line of the revolve and engages a similar hole drilled in the stage floor. To prevent the kingpin from enlarging these holes, rectangular washers made of strap iron are drilled to fit the kingpin. Smaller holes are also drilled to admit the screws that hold the washers in place.

If the scene shifts occur while the front curtain is closed, the semicircle can be turned manually by using a simple pull rod that engages a socket in the floor of the revolve. No matter how the turn is effected, a masking riser made of $1/4''$ plywood is nailed to the flooring edges to conceal the castors. A $3/4''$ clearance must be left between the bottom of the riser and the stage floor.

When the curtain is open and the shifts are made in view of the audience, the semicircle can be turned by using cables operated by a winch located in an offstage position. However, turning the revolve by winch-operated cables has one disadvantage. The masking riser will foul the cables. A possible exception may occur if the semicircle is small enough that it can be handled with a $1/8''$ wire cable or a rubber-covered extension cord that is served around the outside of the masking riser. If this is attempted, the riser must be substantially reinforced to withstand the strain. Riser and cable are painted the same color to reduce the contrast between the two.

There is another alternative for powering a semicircle if it is to be shifted in view of an audience. However, it involves the use of an expensive piece of equipment and as such may be beyond most budget limits. This equipment is a reversible electric motor with a gear box and rubber-tired drive wheel that is mounted within the framework of the semicircle.

VERTICAL FRAMING FOR PAINTING A FLOWN DROP

There are occasions when a scene painter may not be able to paint a drop on the paint frame or be able to lay the drop on the floor and paint it in that position. An adequate solution to this problem is to stretch the drop using two counterweighted battens and an anchor pipe. A major concern in painting a vertical drop suspended in this manner is overcoming the problem of shrinkage of the drop fabric unless its sides can be stapled to vertical battens. There is no great problem in side framing a drop when it is extended to its full height. Usually $1'' \times 6''$s are used for this purpose. These vertical battens are screwed to the back of top and bottom horizontal drop battens and the fabric is stapled to them. The drop can then be painted without shrinkage distorting the vertical lines of the design. However, this method of framing forces the painter to work from ladders or a boomerang in order to reach the top of the drop.

Plate 167 illustrates a method of dividing the vertical side framing into short sections that will permit the scene painter to accomplish all painting from floor level. Batten clamps are used to attach the drop to two adjacent pipe

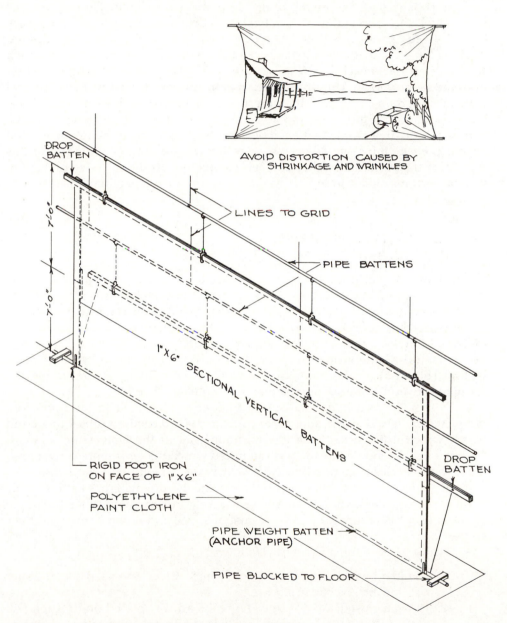

AVOID DISTORTION CAUSED BY
SHRINKAGE AND WRINKLES

DROP
BATTEN

LINES TO GRID

PIPE BATTENS

1" X 6" SECTIONAL VERTICAL BATTENS

DROP
BATTEN

RIGID FOOT IRON
ON FACE OF 1" X 6"

POLYETHYLENE
PAINT CLOTH

PIPE WEIGHT BATTEN
(ANCHOR PIPE)

PIPE BLOCKED TO FLOOR

Plate 167   Vertical Framing for Painting Flown Drop

battens. To prevent the drop from swaying while it is being painted and to hold the material taut, a pipe is placed at the drop fold and blocked to the stage floor. To avoid the possibility of rust from the pipe discoloring the paint job, wrap the pipe with polyethylene sheeting and tape it in place.

Start painting from the top of the drop and work down. The two battens from which the drop is flown are adjusted to the proper height; this may vary from 5'-0" to as much as 7'-0". Two lengths of 1" × 6" are cut to the desired working height and attached to the back of the wooden drop batten, one at each side. The bottom of each 1" × 6" is anchored to the stage floor by means of a foot iron and stage screw. The drop material can now be stapled to these vertical battens. When this section of the drop has been painted remove the foot irons and raise the drop until two additional 1" × 6" battens can be attached to the bottoms of the first two by battened butt joints. Again attach the foot irons and anchor them to the stage floor with stage screws. Continue painting until this section of the working height has been completed. Additional sets of 1" × 6" vertical sections can be added in this manner until the full height of the drop has been reached.

AN ADJUSTABLE, COLLAPSIBLE
HORIZONTAL PAINT FRAME

Elbin Cleveland, Technical Director of the Department of Theatre and Speech at the University of South Carolina has designed a portable, adjustable, floor-mounted paint frame (Plate 168). The frame operates on the principle of the curtain stretcher upon which grandma used to dry her lace curtains. The drop material is attached to both the horizontal support battens and then is stretched by drawing the battens apart through the use of the cables and hand-operated winch. The width of the frame can be varied by increasing or decreasing the length of the horizontal support battens as detailed in Plate 168.

One of the two horizontal support battens is fastened to the floor. The other, which serves as the adjustable stretcher, is attached by cables to a hand winch which is mounted on a low partition wall in the University of South Carolina installation. While the wall-mounted winch makes it more convenient, the winch will also operate efficiently if it is floor mounted. The lengthwise battens are slotted on 8'-0" centers to accept the 24'-0" long cross battens. This permits the adjustable stretcher to slide back and forth on them. When the frame is not in use, the parts neatly stack against one wall and require only 8" of floor space.

Further explanations and details follow:

1. The hand winch can be any small winch. Cleveland used a boat trailer winch which he had in stock.
2. The cable used was ⅛" since no real load was placed on it. Rope will not work because it stretches and fails to hold the drop square.
3. The cables are attached to the frame with ¼" × 8" eye bolts. Each line is connected to a clew plate with a 4" turnbuckle for adjusting. This provides an easier method of making adjustments than does shortening the cables at the eye bolts.
4. It is essential to have as much free line as will be required to pay out enough line to form the smallest horizontal paint frame. Since it was

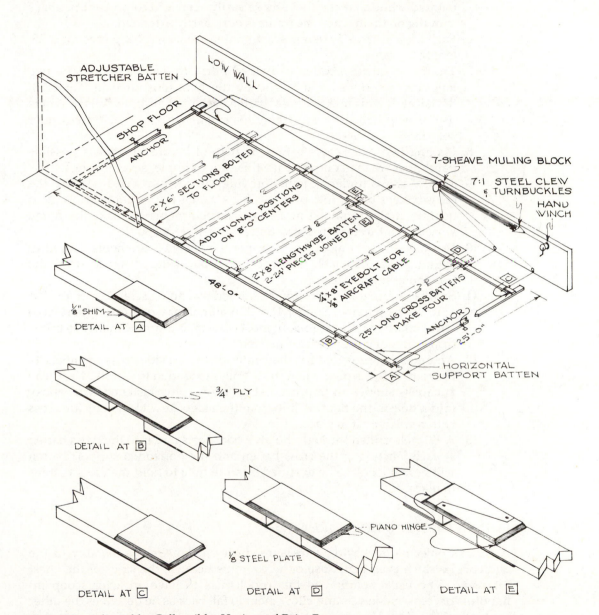

ADJUSTABLE
STRETCHER BATTEN

LOW WALL

SHOP FLOOR

ANCHOR

2"X6" SECTIONS BOLTED TO FLOOR

ADDITIONAL POSITIONS ON 8'-0" CENTERS

2"X8" LENGTHWISE BATTEN
2-24' PIECES JOINED AT B

48'-0"

¼"X8" EYEBOLT FOR ⅛" AIRCRAFT CABLE

25'-LONG CROSS BATTENS MAKE FOUR

7-SHEAVE MULING BLOCK

7:1 STEEL CLEW & TURNBUCKLES

HAND WINCH

ANCHOR

25'-0"

HORIZONTAL SUPPORT BATTEN

⅛" SHIM

DETAIL AT A

¾" PLY

DETAIL AT B

DETAIL AT C

⅛" STEEL PLATE

DETAIL AT D

PIANO HINGE

DETAIL AT E

Plate 168   Adjustable, Collapsible, Horizontal Paint Frame decided to have 8' as a minimum size, there is 16' between the winch and the muling block.

5. The individual line muling blocks are mounted as close to the floor as possible so that the cables can be close to the floor. The cables are painted white to make them more easily seen and to prevent people's tripping on them when the frame is only partly extended.

6. Each 2" × 6" cross batten is scarf-jointed from two 14' pieces for a 25' length.

7. The 48' lengthwise batten is divided into two equal lengths. The two lengths are fastened end to end by the joint illustrated in Plate 168, 'Detail at E.' This makes the 48' batten easier to handle and also permits use of only half the paint frame for smaller drops. It also frees floor space for other uses.

8. Making two extra cross battens is helpful because it makes possible painting more than one item at a time, for example, several wings.

9. The ⅛" shims under all joints provide the necessary clearance for the cross battens to slip into place easily. Also it is important to select good quality, straight-grained lumber as warped members make the frame very difficult to use and may defeat its entire purpose.

10. Marking all cross members with permanent measurements simplifies aligning the adjustable stretcher at a particular distance from the horizontal support batten.

11. Smaller or irregular drops can be framed by adding scrap 1" × 3" or 1" × 4" to the base frame. Longer 1" × 3" material may require support from wires attached to the frame. In most cases, it is a simple matter to frame in any irregular shape that is needed.

12. An anchor is provided for the center of the outside cross members to prevent their warping when the frame is extended to its full 24'-0". The anchor is simply an improved stage screw plug fastened with epoxy into a hole in the floor. A line from the stage crew to the outside cross batten will hold it in place.

13. A ⅜" hole drilled through the plywood cleats and into the cross batten at each junction of the cross batten and the horizontal support batten will permit a bolt to be dropped into the hole to hold the cross battens in place.

INSTANT-REVEAL TREASURE CHEST

A serious objection to having a treasure chest on stage is the inability of the audience to catch even a glimpse of its contents because the sides of the chest intervene. The usual solution to this problem is to have an actor scoop up handfuls of coins and jewels and allow them to fall back as he describes the other contents of the chest. This is nowhere near as exciting for an audience as seeing for themselves. Joseph Farell, an M.F.A. student from Florida State University, working in the property department of the Asolo Theatre, solved this problem with two mouse traps, two rat traps, and considerable ingenuity. (See Plate 169.)

The chest was constructed so that when the unhinged top was removed, all four sides of the chest fell away simultaneously to reveal the contents. This was accomplished by hinging all four sides to the bottom of the chest. To insure that all sides would fall at the same time, they were propelled by compression

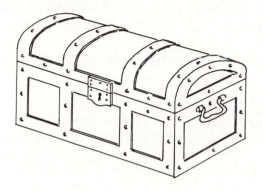

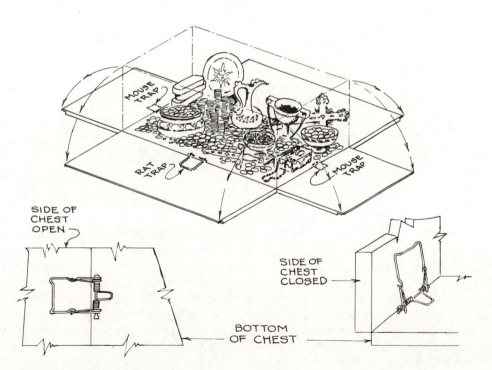

Plate 169 Instant-Reveal Treasure Chest

springs; four spring traps were used. The springs of a mouse trap opened each end of the chest, and the larger springs of a rat trap were used to open the larger front and back panels. The wooden base and the triggers of each trap were removed leaving only the springs and the snap-bar. This spring mechanism was then stapled to the floor of the chest allowing only the snap-bar to exert its pressure against the hinged sides. The interior of the chest was covered with black velour, providing a perfect background for the glittering gold and jewels. A coat of flat black paint on each of the four traps made them all but invisible.

TENSION TAKE-UP FOR WINCH UNIT

A problem associated with the wooden winch (page 372, Plate 152) was preventing the cables from slipping. If the cable became loose, it slipped or overlapped on the revolve it was supposed to turn; or sometimes it fouled on the muling block that guided the cable to the revolve. Tightening the cable presented no major problem, but it did require a screwdriver, a hammer, and a little time. When it was necessary to tighten the cable on the original winch, the screws were removed from the base plate and the whole winch assembly was pulled away from the revolve until the cable was taut; the base was then once more screwed to the floor.

A very clever improvement for tightening the cable, without the need of tools, was developed by Michael Griffith of Miami University Theatre of Ohio (Plate 170). Griffith widened the base plate of the winch so that it extended $1^1/2''$ on either side beyond the vertical supports of the winch top. Overlapping these extensions on either side was a simple track made from two lengths of $1'' \times 4''$ placed face to face with an $^1/8''$ shim between them for clearance. The tracks were screwed to the stage floor but the winch was free to move between them. Two turnbuckles were attached to the back of the winch base plate with eye bolts; the nuts of the eye bolts are countersunk to prevent them from snagging on the floor cloth. Lag bolts anchored the opposite ends of the turnbuckles to the floor. Tightening the cable was thereby reduced to the simple operation of turning the bodies of the turnbuckles.

WOODEN SCREW JACK

A wooden screw jack as designed by Michael Griffith of Miami University can provide a solution to many of the problems arising in theatres, schools, or municipally owned facilities which have floors and low ceilings that must remain untouched by stage screws or any other hardware. The jacks provide a strong vertical support by pressing against the stage floor and the low overhead ceiling directly above it as shown in Plate 171. When two or more jacks are used in conjunction with a horizontal cross member, the system can be used to support draperies or small lighting instruments. Since the jacks can be moved easily from one position to another, they can be used as the support devices for a series of decorative panels or room dividers. Like so many other simple tools, wooden screw jacks are limited in their usefulness only by the imagination of the user.

The following suggestions may prove helpful in planning and constructing the wooden screw jack:

1. With the jack fully contracted it should measure 2" or $2^1/2''$ less in height than the distance between the floor and the ceiling of the room.

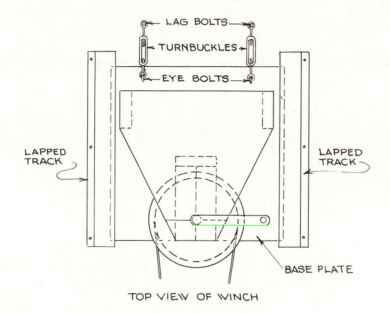

TOP VIEW OF WINCH

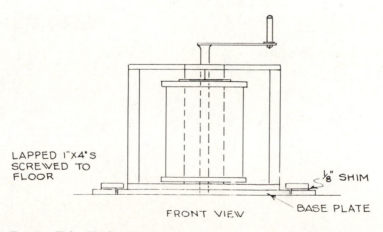

FRONT VIEW

Plate 170 Tension Take-Up for Winch Unit

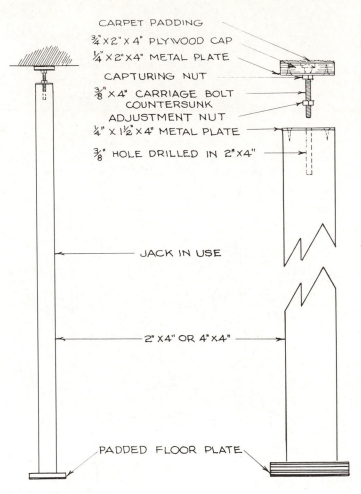

CARPET PADDING
¾" X 2" X 4" PLYWOOD CAP
¼" X 2" X 4" METAL PLATE
CAPTURING NUT
⅜" X 4" CARRIAGE BOLT
COUNTERSUNK
ADJUSTMENT NUT
¼" X 1½" X 4" METAL PLATE
⅜" HOLE DRILLED IN 2" X 4"

JACK IN USE

2" X 4" OR 4" X 4"

PADDED FLOOR PLATE

Plate 171   Wooden Screw Jack

2. Padding made from a scrap of carpeting should be glued on the plywood cap to prevent scratching or marring the ceiling.
3. A reinforcing plate of ³/₁₆″ or ¹/₄″ steel should be screwed to the underside of the cap. Tightening the capturing nut against the reinforcing plate will reduce the chances of splitting the wooden cap.
4. A metal bearing plate should be fitted to the top of the wooden upright. The adjustment nut works against this metal plate when the jack is being locked in position.
5. The floor plate should be fitted with padding made from a rubber mat to keep the jack from slipping on the floor.
6. Care should be exercised to place the top end of the jack on a solid bearing surface such as a floor or ceiling joist, rather than an unsupported area of ceiling drywall or plaster.

REMOTELY CONTROLLED "MAGIC" STOOL

The stage directions of the play *Knights of the Round Table* specify that a stool move, without visible means of propulsion, from its position beneath a window to a table at center stage. Later the stool just as mysteriously moves back to its original position. At a production meeting where several different solutions to this problem had been discussed, the director remarked, "I wish there was some way to move that stool without having it roll along a straight line as it obviously will if it is to be guided by a track." The eventual solution of this problem was developed by Elbin Cleveland, at that time a graduate assistant in technical theatre at the University of Iowa. Cleveland developed a remote-controlled, electrically driven stool that wandered about the stage on cue much to the delight of both director and audience.

The unit, illustrated in Plate 172, was driven by two wiper motors which independently powered the two drive wheels. Power for the motors was supplied by two 12 VDC motorcycle batteries. Steering was accomplished by running only one drive wheel so that the stool pivoted around the other or "dead" drive wheel. Control for the motors was provided by a single channel radio control unit such as those used in model airplanes.

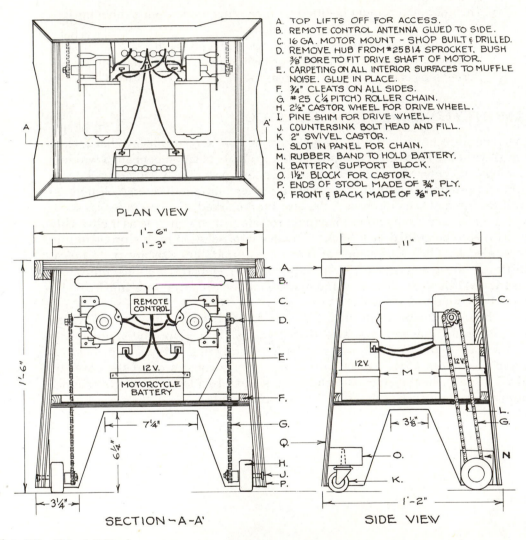

A. TOP LIFTS OFF FOR ACCESS.
B. REMOTE CONTROL ANTENNA GLUED TO SIDE.
C. 16 GA. MOTOR MOUNT - SHOP BUILT & DRILLED.
D. REMOVE HUB FROM #25B14 SPROCKET. BUSH ⅜" BORE TO FIT DRIVE SHAFT OF MOTOR.
E. CARPETING ON ALL INTERIOR SURFACES TO MUFFLE NOISE. GLUE IN PLACE.
F. ¾" CLEATS ON ALL SIDES.
G. #25 (¼ PITCH) ROLLER CHAIN.
H. 2½" CASTOR WHEEL FOR DRIVE WHEEL.
I. PINE SHIM FOR DRIVE WHEEL.
J. COUNTERSINK BOLT HEAD AND FILL.
K. 2" SWIVEL CASTOR.
L. SLOT IN PANEL FOR CHAIN.
M. RUBBER BAND TO HOLD BATTERY.
N. BATTERY SUPPORT BLOCK.
O. 1½" BLOCK FOR CASTOR.
P. ENDS OF STOOL MADE OF ¾" PLY.
Q. FRONT & BACK MADE OF ⅜" PLY.

PLAN VIEW

SECTION-A-A'

SIDE VIEW

Plate 172 "Magic" Stool

16

Backstage Organization and Management

The last few days immediately preceding the opening of a production are traditionally depicted as nerve wracking and harrowing. Movie and TV script writers have done an excellent job of showing this period filled with frantic all-night sessions, exhausted actors and crew members, crisis heaped upon crisis, and a supervising director on the verge of a nervous breakdown. Unfortunately, within a field as universal as that of play production, there will always be a small percentage of individuals whose warped sense of the dramatic so far outweighs their common sense that their dress rehearsals are like those just described—chaotic. However, this is the exception rather than the rule, and it is easy to put the blame right where it belongs—lack of proper organization and planning.

The dress rehearsal period is intended for one purpose: synchronizing and polishing all elements into a production with unity. This presupposes that the elements of scenery, props, lights, and costumes have all been completed according to the plan of their individual work schedules and are ready to be integrated. There is then an orderly sequence of operations that avoids last-minute congestion and confusion. As an example, the technician's work schedule may have called for all construction to be finished by the 20th; the next three days are allowed for painting; the 24th and 25th are set aside for assembly,

413

rigging, and preliminary work on lighting; the 26th and 27th are to be devoted to assembling properties, trimming sets, and to final adjustments on lighting. Should the scene shift be especially complicated, a part of the 27th could well be used for a technical rehearsal, which is best described as a performance without benefit (or hindrance) of audience or actors. Just as the technician's work schedule has pinpointed possible troublesome details in advance and provided time for their correction, the costumer's schedule may have set aside a time for a dress parade that provides the actors with an opportunity to try out their costumes and makeups against the scenery and under the lights in advance of dress rehearsals. There is then time to make any necessary changes or adjustments before dress rehearsals begin. If the mechanical aspects of the production have been worked out in advance, there is no reason why the first dress rehearsal should not be devoted to the purpose for which it was intended: namely the polishing of the production.

THE STUDENT STAGE MANAGER

The stage manager is the key to backstage organization. He or she is usually one of the more experienced and older students, selected as much for tact, diplomacy, and ability to get along in trying situations as for any other qualities. The stage manager becomes the director's representative backstage and is responsible for the smooth running of the production through the rehearsal period and during the run of the play.

Unlike the professional stage manager, who is in attendance at all rehearsals from the time of casting till the close of the production, the stage manager of the educational theatre usually assumes his duties only shortly before the first technical rehearsals. Just how soon and how long the stage manager attends rehearsals will depend upon the complexity of the production and the director's need for his services. It is obvious that the value of the student manager to the director is in direct proportion to knowledge of the script, the actors, and the established stage business. Such knowledge can be assimilated only through attendance at a series of rehearsals. During this period while he is learning the script, he is busy making notes on a series of details that will later become his responsibility to supervise: the sequence of scenes, opening and closing curtain cues, and at what points the director wants the act breaks and intermissions. The stage manager's notes will also include all of the information required for compiling the actor's checklist, and at what time music and sound cues are required. He will make a furniture plan for each scene, note where each major prop must be placed, and whether doors and windows are closed or open at the beginning of a scene. He is aware of any special effects involving either lighting or sound, and he will know the cues for them, and how they are to be timed to the stage business.

Because of his knowledge of the production the stage manager can, in the absence of the director, provide the technician and lighting specialist with needed information during the rigging and lighting of the production. He is able to show the technician where each item of furniture is to be placed for a special piece of stage business; he can explain why certain parts of the setting may need additional bracing; or he can show the lighting specialist which acting areas must receive special attention. Since the stage manager frequently serves as head of the stage crew, he helps the technician plan the details of each shift and make individual crew assignments. By the date of the first technical rehearsal, the stage manager has become thoroughly conversant with every phase of the production; he knows how, where, and when each physical aspect of the play will occur. He has become an able backstage assistant to the director.

Actor's Checklist

During the rehearsal period and the run of the production there is little time for the stage manager to use an elaborate set of notes. However, any chart or diagram that will provide her with needed information at a glance can prove extremely helpful. Such a chart is the actor's checklist. This chart takes two forms: a simplified version that is checked by the actors as they enter the theatre, and a more detailed chart that is again checked by the actors when they report to the stage for their entrances.

The simplified version is a listing of characters by order of appearance on stage, followed by the actor's name, his phone number, and a series of spaces representing the dates of dress rehearsals and performances (Plate 173). This list is posted by the stage entrance or near the dressing rooms; the actors check their names on this list to indicate that they have arrived at the theatre and are busy with their makeups and costumes.

The second chart is posted on the bulletin board near the stage manager's desk; a check opposite an actor's name on this chart indicates that she has reported to the stage and is ready for her entrance. This chart is more detailed than the first; it not only carries all of the information listed on the first, but lists the names of the characters and actors in the order of their appearance for each act and scene. Also listed is the playing time for each act and scene and the time required for each scene shift and intermission (Plate 174).

These charts inform the stage manager at a glance if all actors have reported to the theatre, if each is ready for his entrance, and who should be onstage for the opening of each scene. By consulting this chart both cast and crews can be kept informed regarding the length of time remaining before their next appearance or assignment.

Stage Manager's Script Copy

The stage manager's need to make extensive use of a play script will vary from production to production. With a comparatively simple play that has few light or sound cues there is little need for a script once the play has progressed past the dress-rehearsal period. On elaborate productions the stage manager may find it simpler to follow the dialogue onstage, line by line, in her own script. Along the margins of each page are her penciled notes specifying the proper place for warning cues and action cues for lights, sounds, music, entrances, or special effects. The action cues are usually underscored in colored pencil so that they may be easily spotted.

Time Schedule

One of the most valuable charts kept by the stage manager is the time schedule. By noting the exact time when the curtain is opened and closed, this chart provides a simple way for the manager to keep an accurate record of the playing time for each act or scene. If this record is correct, it will automatically give the

PICNIC													
CHARACTER	ACTOR	PHONE	REHEARSAL			PRODUCTION DATES							
			10/13	10/14	10/15	10/16	10/17	10/18	10/22	10/23	10/24	10/25	
HELEN POTTS	RUTH CANFIELD	7392											
HAL CARTER	ED WELLS	X 3291											
MILLIE OWENS	JOAN HUMMER	5219											
BOMBER	BOB HALL	4716											
MADGE OWENS	ALICE BONNER	X 2241											
FLO OWENS	DEE YOUNG	X 2340											
ROSEMARY SIDNEY	VIRGINIA DE LILLO	7418											
ALAN SEYMOUR	KENNETH HILL	5521											
IRMA KRONKITE	PEGGY SPRAGUE	6593											
CHRISTINE SCHOENWALDER	MARAGRET KEYS	3361											
HOWARD BEVANS	WILLIAM KELLY	4432											

Plate 173   Actor's Checklist

			PICNIC											
CHARACTER	ACTOR	PHONE	PLAYING TIME	ACT BREAK	REHEARSAL			PRODUCTION DATES						
ACT I			34 MIN.	10 MIN	10/13	10/14	10/15	10/16	10/17	10/18	10/22	10/23	10/24	10/25
POTTS	CANFIELD	7392												
CARTER	WELLS	X 3291												
MILLIE	HUMMER	5219												
BOMBER	HALL	4716												
MADGE	BONNER	X 2241												
FLO	YOUNG	X 2340												
ROSEMARY	DE LILLO	7418												
ALAN	HILL	5521												
IRMA	SPRAGUE	6593												
CHRISTINE	KEYS	3361												
ACT II			35 MIN.	12 MIN.										
MILLIE	HUMMER													
MADGE	BONNER													
FLO	YOUNG													
IRMA	SPRAGUE													
CHRISTINE	KEYS													
ROSEMARY	DE LILLO													
POTTS	CANFIELD													
HOWARD	KELLY	4432												
CARTER	WELLS													
ALAN	HILL													
ACT III SCENE I			11 MIN.	2 MIN.										
HOWARD	KELLY													
ROSEMARY	DE LILLO													
CARTER	WELLS													
MADGE	BONNER													
ACT III SCENE II			17 MIN.											
FLO	YOUNG													
MILLIE	HUMMER													
POTTS	CANFIELD													
ROSEMARY	DE LILLO													
IRMA	SPRAGUE													
CHRISTINE	KEYS													
BOMBER	HALL													

Plate 174   Actor's Checklist, Stage Manager's Copy

total elapsed time for each act break—the difference between the closing time of one scene and the opening of the next. If it is considered desirable, the actual scene shift can be more accurately timed by noting the elapsed time between the closing of the curtain and the moment when the last crew head reports to the stage manager that his crew has completed its assignment and is "set." Usually space is reserved on the chart to note the cause for any delay that might affect the over-all time of the act break. A misplaced prop, a flickering spotlight, or a difficult costume change may cause a delay of from one to several minutes. If these delays are recorded and their causes noted, proper steps can be taken to overcome them (Plate 175).

Keeping an accurate time record of the production is not a needless piece of busy work; it provides the director, the house manager, and all crew heads with needed information. It provides the director with a perfect method of checking the playing time of one performance against another. It can be done scene by scene and act by act, or by comparing total elapsed playing times. Detecting when actors have been racing their lines or unnecessarily prolonging stage business becomes a simple matter of comparing performance records. Faults of this type can be easily corrected if the director knows exactly when it occurred and how long it lasted. "What time is the play over?" is a question asked of the house manager many times a night by taxi drivers or others who are meeting friends after the play. If there is an emergency call for a member of the audience, knowing just when there will be an act break helps the house manager locate the individual with a minimum of disturbance to the rest of the house. When heads of prop, costume, light, and sound crews know just how long the stage crew requires to complete a shift, their own assignments can be planned accordingly. If the time of the shift is very short, say 1 or 2 minutes, this may mean that additional crew members will be needed or a different method must be devised to complete their assignments in the allotted time.

THE STAGE CREW

Selecting the members to form the stage crew is a responsibility of the scene technician. Frequently the stage manager will be called into conference by the technician and the two of them will discuss each shift in detail, deciding on the desired number of crew members. On simple one-set productions a stage manager, an assistant manager, and a curtain man may be all that are needed. On heavier productions with several settings a full crew of 8, 10, 12, or more may be required. Usually the crew is divided into three sections, each assigned to handle the scenery on some particular part of the stage such as stage right, center rear, or stage left.

At this point, just before the first technical rehearsal, the technician calls the crew together to explain the general scheme of shifting and to make individual crew assignments. Certainly one of the easiest ways of accomplishing this task is to draw a floor plan of each setting on a blackboard, explaining in detail the order in which the setting will be struck and just where each unit of scenery will be stored. Since the word "shift" implies the dismantling of one set and the assembly of another to take its place, the technician will explain where the various parts of the second set have been stored and in what order they should be assembled. Individual assignments can be given at this time. If the crew is inexperienced, it is best to discuss one shift at a time, preferably just

PRODUCTION — PICNIC						DIRECTOR — GEE	
DATE	ACT	CURTAIN UP	CURTAIN DOWN	PLAYING TIME	ACT BREAK	SHIFT	DELAY
WED 10/16	I	8:10	8:44	34	10		
	II	8:54	9:29	35	12		2 MIN. REFOCUS SPOT
	III-1	9:41	9:52	11	2		
	III-2	9:54	10:11	17			
	TOTAL			1:37	24		
TOTAL PRO. TIME			2 HRS. 11 MIN.				
						STAGE MANAGER — TILTON	

Plate 175 Time Schedule

before the crew members go to the stage to try out their assignments. The crew should be reassembled at the completion of the shift and each step reviewed. Sometimes it may be necessary to alter the operational steps or to change individual assignments; and always there are questions to be answered and suggestions to evaluate.

It is advisable to have the heads of both the lighting crew and the property crew present at these briefing sessions. Frequently their crew assignments are so interrelated with those of the stage crew that it is impossible to plan the shift without taking them into consideration. One point should be stressed at these first meetings: the importance of cooperation between crews, and a complete understanding by all crew members of the sequence of steps to be performed in accomplishing the shift. A quick, quiet shift can be obtained only if all crew members know when, how, and where their assignments must be completed.

The Operational Sequence of a Scene Shift

The pattern used in planning the shifts of most conventional settings generally follows the outline below. Note that the order of the strike involves the removal of all upstage units first, moving progressively from the back wall down to the tormentors. If this pattern is followed and the scenery is stacked in that order, it is automatically in the right order for reassembly.

1. The stage manager warns the crew members to take their respective positions shortly before the close of the curtain.
2. The main curtain is closed.
3. Switching on the stage work lights is the silent command for the strike to begin.
4. The cyclorama is raised. This operation both protects the cyc and clears the stage floor for the free movement of scenery, props, and lights.
5. The ceiling is raised.
6. The prop crew removes all decorative and practical props from the walls of the set. Floor props are pulled into the downstage center area to clear them from the folding or the movement of the walls.
7. The stage crew strikes all backings, cutouts, and set pieces.
8. The light crew disconnects and removes all light fixtures from set walls. All floor and table lamps are disconnected and removed.
9. The stage crew removes all three-dimensional architectural trim (removable doors, windows, fireplaces, etc.).
10. The rear wall is struck.
11. The larger floor props are removed.
12. The side walls are unbraced and struck.
13. The large floor props for the second setting are moved to downstage center.
14. The side walls are run in and braced.
15. The back wall is joined to the side walls and braced.
16. Three-dimensional architectural trim is placed in position.
17. Floor props are placed. Light fixtures and decorative props are fitted to the set walls.
18. The ceiling is lowered.
19. Backings, set pieces, and cutouts are placed in position.

20. The cyclorama is lowered.
21. All backstage lights are tested.
22. Prop, light, and costume crew heads report to the stage manager that their assignments are completed and they are "set."
23. The crews clear stage, the stage manager gives the command of "Places," checks with the control-board operator, and, if she is ready, gives the cue for the opening of the scene.

There is always a possibility of combining several of these operations so that they can be performed at the same time. On the strike, for instance, operations 4 to 9 could be carried out simultaneously, and on the assembly, steps 14 to 20 could be combined.

The Blackout Scene Shift

There are occasions in some productions when the scene shift must be performed without benefit of a closed front curtain and without work lights. Impossible as it may sound, this can be accomplished quietly and quickly. Just how successfully it is done depends upon two things: how well the shift has been planned and how thoroughly it has been rehearsed.

The following procedural steps will help in planning a successful blackout scene shift:

1. The fastening devices used in joining units of scenery together or in locking them into place must be simplified to the point that the joining or locking can be accomplished more by a sense of touch than by a sense of sight.
2. A smaller and more specific shifting assignment for each crew member may be necessary when working without lights, for example, two members working the stage right area will handle only unit A and two others will be responsible only for unit B; they will have no other duties. The more they know about the way a particular unit handles, joins to another unit, or locks in place, the easier it becomes to do this in the dark.
3. Stress the importance of *what, when* and *where* each scenic unit and each large floor prop is to be moved. If the pattern established by the three Ws is followed, much of the congestion and most of the conflicts of a blackout scene shift can be eliminated.
4. The positions for all scenic units and floor props must be spiked with luminous tape.
5. After giving the shifting assignment to each crew member, practice the scene shift with the work lights on. Repeat the shift until everyone is certain of his assignment and has learned just how, when, and where each object is to be moved. Once smoothness and the desired speed has been achieved, turn the work lights off and begin to practice the same procedure in the dark. Repeat as often as necessary to achieve the same results.
6. All crew members should wear black or other very dark clothes.
7. If crew members will avoid looking directly at stage lights and will keep their eyes closed for one or two minutes just prior to the shift, their eyes will adapt faster to complete darkness.

THE PROPERTY CREW

The property master and her crew have assembled or constructed all the required props under the supervision of the director and the designer. The director must pass on their acceptability for stage business, while the designer is concerned about their correctness as to period, form, and color. Once properties have been approved they become the responsibility of the property master and her crew. Details regarding their placement on stage and manner and order of shifting them are determined at early briefing sessions with the stage manager. He will see to it that the shifting of the props is coordinated with the other activities of the scene shift.

The property master will use many tricks to reduce the time required for the removal or assembly of props. When possible, and if it can be done without damage, heavy floor props can be stacked on a low dolly and wheeled to and from the stage. Props can also be loaded on wagons and rolling platforms used for shifting scenery. Two chairs can be stacked seat to seat and carried as one, or they can be laid on a sofa or table and all carried at once. Small decorative props placed on tables, buffets, shelves, and so forth, must be cleared before the furniture can be moved. This can be done rapidly by two crew members who make a circuit of the set, collecting all such items and placing them in a large container such as a wicker clothesbasket. Wall hangings, pictures, and fixtures are all marked for ready identification with their proper positions on the set walls. "Spike marks" of chalk, scene paint, or tacks on the stage floor are frequently used to spot the floor props in exactly the correct position. If spike marks are inadvisable for some reason, the position can be established by two measurements taken from some distinctive feature of the setting. For example, a table can be aligned with the door in the right wall and a window in the rear wall.

Hand properties, at least those that are carried onstage or offstage by the actors, are usually dispensed and collected from a table placed offstage near the main entrance of the setting. A crew member assigned to this table, whose principal duty is to collect the props from the actors as they leave the stage, will eliminate the exasperating job of locating missing hand props after a performance.

THE LIGHT CREW

Details concerning the division of the light crew into various sections were discussed in Chapter 1. The floor crew is the only section of the light crew that is likely to be directly involved with the actual scene shift. As such, their duties and the order in which they are to be accomplished fall under the supervision of the stage manager, who must coordinate them with the other activities of the shift.

The actual duties of the light crew during the shift are few, compared with those of the stage or property crew. Although they may be considered minor in respect to the number of assignments per crew member, they are nonetheless important. Failure to disconnect and remove light fixtures from the setting can delay the stage crew many seconds, just as a barrier of horizon strips can block the movement of scenery either onstage or offstage. Electrical cables must be disconnected from all wagons before those units can be moved, and all electrical cables that lie on the floor must be coiled out of the way in order to prevent their fouling rolling scenery and to avoid damage to the cables themselves.

THE COSTUME CREW

Unless there are fast costume changes that demand temporary onstage dressing rooms, the shift is not likely to be much affected by the activities of the costume crew. However, temporary dressing rooms occupy valuable space that would otherwise be available for storage of scenery or props, and do concern the stage manager. It becomes his duty to designate the area that can best be used for the purpose. Occasionally, even with the aid of dressers, a particularly complicated costume and makeup change cannot be accomplished within the specified time of the shift. In such cases the costumer will notify the stage manager, who will make proper allowances for it on the time schedule.

SUMMARY OF THE STAGE MANAGER'S DUTIES AND OPERATIONAL CHECKLIST FOR RUNNING A UNIVERSITY THEATRE PRODUCTION

Since the duties of the stage manager are so numerous and varied, some kind of list should be prepared for the student manager, summarizing the principal duties and responsibilities expected of an efficient stage manager. Where this practice has been established, there is a noticeable decrease in the number of mistakes that occur because the student was unaware of what was expected of him. Some additions or deletions would have to be made in this list to make it conform to the pattern of production used by different próducing organizations; but, whatever the schedule may be, it is important to have it down in black and white so that it may be given out at the time the stage manager is appointed. Information contained on the chart of a stage manager's duties and the operational checklist used at the University Theatre at Iowa follows.

Stage Manager's Duties

1. Secure a copy of the play and study the script before attending rehearsals. Use this script for underscoring warning cues, action cues, sound cues, light cues, and so forth.
2. During the absence of the director or any staff member backstage, the stage manager has full authority over actors and crew members.
3. The length of time the stage manager attends rehearsals preceding the first technical rehearsal depends upon the director's need for his service and the complexity of the production. In all cases he must attend rehearsals, in advance of the technical rehearsals, a sufficient number of times to become familiar with the sequence of scenes, the actors, stage business, use of props, and placement of furniture.
4. Make out an actor's checklist containing the name of the actor, the character he plays, and his telephone number. (See Plate 173.) Post a copy of the list on the board by the dressing-room doors. Insist on all actors checking in as they enter the theatre. Post the stage manager's copy of this list on the bulletin board by your desk on the stage.

5. Make out a crew checklist containing the names, telephone numbers, and addresses of students serving as crew heads, control-board operators, curtain man, and so forth.

6. Draw a plan of the property and furniture layout for each scene. Pay attention to each key prop such as a fan, letter, and so forth, that must be placed by the prop crew before the opening of the scene. Check, and note on your plan, the position of doors and windows. Are they to be open or closed for the beginning of the scene?

7. Check sound effects controlled from backstage. Telephone buzzers are usually operated backstage by the prompter. All other sound effects are usually controlled from the light booth by members of the sound crew, using the public address system.

8. Become familiar with the operation of the following stage equipment before the first rehearsal.
   a. House lights.
   b. Lights controlled from the stage manager's desk.
   c. Warning bell for audience.
   d. Controls for the main curtain.
   e. Asbestos curtain.
   f. Controls for the revolving stage.
   g. Fire hose and fire extinguishers.
   h. Fire doors.
   i. Cyclorama.
   j. Backstage work lights.
   k. House phone system.
   l. First-aid supplies.

9. Keep an accurate time schedule of all dress rehearsals and performances, showing opening and closing times of each scene, elapsed time between scenes and acts, and the reason for any delay during a scene shift. For example:

Curtain	Up	Down	Playing Time	Shift	Delay
Act I	8:10	9:00	50	5	1 min. props
Act II	9:05	9:45	40	12	Intermission
Act III	9:57	10:32	35		
			125	17	

TOTAL PLAYING TIME	2 hours and 5 minutes
TOTAL SHIFT TIME	17 minutes
TOTAL PRODUCTION TIME	2 hours and 22 minutes

Operational Checklist

1. Check the forestage to see that no classroom equipment or rehearsal furniture has been left on the apron in front of the asbestos.

2. Make certain that the beam work lights over the auditorium are out. It is easy to overlook these with the auditorium lights on.

3. Give the first warning call to the actors 30 minutes before the curtain, a second call 15 minutes later. Last call is given at 8 o'clock, when all actors who open the play should be on stgae.

4. Between the first and last warning calls, the stage manager should check all scenery, lights, and props for the opening act.
5. As the actors come to the stage from the dressing rooms have them check their names on the actor's checklist which is posted to the left of the stage manager's desk. After an actor has checked in for a scene do not permit him to leave the stage without notifying you or your assistant.
6. Under no circumstances should the play be opened until the majority of the audience is seated. Information on the condition of the house is obtained by calling the ticket office or by word from the director.
7. At 8 o'clock, the asbestos curtain is raised and tied off. It will not be lowered again, except in an emergency (it can be used as a substitute for the main curtain should it fail) until the end of the play.
8. The usual curtain time is 8:10, but this varies a little, depending upon the length of the play and whether the audience is slow in assembling and getting seated.
9. After receiving word from either the house manager or the director that the audience is in and seated, the command "Places" is given. All crew members clear stage, and the actors take their positions for the opening scene.
10. Turn off all backstage work lights. This is easy to overlook, especially if the bridge and cyc lights are on. Flick the work lights off and on several times as a silent warning to those who may not have heard the call of "Places." This should remind you to turn them off.
11. Over the headphones call the control-board operator for a last-minute check on lights, and if she is ready, ask for the house lights to be dimmed out.
12. When the house lights are completely out, give the cue for the opening of the curtain. Should the director want the play to open on a black stage, it will be necessary to notify the control-board operator when the curtain is open because it will be impossible for her to see it.
13. Enter on the time schedule the exact time the curtain was opened.
14. The curtain is closed at the end of the act on a cue determined by the director during the dress rehearsals.
15. Enter on the time schedule the exact time when the curtain closed at the end of the scene.
16. Do not turn on the work lights backstage for the scene shift until the auditorium lights are up. This can create a bad light spill across the apron or under the front curtain.
17. During dress rehearsals the stage crews will not begin a shift until the command "Strike" is given by the stage manager; the director may want to repeat a part, or all of an act. During the run of the performance, the switching on of the work lights is the silent command for the shift.
18. When the director has chosen to close a scene by dimming or blacking out all stage lights, the stage manager must notify the control-board operator when the front curtain is closed. This will be her cue to bring up the house lights. When scenes are to be handled in this manner the stage manager must see that all backstage lights not controlled by the board are out, including the light over the stage manager's desk, the prompter's lights, and so forth.

19. The average time for a shift of scenery and props is 5 to 6 minutes between acts and 3 minutes or less between scenes of an act. The act break selected by the director for the intermission is usually about 10 to 12 minutes.
20. Three minutes before the end of the intermission, sound the audience warning chimes three times.
21. Note the exact closing time of the play on the time schedule. Compute the total playing time and total shift time. Give the director a copy of this record.
22. Before leaving the theatre after a rehearsal or performance, make sure that the cyclorama has been raised, the fire doors above the grid closed, the asbestos lowered, and all backstage lights turned off.

DISMANTLING SCENERY AFTER THE LAST PERFORMANCE

Immediately after the last curtain call on the last night of a production's run it is traditional to strike the settings. The scenery is dismantled and stripped of all its hardware, salvageable materials are set aside, and everything is properly stored. The question may well be asked, "But why must it be done so late at night? Why not just wait until tomorrow when there's more time?" As is true with many other theatrical traditions, this one is based on common sense and when carried out in the manner described below results in a saving of both time and energy. The reasons are obvious once they are pointed out.

1. The crews that have been responsible for handling the scenery during the run of a production are already in the theatre, so no time is lost in recalling them. If additional crew members are needed for the strike, they can be called without encountering the problems of conflicting classes and/or work assignments.
2. The regular running crews are familiar with each property and unit of scenery; they know how to handle it and how it was joined to other units. As a result of this knowledge they are able to disassemble it with the least possible wasted motion.
3. Removing the current production from the stage and the shop frees these two areas and gives the following production free use of the space.

Because no two productions are exactly alike, no hard and fast rules can be set down for listing the steps that govern a final strike. One plan never would apply equally well to any two productions.

The problem of coordination of all activities is greatly simplified if there are several supervisors for the many crew members working at the same time on different phases of a strike in different sections of the backstage area. For this reason the technician together with the crew heads, the stage carpenter, the shop foreman, and the technical assistants plan the strike in advance so that each of them will have a clear understanding of what is to be done first and the order to be followed in conducting each phase of the strike. It is often surprising to the uninitiated to see how smoothly and quickly the strike of even a multiset production can be completed.

Glossary

Acrylic. A clear sheet plastic that is primarily used as a glass substitute. Also available in other shapes and colors.

Aniline Dye. See *Scene Paint*.

Apron. The part of the stage floor extending beyond the proscenium arch into the auditorium; forestage.

Arbor. A metal frame that holds the counterweights used to balance the weight of flown scenery; synonymous with carriage and cradle.

Asbestos Curtain. A fireproof curtain hung just upstage of the proscenium arch to prevent the spread of fire.

Back-Flap Hinge. See *Hinge*.

Backing. Any type of two- or three-dimensional scenery placed in back of an opening to screen the backstage area from the audience.

Batten Clamp. A piece of stage hardware used to attach drops or borders to a pipe batten.

Black Powder. An explosive powder that gives a brilliant flash of light with a considerable amount of smoke. See also *Flash Powder*.

Block. A grooved pulley or sheave housed in a wooden or metal frame provided with a hook, eye, or strap by which it may be attached to other objects.

Board Foot. A unit of measure by which lumber is sold. Each unit represents a piece of lumber 1" thick, 12" wide, and 12" long.

Bobinette. A very lightweight cotton netting.

Bolt:

    Carriage. A threaded shaft with a round head. The shaft graduates into angular shoulders just beneath the head; these prevent the bolt from turning when driven into wood.

> *Machine.*   A threaded shaft with a square or hexagonal head.
>
> *Stove.*   A threaded shaft with a head that is slotted like a screw.

Book Ceiling.   See *Ceiling.*

Boomerang.   A multileveled rolling platform on which workmen can stand.

Borders.   Strips of fabric hung horizontally above the stage to mask overhead space and equipment.

Brace Cleat.   A metal plate 2″ wide by 4″ long drilled with holes; used in conjunction with a stage brace and a stage crew to brace scenery.

Breasting.   The process of pulling a flown object out of its normal vertical path by means of a special line and blocks.

Butt Hinge.   See *Hinge.*

Butt Joint.   See *Joint.*

Cabinet Drawing.   Cabinet drawing is similar to an oblique drawing in all details except one. All dimensions shown on the oblique angles are reduced one-half.

Carpet Hoist.   A type of rigging used to transfer weight from one counterweight arbor to another by means of special brackets.

Carriage.   (1) The supporting member of a run of stairs. (2) Synonym for arbor and for cradle.

Carriage Bolt.   See *Bolt.*

Casein paint.   See *Scene Paint.*

Casing.   The enclosing framework around a door or window opening.

Ceiling:

> *Book.*   A ceiling piece so constructed and rigged that its two halves fold face to face for compact storage in the flies.
>
> *Roll.*   A ceiling piece so constructed that it can be easily dismantled and rolled into a compact bundle.

Ceiling Plate.   A metal plate 2½″ wide and 7″ long, fitted with a metal ring and drilled to receive bolts. Used in joining the cross battens to the lengthwise battens of ceilings.

Celastic.   A trademarked plastic-impregnated felt cloth. When dipped in acetone it becomes limber and can be formed as desired. When the acetone evaporates the material becomes rigid.

Cel-O-Cloth.   A thin sheet of cellophane with a backing of loosely woven threads. Used as a substitute for glass.

Cel-O-Glass.   Screen wire that has been treated with a coating of cellophane to make it completely translucent. Used as a substitute for glass.

Cellulose Acetate.   A chemical compound having the appearance and most of the properties of glass. Occasionally used as a substitute for glass; more frequently used in making curved slides for projectors.

Clout Nail.   A nail with a tapering wedge-shaped shaft used for joining keystones and corner blocks to flat frames. The points of these nails are easily bent or clinched for a stronger anchor.

Column.   A supporting shaft or pillar.

Continental Parallel.   See *Parallel.*

Corner Block.   A ¼″ thick piece of plywood in the shape of a right triangle with 10″ sides, used to reinforce and join right-angle butt joints.

Corner Plate.   An L-shaped right-angle metal plate used to reinforce the butt joints of a window or door unit.

Cotton Canvas Duck.   The most commonly used covering material for flat frames.

Cotton Rep.   An inexpensive, heavy-duty, ribbed cotton material obtainable in colors.

Counterweight, Multiple Speed.   Used in flying scenery; employs a 2 to 1 mechanical advantage in its rigging. The batten moves twice as far and twice as fast as the arbor.

Counterweight System.   A method of raising scenery vertically by means of steel cables, blocks, pipe batten, and weights placed in an arbor.

Cradle.   A metal frame for holding counterweights. Synonym for arbor and carriage.

Curtain:

> *Draw.*   A curtain that parts in the center; each section pulls to the sides in back of the proscenium arch.
>
> *Fly.*   A curtain that is opened and closed by raising and lowering it by means of the counterweight system or rope-line rigging.
>
> *Main.*   The front curtain that separates the stage from the auditorium.
>
> *Roller.*   A curtain that is opened by winding it around a long wooden roller that is usually attached to the lower hem.
>
> *Tab.*   A two-sectioned curtain rigged to open diagonally, presenting a decorative draped effect.

Cut-Line.   A special line used to hold the asbestos curtain in the open position. Cutting or releasing this line will automatically lower the asbestos.

Cyclorama:

> *Fly.*   A U-shaped expanse of light-blue canvas enclosing the acting area on three sides. It is raised and lowered by the counterweight system. Used for sky effects.
>
> *Trip.*   Similar to a fly cyc, but so rigged that it will fold as it is raised, thus requiring less grid height.
>
> *Linnebach.*   Serves the same purpose as the fly or trip cyc but operates differently. It is suspended from a curved track and moves horizontally to store in a rolled position around a truncated cone. Named after the inventor, Adolph Linnebach.

Dado Joint.   See *Joint.*

Designer's Plans.   Scaled mechanical drawings for exact representation of a setting. They include the ground plans, front elevations, detail, and sight-line drawings.

Designer's Sketch.   Usually a colored perspective drawing showing the proposed setting as it will appear to a member of the audience seated about halfway back in the auditorium.

Detail Drawings.   Mechanical drawings, made to a large scale showing the top, front, and side views of three-dimensional objects.

Diagonal Brace.   A brace made of $1'' \times 2''$ lumber and placed at an angle between the stile and rail of a wide flat to strengthen the frame.

Dolly.   A small low platform mounted on wheels or a single roller; used in moving heavy objects.

Dome, Plaster.   Similar in shape and use to a cyclorama but made of steel screening and covered with plaster. It cannot be shifted. It may partially or completely enclose the acting area on three sides.

Double Luff.   An arrangement of rope and pulleys used to provide a mechanical advantage of 4 to 1.

Double Whip.   An arrangement of rope and pulleys used to provide a mechanical advantage of 2 to 1.

Doweled Joint.   See *Joint.*

Downstage.   The front of the stage, toward the audience.

Draperies, Stage.   A set of draperies used to mask the backstage area when no scenery is being used.

Drapery Hangers.   Steel sockets and hooks used to support door and window draperies. Hooks are attached to a drapery pole, sockets to the scenery.

Draw Curtain.   See *Curtain.*

Drop.   A large unframed expanse of cloth supported by a heavy wooden batten at the top with a lighter batten at the bottom to hold the material free of wrinkles.

Drop, Cutout.   A standard drop with sections removed to give it a distinctive shape.

Dutchman.   A strip of muslin 5" wide that is glued and tacked or stapled over the hinges and crack formed when two flats are hinged together.

Electric Glue Pot.   An electrically operated thermostatically controlled device for heating animal glue in the scene shop. Will not burn the glue.

Eyebolt.   A threaded shaft with one end formed into a solid ring.

Fall.   That part of the rope of a tackle rigging to which the power is applied in hoisting.

False Proscenium.   A decorative silhouette usually made of two-dimensional scenery, placed just upstage of and parallel with the regular proscenium arch.

Fiberglass.   The general term for fiberglass reinforced plastics. The fiberglass reinforcement (cloth, mat, strands, powder) is coated with polyester or epoxy resin to create very strong structures. Used for scenic, costume, and property construction.

Flash Effect.   A general term covering all types of special effects that give a flash at detonation. Includes flash and black powder effects as well as flashbulbs and strobe lights.

Flash Powder.   An explosive powder that gives a brilliant flash of light with little smoke. See also *Black Powder.*

Flat:

   Archway.   A flat frame with the structural members arranged to form a door or window opening with a curved or shaped top.

   Door.   A flat frame with the structural members so arranged as to form a door opening.

   Irregular.   Flats whose shape is other than rectangular.

   Jog.   A narrow plain flat; usually any flat less than 3'-0" wide.

   Plain.   A rectangular frame covered with an unbroken expanse of canvas, muslin, or compositional material.

   Window.   A flat with its structural members placed to form a window opening.

Flies.   The space above the acting area where scenery can be flown for storage.

Float.   To lower standing scenery to a horizontal position on the floor by blocking the lower rail and allowing the flat to fall.

Floor Cloth.   A covering of heavy canvas for the stage floor, usually dark-brown in color.

Flux.   A material used in soldering and welding that cleanses the metal of impurities. It aids in creating a strong solder or weld joint.

Fly Curtain.   See *Curtain.*

Fly Cyclorama.   See *Cyclorama.*

Fly Gallery. A platform attached to the side wall of the stagehouse about 15'-0" to 25'-0" from the floor. Used by workmen when flying scenery by the rope-line and sandbag method.

Flying. Shifting scenery by raising it vertically over the acting area by rope-line rigging or the counterweight system. The fastest and quietest method of shifting.

Fog Machine. A device to produce lingering smoke or fog onstage.

  Dry Ice. This machine plunges dry ice into hot water to create a low lying, fast dissipating, odorless fog.

  Oil Heater. Passes mineral oil vapor over a heating element to create smoke. Leaves an oily residue and has an odor.

Folding Jack. See *Jack.*

Forestage. The part of the stage floor extending beyond the proscenium arch into the auditorium. Synonym for apron.

Foot Iron, Hinged. A steel brace used in bracing the bottom of scenery. The two legs of this brace can be adjusted to different angles.

Foot Iron, Rigid. A right-angle steel brace fastened to the bottom of scenery to brace or lock it to the stage floor.

Front Elevation. Scaled mechanical drawing representing a front view of the setting as it would appear when drawn in a single plane.

Glue Block. A miter-cut piece of hardwood used to brace and strengthen the various elements in a wood joint.

Glue Pot. See *Electric Glue Pot.*

Grid, Gridiron. A framework of metal or wooden beams extending over the stage area and located about 6'-0" below the roof of the stagehouse. On it are bolted the head and loft blocks of the counterweight or rope-line rigging systems.

Ground Plan. A scaled mechanical drawing representing the top view of a setting in position on stage.

Grommet. A reinforcing metal eyelet used to protect the edges of a hole cut in fabric.

Gun Tackle. An arrangement of rope with one single and one double pulley that provides a mechanical advantage of 3 to 1.

Gusset. A triangular piece of material usually wood or metal used to brace the intersection of two elements of a structure such as the post and lintel of an archway.

Halved Joint. See *Joint.*

Hanger Iron. A steel strap 1^1/$_8$" wide by 7^1/$_2$" long fitted with a metal ring. Used in flying scenery.

Hinge:

  Back-Flap, Loose-Pin. Hinges designed especially for joining flats. They come in two sizes, 1^1/$_2$" by 3^1/$_2$" and 2" by 4^3/$_8$". Pins can be easily removed to separate flats.

  Back-Flap, Tight-Pin. Same as above except that the pins cannot be removed.

  Butt. Each half, or leg, of this hinge is rectangular in shape and wider than it is long.

  Strap. The legs of this hinge are elongated and tapering.

Head Block. Several grooved wheels, or sheaves, turning on a single axle and housed in a common metal frame. It is bolted to the eyebeams above the grid.

Hook Hanger Iron. A steel strap with a metal ring attached to one end, the other end shaped to receive the lower rail of framed scenery. Used in conjunction with a hanger iron for flying scenery.

Isometric Drawing. A scaled, mechanical drawing of an object on a single plane (the plane of the paper) with the object so placed that three of its faces can be shown in a single drawing.

Jack:

    Folding. A triangular frame of 1" × 3" placed on the back of scenery to brace it. It is hinged so as to fold parallel with the scenery as an aid in shifting and storage.

    Modified. A 1" × 3" frame built to brace irregularly shaped scenery and conforming to its shape.

    Rigid. Made in the same way as a folding jack, but held rigidly at right angles to the flat frame by hinges placed on both sides of the jack.

Jackknife Stage. A large platform mounted on rigid castors; one corner is locked to the floor by a pivot pin. The stage moves in a quarter arc to bring the setting in alignment with the proscenium. Two such stages are generally used, one on each side of the stage.

Jog. See *Flat*.

Joint:

    Butt. Two pieces of wood squared off and joined at a true right angle.

    Dado. The end of one piece of wood fits into a slot cut into the side of another. The slot can be speedily cut with a dado attachment for a circular saw.

    Doweled. Matched holes are drilled into the pieces of wood to be joined. Hardwood pegs, called dowels, are covered with glue and inserted into the holes.

    Halved. A method of joining two pieces of lumber without increasing the thickness. One-half the thickness is removed from the ends of two pieces of lumber, and they are then glued together.

    Lap. The simplest of all wood joints. One piece is laid over another and nailed or screwed in place.

    Mortise and Tenon. A rectangular hole, the mortise is cut in one piece of lumber. A projecting peg, the tenon, is cut into the other. The tenon fits into the mortise and is held by glue.

    Notched. This joint is similar to the dado joint, except that the notch is cut in the edge of the lumber rather than across the face.

    Scarf. A method of joining two pieces of lumber end to end without increasing the thickness of the lumber at the joint. Wedges 18" long are removed from the faces of both pieces, the cuts are covered with glue, and one piece is placed upon the other and held in place with nails or screws until the glue has dried.

Keeper or S-Hook. Strap iron shaped into a double hook. One side of the hook is placed over a toggle bar and a stiffening batten is placed in the other side of the hook. Used in bracing scenery.

Kerf. A cut or notch made by a saw blade.

Keystone. A piece of ¼" plywood 8" long, tapered from 4" wide at one end to 2¾" at the other. Used for joining butt joints between stiles and toggle bars.

Lap Joint. See *Joint*.

Lash Line. A length of ¼" sash cord used to lace two flats together.

Lash-Line Cleat.   Metal cleats attached to the inner edges of flat stiles to engage the lash line when flats are to be joined by lashing.

Lash-Line Eye.   A metal cleat fitted with a ring at one end and drilled to receive a screw on the other. Provides a method of attaching a lash line to a flat. Line is passed through the ring and knotted.

Lash-Line Hook.   A strap of metal drilled to receive two screws and with a hook formed at one end. Used as a substitute for standard lash cleats when the latter cannot be used.

Lengthwise Batten.   The outside framing members that extend the full length of either a roll or a book ceiling.

Lift Jack.   A device used for shifting scenery. A lever lifts the weight of the scenery onto castors so that it can be rolled.

Light Bridge.   A metal framework about 2′ wide, located upstage from the proscenium arch and extending a few feet past the limits of the arch on each side. It is suspended from the counterweight system so that it can be raised and lowered, and is usually powered by an electric winch. On it are mounted spotlights and other lighting equipment.

Linen Canvas.   The best, and most expensive, material for covering flat frames.

Linnebach Cyclorama.   See *Cyclorama.*

Loading Platform.   A metal gallery supported by the grid. It provides a working platform where counterweights can be loaded into the arbors.

Locking Rail.   A metal framework bolted to the wall and floor along one side wall of the stagehouse. On it are the rope locks of the counterweight system.

Loft Block.   A single-grooved wheel mounted in a metal housing and bolted to the grid. Over these wheels run the ropes or cables of the flying system.

Machine Bolt.   See *Bolt.*

Main Curtain.   See *Curtain.*

Marquisette.   A sheer, somewhat lustrous, cotton netting.

Masking.   Placing either framed or unframed scenery in a position to prevent the audience from seeing the backstage area.

Mechanical Advantage.   Increasing an applied force by mechanical means, as through the use of a block and tackle or a winch.

Mechanical Drawing.   A type of drawing made with the aid of instruments, generally made to scale.

Mortise and Tenon Joint.   See *Joint.*

Muling.   Changing the direction of a cable or rope by passing it around a specially mounted horizontal block.

Muslin.   Heavyweight unbleached cotton material used for covering flat frames or in the construction of drops when economy is a prime requisite.

Notched Joint.   See *Joint.*

Oblique Drawing.   A method of drafting similar to an isometric drawing, but with one face of the object placed at right angles to the observer's view. The other two faces are drawn at any convenient angle.

Operating Line.   (1) The rope used to raise and lower the arbor of the counterweight system. (2) The rope used to open or close different types of curtains, such as the draw, tab, or roller curtains.

Orthographic Projection.   A scaled, mechanical drawing representing an object by three separate views—top, front, and side views.

Outrigger.   A skeletal platform of irregular shape mounted on castors with scenery attached to one of its faces.

Paint Frame:
> *Counterbalanced.*   A large wooden frame to which scenery is temporarily nailed to hold it in a vertical position while it is being painted. The frame can be lowered into a slot in the floor so that all painting can be done from the floor level.
> *Vertical.*   A frame which is attached to a wall in the scene shop. Scenery to be painted is nailed to the frame. Painting is done from a boomerang or ladder.
> *Horizontal.*   A portable horizontal paint frame used to stretch drops for horizontal painting.

Paint Pallet, Rolling.   A metal-topped rolling worktable on which small quantities of paint are mixed.

Papier-mâché.   A technique using wheat paste and strips of newspaper or paper pulp to build up a shape over a basic form.

Parallel, Continental.   A folding platform with a removable top and inside supporting frames. When folded the outside frames form a compact unit.

Parallel, Standard.   A folding platform with a removable top. The folded supporting frames of this parallel are awkward to handle.

Picture Hook and Eye.   Lightweight steel sockets and hooks used for attaching objects to scenery that must be shifted rapidly.

Pilaster.   An upright support that is structurally a part of the wall but projects out from it by a distance equal to one-third the width of the support.

Pinrail.   A part of the rope-line rigging system consisting of a metal pipe or wooden beam attached to the fly gallery and fitted with removable pins used in tying off the ropes.

Pipe Batten.   The part of the counterweight system to which the scenery is attached for flying.

Platform, Rigid.   A weight-bearing platform that may be varied in height by attaching different sets of supporting legs.

Plywood.   A compositional material made of three or more layers of wood glued together, each layer laid with the grain at right angles to that of the others. Sold in sheets 4' wide in varying thicknesses and lengths.

Polyester.   A generic name for a plastic used in two basic forms for theatrical construction.
> *Saturated Polyester.*   The main form of saturated polyester in the theatre is polyester film. From it such products as Mylar, recording tape, and colored media for lighting instruments are manufactured.
> *Unsaturated Polyester.*   Unsaturated polyester resin is the binding agent in fiberglass reinforced plastics. It also has many other applications such as glue, paint, and surface treatment.

Polyethylene.   Polyethylene products are used in three basic forms in scenic and property construction.
> *Polyethylene Film.*   A thin sheet, generally .002 to .006 inches thick, used as a drop cloth and occasionally as a decorative material.
> *Polyethylene Foam.*   Generally known by the tradename "Ethafoam," it is a flexible foam material primarily used in rod form. Easily curved, it is used as a substitute for decorative wrought iron and similar applications.
> *Polyethylene Pipe.*   Commonly available as flexible black water pipe, it can be used as a waterpipe and also as the material from which compound curved handrails on staircases are made.

Polystyrene.   There are two principal theatrical applications of plastics from the polystyrene family.
> *High Impact Polystyrene.*   This plastic becomes very flexible when heated and retains the shape to which it is formed after it cools. This property makes it the primary material used in heat or vacuum forming.
> *Expanded Polystyrene Foam.*   Known by the tradename Styrofoam it is the primary foam used in theatrical construction. Available in a variety of densities it can be carved with knives, saws, or hot-wire cutters.

Polyurethane Foams.   One of the most versatile plastics in the technician's repertoire. Available in manufactured shapes as well as pour-in-place and spray components for mixing in the shop. Variations in the formulation of the mixture allows the foam to be either rigid or flexible. It can be cut by mechanical means. It should never be burned or heated as the burning releases a toxic gas.

Properties:
> *Breakaway.*   A property that is supposed to break as part of the action onstage. Furniture, crockery, and glass should be prebroken and lightly reglued so that it will break at the appropriate place and at the right time.
> *Decorative.*   Furniture or objects on stage that serve no practical purpose but help to give character to the setting.
> *Floor.*   All the furniture normally used by the actors.
> *Hand.*   Small objects carried to or from the stage by the actors or handled by them while on stage.

Proscenium Arch.   The opening in the wall between the stage proper and the auditorium.

Proscenium Doors.   Doorways located on either side of the forestage and usually on the auditorium side of the proscenium arch.

Pull Rod.   A ³/₈" iron rod with a handle at one end and a hook at the other, used in pulling wagon stages or turning a revolving disc.

Pull Ropes.   Short lengths of knotted ropes attached to low wagon stages and used in pulling them.

Rail.   The top and bottom horizontal members of a flat frame.

Reeve.   To pass a rope over a sheave in a block or pulley.

Revolving Disc.   A low circular platform supported by the stage floor. Usually designed for a particular production and carries but a portion of a setting.

Revolving Stage.   A circular section of the stage floor that revolves and is supported from beneath. It is usually electrically driven. Used for shifting entire settings.

Rigging.   All of the activities associated with the initial assembly of a setting when it is first taken to the stage. Rigging also readies a set to be shifted.

Rigid Platform.   See *Platform.*

Riser.   The vertical face of a step.

Roll Ceiling.   See *Ceiling.*

Roller Curtain.   See *Curtain.*

Rolling Scenery.   Scenery mounted on castors or wheels to be shifted manually or by power.

Rope Lock.   A lever that activates a pawl housed in a metal frame so as to apply pressure on the operating line of a counterweight unit.

Running.   Shifting or moving scenery manually.

Saddle.   Obtaining multiple points of support from a single line. Both ends of a short line are tied off to an object and the lifting line is then attached to the center of the saddle thus made.

Sandbag. A heavyweight canvas bag enclosed by ropes and filled with sand, used for balance in rope-line rigging.

Sash Cord. The ¼" thick braided cotton cord used in making lash lines.

Sateen. A shiny cotton material, not very strong, but inexpensive.

Scarf Joint. See *Joint.*

Scene Dock. The area and racks where two-dimensional scenery can be stored.

Scene Paint:

    Aniline Dye. A dye made of a variety of materials. Available in a wide range of colors, it is dissolved in boiling water. It is the principal dye used in scene painting.

    Casein Paint. A water-based, flat finish, protein resin, concentrated pulp paint. Water is added to the pulp to bring the paint to the appropriate consistency. It does not need an additional binder.

    Dry Pigment and Binder. Powdered pigment is added to size water to form a paint used in scene painting. The amount of glue in the size water varies with the type of pigment.

    Latex Paint. A water-based paint that uses a synthetic rubber or latex as the binder. Can be thinned slightly for use in scene painting. The finish usually has a slight sheen.

    Shellac. A clear or slightly amber organic resin finish coat that dries to a gloss finish. It can also be used as a sealer coat to prevent underlying coatings or materials from bleeding through the succeeding coats.

    Size Water. A mixture of synthetic or animal glue and water. A standard mixture is 14 parts water to 1 part glue. Used as the binder in dry pigment and binder scene paint. The ratio of glue to water can be varied as appropriate.

    Varnish. A clear synthetic or organic resinous finish coat. Available in a variety of surface finishes: matte, satin, and gloss. Varnish is available in water-, alcohol-, and oil-based vehicles.

    Vinyl Acrylic. A water-based pulp type scene paint that uses vinyl acrylic as the binder. An extremely flexible paint, it will adhere to many surfaces that reject other paints. The general mixture is 2 parts water to 1 part paint, although more water can be used without adverse effects.

Scene Shift. The striking of one setting and assembly of another.

Scene Shop. The area used for the construction, covering, joining, and painting of scenery.

Segment Stage. A pie-shaped rolling platform used in shifting scenery.

Semicircle. A low semicircular platform mounted on castors and pivoted from the center of the straight side.

Sharkstooth Scrim. A netting with a rectangular weave; it is stronger and has greater opacity than bobinette.

Sheave. A grooved wheel in a block or pulley.

Shellac. See *Scene Paint.*

Sight Line. An imaginary line extending from any seat in the auditorium past the proscenium arch to any position on stage to determine how much of the stage will be visible from that point.

Sill Iron. A reinforcing length of strap iron, ¼" thick by ¾" wide, joining the two legs of a door flat.

Size Water. See *Scene Paint.*

Slip Stage. A very large platform riding on flanged wheels and tracks. It can carry a full setting and all properties.

Snap Hook. A steel hook with a spring trigger that closes its throat. Attached to the end of snatch lines it eliminates the need for rope knots.

Snatch Line. Length of rope, piano wire, or chain used in attaching scenery to a batten of the rope-line or counterweight flying system.

Soldering. The process of melting an alloy of tin, zinc, and lead (solder) to bind together two or more metal surfaces. The solder melts at a lower temperature than the metal to be joined and flows over and bonds to the surface of the metal.

Spotline. A rope line passing over special blocks on the grid to fall to the stage floor at a given point.

Stage Brace. Used in bracing scenery. Metal loops hold two overlapping lengths of hardwood that can be adjusted in length and locked in position with a thumbscrew. One end of the brace is fitted with a double hook, the other with an angular or curved foot iron.

Stage Left. That part of the stage that lies to the left of the actor as he faces the audience.

Stage Right. That part of the stage that lies to the right of the actress as she faces the audience.

Stage Screw. A large steel screw with a handle in place of a slotted head. It can be driven into the stage floor by turning and hand pressure.

Standard Parallel. See *Parallel.*

Stiffening Batten. Length of 1″ × 3″ or 1″ × 4″ lumber used to brace and strengthen a series of flats that have been joined by hinging.

Stile. A vertical outside member of a flat frame.

Stock Scenery. Flat frames, standardized in height, that are kept for possible alterations and reuse.

Stop Block. Short length of 1″ × 1½″ wood used to prevent one flat from slipping past another when making an inside lashing.

Stop Cleat. A small metal cleat ¾″ × 3″ that is screwed to the back of a stile and allowed to project ¾″ to ensure the vertical alignment of flats joined by an outside lashing.

Stove Bolt. See *Bolt.*

Strap Hinge. See *Hinge.*

Strap Iron. Strips of malleable iron, ³/₁₆″ or ¼″ thick and ¾″ wide, used in making sill irons for door flats.

Straps, Plywood. Rectangular pieces of ¼″ plywood 8″ long and 2¾″ wide. Used for the same purpose as keystones.

Strike. Command given by the stage manager to signal the beginning of a scene shift. Also used at the close of a production for the operation of dismantling all scenery and stripping it of hardware preparatory to storing it.

Sweeps. The curved or shaped structural members of an archway flat that give it its distinctive shape.

Swivel and Hook. Stage hardware used to help in flying scenery placed on stage at an angle other than parallel with the pipe battens.

T-Bar Track. Vertical metal tracks mounted against the side wall of the stagehouse to guide the arbors and prevent sidesway.

Tab Curtain.   See *Curtain*.

Tackle Rigging.   The method of arranging rope and pulleys for the purpose of lifting or moving heavy objects.

Teaser.   A horizontal masking border that usually matches the main curtain in color and material. It can be raised or lowered to mask the space above settings of different heights.

Tee Plate.   A steel plate shaped like the letter T, used in place of a keystone when greater strength is required.

Template Bench.   A workbench especially suited for the assembly of flat frames.

Tension Pulley.   A special pulley mounted on the T-bar track below the locking rail and around which the operating line passes.

Tie-Off Cleats.   Cleats placed opposite each other on the stiles at the 3'-0" level, around which the lash line is tied off.

Tip Jack.   A device used for shifting heavy or awkward units of scenery. It is similar to a rigid jack but is mounted on castors with the vertical member at less than a 90-degree angle to its base. Two jacks are required for each unit of scenery to be so shifted.

Thickness Pieces.   Structural members that give the appearance of depth and solidity to all openings in two-dimensional scenery.

Toggle Bar.   The inside cross member of a flat frame.

Tormentors.   Vertical masking pieces, usually of plain flat construction, placed on either side of the proscenium just upstage of the teaser.

Track, Curtain.   The hollow supporting frame, either metal or wood, from which the draw curtain is suspended and on which it moves.

Trap.   A removable section of the stage floor.

Tread.   The horizontal plane of a step unit.

Trial Setup.   The process of assembling the various parts of a setting for the first time.

Trim.   Adjusting flown units of scenery so that the lower rails or battens are parallel with the stage floor.

Trip Cyclorama.   See *Cyclorama*.

Tripping.   To fold, by special lines, a flown unit such as a drop or a cyc to reduce the amount of height required to raise it above sight lines.

Truss.   An assemblage of members or beams combined and reinforced by triangular bracing to form a rigid framework.

Tumbler.   A vertical length of 1" × 3" lumber hinged to two flats of a three-fold unit that will permit three flats of the same width to fold into a compact stack.

Turnbuckle.   A steel loop fitted with a threaded eyebolt at one end and a threaded hook bolt at the other. By turning the loop the bolts are drawn together or extended.

Two-Dimensional Scenery.   Framed or unframed scenery that has width and height but no depth other than that of the material from which it is made.

Upstage.   A position away from the audience and toward the back of the stage.

Varnish.   See *Scene Paint*.

Velour.   A heavy deep-piled fabric used for main curtains.

Vinyl Acrylic Paint.   See *Scene Paint*.

Wagon Stage.   A platform mounted on castors on which heavy sections of a setting can be shifted.

Walk It Up. Raise a framed two-dimensional unit from a horizontal to a vertical position by blocking the lower rails and lifting the upper rails until the stagehands can reach the stiles. They then walk hand over hand along the stiles until the unit is upright.

Webbing. Strips of strong fabric used to reinforce the top hem of curtains and stage draperies.

Welding. The process of heating metal to its melting point so that adjacent surfaces or edges fuse together to form a permanent bond.

  Arc Welding. Uses an electrical arc to generate the heat necessary to accomplish the welding process. Uses a flux coated consumable welding rod.

  MIG. Metal inert gas arc welding is an arc-welding process that bathes the weld zone with an inert gas to shield the weld from the oxidizing effects of the atmosphere. Uses a consumable wire electrode that is automatically fed through the electrode handle to the weld-contact area.

  Oxy-acetylene Welding. A gas-welding process that uses a mixture of oxygen and acetylene to create an intensely hot flame to heat the metal. A consumable welding rod is used to help fill the weld. It is usually dipped in flux to aid in making a solid weld.

  TIG. Tungsten inert gas arc welding uses a basically nonconsummable tungsten electrode which is bathed in an inert gas environment to prevent contamination of the weld. A filler rod is used with TIG welding.

Winch, Powered. A power-driven piece of machinery consisting of a set of gears that turn a drum or cylinder on which a rope or cable is coiled. Used in hoisting heavy objects.

Window Stiles. The vertical members of a flat that form the sides of a window opening.

Work Schedule. A calendar of operational steps to be followed in mounting a production.

Working Drawings. The scaled mechanical drawings that show the carpenter what to build and how to build it.

Wing Nut. A threaded nut with extensions or wings on each side that make it possible to tighten or loosen it with the fingers.

Selected References

Baldwin, John. *Contemporary Sculpture Techniques*. New York: Reinhold, 1967.

Bowman, Ned. *Handbook of Technical Practice for the Performing Arts*. Winkinsbury, Pa.: Scenographic Media, 1972.

Bryson, Nicholas L. *Thermoplastic Scenery for the Theatre*. New York: Drama Bookshop Specialist, 1970.

Burris-Meyer, Harold, and Edward C. Cole. *Scenery for the Theatre*, 2nd ed. Boston: Little, Brown, 1972.

Burris-Meyer, Harold, and Edward C. Cole. *Theatres and Auditoriums*, 2nd ed. New York: Van Nostrand Reinhold, 1964.

Cadillac Plastic and Safety Buyer's Guide. Cadillac Plastic and Chemical Co., 1978.

French, Thomas E., and Charles J. Vierck. *A Manual of Engineering Drawing for Students and Draftsmen*, 9th ed. New York: McGraw-Hill, 1960.

Friederich, Willard J., and John H. Fraser. *Scenery Design for the Amateur Stage*. New York: Dryden, 1941.

Gruver, Bert. *The Stage Manager's Handbook*. New York: Harper & Row, 1953.

Henderson, Kenneth A. *Handbook of American Mountaineering*. Boston: Houghton Mifflin, 1942. (Rope knots.)

Hewitt, Barnard, J. F. Foster, and Muriel Sibell Wolle. *Play Production Theory and Practice*. Philadelphia: Lippincott, 1952.

Meyers, L. Donald. *The Furniture Lover's Book*. New York: Dutton, 1977.

Newman, Jay Hartley, and Lee Scott Newman. *Plastics for the Craftsman*. New York: Crown, 1972.

Parker, W. Oren, and Harvey K. Smith. *Scene Design and Stage Lighting*. New York: Holt, Rinehart and Winston, 1979.

Pecktal, Lynn. *Designing and Painting for the Theatre*. New York: Holt, Rinehart and Winston, 1975.

Plymouth Cordage Company. *Manual of Rope Usage, How to Put Rope to Work in Industry; and Useful Knots and How to Use Them.* Plymouth, Mass.: Plymouth Cordage Company, 1948.

Selden, S., and H. Sellman. *Stage Scenery and Lighting,* 3rd ed. New York: Appleton-Century-Crofts, 1959.

Southern, Richard. *Changeable Scenery: Its Origin and Development in the British Theatre.* London: Faber & Faber, 1952.

Stell, Joseph W. *The Theatre Student: Scenery.* New York: Richard Rosen Press, 1970.

Taylor, Douglas C. *Metalworking for the Designer and Technician.* New York: Drama Book Specialists, 1979.

Wade, Robert J. *Designing for TV.* New York: Farrar and Straus, 1952.

Whiting, Frank. *An Introduction to the Theatre,* rev. ed. New York: Harper & Row, 1961.

Wilke, Bernard, MBKS. *The Technique of Special Effects in Television.* New York: Communication Arts Books, Hastings House, 1971.

Index

87 88 89 9 8 7 6 5